EMPEROR OF THE WORLD

T0366659

EMPEROR OF
THE WORLD

CHARLEMAGNE AND
THE CONSTRUCTION OF
IMPERIAL AUTHORITY,
800–1229

ANNE A. LATOWSKY

CORNELL UNIVERSITY PRESS
Ithaca and London

First published 2013 by Cornell University Press

First paperback printing 2020

Library of Congress Cataloging-in-Publication Data

Latowsky, Anne Austin.
    Emperor of the world : Charlemagne and the construction of imperial authority, 800–1229 / Anne A. Latowsky.
        p. cm.
    Includes bibliographical references and index.
    ISBN 978-0-8014-5148-5 (cloth)
    ISBN 978-1-5017-4851-6 (pbk.)
    1. Charlemagne, Emperor, 742–814—Legends—History and criticism.   2. Charlemagne, Emperor, 742–814—Influence.   3. Holy Roman Empire—Kings and rulers.   4. Literature, Medieval—History and criticism. 5. Authority in literature.   6. East and West in literature. 7. East and West—History—To 1500.   I. Title.
    PN687.C5L38 2013
    809'.93351—dc23   2012025569

For David, Julia, and Jonathan

❧ Contents

❧ ACKNOWLEDGMENTS

Three days before I sent the first full manuscript of this book to Cornell University Press for consideration in May 2011, I learned that my mentor and friend, Eugene Vance, had died in a solo plane crash. I had been waiting to tell him that I had finally completed the book, but never got the chance. Gene was a passionate reader of the medieval world, and it is my hope that this book will in some way bear witness to his legacy as a teacher. During my years in graduate school, he always allotted me the freedom to plot my own course, happily tolerating the time I spent in the classics department, and, even more so, the time I spent in the history department with Robert Stacey, who taught me to be a medieval historian. My aim in this book has been to navigate the often murky waters between literature and history, and I look back with gratitude to those who prepared me for that endeavor.

At the University of South Florida, my colleagues have patiently given me the time and space I have needed to write this book. I am particularly grateful to Christine Probes for her generosity and friendship over the years. Among the historians who have welcomed me into their fold, I wish to acknowledge Matthew Gabriele, Jace Stuckey, Eric Goldberg, Paul Dutton, David Ganz, Patrick Geary, Paul Hyams, Jinty Nelson, and Damien Kempf, who has been kind enough to share work in progress. I especially want to thank Valerie Garver, who has been a great help in the publication process, and Tom Noble for his support over the past five years.

This book would not have been possible without the support of a National Endowment for the Humanities Faculty Research fellowship in 2009–10, which allowed me a year to regroup and write what turned out to be a different book than the one I had intended. I wish to thank the Humanities Institute of the University of South Florida for an important summer of funding for research in 2008. The Department of World Languages at USF has also contributed generously to the publication of this book. The University of Wisconsin Libraries at Madison have provided me with a summer home on several occasions. Without their generous policies for temporary patrons, my research would have been far less productive during those intensive weeks in the Greek and Latin Reading Room. Finally, I would like to thank Marc Du Pouget for granting me permission to read his important doctoral dissertation in the National Archives in Paris.

I owe much to the patient interlibrary loan staff at the University of South Florida in Tampa and at the Jane Bancroft Cook Library of New College of Florida in Sarasota. They have endured my endless borrowing requests for years, and even forgave me when a book from a German library fell into my recently unpacked Kalamazoo bag for an entire year before reappearing as I readied my annual pilgrimage to the north. I would also like to express my gratitude to those who have undertaken the digitization of the Monumenta Germaniae Historica, an endeavor that has made an enormous difference to scholars attempting to do research in medieval studies from schools that simply cannot offer the resources necessary to complete a study of this kind.

In some ways, this book has been long in coming, but in other ways *Emperor of the World* is a relatively recent development. The first two chapters have recognizable antecedents in my 2004 dissertation. An early version of a portion of chapter 1 was published as "Foreign Embassies and Roman Universality in Einhard's Life of Charlemagne" in *Florilegium,* the journal of the Canadian Society of Medievalists / Société canadienne des médiévistes, in 2005. My thanks go to Christa Canitz for her kindness and encouragement.

Among my Florida medievalist colleagues, I wish to first thank David Rohrbacher (a classicist), Carrie Beneš, and Thomas McCarthy for their willingness to read the whole manuscript. James D'Emilio and Florin Curta have offered steady advice and encouragement over the years, and Felice Lifshitz (now a Canadian medievalist) gave me a crucial reminder at a key moment. Tison Pugh and Mary Jane Schenck have shared this journey with me over the years, as have Greg Milton and Shira Schwam-Baird. Finally, I would like to thank Peter J. Potter, the wonderful editorial staff at Cornell University Press, and the anonymous readers, all of whom have helped me make this a better book.

My family and friends have been loving and encouraging throughout this process, especially my mother, Julie Hayward. Throughout *Emperor of the World,* readers will hear much talk of rhetorical topoi relating to the theme of Roman universalism. A different rhetorical device bears mention here, and that is the topos of inexpressibility, since I lack the words to properly express the debt of gratitude that I owe to my husband, David, for his unflagging support all along the way. This book is dedicated to him, and to our children, Julia and Jonathan.

❧ ABBREVIATIONS

Ad Hein.	Benzo of Alba. *Libri ad Heinricum IV Impera-torem.* Ed. Hans Seyffert. MGH *SRG* 65. Hanover, 1996.
Adso, *De ortu*	Adso of Montier-en-Der. *De ortu et tempore antichristi: Necnon et tractatus qui ab eo dependent.* Ed. Daniel Verhelst. Turnhout, 1976.
Annales Marbacenses	*Annales Marbacenses.* Ed. Hermann Bloch. MGH *SRG* 9. Hanover, 1907.
Archpoet, *Kaiserhymnus*	Archpoet. *Die Gedichte des Archipoeta.* Ed. Heinrich Watenphul and Heinrich Krefeld. Heidelberg,1958.
ARF	*Annales regni francorum.* Ed. Friedrich Kurze. MGH *SRG* 6. Hanover, 1895.
Benedict, *Chron.*	Benedict of Mount Soracte. *Il Chronicon di Benedetto monaco di Santo Andrea al Soratte.* Ed. G. Zucchetti. *Fonti per la Storia d'Italia* 55. Rome, 1920.
CC	*Corpus Christianorum*
CSEL	*Corpus Scriptorum Ecclesiasticorum Latinorum*
Desc.	*Descriptio qualiter Karolus Magnus clavum et coro-nam Domini a Constantinopoli Aquisgrani detulerit qualiterque Karolus Calvus hec ad Sanctum Dionysium retulerit.* Ed. Gerhard Rauschen. In *Die Legende Karls des Grossen im 11. und 12. Jahrhundert.* Leipzig, 1890.
Einhard, *VK*	Einhard. *Vita Karoli Magni.* Ed. O. Holder-Egger. MGH *SRG* 25. Hanover and Leipzig, 1911.
EL, **Ado of Vienne**	Ado of Vienne. *Martyrologium. PL* 123, col. 875.
EL, **Avitus**	Avitus of Braga. *Epistola ad Palchonium, de Rel-iquiis Sancti Stephani, et de Luciani epistola a se e graeco in latinum versa. PL* 41, cols. 805–7.

EL, Fleury	*Epistola Luciani ad Omnem Ecclesiam, de Revelatione Corporis Stephani Martyris Primi et Aliorum. PL* 41, col. 807.
EPJ	*Epistola presbiteri Johannis.* Ed. Bettina Wagner. In *Die "Epistola presbiteri Johannis" lateinisch und deutsch: Überlieferung, Textgeschichte, Rezeption und Übertragungen im Mittelalter.* Tübingen, 2000.
Eusebius, *VC*	Eusebius. *Life of Constantine.* Trans. Averil Cameron and Stuart G. Hall. Oxford, 1999.
Eutropius, *Brev.*	Eutropius. *Breviarium ab urbe condita.* Ed. and trans. Joseph Hellegouarc'h. Paris, 1999.
Exhortatio	*"Exhortatio ad proceres regni."* Ed. Georg Waitz. *Neues Archiv* 1. Hanover, 1876.
Falschen Investiturprivilegien	*Die falschen Investiturprivilegien.* Ed. Claudia Märtl. MGH *Fontes* 13. Hanover, 1986.
Florus of Lyons, *Querela*	Florus of Lyons. *Querela de Divisione Imperii.* Ed. Ernst Dümmler. MGH *Poet. Lat.* 2. Berlin, 1884.
GF	Otto of Freising and Rahewin. *Gesta Friderici I imperatoris.* Ed. Roger Wilmans. MGH *SS* 20. Hanover, 1868.
Godfrey of Viterbo, *Memoria Seculorum*	Godfrey of Viterbo. *Memoria Seculorum.* Ed. Georg Pertz. MGH *SS* 22. Hanover, 1872.
Godfrey of Viterbo, *Pantheon*	Godfrey of Viterbo. *Pantheon.* Ed. Georg Pertz. MGH *SS* 22. Hanover, 1872.
Godfrey of Viterbo, *Speculum Regum*	Godfrey of Viterbo. *Speculum Regum.* Ed. Georg Pertz. MGH *SS* 22. Hanover, 1872.
Hillin-Briefe	*Hillin-Briefe.* Ed. Norbert Höing. In "Die 'Trierer Stilübungen.' Ein Denkmal der Früzeit Kaiser Friedrich Barbarossas," *Archiv für Diplomatik, Schriftgeschichte, Siegel- und Wappenkunde* 1 (1955): 257–329.

Hist. Aug.	*Scriptores Historiae Augustae.* Ed. Ernst Hohl. 2 vols. Leipzig, 1927.
HdDC	Otto of Freising. *Ottonis episcopi Frisingensis Chronica sive Historia de duabus civitatibus.* Ed. Adolf Hofmeister. MGH *SRG* 45. Hanover, 1912.
Hist. Lang.	Paul the Deacon. *Historia Langobardorum.* Ed. L. Bethmann and Georg Waitz. MGH *SRL* 1. Berlin, 1878.
Karlsprivileg	*Karlsprivileg.* Ed. Erich Meuthen. In *Aachener Urkunden 1101–1250.* Bonn, 1972.
Karolinus	Giles of Paris. *Karolinus.* Ed. M. L. Colker. In "The 'Karolinus' of Edigius Parisiensis," *Traditio* 29 (1973): 199–325.
KMLP	*Karolus Magnus et Leo Papa.* Ed. Ernst Dümmler et al. MGH *Poet. Lat.* 1. Berlin, 1881.
Ludus	*Ludus de Antichristo.* Ed. Karl Young. In *The Drama of the Medieval Church.* Oxford, 1962.
MGH	Monumenta Germaniae Historica
Fontes	*Fontes Iuris Germanici Antiqui in usum scholarum separatim editi.* Hanover, 1909–86.
Poet. Lat.	*Poetae Latini Aevi Carolini.* Hanover, 1881–99.
SRG	*Scriptores Rerum Germanicarum in usum scholarum separatim editi.* Hanover, 1871–1987.
SRL	*Scriptores Rerum Langobardorum et Italicarum, saec. 6–9.* Hanover, 1878.
SS	*Scriptores.* Hanover, 1824–1924.
Neues Archiv	*Neues Archiv der Gesellschaft für ältere deutsche Geschichtskunde.*
Notker, GK	Notker of Saint Gall. *Gesta Karoli Magni.* Ed. Reinhold Rau. In *Quellen zur karolingischen Reichsgeschichte,* vol. 3. Berlin, 1963.
Orosius, *Hist.*	Orosius. *Pauli Orosii historiarum adversum paganos libri VII; accedit eiusdem, Liber Apologeticus.* Ed. Karl Friedrich Wilhelm Zangemeister. *CSEL* 5. Vienna, 1882.
Pan. Lat.	*In Praise of Later Roman Emperors: The "Panegyrici Latini."* Ed. and trans. C. E. V. Nixon and Barbara Saylor Rodgers. Berkeley, CA, 1994.

Paulinus of Nola,
Carmina   Paulinus of Nola. *Sancti Pontii Meropii Paulini*
                            Nolani Opera. Pars 2, Carmina. Ed. Wilhelm
                            von Hartel and Margit Kamptner. *CSEL* 30.
                            Vienna, 1999.

Pierre de Beauvais,
French *Desc.*   Pierre de Beauvais. French *Descriptio.*
                            Ed. Ronald N. Walpole. In "Charlemagne's
                            Journey to the East: The French Translation of
                            the Legend, by Pierre of Beauvais." *Semitic and*
                            Oriental Studies 9 (1951): 445–52.

PL   *Patrologia Cursus Completus, Series Latina.*
                            Ed. J.-P. Migne. 221 vols. Paris, 1841–66.

Poeta Saxo   Poeta Saxo. *Annalium de gestis Caroli Magni*
                            imperatoris libri quinque. Ed. Paul von
                            Winterfeld. MGH *Poet. Lat.* 4. Berlin, 1899.

RHC Occ.   *Recueil des historiens des croisades, Historiens*
                            occidentaux. Vol. 3. Paris, 1841–95.

Suetonius, *Aug.*   Suetonius. *Vita Augusti.* In *C. Suetoni Tran-*
                            quilli Opera. Vol. 1, *De Vita Caesarum Libri VIII.*
                            Ed. M. Ihm. Leipzig, 1907.

TSD   *Translatio Sanguinis Domini.* Ed. Georg Waitz.
                            MGH *SS* 4:445–49. Hanover, 1891.

Victor, *De*
Caesaribus   Sextus Aurelius Victor. *Liber de Caesaribus.*
                            Ed. Franz Pichlmayr. Leipzig, 1961.

VKM   *Vita Karoli Magni.* Ed. Gerhard Rauschen. In
                            Die Legende Karls des Grossen im 11. und 12.
                            Jahrhundert, 1–93. Leipzig, 1890.

Widukind, *Rer.*
Gest.   Widukind of Corvey. *Rerum Gestarum*
                            Saxonicum. Ed. P. Hirsch, MGH *SRG* 60.
                            Hanover, 1935.

Introduction

> Let neighboring nations, having heard tell of your
> excellence, either hasten to submit themselves to
> you or waste away trembling. Let the Slav groan,
> the Hungarian shriek, and the Greek be awed and
> dumbstruck. May the Saracen be unsettled and flee.
> May the African offer you tribute, the Spaniard seek
> your help, the Burgundian venerate and cherish you,
> and the joyful Aquitanian run to you.
>
> —Odilo of Cluny to Emperor Henry III, 1046

Not long after the death of Charlemagne in
814, Einhard recalled in his *Life of Charlemagne* the arrival at court of an
elephant sent from the caliph Harun al Rachid.[1] The biographer describes
the extravagant gift in a chapter devoted to the friendly relations that the
Frankish king had enjoyed with foreign nations once he became emperor,
even with the rival Greeks, who sought a friendly alliance with him out of
fear. Of the various memorable chapters in the life of Charlemagne, his diplomatic relations with the East proved to be one of the most persistent. Hundreds of years later, for instance, near the turn of the fourteenth century, the
Flemish poet and chronicler Jean d'Outremeuse provided a new account of
the arrival of the elephant from the East. Drawing on a variety of Latin and
vernacular sources, Jean tells of how a hideous and vengeful dwarf from the
court of Harun, a man fluent in Persian, Greek, Saracen, French, and Flemish,
had ridden the elephant all the way to the Carolingian court. Incensed over
a previous slight by the queen, whom he had once coveted, the dwarf exacts
his revenge by gaining entry into the intimate sleeping quarters of the royal
couple and slipping between the sheets after Charlemagne's departure for
Mass. When the king returns to discover the seemingly adulterous scene, he

---

1. Einhard, *VK,* 16.

threatens the execution of his Byzantine queen, the daughter of the emperor of Constantinople. Ultimately the queen and her unborn baby are saved from the wrath of her unjust husband, and political order is restored by the hero of Jean's chronicle, the warrior of vernacular epic named Ogier the Dane.[2] This book, I almost hesitate to say now, has nearly nothing to with elephants, dwarfs, or the goings-on in Charlemagne's bedroom. *Emperor of the World* promises instead to be an exploration of the role of "Charlemagne and the East" as an episode in the imagined life of the Frankish king, one of the most influential narratives of the European Middle Ages.[3]

Although Charlemagne never traveled east of the Italian peninsula, a story based on a single passage in Einhard began to be told in the tenth century of how he had traveled to Jerusalem and Constantinople to meet with the leadership in the East. In a document known as the *Descriptio,* the most widely known version of the story, the narrator tells of how the emperor of Byzantium had received a divine vision instructing him to call on Charlemagne to help him with the deteriorating situation in the Holy Land.[4] Charlemagne answers the call by bringing a large army to Jerusalem, an expedition that involves no battles, since the occupying pagans flee the Holy City upon his arrival. Both emperors understand that God has shown his preference for the new emperor in the West over the Greeks in the East as his vicar on earth and protector of Christendom. The Greek emperor offers the Frank lavish rewards for his deeds, which he piously refuses. At the insistence of his host that he accept some evidence of the favor of God that he had enjoyed in Jerusalem, Charlemagne asks for and receives relics of the Passion to bring back to the West.

The tale of Charlemagne's encounters in the East gained wide currency throughout the Middle Ages in various guises and in an array of narrative contexts, including royal biography, *res gestae,* chronicles, universal histories, royal histories, relic authentication texts, imperial decrees, hagiographies, stained-glass windows, and vernacular verse and prose. Any exploration of the various facets of the legendary Charlemagne must therefore take into account the striking diversity of cultural productions in which the story appeared. As a motif, the story was portable, mutable, and enduring, yet neither the nature of the episode nor the reasons behind its persistence over time have ever been properly accounted for. The account of his journey to the East serves, more

---

2. Jean d'Outremeuse, *Ly myreur des histors: Fragment du second livre (années 794–826),* ed. André Goosse (Brussels, 1965), 42.

3. Matthias Tischler, *Einharts Vita Karoli. Studien zur Entstehung, Überlieferung und Rezeption* (Hanover, 2001). Tischler has shown in this monumental study that Einhard's biography was one of the most often copied and well diffused texts in the medieval West.

4. *Desc.*

often than not, as the backdrop for a relic authentication narrative.[5] What is extraordinary about this particular exchange of relics, however, is the fact that the transfer occurs between the emperors of the newly divided Christian empire and generally involves relics of the Passion, the most symbolically potent of all sacred objects. Given the implications of the encounter that it stages between the two sides of Christendom, Charlemagne's journey to the East, an episode born of Einhard's spare discussion of the emperor's dealings with Eastern nations after his coronation, proves to be far more engaged in the politics of empire than has been previously recognized.

This is not the book that I imagined I would write about Charlemagne's apocryphal encounters with Byzantium and the Holy Land. As a French medievalist, I had long been wrestling with the enigmatic Anglo-Norman poem *The Voyage of Charlemagne to Jerusalem and Constantinople,* trying to establish a place for it within both vernacular and Latin textual traditions.[6] Following the conventional theory that Charlemagne had functioned as a sort of idealized royal proto-crusader in the culture of medieval France, a *Charlemagne croisé,* I plotted a path that began with Einhard and progressed through the centuries toward the late twelfth century in France.[7] The First Crusade had been a largely Frankish and Francophone endeavor, so it was not surprising that the association between France and Charlemagne as a Holy Land crusader *avant la lettre* became so engrained. In my explorations of the origins and ramifications of the legend of Charlemagne and the East, I found, however, to my surprise, that the elements of the prevailing theory of Charlemagne as Holy Land crusader in French cultural memory simply did not cohere.[8]

---

5. For narratives accompanying relics, see Patrick J. Geary. *Furta Sacra: Thefts of Relics in the Central Middle Ages* (Princeton, NJ, 1978).

6. *The Journey of Charlemagne to Jerusalem and Constantinople,* ed. and trans. Jean-Louis G. Picherit (Birmingham, AL, 1984).

7. Important examples of this approach to the legend include Robert Folz, *Le souvenir et la légende de Charlemagne dans l'Empire germanique médiéval* (Geneva, 1973), 138; Paul Rousset, *Les origines et les caractères de la première croisade* (Neuchâtel, 1945), 133; Jean Flori, *La guerre sainte: La formation de l'idée de croisade dans l'Occident chrétien* (Paris, 2001), 31; Carl Erdmann, *The Origin of the Idea of Crusade,* trans. Marshall W. Baldwin and Walter Goffart (Princeton, NJ, 1977), 298; Robert Morrissey, *L'empereur à la barbe fleurie: Charlemagne dans la mythologie et l'histoire de France* (Paris, 1997), 92; Gabrielle M. Spiegel, *The Past as Text: The Theory and Practice of Medieval Historiography* (Baltimore, 1997), 124; Werner Goez, *Translatio Imperii: Ein Beitrag zur Geschichte des Geschichtsdenkens und der politischen Theorien im Mittelalter und in der frühen Neuzeit* (Tübingen, 1958), 42; Federica Monteleone, *Il viaggio di Carlo Magno in Terra Santa* (Fasano di Brindisi, 2003), 36.

8. The Charlemagne who battles enemies of the faith in Spain in the *Pseudo-Turpin Chronicle* and the *Song of Roland* raises a set of questions far too complex to treat sufficiently as a side issue to the matter of his encounters in the East. Although the two episodes began to appear in tandem in the saintly *Vita* of Charlemagne sometime after 1170, the traditions need to be considered separately. For the Spain tradition and crusading, see William J. Purkis, *Crusading Spirituality in the Holy Land and*

The fortunes of "Charlemagne and the East" in the French-speaking world after the First Crusade prove, in fact, to have been relatively meager. Instead, I was able to show that this invented chapter in the Carolingian past was fundamentally concerned with the continuity of the Roman Empire and the establishment of Frankish authority after the coronation of 800. To respond to the questions of how and why the episode had evolved as it did, I needed to look not to the literature of the kingdom of France, but to the promotion of the German inheritance of the Roman Empire beginning in the tenth century. Charlemagne's peaceful envelopment of the East into the fold of his theoretical Christian empire began in Einhard as the product of medieval biographical practice, and never really ceased to be an example of the rhetorically governed practice of commemorating royal deeds and virtues, but it flourished in the propagandistic literature of the German empire, far more so than in France. The episode did eventually play a role in the construction of France's Carolingian past, but, as I demonstrate in my final chapter, that phenomenon occurred both later and differently than has previously been argued. The majority of the pages that follow are therefore concerned with Charlemagne's invented encounters with Byzantium and the Holy Land in the literature and propaganda of the Carolingian Empire and its Teutonic successors between the ninth and the early thirteenth centuries.

While the historical Charlemagne has rarely suffered from scholarly neglect, the Charlemagne of legend, especially outside of the vernacular Romance epic, has yet to be satisfactorily understood. Robert Folz's 1950 *Le souvenir et la légende de Charlemagne dans l'Empire germanique médiéval,* reissued in 1973, is an undeniable monument to the study of the memory of Charlemagne, for which I am consistently grateful. Stephen G. Nichols, Amy Remensnyder, Gabrielle Spiegel, and Robert Morrissey have all shed invaluable light on the various functions of the Charlemagne of legend within the historiographical and artistic traditions of medieval France. Most recently, Matthew Gabriele, in his 2011 *An Empire of Memory: The Legend of Charlemagne, the Franks, and Jerusalem before the First Crusade,* offers a lucid testament to the formation of a concept of Frankish identity based on the recapturing of a version of the Carolingian past that emerged after the real emperor's death in 814. Another recent work, Courtney Booker's *Past Convictions: The Penance of Louis the*

Iberia, c. 1095–c. 1187 (Woodbridge, UK, 2008), 164–165; Jace Stuckey, "Charlemagne as Crusader? Memory, Propaganda, and the Many Uses of Charlemagne's Legendary Expedition to Spain," in *The Legend of Charlemagne in the Middle Ages: Power, Faith, and Crusade,* ed. Matthew Gabriele and Jace Stuckey (New York, 2008), 139; Barton Sholod, "Charlemagne—Symbolic Link between the Eighth and Eleventh Century Crusades," in *Studies in Honor of M. J. Benardete (Essays in Hispanic and Sephardic Culture),* ed. Izaak A. Langnas and Barton Sholod (New York, 1965), 33–46.

Pious and the Decline of the Carolingians, skillfully dismantles the long-standing historical narrative of Carolingian decline by offering a fresh evaluation of the complex formation and varying receptions of the competing sources for the penance of Louis the Pious in 833.[9] *Emperor of the World* joins these recent efforts to offer new approaches to the written sources on which we depend, so that we may better understand the rhetorically complex figure of Charlemagne as it traversed the historical, political, ecclesiastical, and literary discourses of the medieval Latin West.[10]

Charlemagne's diplomatic exchanges with the East have long been of interest to scholars concerned with the role of pseudo-historical material in the promotion of Capetian kingship, in the construction of the memory of the early crusading movement, and in the development of the Romance epic tradition. The Charlemagne who traveled to the Holy Land has been viewed as a church builder, relic donor, and proto-crusading figure, but that image has been aptly described as "veiled in imprecision."[11] The Charlemagne who goes to the East has also persisted in modern scholarly memory (especially French) as a French cultural phenomenon that was appropriated by the Germans who sought to wrest the memory of the emperor from its overly successful Capetian cultivators.[12] This book argues that the journey to Jerusalem and Constantinople served as an assertion of symbolic victory for the West, and that this fantasy of Frankish protective custody of all of Christendom was the product of an imperial rather than a royal mindset. The evidence for this distinction becomes more pronounced in the late eleventh century when the Charlemagne who was chosen by God to protect all Christians began to function as an imperialist retort to reformist narratives of the papal origins of Carolingian imperial authority. Rather than affirming Constantine the Great's relinquishing of imperial authority to the Holy See, "Charlemagne and the East" offered an antidote to memories of eighth- and

---

9. Courtney M. Booker, *Past Convictions: The Penance of Louis the Pious and the Decline of the Carolingians* (Philadelphia, 2009); see also Mayke De Jong, *The Penitential State: Authority and Atonement in the Age of Louis the Pious, 814–840* (Cambridge, UK, 2009).

10. Stephen G. Nichols describes the evolving mythos of the Carolingian king as a phenomenon that moved beyond simple historical narrative to become a symbolic system and meaning-producing source that paralleled that of Christ himself; see Nichols, *Romanesque Signs: Early Medieval Narrative and Iconography* (New Haven, CT, 1983), 94. Eugene Vance evokes the idea of "an ideological discourse named 'Charlemagne,'" in "Semiotics and Power: Relics, Icons, and the *Voyage de Charlemagne à Jérusalem et à Constantinople*," *Romanic Review* 79 (1988): 170–71.

11. Elizabeth A. R. Brown and Michael W. Cothren, "The Twelfth-Century Crusading Window of the Abbey of Saint-Denis: *Praeteritorum enim Recordatio Futurorum est Exhibito*," *Journal of the Warburg and Courtauld Institutes* 49 (1968): 15.

12. Folz, *Le souvenir,* 207; Peter Munz, *Frederick Barbarossa: A Study in Medieval Politics* (Ithaca, NY, 1969), 243.

FIGURE 1.   Procession of surrendering foreign nations before an enthroned Otto III, Gospels of Otto III, c. 1000, Bayerische Staatsbibliothek, Munich

ninth-century popes legitimating the temporal authority of the Franks. Instead, the Charlemagne who symbolically conquered the East offered a model of divinely elected lay protection of the Christian imperium.

Beginning with Einhard's *Life of Charlemagne,* the Frankish king's diplomatic exchanges with the East occur as if in reaction to his coronation by Pope Leo III. This implied sequence gives the episode special value as the moment of reckoning between the two sides of the newly divided empire after the imperial investiture. The invented story takes on further significance, however, when considered in light of the fact that the Carolingian biographer constructed the episode based on a commonplace of classical imperial biography

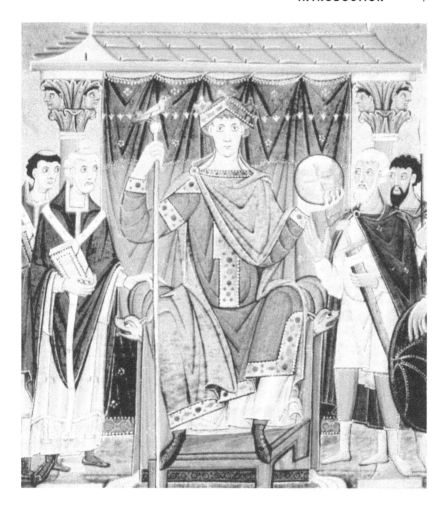

that connoted Roman universal dominion. The classical motif of surrendering foreign nations, to which I will refer using variations on the term
"foreign embassy topos," is exemplified by a scene in *Aeneid* 8, where Vergil
describes the shield given to Aeneas on which are depicted vanquished foreign nations parading before the emperor of a triumphant Rome.[13] Versions
of that motif became a commonplace in the discourse of empire and Roman
renewal throughout the Middle Ages.[14] In an example from a tenth-century

---

13. Vergil, *Aeneid* 8.720–23. The emperor Augustus adopted the topos for his own self-
celebratory inscription in his *Res Gestae Divi Augusti,* 31–32. See also the fourth-century biographer
Sextus Aurelius Victor on Augustus, *De Caesaribus* 1.

14. See Robert Holtzmann, *Der Weltherrschaftsgedanke des mittelalterlichen Kaisertums und die Souveränität des europäischen Staaten* (Darmstadt, 1953), 8; Karl J. Leyser, "Frederick Barbarossa, Henry II

chronicle of the deeds of the Saxons, Widukind of Corvey celebrates the transfer of empire to Otto I, to whom the Romans, Greeks, and Saracens all signal their surrender with exotic gifts and never-before-seen animals.[15] A splendid version of the motif appears in the dedication of the Gospel Book of Otto III from Reichenau, in which the emperor sits in majesty as representatives of various surrendering peoples, with heads bowed, process before him bearing gifts and tribute.[16] The passage from Odilo of Cluny in the epigraph that heads this introduction also provides a vivid example of the topos as it appeared within a stylized letter praising the Salian emperor Henry III, who had been crowned emperor in 1046 immediately following the elevation of Pope Clement II.[17]

When the foreign embassy motif appeared in classical and late antique biographies, such as Suetonius's *Life of Augustus,* or Eusebius's *Life of Constantine,* the allusion to foreign peoples surrendering to the emperor occurred within the enumeration of the victories that the emperor had achieved without battle as part of his attainment of universal dominion. In adopting this classical ideal of bloodless victory, Einhard and his successors faced an obstacle to the creation of an idealized picture of imperial unity not encountered by their classical predecessors, since the Byzantines, their fellow Christians, were the actual, titular Roman emperors. Those who articulated the theme of Roman imperial unity in the literature of the Latin West after 800 thus had to contend, in some way or other, with the contested inheritance of the leadership of the empire. For his part, Einhard invented an episode in Charlemagne's life that functioned as the next step after his investiture with the imperial title. As such, it provided a logical site for the discussion of the meaning of his coronation at Rome. And, like the coronation itself, the theoretical establishment of Charlemagne's authority in the divided empire offered a locus of memory ripe for multiple interpretations.[18]

---

and the Hand of Saint James," in *Medieval Germany and Its Neighbours (900–1250)* (London, 1983), 215, 218.

15. Widukind, *Rer. Gest.,* 135.

16. Henry Mayr-Harting, *Ottonian Book Illumination: An Historical Study* (London, 1999).

17. "Vicinae nationes aut se subdere vobis festinent aut preconiis vestrae virtutis auditis tremefactae tabescant. Slavus grunniat, Ungarus strideat, Grecus miretur et stupeat. Sarracenus turbetur et fugiat. Punicus persolvat tributum, Hispanus requirat auxilium, Burgundio veneratur et diligat, Aquitanus letabundus accurrat." In "Ein Schreiben Odilos von Cluni an Heinrich III. Vom October 1046," ed. Ernst Sackur, *Neues Archiv* 24 (1899): 732–35. The date and authorship are not certain. See Giles Constable, *Crusaders and Crusading in the Twelfth Century* (Aldershot, 2009), 188. For the politically contentious situation surrounding the papal election of 1046, see Stefan Weinfurter, *The Salian Century: Main Currents in an Age of Transition* (Philadelphia, 1999), 90–91.

18. For the notion of realms of memory, see Pierre Nora's prologue to *Realms of Memory: Rethinking the French Past* (New York, 1996), 1:1–20.

Over the centuries, as authors and scribes borrowed from and elaborated on the biographer's description of the symbolic surrender of the East to Charlemagne, the act of reproducing those diplomatic encounters allowed them to confront the implications of the shared custody of the Christian imperium.

The Christianization of the concept of eternal Rome that occurred during late antiquity had left as a legacy to the Middle Ages a vision of the Roman Empire as an instrument of divine providence, with the emperor as vicar of Christ on earth.[19] The imperial coronation of 800 was the first time a pope had claimed a role in selecting an emperor, and debates persisted for centuries over what the ceremony had implied about the competing roles of the papacy and lay leadership in the election and coronation of emperors in the Christian West. In an example of the contested nature of imperial coronations in the eleventh century, an image of the coronation of Henry III in 1046 depicts an enthroned Christ, not Clement II, crowning the kneeling German king and his wife as emperor and empress, while announcing that they will rule through him.[20] Just as medieval authors created conflicting versions of the events of Christmas 800, they also re-created Charlemagne's post-coronation diplomatic encounters with the imperial East and the Holy Land as part of the larger discussion of the Frankish inheritance of Rome. Since Einhard had established those exchanges as having occurred just after the coronation, they came to represent an essential step in the process of defining Christian imperial authority in a newly divided realm. This was particularly the case during the Investiture Contest of the late eleventh century, when the question of Pope Leo's role in the coronation of Charlemagne and the nature of the accompanying transfer of imperial authority became matters of intense partisan debate.

The versions of Charlemagne's encounters with the East that occur in works written prior to the Investiture Contest all affirm the Frankish king's indebtedness to the Holy See for his status as emperor. They also emphasize a spirit of cooperation between Charlemagne and Leo in their mission to protect Christendom. Beginning in the late eleventh century, a new scenario supplanted this vision of cooperation, and Charlemagne's status as imperial protector began to be portrayed as having been ordained by God and granted by the Roman people, without mediation by the papacy. This vision was in line with the claims of imperialist theorists at the time, who were working against assertions by the Holy See of its own brand of universal authority in

---

19. François Paschoud, *Roma Aeterna: Étude sur le patriotisme romain dans l'Occident latin à l'époque des grandes invasions* (Rome, 1967), 330.

20. Weinfurter, *Salian Century,* 92–93.

the empire. As Brett Whalen ably demonstrates in his recent book, the estab-lishment of the papacy as the center of Christendom defined as the Roman Empire became an ongoing project for the church.[21] Evidence from the period of most-intense conflict in the late eleventh century, especially Benzo of Albo's panegyric to Henry IV, the *Ad Heinricum,* reveals that in an atmo-sphere of competing expressions of imperial universalism, the Charlemagne who providentially united East and West ran counter to reformist visions of the pope at the helm of the Christian imperium.

In the mid-twelfth century, this new Charlemagne, whose imperial authority was God-ordained and unmediated by Rome, appealed to the promoters of Frederick Barbarossa during his conflict with the Holy See. Barbarossa's unsanctioned canonization of the Carolingian emperor in 1165 with the creation of a liturgical cult in honor of the new saint centered at Aachen marked the high point of his celebration of Charlemagne as a model Christian emperor and ideal forerunner of the German emperors. Scholars have often argued that the audacious act was intended as a means of reclaim-ing the Frankish emperor from the French.[22] This theory conforms to a more general historical narrative of rivalry between the German empire and the kingdom of France, but it does not account for the fact that the Capetian monarchy and its spokesmen at the royal abbey of Saint-Denis actually did relatively little to cultivate the memory of Charlemagne as emperor during the twelfth century. Frederick's actions are better understood when viewed within the context of generations of creative appropriation of episodes in Charlemagne's biography, especially those that could be altered to nourish a vision of the primacy of lay authority in the empire.

Reading Biographically

In the written life of an emperor, scenes such as the imperial investiture or the surrender of foreign nations were understood to be linked to other typologically similar episodes in other imperial *Lives.* As an episode from Charlemagne's legendary life, the reckoning with the imperial East offers an example of the practice of medieval biographical composition that Ruth Morse has elucidated.[23] Morse describes how written lives were constructed

21. Brett Edward Whalen, *Dominion of God: Christendom and Apocalypse in the Middle Ages* (Cam-bridge, MA, 2009), 41.

22. Folz, *Le souvenir,* 207.

23. Ruth Morse, *Truth and Convention in the Middle Ages: Rhetoric, Representation and Reality* (Cam-bridge, UK, 1991).

according to episodes, and argues that, more often than not, the value of a particular episode lay in its rhetorical pertinence. The importance of historical truth was therefore often secondary to rhetorical styling and intertextual play. Medieval biographical writing, whether secular or hagiographical, was built not on a series of facts, but on rhetorical topoi, the recognizable commonplaces that functioned as building blocks of the genre. Biographers wrote by compiling scenes and stories with the expectation that readers would recognize the commonplaces that were employed and then compare them to other instances of their usage. The units of composition were often altered, transformed, and amplified, while still claiming to represent the essential narrative of the life of the subject. Moreover, the events in the life of a subject regularly pointed outward to similar episodes in other biographies rather than inward to the personality and actual life of the subject.[24] The invention and reproduction of Charlemagne's post-coronation encounters with the East richly exemplify these literary processes.

Einhard's biography, where the encounters with the East originated, was both a popular work in itself and a source text for frequent copying and elaboration.[25] Richard Landes, in his work on Ademar of Chabannes's treatment of the life of Charlemagne, usefully describes these processes as the "embroidering of a mythical past."[26] Over time, a body of related fictions about the Frankish king emerged, which included new versions of key moments in his life, including his coronation and the subsequent reckoning with the rival Greeks. The story of his alliances with foreign leaders in the East is usually recounted as a series of ambassadorial exchanges. These elaborated passages constitute not just topoi but type-scenes, a conventional feature of medieval historiographical narrative that Joaquín Martínez Pizarro has shown to have allowed authors to address unresolved ideological conflicts with increased dramatic emphasis.[27] The depiction of Charlemagne's encounters with the East in the form of embassies allowed for the presentation of both written and verbal communication, and therefore a variety of narrative devices, including invented letters. Within these sometimes tense exchanges between foreign

---

24. Ibid., 127–28.

25. See generally Tischler, *Einharts Vita Karoli;* Matthew S. Kempshall, *Rhetoric and the Writing of History, 400–1500* (Manchester, 2011), 159.

26. Richard Landes, *Relics, Apocalypse, and the Deceits of History: Ademar of Chabannes, 989–1034* (Cambridge, MA, 1995), 141. Cf. Amy Remensnyder, "Topographies of Memory: Center and Periphery in High Medieval France," in *Medieval Concepts of the Past: Ritual, Memory, Historiography,* ed. Gerd Althoff, Johannes Fried, and Patrick J. Geary (Cambridge, UK, 2002), 208–14.

27. Joaquín Martínez Pizarro, "The King Says No: On the Logic of Type-Scenes in Late-Antique and Early-Medieval Narrative," in *The Long Morning of Medieval Europe: New Directions in Early Medieval Studies,* ed. Jennifer R. Davis and Michael McCormick (Aldershot, 2008), 182, 191–92.

envoys and the leaders to whom they bring messages, theoretical problems related to the meaning of the Frankish inheritance of Rome come to the fore. Authors were thus able to dramatize the issue of the divided empire within an imagined world of East–West diplomacy that is essentially the foreign embassy motif brought to life through dialogue and narrative intervention.

After the crumbling of the Carolingian Empire in the late ninth century, Charlemagne increasingly appeared as a protector of Christendom, ecclesiastical benefactor, and transporter of relics, an evolution that culminated in his canonization in 1165 and in the production of his saintly vita around 1180. His return from the East with relics is a wholly invented moment in his life, a circumstance that has often inspired historians to treat the episode too narrowly as a matter of naïve hagiographical invention and falsehood. But a more nuanced approach to the interpretation of hagiographical discourses can enrich our understanding of the function of Charlemagne as a procurer of relics and peaceful subjugator of nations in the East. Felice Lifshitz has argued, for instance, that when reading medieval hagiography, we must avoid seeing the genre as somehow false, and resist the secularizing instinct to divide fact from fiction so that we may then dismiss the fiction. "First we have to recognize re-visions and re-writings as historiographical," she argues, since medieval historians revised their pictures of the past to bring them in line with contemporary concerns.[28] Similarly, Jean Claude Schmitt writes in his presentation of the debates surrounding the unknown authorship of the autobiography of Herman the Jew, "One can hardly overstate the extent to which the insoluble contradiction of 'truth against fiction' is devoid of meaning."[29] My own approach to the alleged falseness of episodes in the evolving biography of Charlemagne also refuses this dichotomy, looking instead toward an improved understanding of the rhetorical function of fabricated memories in the various contexts in which they appear.

At the end of his summary of Philippe Buc's contribution to the valuable collection of essays entitled *Medieval Concepts of the Past: Ritual, Memory, Historiography,* editor Gerd Althoff writes, "The medievalist is imprisoned in texts, and must not forget that attempts to read rituals as texts amounts to reading texts as rituals."[30] It goes without saying, however, that the fact that written

28. Felice Lifshitz, "Beyond Positivism and Genre: 'Hagiographical' Texts as Historical Narrative," *Viator* 25 (1994): 99, 104. See also Thomas J. Heffernan, *Sacred Biography: Saints and Their Biographers in the Middle Ages* (Oxford, 1988).

29. Jean Claude Schmitt, *The Conversion of Herman the Jew: Autobiography, History, and Fiction in the Twelfth Century* (Philadelphia, 2010), 32.

30. Althoff, Fried, and Geary, *Medieval Concepts of the Past,* 12. See also Geoffrey Koziol, *Begging Pardon and Favor: Ritual and Political Order in Early Medieval France* (Ithaca, NY, 1992), and cf.

sources do not allow for unmediated access to past events need not keep us from pursuing a better understanding of their composition, especially when these sources depict ritualized events such as diplomatic encounters.[31] Booker's approach is helpful in this regard, as he seeks to move beyond the simple evaluation of competing narratives of the past, to the recognition of the rhetorical elements of those narratives, and ultimately to an "understanding of the historical beliefs and value systems that justified and informed them."[32] This current study does not confront the coronation of Charlemagne itself, nor is it interested in the real diplomatic exchanges with Byzantium that followed it. The possibility of accessing the truth and meaning behind ritual in the early medieval world is a matter for others to continue to debate.[33] For my purposes, I insist on the idea that the writing and rewriting of ritualized events such as the coronation, or the fabrication of politically significant diplomatic encounters, constituted its own sort of historical act. The reconceptualization of an event or the invention of a new one, such as the symbolic surrender of Byzantium, represent actions designed to change the perception of the past for present and future audiences. In this sense, by its very occurrence, an ideologically motivated act of writing or rewriting sheds light on the context of its own creation. My interest, therefore, is in the invention of events within biographical literature broadly defined, and more specifically encomiastic literature, which then allows me to consider the ways in which Charlemagne's symbolic conquest of the East after his coronation functioned over time and across multiple written and visual genres.

Prophecy as Praise: The Franks and the Fourth Kingdom

While Charlemagne's Carolingian encomiasts had looked to the classical and late antique past for imperial models, the revisers of the "Charlemagne and the East" episode, starting in the tenth century, chose to link the Frankish king typologically to another model of Roman universalism, the last Roman emperor of the sibylline tradition. Since late antiquity, the attainment of

---

Philippe Buc, *The Dangers of Ritual: Between Early Medieval Texts and Social Scientific Theory* (Princeton, NJ, 2001).

31. Martínez Pizarro deems type-scenes and other narrative formulae "priceless documents of the political and historical imagination, and thus a crucial chapter in the history of mentalities." In "King Says No," 191.

32. Booker, *Past Convictions,* 10.

33. See Geoffrey Koziol, "The Dangers of Polemic: Is Ritual Still an Interesting Topic of Historical Study?" *Early Medieval Europe* 11 (2002): 367–88.

Roman *dominium mundi* and world unity had been part of the teleological narrative of Christian history, and certain prophetic traditions demanded the eventual reunification of the divided empire before the end of time.[34] By the age of Charlemagne, anticipation of the "end time" and the fortunes of the Roman Empire had long been tied to exegesis on the Pauline statement in 2 Thessalonians 2, in which the apostle predicted the *discessio* or the "falling away" that would precede the appearance of the Son of Perdition who would capture the sanctuary of the Lord. Interpreters of the cryptic passage, most famously Jerome, linked Paul's *discessio* to the inevitable dissolution of Roman power, and announced that the decline of Roman imperial unity would herald the arrival of Antichrist.[35] As a result, the maintenance of unified Roman power came to be seen as necessary for the prevention of the coming of Antichrist. The vision of Rome as the force pushing back against the end of time contravened Augustine's warnings against viewing the empire as a transcendent entity, rather than as the mere political order that he believed it to be. The eschatological view of Rome exemplified by Jerome, with the empire as the restraining power working against the coming of Antichrist, was nonetheless quite popular in the Middle Ages.[36] At the time of Charlemagne's coronation, certain signs, such as the assumption of the imperial title in the East by a woman, Irene, had been taken as premonitions of the final dissolution of the Roman Empire.[37] For some, then, Charlemagne's coronation had been a God-ordained transfer of authority away from the Greeks to the Franks that had allowed for a postponement of the dissolution that Paul had predicted. The survival of the empire under the Franks thus served as the barrier against the end of time.[38]

Beginning with Notker the Stammerer, the ninth-century monk of Saint Gall, Charlemagne's rise to the status of emperor became more explicitly eschatological. Notker was the first author to dramatize Einhard's brief suggestion of world unity under Charlemagne that had been achieved through

---

34. See Ernst H. Kantorowicz, "The Problem of Medieval World Unity," *American Historical Association, Annual Report* 3 (1944): 31–37.

35. Benjamin Arnold, "Eschatological Imagination and the Program of Roman Imperial and Ecclesiastical Renewal at the End of the Tenth Century," in *The Apocalyptic Year 1000: Religious Expectation and Social Change, 950–1050,* ed. Richard Landes, Andrew Gow, and David C. Van Meter (Oxford, 2003); Richard Landes, "Lest the Millennium Be Fulfilled: Apocalyptic Expectations and the Pattern of Western Chronography, 100–800 C.E.," in *The Use and Abuse of Eschatology in the Middle Ages,* ed. Werner Verbeke, Daniël Verhelst, and Andries Welkenhuysen (Louvain, 1988); Marie Tanner, *The Last Descendants of Aeneas: The Hapsburgs and the Mythic Image of the Emperor* (New Haven, CT, 1993), 120.

36. Paschoud, *Roma Aeterna,* 332–34.

37. Landes, "Lest the Millennium Be Fulfilled," 201–3.

38. Arnold, "Eschatological Imagination," 273.

the bloodless alliances with the Greeks and the Persians. In the opening to his *Deeds of Charlemagne,* the monk ties the Frankish assumption of the imperial title to the persistence of Rome defined as the Fourth Kingdom, the last of the four world monarchies moving from East to West according to Jerome's reading of the dream of Nebuchadnezzar in Daniel 2.[39] Interpretations such as Notker's were not a matter of real political or territorial boundaries, to be sure, but of the continuing redefinition of eternal Rome in the literature of empire. The matter of who was to be at the helm as its unifier was therefore much more than a question of simple rivalry between Byzantium and the Franks for supremacy. The encounters with the East, when placed within an eschatological schema, become the defining moment after the coronation that establishes the authority of Charlemagne as the leader of Rome defined as the fourth and therefore last kingdom before the end of time. According to this theory, the duration of human history is governed by the survival of that final kingdom.

Not long after the Saxon assumption of the imperial title in 962, Charlemagne's encounters with the East began to incorporate elements of the sibylline prophecy of the Last Emperor.[40] In making the journey to the East himself, Charlemagne rehearses certain major aspects of the projected final journey of the prophetic leader, who was predicted to defeat all enemies of the faith, compel the conversion of the infidel, reunite East and West, and then lay down his regalia at Jerusalem before the coming of Antichrist. In the *Chronicon* of Benedict of Mount Soracte, the first known work to describe Charlemagne's own voyage to Jerusalem and Constantinople, the author states openly that the emperor returned home having subjugated many foreign nations. Charlemagne thus unites East and West through symbolic defeat, bringing Jerusalem under his jurisdiction, and he even decorates the Holy Sepulcher with gifts. He does not give up his title, however, nor does he relinquish his regalia. Instead, he returns to the West in triumph bearing relics and enjoys the acclamation of the Roman people. The journey thus marks a political beginning, not an end, to the Frankish leadership of the Roman Empire.

Rather than mimicking the pursuit of the millennium, the Charlemagne who recalls the Last Emperor embodies the glory of imperial unification

---

39. Jerome interprets the dream by stating that the head of gold is Babylon, the silver represents the Medo-Persians, the bronze the Macedonian empire of Alexander and his successors, and the iron, which breaks into many pieces, is Rome, which overcomes all previous empires. *Hieronymus: Commentariorum in Danielem libri III,* ed. F. Glorie, *CC* 75A (Turnhout, 1964). Orosius, on the other hand, lists them as the Babylonian, Carthaginian, Macedonian, and Roman. See David Rohrbacher, *The Historians of Late Antiquity* (London, 2002), 145–46.

40. Bernard McGinn, *Visions of the End: Apocalyptic Traditions in the Middle Ages* (New York, 1998), 44–50.

described in the prophecy, but as a celebration of imperial renewal, not end time speculation. There were competing attitudes toward the coming end time in the Middle Ages, some characterized by the desire to hasten the Last Judgment, others by feelings of dread and a desire for its delay.[41] The creation of a Charlemagne who reflected elements of imperial apocalyptic tradition did not fit into either of these categories. Over a century ago, Franz Kampers argued that the competition for the symbolic leadership of the Christian Roman Empire truly took hold in the eleventh century with the proliferation of Greek, Frankish, and German-friendly sibyls predicting the arrival of the Last Emperor.[42] As early as the mid-tenth century, however, evidence reveals that the elision of the Frankish emperor with the apocalyptic Last Emperor had already begun to function as a tool in the political discourse on the leadership of the empire. Charlemagne's quasi-apocalyptic journey to the East served to praise the preservation and prolonging of the empire, an encomiastic function of the episode that persisted for centuries to come.

Beginning with Benedict's imagined journey, Charlemagne's symbolic subjugation of the East came to reflect a combination of two conflicting medieval conceptions of apocalyptic Roman universalism. One was based on an ideal of peace that had evolved from the prediction of the Cumaean Sibyl that a peaceful end to all wars would be followed by a golden age, a prophecy made famous in Vergil's fourth eclogue.[43] That ideal was often seen to have been fulfilled by the peace of Augustus, to whom biographers and historians applied the foreign embassy motif as an expression of the bloodless and willing surrender of all nations to his universal and peaceful rule. The other prevalent model of *dominium mundi* derived from the sibylline Last Emperor prophecy, as told in the text of the Tiburtine Sibyl and later in the *Revelations* of Pseudo-Methodius. In its various guises, the prophecy foretold the violent conquest of all enemies of the faith to bring imperial unity before the end of time.[44] The late Roman sibyls had been preoccupied with the emperor's annihilation of barbarians, and so, too, the medieval sibyl celebrates the emperor's crushing and forced conversion of all enemies before the

---

41. Adriaan Hendrik Bredero, *Christendom and Christianity in the Middle Ages: The Relations between Religion, Church, and Society* (Grand Rapids, MI, 1994), 66.

42. Franz Kampers, *Die Deutsche Kaiseridee in Prophetie und Sage* (Munich, 1896), 49–53; Bredero, *Christendom*, 68.

43. Jan M. Ziolkowski and Michael C. J. Putnam, eds., *The Virgilian Tradition: The First Fifteen Hundred Years* (New Haven, CT, 2008), 487–503.

44. Jay Rubenstein, *Armies of Heaven: The First Crusade and the Quest for Apocalypse* (New York, 2011), 51–52.

consummation of his reign at Jerusalem.[45] It is my contention that the Charlemagne of legend was defined at a basic level by the intersection of these two competing ideals. Was he a conquering emperor or a humble pilgrim? He was both and neither. The two models are seemingly incommensurate, but authors managed to preserve certain more favorable elements of the Last Emperor tradition, such as his unification of East and West, while eschewing its violence. Although Charlemagne is famously a warrior and conqueror of non-Christian peoples, he is almost never depicted as a conqueror in the East. Instead, those who sought to cast him as a universalizing imperial figure chose to adhere to the classical ideal by avoiding references to battles in the Holy Land and by describing his peaceful pilgrimages. Authors were able to pacify the violence implied by the prophecy by rewriting his victories as symbolic, and by placing in his hands the relics that symbolized those bloodless victories, and therefore his new spiritual authority in the empire.

Charlemagne, when presented as a unifier of East and West, functions as the embodiment of imperial continuity under the Franks after the *translatio imperii* away from the Greeks. In this way, he appears as a sort of forerunner of the predicted Last Emperor, but he is clearly a figure of the past whose memory is invoked as a tool of political commentary. Roman universalism had been tied to Christian eschatology since late antiquity, but the emergence of a Charlemagne whose actions mimicked those of the projected Last Emperor only began after the Ottonian assumption of the imperial title. Although the "Charlemagne and the East" narrative became increasingly imbued with end time themes, these shades of eschatological discourse were related to dynastic politics in the empire rather than end time speculation.[46] At the end of the ninth century, Notker had praised Charlemagne by portraying his imperial reign as the inauguration of the Frankish hold over the Roman Empire according to the schema of the Four Kingdoms. The authors who depicted Charlemagne as an avatar of the last Roman emperor also did so as a means of commenting, sometimes positively and sometimes negatively, on the imperial pretentions of the regimes under which they wrote. As one scholar notes, the apocalyptic myth was broad enough to "provide symbolic resources for both the legitimation and the critique of religious and secular power."[47]

45. David S. Potter, *Prophets and Emperors: Human and Divine Authority from Augustus to Theodosius* (Cambridge, MA, 1994), 140.

46. For the importance of prophecy in secular politics and the relative lack of importance of it in ecclesiastical politics, see Robert E. Lerner, "Medieval Prophecy and Politics," *Annali dell'Istituto storico italo-germanico in Trento* 15 (1999): 423.

47. Stephen D. O'Leary, *Arguing the Apocalypse: A Theory of Millennial Rhetoric* (New York, 1994), 57–58.

Despite the prominence of apocalyptic themes in nearly all iterations of "Charlemagne and the East," the function of the episode was primarily enco-miastic. The episode spoke to elite political concerns rather than popular apoca-lyptic speculation by affirming the continuation of the Roman Empire under the aegis of the West as it passed from one dynasty to the next, beginning, not ending, with Charlemagne. The projection onto the past of an idealized vision of Charlemagne as an emperor of all Christians elected by God to unite and protect the Christian imperium was intended to nourish the rhetoric of Roman renewal rather than to fuel crusading fervor or to herald the end of days. For whatever similarities he bore to the prophesied Last Emperor, the Charlemagne who returned from the East with relics was not a messianic figure. His trium-phal journey does not signal the end of history, but offers, through the invoca-tion of its memory, a locus of commentary on the state of the empire.

This book begins with Einhard's early ninth-century invention of the friendly transfer of custody of holy sites in Jerusalem to Charlemagne after his coronation. It ends with a letter written by the Hohenstaufen emperor Frederick II to the king of England in 1229, in which the controversial Ger-man leader vaunts his recent recuperation of the Holy Land for the Christian West through peaceful negotiation with the sultan of Egypt. For a variety of reasons, I have limited my inquiry to Latin texts, but not out of any disregard for the rich vernacular tradition of Charlemagne's legendary expeditions to the Holy Land and Spain. On the contrary, this book has turned out to be, in many ways, the prologue I had been seeking to my work on the Charlemagne of the Old French tradition. As medievalists, we still wrestle with what to do with obvious fictions when they seem to invade an otherwise "historical" document. In the not-so-distant past, authors such as Notker the Stammerer and Benzo of Alba were condemned for their indulgence in creative inven-tion, often by the very people who mined their works for nuggets of historical information. Notker and Benzo have been, for me, some of the richest sources of insight into the meanings of Charlemagne. Scholars of medieval historio-graphical writing have certainly moved beyond such simplistic approaches to their sources, but questions still remain about how we should best interpret the fictions and fabrications that inform our understanding of the medieval past. In this journey over several centuries, I hope to have offered a new understanding of one of the medieval West's most enigmatic political fictions.

 CHAPTER 1

Carolingian Origins

Einhard

The apocryphal travels of Charlemagne to Jerusalem and Constantinople have their roots in the Carolingian sources of the eighth and ninth centuries. The story begins with chapter 16 of Einhard's *Life of Charlemagne*, in which the biographer elaborates the ways in which foreign leaders sought the friendship of the Frankish king after his imperial coronation and willingly offered themselves as his subjects.[1] Charlemagne increased the glory of his kingdom, Einhard explains, by winning over kings and peoples through friendly means. One of the surrendering kings was Alfonso, the king of Galicia and Asturias, who sent envoys charged with delivering letters and the message that the Spanish leader wished to be referred to as Charles's subject. The Irish kings, moved by the Frankish king's generosity, also declared him to be their lord, and were eager to serve as his willing subjects. The biographer even claims that some of the letters that were sent to Charles still survive as evidence of the esteem in which he was held.

---

1. The biography circulated anonymously from the 820s to the 840s until Walafrid Strabo added an introduction and divided the work into chapters. See Matthew Innes and Rosamond McKitterick, "The Writing of History," in *Carolingian Culture: Emulation and Innovation*, ed. Rosamond McKitterick (Cambridge, UK, 1994), 213.

Einhard then describes the emperor's exchanges with Harun al Rachid, the king of the Persians, who held almost the entire East, except for India. Harun was so eager to count Charlemagne among his friends, the reader learns, that when Frankish envoys came to the East, the Persian king sent them home with many gifts from the Holy Sepulcher. Harun also allowed the envoys to complete their mission at the site of the Resurrection. The biographer then makes the oblique suggestion that Harun had allotted to Charlemagne authority over certain sites in the Holy Land, stating that he "even handed over the sacred and salvific place, so that it might be considered as under Charles's control." Harun then sends his own representatives back with the Frankish envoys, laden with magnificent gifts including robes, spices, and other riches of the East. A few years earlier, Einhard adds, Harun had honored Charles's request that he send him an elephant.[2] The biographer completes his portrait of diplomatic encounters with the East by relating that the Greek emperors had previously sought a treaty to allay their fears that the Frankish leader wished to annex their empire in the wake of his coronation. He lists three emperors of Constantinople—Nicephorus, Michael, and Leo—all of whom, he insists, had voluntarily sought Charles's friendship, as well as an alliance, by sending multiple embassies to the Frankish leader. The passage closes with Einhard's comment that the Romans and Greeks are always suspicious of Frankish power, which explains the continued popularity of the Greek proverb that says, "Have a Frank as a friend, never as a neighbor."[3]

The harmonious relationship between Charlemagne and Harun al Rachid has long been a prized piece of Carolingian historical memory, one made more fascinating, no doubt, by the story of Harun's gift of an elephant. For centuries, the tale of his concession of jurisdiction over holy sites in Jerusalem was borne along by the popularity of the Frankish sources and Einhard's biography, as well as by the more explicit articulations of the story found in such works as the versified deeds of Charlemagne by the Saxon Poet and

---

2. Lawrence Nees, "Charlemagne's Elephant," *Quintana: Revista do Departamento de Historia da Arte, Universidade de Santiago de Compostela* 5 (2006): 13–49.

3. Einhard, *VK*, 16. See also Paul Edward Dutton, *Charlemagne's Courtier: The Complete Einhard* (Peterborough, ON, 1998), 25–26, and *Charlemagne and Louis the Pious: Lives by Einhard, Notker, Ermoldus, Thegan, and the Astronomer*, trans. Thomas F. X. Noble (University Park, PA, 2009), 35. Michael McCormick translates the proverb as "If you have a Frank who is a friend, you don't have him for a neighbor," and proposes that it was a saying coined by Byzantines in Rome; see "Diplomacy and the Carolingian Encounter with Byzantium Down to the Accession of Charles the Bald," in *Eriugena: East and West*, ed. Bernard McGinn and Willemin Otten (Notre Dame, IN, 1994), 22.

Notker the Stammerer's *Deeds of Charles the Great*.[4] The *Royal Frankish Annals* (*Annales regni francorum*) made no mention of this specific concession, but furnished instead the well-known account of how the patriarch of Jerusalem had sent keys to the Holy Sepulcher and a banner to the newly invested Frankish emperor.[5]

While Charlemagne does indeed seem to have received an elephant from Harun, the claims of a transfer of custody of sites in Jerusalem have failed to pass historical muster. Some noted scholars, such as Louis Bréhier, mounted valiant efforts in the early twentieth century to verify the protectorate story.[6] In an assessment of Einhard's biography as a source for the historical life of Charlemagne, Louis Halphen, in contrast with Bréhier, puzzled over the tendentious nature of chapter 16 and wondered whether Einhard was not guilty of mixing up a collection of rather vague memories.[7] Halphen questioned the existence of the letters from the Spanish and Irish kings and raised grave doubts about the presentation of relations with Harun.[8] The 1930s witnessed a flurry of scholarly debate over the concession of territory in Palestine, and scholars tended to concur, with some exceptions, that the protectorate story was a legend.[9] In an article from 1981, Aryeh Graboïs summarized the debate, concluding that scholars had yet to reach much agreement about the "goals and meanings" of the information in the Frankish sources concerning the Frankish relationship to Baghdad.[10] Graboïs cited Steven Runciman extensively in his notes, including the latter's forceful proclamation on

4. Poeta Saxo, verses 88–91. "Nam gemmas, aurum, vestes et aromata crebro / Ac reliquas orientas opes direxerat illi / Ascribique locum sanctum Hierosolimorum / Concessit propriae Caroli semper dicioni."

5. *ARF, sub annis* 799, 800.

6. Louis Bréhier, "Les origines des rapports entre les Francs et la Syrie: Le protectorat de Charlemagne," in *Congrès français de la Syrie*, vol. 2 (Marseille, 1919). Another major proponent was F. W. Buckler, in *Harunu'l-Rashid and Charles the Great* (Cambridge, UK, 1931).

7. Louis Halphen, *Études critiques sur l'histoire de Charlemagne: Les sources de l'histoire de Charlemagne, la conquête de la Saxe, le couronnement impérial, l'agriculture et la propriété rurale, l'industrie et la commerce* (Paris, 1921), 97. "Mais il est difficile d'expliquer les dires étranges d'Einhard autrement que par toute une série de confusions."

8. Ibid., 96–98.

9. Einar Joranson, "The Alleged Frankish Protectorate in Palestine," *American Historical Review* 32 (1927): 241–61; Arthur Kleinclausz, "La légende du protectorat de Charlemagne sur la Terre Sainte," *Syria* 7 (1926): 211–33; Steven Runciman, "Charlemagne and Palestine," *English Historical Review* 50 (1935): 606–19. Buckler, *Harunu'l-Rashid*, is an exception.

10. Aryeh Graboïs, "Charlemagne, Rome and Jerusalem," *Revue belge de philologie et d'histoire* 59 (1981): 792–95. For other modern discussions of the debate, see Michael Borgolte, *Der Gesandtenaustausch der Karolinger mit den Abbasiden und mit den Patriarchen von Jerusalem* (Munich, 1976); Karl Schmid, "Aachen und Jerusalem: Ein Beitrag zur historischen Personenforschung der Karolingerzeit," in *Das Einhardkreuz: Vorträge und Studien zum Münsteraner Diskussion zum arcus Einhardi*, ed. Karl Hauck (Göttingen, 1974), 140–42.

the protectorate controversy: "It is time that its ghost were laid."[11] While Runciman's call to have the protectorate story put to rest has been largely answered, some have continued to breathe life into the tale by depicting it as a moment of symbolic exchange of territory or cementing of friendship.[12] None, however, has brought any new historical evidence to bear.

The origins of this episode lie outside of history, I contend, and are to be found instead in the literary construction of the aftermath of Charlemagne's imperial coronation. That investigation leads back to the skeptical Halphen and his charge that chapter 16 of the *Life of Charlemagne* constituted a confused jumble of unverifiable facts.[13] The French scholar was right to be skeptical about the veracity of the events that Einhard described, but he was mistaken in charging the biographer with "une série de confusions." The spare and somewhat cryptic chapter, while indeed not based on historical fact, proves to be a meticulously constructed piece of imperial biography.[14] Far from throwing together mixed-up facts of questionable value, Einhard presented a series of events that he had deliberately assembled. His depiction of the emperor's diplomatic exchanges with rulers from the four corners of the world offers a careful refashioning of Frankish historiographical materials to conform to a classical and late antique encomiastic topos

---

11. Graboïs, "Charlemagne, Rome and Jerusalem," 795; Runciman, "Charlemagne and Palestine," 619.

12. Matthias Becher states that Harun transferred administrative control of the Holy Sepulcher to Charlemagne ("Verfügungsgewalt über das Grab Christi") in 802; see Becher, *Karl der Grosse* (Munich, 1999), 88. Alessandro Barbero's 2002 biography also depicts the transfer as a symbolic gift, although he clarifies that the passage referred to the land on which the Holy Sepulcher stood; see Barbero, *Charlemagne: Father of a Continent*, trans. Allan Cameron (Berkeley, CA, 2004), 100–101. Tomaz Mastnak presents the exchanges uncritically, echoing Buckler's idea that had the Carolingian Empire lasted longer, Christian and Islamic cultures "might have been on better terms"; see Mastnak, *Crusading Peace: Christendom, the Muslim World, and Western Political Order* (Berkeley, CA, 2002), 68. Roger Collins makes no mention of the protectorate story in his *Charlemagne* (Toronto, 1998), 152; nor does Rosamond McKitterick, *Charlemagne: The Formation of a European Identity* (Cambridge, UK, 2008). See Borgolte, *Der Gesandtenaustausch der Karolinger*, 82–83. Dieter Hägermann refers to the "angeblichen Übergabe" in *Karl der Grosse: Herrscher des Abendlandes* (Berlin, 2000), 409 and 518.

13. Louis Halphen, *Éginhard: Vie de Charlemagne* (Paris, 1947), 49.

14. For studies of the painstaking art of Einhard the biographer, see Walter Berschin, *Biographie und Epochenstil im lateinischen Mittelalter III: Karolingische Biographie 750–920 n. Chr.* (Stuttgart, 1991), 199–219; David Ganz, "Einhard's Charlemagne: The Characterization of Greatness," in *Charlemagne: Empire and Society*, ed. Joanna Story (Manchester, 2005), 38–51; David Ganz, "The Preface to Einhard's 'Vita Karoli,'" in *Einhard: Studien zu Leben und Werk dem Gedenken an Helmut Beumann gewidmet*, ed. Hermann Schefers (Darmstadt, 1997), 299–310; Matthew S. Kempshall, "Some Ciceronian Models for Einhard's *Life of Charlemagne*," *Viator* 26 (1995): 11–37; Heinz Wolter, "Intention und Herrscherbild in Einhards 'Vita Karoli Magni,'" *Archiv für Kulturgeschichte* 68 (1986): 317; Lawrence Nees, *A Tainted Mantle: Hercules and the Classical Tradition at the Carolingian Court* (Philadelphia, 1991), 114; Jason Glenn, "Between Two Empires: Einhard and His Charles the Great," in *The Middle Ages in Texts and Texture: Reflections on Medieval Sources* (Toronto, 2011), 105–18.

that symbolized the achievement of Roman universal dominion. Einhard's use of this biographical motif then became the framework on which the literature surrounding "Charlemagne and the East" would be built for centuries to come.[15]

In the classical tradition, the foreign embassy topos, which often features envoys arriving from far-off lands with sumptuous offerings and exotic beasts, functions as a celebration of a unified empire at peace. By listing the embassies sent from places such as India, Britain, or Scythia, the author signals that the emperor's dominion now stretches as far to the east, west or north as possible. The commonplace also functions as a celebration of imperial victories gained without war, and serves as a rhetorical device designed to praise the emperor for his ability to elicit the willing submission of distant nations through the power of his worldwide reputation. The motif is famously illustrated at the end of *Aeneid* 8 where Vergil describes the shield given to Aeneas that is resplendent with images of the future triumphs of imperial Rome. The poet presents a parade of vanquished nations, as diverse in their languages as they are in their dress, processing before an enthroned emperor.[16] Numerous other instances of the topos occur in works by authors who either were known or could have been known to Einhard, including Suetonius, Florus, Eutropius, and Orosius. Versions of it also exist in praise of Constantine in Eusebius's *Life of Constantine* and in the fourth-century *XII Panegyrici Latini*, both of whose influence on Einhard cannot be concretely attested, but which are nonetheless crucial for the understanding of the Christianization of this classical rhetorical construction. And finally, the biography of the emperor Aurelian in the so-called *Historia Augusta*, written around 400, offers an extravagant example of the rhetoric of Roman universalism in imperial biography in a work that parodies the Suetonian model.

Augustus

Einhard provides no dates for Charlemagne's diplomatic relations with foreign princes, but instead arranges the material from the Frankish sources to convey that the events had occurred in reaction to the recent coronation at Rome. In doing so, he highlights the new emperor's ability to elicit the willing surrender of foreign nations, a well-known form of praise for a new Caesar in the Roman tradition. Other Roman emperors, such as Augustus

---

15. An earlier version of this argument appeared under the title "Foreign Embassies and Roman Universality in Einhard's *Life of Charlemagne*," *Florilegium* 22 (2005): 25–57.

16. Vergil, *Aeneid* 8.720–23.

and Constantine, whose reigns held providential meaning for the history of the Christian Roman Empire, had received similar praise. Suetonius is certainly one source for Einhard's adaptation of the foreign embassy motif, but he was likely not the only one.[17] The relationship between *The Life of Charlemagne* and *The Lives of the Caesars* is well established, but the passages in chapter 16 attest to the biographer's ample independence from the Roman model. Suetonius's version of the Roman universality topos is found, not surprisingly, in the *Life of Augustus*: "The reputation for prowess and moderation which he thus gained led even the Indians and Scythians, peoples known to us only by hearsay, to send, on their own accord, envoys to seek his friendship and that of the Roman people."[18] Just prior to this passage Suetonius offers an enumeration of conquests, but then tempers the triumphal mood with discussion of the far-off nations that peacefully sought the friendship of the emperor. This sequence, which places a catalog of "deeds in war" just prior to a list of "deeds in peace," corresponds to a conventional sequence of biographical themes in a panegyrical work, and is designed to illustrate the vastness of the emperor's domain.[19]

Suetonius's catalog of deeds in peace emphasizes that Augustus did not aim to expand the empire or increase his glory strictly through war, an ideal that Einhard echoes on behalf of Charlemagne. With his construction of chapter 16, the Carolingian biographer adheres to the convention of "deeds in peace" in a section that he clearly demarcates as distinct from the previous section containing a lengthy enumeration of Charlemagne's conquests. At the end of chapter 15, Einhard closes the catalog of military victories with the assertion that, despite Charles's many conquests, "other peoples [living there], who far outnumbered them, simply surrendered." Chapter 16 then begins with his statement that the king had increased the glory of

17. For Einhard's use of Suetonius, see Helmut Beumann, "Topos und Gedankengefüge bei Einhard," *Archiv für Kulturgeschichte* 33 (1951): 337–50; Sigmund Hellman, "Einhards literarische stellung," *Historische Vierteljahrschrift* 27 (1932): 81–82; Matthew Innes, "The Classical Tradition in the Carolingian Renaissance: Ninth-Century Encounters with Suetonius," *International Journal of the Classical Tradition* 3 (1997); F. L. Ganshof, *The Carolingians and the Frankish Monarchy: Studies in Carolingian History*, trans. Janet Sondheimer (Ithaca, NY, 1971), 19; Berschin, *Biographie und Epochenstil*, 212–19.

18. Suetonius, *Aug.* 21.6. "Qua virtutis moderationisque fama Indos etiam ac Scythas auditu modo cognitos pellexit ad amicitiam suam populique Romani ultro per legatos petendam."

19. For conventions of panegyric, see *In Praise of Later Roman Emperors: The "Panegyrici Latini,"* ed. C. E. V. Nixon and Barbara Saylor Rodgers (Berkeley, CA, 1994), 11–12; Eusebius, *VC*, 191. See also Tomas Hägg and Philip Rousseau, *Greek Biography and Panegyric in Late Antiquity* (Berkeley, CA, 2000), 1–5.

his kingdom through his alliances with other kings and peoples.[20] Einhard also imitated Suetonius by emphasizing the importance of the emperor's reputation in his achievement of peace in the empire. Suetonius invites the reader to infer that Augustus's worldwide renown intimidated rulers of distant nations so much that they eagerly sent friendly legations from across the globe to seek his clement friendship. Building on Suetonius, the fourth-century historian Eutropius later claimed that until the reign of Augustus, the name of "Romans" had been unknown to the Scythians and the Indians, who then sent envoys and gifts.[21] Einhard likewise emphasizes the power of the emperor's reputation by boasting that the leaders who sent letters and declarations of loyalty had never seen Charles, but that once he was crowned emperor, his reputation spread quickly, leading foreign nations, in particular the Greeks, to seek his friendship out of fear.

Orosius, whose work was well known to the Carolingians, viewed the creation of a Christian Roman Empire everywhere at peace as the culmination of God's plan. For him, the coincidence of the peace under Augustus during the lifetime of Jesus had been established by God for the benefit of Christians.[22] Building from Eutropius, Orosius created an elaborate version of the topos of surrendering nations in his highly influential *Seven Books of History against the Pagans*. After describing the conquests of Augustus, he announces the arrival of envoys representing peoples from all corners of the earth and makes a comparison to Alexander the Great that implicitly conveys that the current Roman emperor has surpassed the famous Greek. Envoys of the Indians and the Scythians traverse the entire world to find the emperor in Tarragona in Nearer Spain. They regale him with stories of the glory of Alexander the Great, who had once, while in Babylon, received an embassy of Spaniards and Gauls seeking peace. Demonstrating that history has since progressed westward, as the eschatological movement of world monarchies dictated it would, Orosius explains how now, the supplicant easterner, the Indian, and the northern Scythian, each bearing gifts from his native land, come seeking peace from the emperor.[23] The Roman emperor then greets

---

20. Einhard, *VK*, 16. "Auxit etiam gloriam regni sui quibusdam regibus ac gentibus per amicitiam sibi conciliatis."

21. Eutropius, *Brev.*, 7.10.1. "Scythae et Indi, quibus antea Romanorum nomen incognitum fuerat, munera et legatos ad eum miserunt." See also Victor, *De Caesaribus*, 1.7. "Felix adeo (absque liberis tamen simulque coniugio), ut Indi, Scythae, Garamantes ac Bactri legatos mitterent orando foederi."

22. Glenn F. Chesnut, "Eusebius, Augustine, Orosius, and the Later Patristic and Medieval Christian Historians," in *Eusebius, Christianity, and Judaism*, ed. Harold W. Attridge and Gohei Hata (Detroit, 1992), 698.

23. Orosius, *Hist.*, 6.21.

the weary travelers from his post in Spain, which is the symbol of the far reaches of the West in the language of praise for a ruler's universal dominion.

Orosius closes 6.21 and the discussion of conquest and then opens 6.22 with the announcement of the universal peace under Augustus: "Therefore in the 752nd year after the founding of the City, Caesar Augustus, with all the nations, from the East to the West, from the North to the South, and over the whole circuit of the Ocean, arranged in a single peace, then closed the doors of Janus for a third time."[24] Then, unlike his non-Christian predecessors, Orosius ties the universal peace under Augustus to the birth of Christ, stating that God had ordained his birth and arranged that God in human form would be counted in the first census of Rome, marking Augustus as the first of all men and the Romans as the rulers of the world.[25] The fact that God allowed himself to be counted as a man in the census taken under Augustus, for Orosius, distinguished him from all previous rulers in human history, for not even the Babylonians or the Macedonians had enjoyed such an honor.[26]

In his presentation of Charles's "deeds in peace," Einhard creates his own version of the foreign embassy motif. He reports the submission of Alfonso, king of Asturias and Galicia, and the Irish kings (*Scottorum*) who sought his friendship by means of letters. As with the exchanges with Harun, here, too, historians have been unable to substantiate Einhard's claims. Alfonso dominates the entry for 798 in the *Royal Frankish Annals*, but does not appear again. In a valiant but fruitless effort to account for the lack of evidence for these offers of surrender, Ganshof advanced the "likely hypothesis" that information about Charlemagne's relationships with Alfonso and the Irish "could" have been gleaned from the archives with access granted under Louis the Pious.[27] If, instead, we read Alfonso of Asturias and the Irish kings metonymically, as symbols of Spain and Britain, both shorthand for the extremes of the far West in the language of Roman universalism, then the content as well as the rhetorical intention of the passage come into much sharper focus. Einhard is not inventing history out of whole cloth, but is rearranging the material from the annals to fit a predetermined pattern for writing imperial praise. After this creative establishment of the western extreme of his geography, the biographer does the same for the East by introducing Harun, king of the Persians, who sends gifts from his native land, followed by the Greeks.

---

24. Orosius, *Hist.*, 6.22. "Itaque anno ab Vrbe condita DCCLII Caesar Augustus ab oriente in occidentem, a septentrione in meridiem ac per totum Oceani circulum cunctis gentibus una pace conpositis, Iani portas tertio ipse tunc clausit."

25. Orosius, *Hist.*, 6.22.

26. Orosius, *Hist.*, 6.22.

27. Ganshof, *Carolingians and the Frankish Monarchy*, 3.

The second-century historian Florus, whose abbreviated history of Rome has been identified as a source for the *Royal Frankish Annals*,[28] provides an expanded version of the foreign embassy topos in the finale to his history. Florus writes that now that the peoples of the West and South had been subjugated, as were the peoples of the North, the ones between the Rhine and the Danube, and the peoples of the East between the Cyrus and Euphrates, the other nations, too, who were not under the rule of the empire, felt the greatness of Rome as the conqueror of the world. The Scythians and the Sarmatians sent ambassadors seeking friendship, as did the Chinese and the Indians, who lived immediately beneath the sun. They brought elephants among their gifts, as well as precious stones and pearls, but regarded their long four-year journey to Rome as the greatest tribute that they rendered.[29] Florus may also shed some light on Einhard's choice of Alfonso of Asturias as the symbol of Spanish surrender, since he names the Astures in his account of Augustus's conquest of Spain. Orosius had likewise singled out the Astures, as well as the Cantabri, as the bravest peoples in Spain in his own list of conquests by Augustus just prior to the announcement of the parade of surrendering nations.[30] Einhard updated the story to conform to contemporary circumstances, but with allusions to his classical models.

Biographies of emperors were not always occasions for unbridled praise, and the celebration of universal dominion under a Roman emperor was ripe for subversion and even parody. This is the case in the outlandish rendition of the foreign embassy motif composed by the author of the late fourth-century series of imperial vitae known as the *Historia Augusta*. This fraudulent and satirical compilation of imperial biographies is a late-antique Latin work whose availability in Carolingian circles in the ninth century and potential influence on Carolingian biography have both been demonstrated.[31] The great procession of vanquished peoples bearing gifts to a universal emperor

---

28. Rogers Collins, "The 'Reviser' Revisited: Another Look at the Alternative Version of the *Annales Regni Francorum*," in *After Rome's Fall: Narrators and Sources of Early Medieval History; Essays Presented to Walter Goffart*, ed. Alexander Callander Murray (Toronto, 1998), 206.

29. Florus, *Epitome of Roman History* 2.34, trans. Edward Seymour Forster (Cambridge, MA, 2005 [1929]), 348–51.

30. Orosius, *Hist.*, 6.21.

31. See André Chastagnol's introduction to *Histoire Auguste: Les empereurs romains des IIe et IIIe siècles* (Paris, 1994). He notes that two ninth-century manuscripts are extant, of which the *Palatinus Latinus 899* now in the Vatican Library is thought to have been written at Lorsch. See also Leighton D. Reynolds, *Texts and Transmission: A Survey of the Latin Classics* (Oxford, 1983), 354–55. Berschin points to evidence of knowledge of the *Historia Augusta* in Thegan's biography of Louis the Pious; see Berschin, *Biographie und Epochenstil*, 386. See also Javier Velaza, "Le *Collectaneum* de Sedulius Scotus et l'*Histoire Auguste*," in *Histoire Augustae Colloquium Argentoratense*, ed. Giorgio Bonamente et al. (Bari, 1998): 339–47.

appears in the life of Aurelian, by whom, in this fictionalized realm, the whole world was restored to Roman jurisdiction.[32] The author satirizes the motif by describing an exaggerated profusion of envoys from foreign nations, with their gifts and exotic animals, and then offers an obvious send-up of praise for the emperor. The scene requires some exposition. In a letter to his archenemy, Zenobia, queen of the East, Aurelian identifies himself as *receptor orientis*, emperor of Rome and "recoverer of the East."[33] In an upside-down version of the Suetonian model, Aurelian scolds Zenobia for failing to surrender willingly and enjoins her to hand over to the Romans her jewels, gold, silver, horses, camels, and silks.[34] Zenobia refuses on the grounds that reinforcements are on their way from Persia, so the angered Roman emperor conquers her, thereby reclaiming the entire East.[35] Among the spoils, Aurelian receives a purple cloak (*pallium*) from the king of the Persians, who hails from the farthest Indies.[36]

When Aurelian returns to Rome in triumph, the parade of vanquished Eastern nations commences in an exaggerated parody of the use of such processions as symbols of Roman universal dominion. The author describes how the new ruler of the entire world, having subdued both the East and the Gauls, marches to Rome, where he intends to present before the Romans a triumph over both Zenobia and Tetricus, which means, the narrator explains, victory over both the East and the West. The triumph proves to be a brilliant spectacle with multiple chariots, twenty elephants, and two hundred various tamed beasts from Libya and Palestine. The parade features tigers, giraffes, elks, and other animals, along with eight hundred pairs of gladiators, and captives from barbarian tribes. The list of surrendering nations, all bearing gifts, includes the Blemmyes, Axomitae, Arabs, Indians, Bactrians, Hiberians, Saracens, Persians, Goths, Alans, Roxolani, Sarmatians, Franks, Suebians, Vandals, and Germans. All are captive, their hands bound.[37] These are foreign nations surrendering to the emperor, but the rhetoric is turned on its head, and the elements borrowed from the Suetonius are highly exaggerated. The list of nations is humorously amplified, and the catalog of beasts that Aurelian is too cheap to feed draws a laugh as well. The clement Augustus who achieved the willing surrender of many nations is travestied here, through play of allusion, as the inclement, stingy, and overly proud Aurelian, who is *severus, truculentus,*

32. *Hist. Aug., Aurelian*, 1.5.
33. *Hist. Aug., Aurelian*, 26.7.
34. *Hist. Aug., Aurelian*, 26.9.
35. *Hist. Aug., Aurelian*, 29.4. "Victor itaque Aurelianus totiusque iam orientis possessor."
36. *Hist. Aug., Aurelian*, 29.2. "Hoc munus rex Persarum ab Indis interioribus."
37. *Hist. Aug., Aurelian*, 32–33.

and *sanguinarius*.[38] Finally, the vanquished peoples in the procession do not arrive willingly, but in chains, and Aurelian, though he has spared Zenobia's life, has killed all her advisers in a clear display of lack of mercy.

The author of the *Historia Augusta* is at play with the recognizable elements with which biographers constructed the lives of Roman emperors. Using encomiastic style, he tells of the rotten reputation of Aurelian as if in the language of praise, and does so within a context associated with Augustan clemency to playfully subvert the traditional function of the parade of foreign nations.[39] Chastagnol explains that this anonymous biographer worked in the manner of a typical biographer or historian, but that the result was a pastiche of allusions that constituted "un clin d'oeil au lecteur éclairé."[40] The life of Aurelian in the *Historia Augusta* illustrates the existence of conscious interplay of recognizable episodes within the world of imperial biography, in particular with regard to the expression of Roman universalism and the unification of East and West. Fruitful interpretation of Charlemagne's symbolic conquest of the East will require similarly "enlightened" readings.

In Praise of Constantine the Great

The enumeration of surrendering foreign nations assumes added significance when articulated in praise of the emperor Constantine the Great. Suetonius and his imitators demonstrate the panegyric structure and primary rhetorical intent of the topos, but late antique versions composed for Constantine help to explain other elements of Einhard's account, such as the evocation of Harun as *rex Persarum*, the concession of holy sites in Jerusalem, and the implied reunification of East and West through the submission of the Greek East. The concept of Roman universalism changed with the Christianization of the empire, and Christian theories of kingship came to regard universal peace under a single ruler as a manifestation of divine will rather than of individual imperial glory. For Eusebius, the first biographer of a Christian emperor, imperium and Pax Romana were closely connected, and Constantine's universal dominion was a crucial aspect of his teleological conception of human history.[41] With its evocation of peaceful Roman universalism, the foreign embassy topos in Christian imperial biography became a providential

38. *Hist. Aug., Aurelian*, 36.3.

39. For the inversion of type-scenes, see Martínez Pizarro, "The King Says No," 186.

40. Chastagnol, *Histoire Auguste*, lvvix.

41. Johannes Van Oort, *Jerusalem and Babylon: A Study in Augustine's "City of God" and the Sources of his Doctrine of the Two Cities* (Leiden, 1991), 155–58.

symbol that placed the biographical subject within the progression of sacred history. For ninth-century authors who were familiar with Eusebius and Orosius, the portrayal of Charlemagne as the receiver of such embassies was therefore much more than an imitation of Roman biographical form.

The foreign embassy motif as an expression of Roman universalism occurs in Eusebius's *Life of Constantine* and in the *XII Panegyrici Latini*, a collection of panegyric speeches also known as the "Gallic corpus," collected in the fourth century for the study of rhetoric and as guidance for orators.[42] There is no direct evidence that Einhard had access to either work, a circumstance that limits, but need not rule out, discussion of the influence of Christian imperial biography on his writing.[43] The biographer was well schooled in both classical and Christian biographical and historiographical traditions, which suggests that he would have been aware of key episodes in the life of Constantine. The description of surrendering eastern nations appears three times in Eusebius's *Life of Constantine*. In 1.7, he writes, "as far as the outermost inhabitants of India and those who live round the rim of the whole inhabited earth, he held in subjection all the toparchs, ethnarchs, satraps and kings of barbarian nations of every kind. All of these leaders spontaneously saluted and greeted him, sending ambassadors with presents, and had high hopes of obtaining his acquaintance and friendship."[44] In 4.50, the biographer illustrates the universality of the Christian empire under Constantine near the time of the emperor's death by describing how Indians who lived near the rising sun arrived with gifts. They brought sparkling jewels and various breeds of animals, many not seen before, in recognition that his power extended as far as the ocean and that he was their sovereign emperor. The first people to subject themselves to him were the Britons, near where the sun sets in the ocean, Eusebius explains, and now it was the Indians who come from where the sun rises.[45]

Carolingian authors also employed this expression of peaceful Roman universalism extending from the West to the East as an expression of God's will. We find it, for instance, in Sedulius Scottus's *On Christian Rulers*, in which he recalls the vast empire and peace under Constantine: "Thus Constantine, because he had been a servant of divine will, extended a peaceful

---

42. *Pan. Lat.*, 10.

43. Carolingian libraries included works of Eusebius in Rufinus's translation, but the *Life of Constantine* does not seem to have been known in Latin. See Rosamond McKitterick, *History and Memory in the Carolingian World* (Cambridge, UK, 2004), 78.

44. Eusebius, *VC*, 1.7.

45. Eusebius, *VC*, 4.50.

reign from the sea of Britain to the lands of the East."[46] Sedulius reminds his reader that imperial victories were ultimately God's, and that rulers served as his vicars on earth. Writing not long after the breakup of Charlemagne's empire in 855, the poet recalls the peace under Constantine as a reflection of the emperor's submission to God. His recollection of Roman universal dominion and Pax Romana serves, in the Carolingian context of division and decline, as a reminder that the victories of Christian kings are part of the larger divine plan.

Both Einhard and the authors of the *Royal Frankish Annals* refer to the caliph Harun al Rachid as *rex Persarum*. The Franks used this title for him, although they also knew his Arabic title of *Amir al-Mu'minin*, or "Commander of the Faithful," and Buckler points out that the Abbasid caliphs would have seen themselves as the inheritors of the great Persian legacy.[47] Whatever the actual diplomatic practices might have been in the ninth century, in biographical practice the pairing of Harun, king of the Persians, with Charlemagne, emperor of the Romans, usefully recalled the grand-scale rivalry with the Persian Empire of the Roman imperial centuries. Eusebius had described Persian envoys seeking the friendship of Constantine, a passage about which Cameron and Hall write, "Here Eusebius places Constantine's dealings with Persia within the panegyrical *topos* of universal peace and in an apologetic context of Christian universalism."[48] Einhard's Harun is a Persian leader proffering gifts, and the Carolingian biographer would not have needed to read Eusebius to be familiar with this commonplace of imperial praise.

Suetonius and his elaborators do not make much, if anything, of the Persians in their versions of the foreign embassy topos. The *rex Persarum* does play a prominent role, however, in the biography of Aurelian in the *Historia Augusta*, which includes the parade of elephants and the gift of a cloak *pallium*, an offering that Einhard also attributes to Harun as *vestes*. The surrendering Persian king is also central to praise for Constantine's universal dominion in the *XII Panegyrici Latini*. The panegyrist Nazarius writes: "The barbarian lies prostrate at the side of Gaul or dispersed in the interior of his territory; the Persians themselves, a powerful nation and second on earth

46. Sedulius Scottus, *Liber de rectoribus christianis*, in *Sedulius Scottus: Quellen und Untersuchungen zur lateinischen Philologie des Mittelalters* 1, ed. Sigmund Hellmann (Munich, 1906), 23. "Hinc ipse, quia minister supernae voluntatis fuerat, a Britannico mari usque ad loca Orientis regnum dilatavit pacificum, et quoniam Omnipotenti semet ipsum subdiderat, cuncta hostilia bella, quae sub eodem sunt gesta, potentialiter atque fideliter superavit."

47. Collins, *Charlemagne*, 152; Buckler, *Harunu'l-Rashid*, 32.

48. Eusebius, *VC*, 312–13.

after Rome's greatness, have with no less fear than affection sought your friendship, greatest Constantine." In their commentary, the editors liken this passage to *Aeneid* 6.794–800, where Vergil uses India as the symbol of the farthest extent of the universal empire before the land beyond the stars.[49] Suetonius and Eutropius follow Vergil in using India to signify the farthest point to the East, while Einhard does something unexpected in chapter 16 when he states that Harun held all of the Orient except for India. Although this reference to India comes in the form of an exception, it provides an enticing demonstration of a conscious manipulation of the Roman motif. Einhard conveys to the reader his awareness of the allusion he is making, but he diverges from tradition in a manner that challenges his audience to consider his ambivalent relationship to the Roman model.

Another sequence from the *Panegyrici Latini* helps to elucidate Einhard's presentation of Harun in the role of the surrendering Persian. Here the panegyrist writes to Diocletian about a certain king who had surrendered in a manner reminiscent of a Persian king. The Persian mode of surrender proves to have some familiar components. The king in question never deigned to confess that he was a mere man, and gave over his whole kingdom, offering marvelous things and wild beasts of extraordinary beauty. After yielding, the man was content to be called "friend," a status he earned by his submission.[50] This model of Persian surrender, with its gift-laden relinquishment of eastern dominion culminating in friendship, finds undeniable echoes in Einhard and his imitators in their presentation of Harun. The Carolingian biographer's Persian king seeks Charlemagne's friendship and offers a concession of territory in Jerusalem, an offer more limited in scope than the entirety of Persia, but crucial to Christian geography. As with the mention of India, Einhard demonstrates adherence to previous models, but creatively stretches his material, although not beyond recognition. Since the underlying panegyric model contains a clear articulation of Persian submission, even without Einhard making explicit Harun's submission to Charles, the allusion to previous examples serves to convey the underlying message of the surrender of the East to the West.

With Constantine, the special relationship of the Roman emperor to Jerusalem became a central component of the vita of a Christian emperor. Eusebius famously celebrates Constantine's construction of the Church of the Holy Sepulcher and praises his generosity toward the church and other holy

---

49. *Pan. Lat.*, 4.38.3.
50. *Pan. Lat.*, 10.6–7.

sites.[51] Scholars have noted that Constantine's actual relations with the Persians were not those described by Eusebius.[52] The norms of biography, with their generous allowance for invention, likewise explain why Charlemagne's encounters with the leadership in the East have remained unverifiable. The assumption of the title of emperor by the Frankish king takes on its own providential significance when Einhard engineers the concession of holy sites in Jerusalem by Harun and the symbolic unification of East and West through the pact with the Greeks. Einhard could hardly compete, however, with Orosius's description of Roman universal peace under Augustus or with descriptions of Constantine's building projects in Jerusalem. In an effort to tie Charlemagne to Constantine, Einhard emphasizes Charlemagne's gifts to the Holy Sepulcher sent at the time of his coronation as emperor and then combines them with his invention of Harun's ceding of jurisdiction over the sacred site. The solicitations of friendship by Harun and the Greek emperors therefore constitute the biographer's own version of a ninth-century reunited Christian imperium in a sort of makeshift Pax Romana.

Einhard drew on the *Royal Frankish Annals* for his *Life of Charlemagne*, but he took ample liberties with his source.[53] A discrepancy in the presentation of embassies to and from Jerusalem in the two works provides further evidence of his efforts to conform to the norms of imperial biography. The annalist tells of gifts sent from the patriarch of Jerusalem in 799, followed by the king's reciprocation with donations for the Holy Sepulcher in 800, and finally of more gifts sent from Jerusalem to Charles later in 800, including keys to sacred sites and a *vexillum* (either a banner or a piece of the true cross).[54] Einhard strikingly removes the patriarch from the story in favor of listing only Harun's gifts to Charlemagne: robes, spices, other gifts, and the elephant. The biographer is clearly rearranging his material, since these gifts do appear in the *Royal Frankish Annals*, but in different years: preparations for the sending of the elephant appear in the 801 entry, while an envoy arrives with other presents from Harun in 802. The arrival of silks, perfumes, ointments, and balsam, an elaborate brass water clock, and "other things too numerous to describe" appears under the entry for 807.[55] Einhard moved and condensed material from the *Royal Frankish Annals* to equate eastern gifts

---

51. Eusebius, *VC*, 3.25–40.

52. *Pan. Lat.*, 384.

53. Collins, "'Reviser' Revisited," 196–97.

54. *ARF, sub annis* 799, 800. The *Annals of Lorsch* tell of the arrival of keys and a *vexillum*: "benedictionis causa claves Sepulchri dominici ac loci Calvarie, claves etiam civitatis et montis cum vexillo." See Runciman, "Charlemagne and Palestine," *English Historical Review* 50 (1935): 610.

55. *ARF, sub anno* 807. See Halphen, *Vie de Charlemagne*, 49.

with the ceding of territory by the Persian leader. His deliberate presentation of the *rex Persarum* rather than the patriarch of Jerusalem as the source of the gifts thus classicizes the story by molding the material to conform more closely to the late antique model of the surrendering Persian emperor.

Reuniting East and West

The task of claiming any sort of universal dominion for the first Carolingian emperor was complicated by the vexing presence of the titular Roman emperor in Constantinople. In the final passage of chapter 16, Einhard diverges strikingly from both contemporary history and the *Royal Frankish Annals* with his presentation of the Greek solicitation of a treaty of friendship out of fear in the wake of Charles's coronation. Halphen was stunned by Einhard's willingness to alter the truth to such an extent, especially given the biographer's knowledge of the correspondence that had led to the eventual Greek recognition of Charles's imperial title.[56] Halphen did not recognize the extent to which the rhetoric of praise had determined Einhard's presentation of events. To conform to the foreign embassy topos, Einhard needed to depict the Greeks as an eastern nation submissively seeking friendship. Although the Byzantines did not take a subservient stance toward the Frankish leader, the assertion that they had sought his alliance would not have required any fabrication. Franco-Byzantine relations in that period were rocky, and, indeed, there were plenty of attempts to settle the festering disputes.[57] Plans for treaties with the Greeks appear in the *Royal Frankish Annals* for the years 802, 809, and 811, until finally a pact was signed in 813.[58] Einhard created an amalgamation of these various events that seems to reflect the spirit of the ratification of the peace treaty of 813, an agreement concluded with Emperor Michael after years of war over territories in the Adriatic. The pact gained the Frankish king a degree of abstract recognition of his imperial status by Constantinople, although only as *imperator Francorum*.[59] The Byzantines finally granted some recognition of an imperial title at the end of his life, but certainly not one of coequal rule.

---

56. Halphen, *Études critiques*, 88.

57. McCormick, "Diplomacy and the Carolingian Encounter with Byzantium," 25.

58. *ARF, sub annis* 802, 809, 813. The 802 mention of a treaty sought by Irene may refer to the failed marriage alliance between the empress and Charlemagne. See Judith Herrin, *Women in Purple: Rulers of Medieval Byzantium* (Princeton, NJ, 2001), 117–18.

59. See generally Peter Classen, *Karl der Grosse, das Papsttum und Byzanz: Die Begründung des Karolingischen Kaisertums* (Sigmaringen, 1985); Michael McCormick, *Eternal Victory: Triumphal Rulership in Late Antiquity, Byzantium, and the Early Medieval West* (Cambridge, UK, 1987), 368; Graboïs, "Charlemagne, Rome and Jerusalem," 799. See also Donald M. Nicol, *Byzantium and Venice: A Study*

Einhard presents the "submission" of the Greeks as a sequence. The two powers enjoyed a relationship of friendly exchange at first, but the coronation at Rome inspired fear in the Greeks, which led them to seek an alliance. Not far below the surface lies the rhetoric of universal dominion implied by the foreign embassy topos: the reputation of the new Roman emperor inspires fear, which then inspires the supplicant behavior of distant leaders. The degree to which the coronation in 800 actually upset relations with Constantinople is a matter of continuing debate, but the Greeks certainly did not submissively solicit a pact with Charlemagne.[60] Moreover, Einhard was not so audacious as to assert a true transfer of imperial dignity from the Greeks to the Franks, in a *translatio imperii a Grecis ad Francos*. In fact, he has relatively little to say about Charlemagne's coronation at Rome or about his imperial reign period. Writing after 817, he would have been well aware of the political wrangling that occurred over the title. To simply declare that Harun and the Greeks had offered submission to the new emperor would have been too blatant a deformation of events in relatively recent memory. Einhard's manipulation of a classical commonplace that conveyed the subservience of the East offered him a more subtle means of conveying Byzantine symbolic surrender without actually asserting it. The model for imperial praise lurks not far beneath the surface as a rich source of tacit evocations based on previous usages, while the biographer avoids creating an overly idealized portrait of his subject.

A sense of anxiety over the meaning of Charlemagne's assumption of the imperial title was not new. Sometime between 804 and 814, the poet Moduin staged a dialogue in one of his eclogues between a boy and an old man that addressed the question of how to properly praise the Frankish Roman *renovatio*. The exuberant boy attempts to write panegyric verses about new Rome under the Franks with Vergilian enthusiasm (24–27), to which the old man responds with criticism of his youthful and exaggerated vision.[61] At a time when the empire of Charlemagne was still a relatively new concept, the elder's hesitance to engage in hyperbolic praise bespeaks a feeling of uncertainty about the appropriateness of employing the rhetoric of Roman triumph for the Frankish king. As the ninth century wore on, however, and Charlemagne's empire fell apart, nostalgia set in, and a poetics of

in Diplomatic and Cultural Relations (Cambridge, UK, 1988), 17–18; Janet Nelson, "Kingship and Empire in the Carolingian World," in *Carolingian Culture: Emulation and Innovation*, ed. Rosamond McKitterick (Cambridge, UK, 1994), 72.

60. James Muldoon, *Empire and Order: The Concept of Empire, 800–1800* (New York, 1999), 46; Herrin, *Women in Purple*, 119–25; McCormick, *Eternal Victory*, 379–81.

61. Moduin, *Ecloga*, in *Poet. Lat.* 1, verses 28–31.

unbridled praise gained prominence in Carolingian literature. In the after-math of the division of the empire among the sons of Louis the Pious, the evocation of an undivided realm under Charlemagne functioned instead as an expression of regret.

The poet Florus of Lyons offers an example of the rhetoric of Roman universalism deployed within the new context of Carolingian decline. Look-ing back longingly to the time when there was one leader, *princeps unus erat* (42), Florus remembers Charlemagne as the bringer of Pax Romana and decries the squandering of the emperor's great achievement.[62] Filled with nostalgia, Florus offers an unabashed deployment of the classical model of foreign nations surrendering in his *Lament on the Division of the Empire*, writ-ten during the discord of the 840s:

> Hence they celebrated the Frankish people throughout the whole world, and the reports of his might reached the furthest ends of the Earth. Foreign kingdoms from far away, barbarians and Greeks alike, sent envoys to the Latin tribunal. Even the race of Romulus yielded to him, and glorious Rome, mother of kingdoms, yielded as well. There the prince assumed the crown of the kingdom, a gift of the pope, trust-ing in the protection of Christ.[63]

In this passage, the poet combines the foreign embassy motif with Char-lemagne's assumption of the imperial title, a connection that is mirrored by Einhard. In a significant evolution of the topos for use in a Carolingian context, the poet highlights the transfer of the imperial dignity from Rome to the Franks. He also implies its transfer away from Greeks by coupling the Greeks with the other barbarians who bring tribute to the new Roman emperor. There is no suggestion of any sharing of imperial power between East and West.

Writing not long after the death of Charlemagne, Einhard was some-where between Moduin and Florus, neither burdened with doubt nor over-whelmed with regret over a lost golden age. His portrait of the king was in

62. See Peter Godman, *Poetry of the Carolingian Renaissance* (London, 1985), 264–65, and Paul Dutton, *The Politics of Dreaming in the Carolingian Empire*, in which he calls the poem a eulogy for the empire (Lincoln, 1994), 121–23.

63. Florus of Lyons, *Querela*, verses 57–64. "Claruit hinc nimium toto gens Francica mundo, / Famaque virtutum fines penetravit ad imos; / Legatos hinc inde suos procul extera regna / Barbara, Graeca simul Latium misere tribunal. / Huic etenim cessit etiam gens Romula genti, / Regnorumque simul mater Roma inclyta cessit; / Huius ibi princeps regni diademata sumpsit / Munere apostolico, Christi munimine fretus."

many ways unique, since it was a secular biography that drew inspiration from classical and Christian models, not unlike the *Life of Saint Martin* of Sulpicius Severus.[64] The dictates of both classical and Christian biography would have given him reason to restrain himself from excessive praise, but he nonetheless created his own brand of measured encomium by only tentatively evoking universal dominion under Charlemagne.[65] One wonders, however, why Einhard selected such an openly triumphal motif only to veil its glorious message. Perhaps he feared that the actual memory of Charlemagne might clash uncomfortably with such lofty rhetoric. Moduin had aired the concern that too much singing about a new universal Rome would invite criticism. The same could be said, but in terms of politics rather than poetry, for Einhard. Paul Dutton has argued that during the decades after his death, Charlemagne's reputation suffered, and that Einhard's biography was more of an apology in the face of criticism than a first and favorable portrait.[66] When viewed in this light, Einhard's reluctance to overtly place his subject in shoes that he could not fill is more comprehensible. The biographer adopts a commonplace of high praise and then diffuses its rhetorical power. In placing Charlemagne so cautiously within the lineage of the greatest of Roman emperors, Einhard both glorifies and burdens his subject's memory. Such a comparison to his predecessors, whether implicit or explicit, necessarily brings to light both the parallels and the discrepancies with previous models. The likening of Charlemagne to Augustus through literary imitation represents a form of tacit praise but, at the same time, the reader may also be reminded of the ways in which the imperial reign of the Frankish leader was unlike that of those who had ruled before him.

Any biographer who evoked Roman universalism in praise of Charlemagne would have confronted hurdles not faced by the biographers of Augustus, Constantine, and Theodosius. Political reality in the ninth-century Carolingian world would have cast dark shadows over any idealized picture of Charlemagne as universal Roman emperor. The Christian Roman Empire was sundered, the Greek East held the imperial title, and the Abbasid caliphate controlled Jerusalem. All of these shortfalls are brought into relief by Einhard's fanciful picture of Charles's peaceful alliances with foreign kings. The foreign embassy topos as it appears in Einhard's biography is certainly intended as praise, but its unusual merging of panegyric structure and historiographical substance makes for a uniquely Carolingian combination of

---

64. Kempshall, *Rhetoric*, 157–59.
65. For the limits of praise, see ibid., 165.
66. Dutton, *Politics of Dreaming*, 56–57.

proud *imitatio imperii* and humble Frankish insecurity. Einhard offers ample celebration of his subject, while protecting the king's memory from critics who might scoff at unrestrained praise. He had also unknowingly created what would become one of the primary episodes in the life of Charlemagne as it was imagined in a wide variety of forms and contexts for centuries to come.

Notker of Saint Gall

During the period prior to the dissolution of the Carolingian Empire in 888, Notker the Stammerer, a monk of the abbey of Saint Gall, adapted Einhard's spare passages concerning Harun and the Greeks into a lively narrative. The first author to build creatively on Einhard's biography, the monk developed a portrait of the Frankish king that now stands as one of the earliest extant manifestations of the Charlemagne of legend. A couple of years before his death in 887, in a state of deep political distress, the Carolingian king and emperor Charles the Fat asked Notker to write about the deeds of his illustrious ancestors.[67] The monk responded with a collection of vignettes known as the *Deeds of Charles the Great (Gesta Karoli Magni)*. In the *Deeds*, the reader encounters a handful of fictionalized ambassadorial scenes between Charlemagne and his counterparts in the East, Harun al Rachid and the Greek emperor Michael. The exchanges play out through a mixture of direct discourse and reported speech, as well as the conveyance of inner thoughts and memories.[68] Based on chapter 16 of the *Life of Charlemagne*, Notker's versions of Charlemagne's diplomatic encounters with the East reveal the monk's awareness of the rhetoric of praise that Einhard had adapted decades earlier. The monk takes the theme of Christian universalism much further, however, portraying a Charlemagne who is at the helm of a Christian Roman Empire that now represents the fourth and last kingdom in the eschatological succession of empires. His East–West ambassadorial exchanges thus create a forum for his meditation on matters such as the meaning of the Frankish assumption of the leadership of the empire and the

---

67. Simon MacLean dates the composition to late 885 and 886, in *Kingship and Politics in the Late Ninth Century: Charles the Fat and the End of the Carolingian Empire* (Cambridge, UK, 2003), 201–4, 225.

68. Hans-Joachim Reischmann describes the phenomenon of Notker's emphasis on psychological conflicts in terms of trivialization, in *Die Trivialisierung des Karlsbildes der Einhard-Vita in Notkers "Gesta Karoli Magni": Rezeptionstheoretische Studien zum Abbau der Kritischen Distanz in der spätkarolingischen Epoche* (Konstanz, 1984), 43. See also Lars Hageneier, *Jenseits der Topik: Die karolingische Herrscherbiographie* (Husum, 2004).

difficult question of how one ought to praise the emperor. In Notker's clever hands, we find the first presentation of Charlemagne's encounters in the East to openly incorporate imperial apocalyptic discourse, a rhetorical strategy that served to fashion the Frankish emperor as a symbol of unity and dynastic continuity in the face of political dissolution in the late ninth century.

Until a generation ago, Notker was more often abused for his failings than appreciated for his erudition and subtle humor. Halphen saw Notker's Charlemagne as a figure of fantasy, and accused other scholars of having been duped by the monk, but modern scholars have been more generous.[69] Some have contrasted Einhard's secular, classicizing biography to Notker's more Christianized work, citing evidence in the latter of the influence of late antique hagiography and Benedictine exempla.[70] Joaquín Martínez Pizarro, for instance, has argued that Notker's depiction of Charlemagne reflects his inversion of the narrative patterns of the *Life of Saint Martin* of Sulpicius Severus to give Charlemagne the "ceremonial precedence" enjoyed by clergy in his hagiographical models.[71] Other scholars, as well as Martínez Pizarro, have turned their focus toward the narrative construction of his anecdotes and the psychological elements of the scenes.[72] The *Deeds* never reached the royal court, and almost nothing is known about the work's reception in the decades after its composition. In fact, no extant versions survive from before the twelfth century.[73] There is little doubt, however, that the collection of stories was intended to be appreciated by readers of Einhard.[74] The vignettes likely circulated with Einhard's biography from the start, and were meant to be read, as David Ganz has shown, as intertextual companion

69. Louis Halphen, *Études critiques*, 104. Cf. Ernst Breisach, *Historiography: Ancient, Medieval and Modern* (Chicago, 1983; reprint, 1994), 100; James Campbell, "Asser's *Life of Alfred*," in *The Inheritance of Historiography, 350–900*, ed. Christopher Holdsworth and T. P. Wiseman (Exeter, 1986), 119. Theodor Siegrist states that Notker's inventive narrative style was meant to inspire political reflection, in *Herrscherbild und Weltsicht bei Notker Balbulus: Untersuchungen zu den Gesta Karoli* (Zürich, 1963), 139, 145. See also MacLean, *Kingship and Politics*, chap. 7; Heinz Löwe, "Das Karlsbuch Notkers von St. Gallen und sein zeitgeschichtlicher Hintergrund," in *Von Cassiodor zu Dante: Ausgewählte Aufsätze zur Geschichtschreibung und politischen Ideenwelt des Mittelalters* (Berlin, 1973).

70. Hans F. Haefele, "Studien zu Notkers Gesta Karoli," *Deutsches Archiv für Erforschung des Mittelalters* 15 (1959): 390–91; Berschin, *Biographie und Epochenstil*, 401. See also MacLean, *Kingship and Politics*, 205; Hageneier, *Jenseits der Topik*, 220–33.

71. Joaquín Martínez Pizarro, "Images of Church and State: Sulpicius Severus to Notker Balbulus," *Journal of Medieval Latin* 4 (1994): 35–36.

72. See generally Joaquín Martínez Pizarro, *A Rhetoric of the Scene: Dramatic Narrative in the Early Middle Ages* (Toronto, 1989) and Siegrist, *Herrscherbild und Weltsicht*; Reischmann, *Die Trivialisierung*, 13.

73. MacLean, *Kingship and Politics*, 229.

74. See Ganz, "Humour as History in Notker's *Gesta Karoli Magni*," in *Monks, Nuns and Friars in Medieval Society*, ed. E. B. King, J. T. Schaefer, and W. B. Wadley (Sewanee, TN, 1989), 177.

pieces to the accompanying biography.[75] The presentation of the extant twelfth-century versions supports this theory, since they appear side by side in histories of the Franks that feature compendia of Charlemagne material.[76]

In structuring his anecdotes, Notker conforms, on the surface, to certain standards of Christian imperial biography, with sections ostensibly devoted to ecclesiastical matters, wars, building projects, and daily life. What falls beneath those familiar rubrics is not what one would expect, though, for often he elects to tell humorous stories about subjects other than the Frankish king. This decision in itself signals to the reader that he was both aware of the norms of biography and prepared to flout them. To appreciate Notker's meditation on Charlemagne as Christian emperor, the reader needed to be able to recognize Einhard's adaptation of the rhetoric of Roman universalism in the passages featuring Harun and the Greeks. In building on Einhard to create his own ambassadorial exchanges with the East, Notker does not "borrow" or "copy" any more than had his predecessor, however. Instead, he uses a familiar framework on which to build a new version of the episode with the same basic set of rhetorical implications. In interpreting this locus of imperial praise, Notker departs from Einhard, however, in that he reveals his awareness of the competing secular and Christian elements that had informed the Carolingian encomiastic tradition. He achieves this through play of allusion to previous models, imposing on his audience the task of recognizing the reference and then considering his innovative portrait in light of the juxtapositions he has created.

Notker was no doubt concerned with the entertainment value of his stories, but he also likely hoped that his work would be appreciated as a political document.[77] He opted for a combination of praise and humor, which was,

75. See Ganz, "Humour as History." For the later manuscript tradition, see Hans F. Haefele, *Notker der Stammler: Taten Kaiser Karls des Grossen* (Berlin, 1962), xxiii–xliv, and, more recently, Matthias Tischler's monumental *Einharts Vita Karoli: Studien zur Entstehung, Überlieferung und Rezeption* (Hanover, 2001). Folz argues that it was likely forgotten until the twelfth century when it became popular again, traveling alongside Einhard's biography; see *Le souvenir*, 15. See also Bernard Guenée, *Histoire et culture historique dans l'Occident médiéval* (Paris, 1980), 273; Robert Morrissey, *L'empereur à la barbe fleurie: Charlemagne dans la mythologie et l'histoire de France* (Paris, 1997), 51–52; MacLean, *Kingship and Politics*, 229; Matthias Tischler, "Tatmensch oder Heidenapostel: Die Bilder Karls des Grossen bei Einhart und im Pseudo-Turpin," in *Jakobus und Karl der Grosse: Von Einhards Karlsvita zum Pseudo-Turpin*, ed. Klaus Herbers (Tübingen, 2003), 7–15.

76. Tischler, *Einharts Vita Karoli*, 48, 291, 307–9.

77. MacLean situates the work in a contemporary political context but also sees it as a mirror of princes, in *Kingship and Politics*, 227. See Ganz, "Humour as History," 172–73. Cf. Innes and McKitterick, "Writing of History," 202; Paul Kershaw, "Laughter after Babel's Fall: Misunderstanding and Miscommunication in the Ninth-Century West," in *Humour, History and Politics in Late Antiquity and the Early Middle Ages*, ed. Guy Halsall (Cambridge, UK, 2002).

needless to say, an original approach to remembering the Frankish leader, and which contrasted with the solemnity of Florus of Lyons or of his closer contemporary, the Saxon Poet, who lamented that there were no more like Charlemagne.[78] Paul Dutton has observed that while Einhard had faced skepticism about Charlemagne's accomplishments in the 820s, by the late ninth century "Notker had no one left to convince. He simply began with God's golden boy."[79] Ganz sums up: "Notker's greatest achievement, in my view, is precisely what he is blamed for doing. He misrepresents the historical Charlemagne. But he no longer lived in the age of Charlemagne. To recapture a vision of that age, Notker and his contemporaries could read Einhard. To measure their distance from that age they needed to read Notker."[80] The nostalgia noted by Dutton and the distance noted by Ganz both contributed to a sense of freedom on the part of the monk to use the memory of Charlemagne as a foundation upon which to build something previously unseen in royal biography.

Notker's approach to celebrating the deeds of Charlemagne reflects an encomiast caught between the competing ideals of classical and Christian biography.[81] The monk was well-read, and his work shows the influence of classical sources, scripture, and the *Lives* of saints such as Benedict and Martin. Notker also shows keen awareness of the anonymous Paderborn epic.[82] In an early model of secular panegyric praise for Charlemagne's kingdom as the new Rome, the poem, otherwise known as the *Karolus Magnus et Leo Papa*, builds toward the climactic meeting of the Frankish king and Pope Leo at Paderborn in 799.[83] For Notker, the unbridled praise inspired by the classical tradition would have gone against the monastic ideal of humility. Moreover, as Simon MacLean notes, by 887, fears about Charles the Fat's waning power had been realized, and therefore flattering rhetoric would have been "embarrassingly out of date."[84] As Moduin's dialogue between the boy and the old man demonstrates, there was open concern during the early years

---

78. Poeta Saxo, 5:88–91.

79. Paul Dutton, *The Politics of Dreaming in the Carolingian Empire* (Lincoln, NE, 1994), 199.

80. Ganz, "Humour as History," 182.

81. Cf. Haefele, "Studien zu Notkers *Gesta Karoli*," 319. MacLean judges his mix of exaltation of his subject and exhortation to better Christian kingship to be "quite traditional," in *Kingship and Politics*, 228–29.

82. By 885, Notker had also written his *Notatio de Viris Illustribus*. See McKitterick, *History and Memory*, 221–22. Susan Rankin argues that he was more familiar with contemporary Christian writing than previously thought, in "Ego itaque Notker scripsi," *Revue Bénédictine* 101 (1991): 293–96. Martínez Pizarro goes further than other scholars in viewing Notker's portrait of Charlemagne as overtly secularist, in "Images of Church and State," 35.

83. *KMLP*, verses 149–53.

84. MacLean, *Kingship and Politics*, 227–29.

of Charlemagne's imperial reign about the limits of acceptable praise. In his own quest for the proper celebratory tone, Notker reflects the incommensurability of secular and Christian praise, offering his subject something that falls between classical encomium and monastic humility. Eschewing lofty hyperbole, he still celebrates his subject's virtues, although he is also willing to put the king in compromising, even humiliating situations.

Notker showed far more interest in the theoretical problem of the Carolingian Empire as Roman *renovatio* than had Einhard, who had little to say on the matter. The material from chapter 16 and the discussion of the Byzantine reaction to the imperial coronation in chapter 28 represent the full extent of Einhard's attention to Charlemagne's assumption of the imperial title. By contrast, Notker opens the *Deeds* with a description of Charlemagne as leader of Rome, in a passage fraught with portentous references to the dream of Nebuchadnezzar, likely suffused with his readings of Jerome's interpretation of Daniel 2:31–33. God has destroyed the great image of the Romans, Notker announces, which had feet of clay and iron, but has raised up among the Franks "the golden head of a second image, equally remarkable, in the person of the illustrious Charles."[85] This is a striking assertion, since, according to Jerome, the golden head was the first of the Four Kingdoms, but Notker's statement was probably not intended to mean that Charlemagne's empire was the new Babylon.[86] Babylon was a kingdom that Orosius had likened to Rome, as a father to a son, but which had come to an end, while Rome, providentially protected by God, would not disintegrate as Babylon had.[87]

Benjamin Arnold has proposed that, for Notker, Charlemagne as the golden head was meant to symbolize postponement of the end time.[88] MacLean, noting the monk's deliberate "elision" of the two emperors named Charles, sees the golden head statement as a warning about what would happen if the empire were to fall away from the Franks, leaving three more empires to follow. Such a warning would have been seen as encouragement of the struggling emperor, who had been crowned emperor in 881, to attend to the looming crisis of succession and preserve Carolingian domination in

---

85. Notker, *GK*, 1.1 "Omnipotens rerum dispositor ordinatorque regnorum et temporum, cum illius admirandae statuae pedes ferreos vel testaceos comminuisset in Romanis, alterius non minus admirabilis statuae caput aureum per illustrem Karolum erexit in Francis."

86. F. Glorie, ed., *Hieronymus: Commentariorum in Danielem libri III, CC* 75A (Turnhout, 1964).

87. Kempshall, *Rhetoric*, 69.

88. Benjamin Arnold, "Eschatological Imagination and the Program of Roman Imperial and Ecclesiastical Renewal at the End of the Tenth Century," in Landes, Gow, and Van Meter, *Apocalyptic Year 1000*, 273.

the realm.[89] In either scenario, the opening passage conveys the desire for the Carolingians to hold on. Notker's Charlemagne, we should then conclude, was the leader of a Frankish Rome now represented by gold, a more durable and unified material than the inherently vulnerable mixture of iron and clay that could not adhere and had already broken. The opening lines of his celebration of Charles the Great as predecessor of Charles the Fat, written before the situation became dire, thus celebrate a vision of Frankish Rome based on a metaphor of unity and stability, a realm not soon to be sundered. He then explores the theme of Christian universalism by incorporating into his presentation of the emperor's diplomatic encounters with the East the idea of symbolic defeat of the Persians and the Greeks based on the theory of the succession of world monarchies.

Charlemagne and the Persians

In the rhetoric of Roman universalism, the dispatching of foreign envoys bearing gifts in surrender occurs in reaction to the unparalleled reputation of the emperor. Notker describes how ambassadors from Harun arrive at the court of Charlemagne bearing gifts so numerous that the envoys seemed to have emptied the East to fill up the West.[90] As Hans-Werner Goetz notes, the scene, in representing the transfer of wealth, also implies the transfer of authority.[91] In his presentation of the embassies sent between Harun and Charlemagne, Notker addresses this central element of the foreign embassy topos by pondering what it means for an emperor to enjoy the esteem of peoples who have only heard of him. For the exchanges with the Persian leader, he constructs a pair of ambassadorial visits that revolve around hunting expeditions, the second of which culminates in Harun's concession of jurisdiction over the Holy Land.[92] In the Carolingian age, descriptions of the royal hunt served as a recognized locus of praise for the royal hunter.[93]

89. MacLean, *Kingship and Politics*, 225–27.

90. Notker, *GK*, 2.8.

91. Hans-Werner Goetz, *Strukturen der Spätkarolingischen Epoche im Spiegel der Vorstellungen Eines Zeitgenössischen Mönchs: Eine Interpretation der "Gesta Karoli" Notkers von Sankt Gallen* (Bonn, 1981), 80.

92. For the contemporary significance of Charlemagne's hunting misadventure, see MacLean, *Kingship and Politics*, 217.

93. Janet L. Nelson, "Kingship and Empire in the Carolingian World," in *Carolingian Culture: Emulation and Innovation*, ed. Rosamond McKitterick (Cambridge, 1994), 60; Peter Godman, "The Poetic Hunt: From Saint Martin to Charlemagne's Heir," in *Charlemagne's Heir: New Perspectives on the Reign of Louis the Pious (814–840)*, ed. Peter Godman and Roger Collins (Oxford, 1990); Paul Dutton, *Charlemagne's Mustache and Other Cultural Clusters of a Dark Age* (New York, 2004), 49.

By having the Persians arrive at court just as Charlemagne is leaving on a
hunt, Notker combines two recognizable sites of praise: the royal hunt and
the arrival of foreign envoys.

The Paderborn epic, for instance, contains a scene that celebrates Charlemagne's love of hunting wild beasts with dogs.[94] The passage is enriched
by the fact that, as Peter Godman has shown, the Vergil-inspired Paderborn
poet frequently secularized and classicized scenes from Christian biography
such as Venantius Fortunatus's *Life of Saint Martin*. The depiction of Charlemagne's killing of a boar in the Paderborn poem is, in fact, a "refashioning"
of a scene in which Saint Martin spares the life of a hare in a demonstration
of kindness toward animals.[95] Such play of allusion between secular and
classical praise goes back even a step further though, since Venantius himself
had been working against Vergilian praise of hunting in his praise of Martin.
The Paderborn poet then returned to the classical model. Notker joins the
Carolingian discourse on the hunt as locus of praise, but avoids having to
choose between secular glory and monastic condemnation. Aware of his
conflicting poetic models, the monk instead uses the hunt as an opportunity
to take a stance somewhere in between. The result is a subtle meditation on
the challenge of praising a Charlemagne who is part Roman emperor and
part ideal Christian king.

In a scene designed to recall the implied surrender conveyed by the foreign
embassy motif, the Persian envoys arrive at court and are overwhelmed by
the sight of Charlemagne in his imperial garb. Notker conveys the bygone
nature of Persian domination by having the emperor describe the envoys to
those in attendance at court as representatives of a people who "once inspired
fear in the whole world." Notker's reader / listener is meant to catch this
reference and to thus see the encounter with the Persian envoys within the
context of the succession of kingdoms.[96] This is also not the only instance
within the encounters with the East of an allusion to the succession of world
empires.[97] Unlike the tense situation with the Byzantines over the shared
imperial title, however, there is no question that the age of Persian domination is over. The narrative voice reinforces this point by explaining that the
envoys' reaction to meeting Charlemagne is characteristic of a people who

---

94. *KMLP*, verses 267–313.
95. Godman, *Poets and Emperors*, 88–89; Godman, "Poetic Hunt," 568, 570, 575.
96. Siegrist also sees the presentation of Harun as king of the Persians as part of the eschatological theme of the succession of world empires, and argues that this passage with the envoys affirms
the lost quality of the Persian empire; see *Herrscherbild und Weltsicht*, 118, and cf. Goetz, *Strukturen
der Spätkarolingischen Epoche*, 77.
97. Goetz, *Strukturen der Spätkarolingischen Epoche*, 80–81.

had never seen an emperor before.[98] The Persians had once been the subject of universal awe, but Charlemagne now enjoys that esteem.

In a variation on the celebration of the emperor's worldwide reputation, as seen in Suetonius, the visit of ambassadors from Persia invites reflection on how Charlemagne is perceived in foreign lands. He offers a warm welcome to the envoys, and they are content to gaze at him and enjoy his hospitality. As the narrator explains, they value the very experience of beholding him more than they would all the wealth of the Orient, a statement that is no simple piece of hyperbole.[99] If Harun was known for one thing in the Carolingian sources, it was his lavish gifts. Notker is referring to the Persian leader's famous generosity, not yet mentioned in the *Deeds*, but well known to readers of the *Royal Frankish Annals* and Einhard's biography. Rather than reinforcing the Persians' gratitude, however, the statement devalues Eastern generosity by having the entire wealth of the East pale by comparison to the mere chance to glimpse the sight of Charlemagne in his imperial garb. The awestruck visitors ultimately declare as they bow before the emperor, in language that recalls the earlier references to the dream of Nebuchadnezzar, that before then they had only seen men of clay, but now they see gold.[100] The scene thus forces the reader to consider whether Notker is praising Charlemagne's inherent imperial qualities or whether he is implying that the king's fancy imperial garb has caused the hapless Persian envoys to swoon. As is often the case with Notker, the answer lies somewhere in between, but further examples of his disdain for the immodesties and excesses of imperial praise will show that the latter scenario is the more likely.

Not long after Harun's envoys arrive at court, Charlemagne invites them to accompany him on a hunt. They accept the offer at first, but are quickly terrified by the strange large animals of the northern forest (a deliberate contrast to the lavish royal hunting park described in the Paderborn epic) and run away. It soon becomes apparent that Notker intends to do something unexpected with this particular hunting scene, which would typically be reserved for the celebration of the king's mastery of his domain. The encounter is no triumph of king over beast, but leads instead to embarrassment for Charlemagne. His sangfroid is tested when he fails to kill a wild animal, loses his boot, and must be saved by a sworn enemy as members of his retinue look on, offering their assistance. He refuses the aid of his men,

---

98. Notker, *GK*, 2.8. "Quibus tamen excellentissimus Karolus ita terrificus videbatur praeomnibus, quasi numquam regem vel imperatorem vidissent."

99. Notker, *GK*, 2.8. Cf. Morrissey, *L'empereur*, 59–60.

100. Notker, *GK*, 2.8.

limping back to his wife for counsel on how he should repay his erstwhile foe.[101] While the Carolingian leader had enjoyed lofty Vergilian praise in the Paderborn poem for his killing of a boar, Notker denies him that honor, though his Charlemagne is no Martin, either, since he shows no Christian pity for animals. Notker refuses to be purely classical or purely Christian, creating his own version of the royal hunt by depicting it as a failure, but still guaranteeing the lack of Persian witnesses to the event, a detail that will prove crucial to the reading of the second hunting expedition in the land of Harun.

During their sojourn at the court of Charlemagne, the Persian envoys are eager to discuss the matter of his reputation. The visitors gradually become too comfortable with their royal host and, one day after too much beer, they lose their inhibitions and announce to the king that although his power is great, it is less than it is reputed to be in the East. Pretending to be unfazed, Charlemagne asks them to explain their claim. Their response offers further evidence of Notker's preoccupation with placing Charlemagne within the eschatological succession of world monarchies: "We, the Persians, or Medes, if you wish, and the Armenians, and Indians, and Elamites, and all eastern peoples fear you much more than our leader Harun. As for the Macedonians or rather the Greeks, what shall we say? Now more than before, they fear that your greatness will overwhelm them more than waves of the Ionian Sea."[102] The envoys list a number of peoples of the East, some of which are related to Jerome's interpretation of the dream of Nebuchadnezzar. For Jerome, the Medo-Persians are the second world empire, the Macedonians are the third, and the Romans the fourth.

By having the Persians describe the fear of Charlemagne among the peoples of the East, Notker implies their recognition of his place at the helm of the current universal empire. There is a distinction to be drawn, however, between the awestruck Persians of the non-Christian East and the Greeks of the eastern half of the Roman Empire, whose fear is more current. Charlemagne has symbolically conquered, by means of his awesome reputation, the Persians and other far-off lands represented by the Indians. The Greeks, although not wholly convinced, are growing more and more fearful. Einhard had intimated something similar by contrasting Harun's unequivocal offer of

---

101. Notker, *GK*, 2.8. MacLean shows how the story of the healing of the rift with Isembard had contemporary resonance and was bound up in the abbey of Saint Gall's relationship to Charles the Fat; see *Kingship and Politics*, 217.

102. Notker, *GK*, 2.8. "Nos Persae vel Medi, Armeniique vel Indi, et Elamitae, omnesque orientales multo magis vos quam dominatorem nostrum Aaron timemus. De Macedonibus autem vel Achivis quid dicamus? Qui iam iamque magnitudinem vestram plus se fluctibus Ionii oppressuram pavitant."

friendship with the Greeks' fearful quest for an alliance. The more expansive Notker uses the exchanges with the Greeks, as we shall see, to defame the Byzantine leadership by dramatizing Charlemagne's superior merit as leader of Christendom.

Although the Persian envoys bow before Charlemagne and confirm the strength of his reputation in the East, Notker has not lapsed into a triumphal mode. Instead, he undermines the encomiastic function of the scene by bringing to light Charles's troubled domestic reputation. The Persian ambassadors explain that those whom they encountered between the East and his own kingdom were keen to obey him, while his own nobles seem to have little respect for him, except when in his immediate presence. Deeply troubled by this news, Charlemagne then deprives the accused nobles and bishops of their lands and levels heavy fines against them. Notker has set up a dichotomy between local and universal reputation, since, despite his robust reputation in India, where no one knows him, Charlemagne lacks respect in his own circles. As with the failed hunt, here again Notker transforms a known site of imperial encomium into a scene of royal dishonor. Charlemagne's reputation is intact in the East, but this is of little consequence if he cannot gain respect at home. Heinz Löwe argues that the envoys' report reflects Notker's attempt to imply that the contemporary Carolingian kings were weak in the face of the nobility in the Frankish west, and MacLean would likely agree.[103] The passage can indeed be read as advice for a king on good governance, and it ought to be read that way, but Notker wrote on multiple levels. His allusive deconstruction of panegyric practice within the anecdotes dealing with the former empires of the East betrays a more theoretical interrogation of the meaning of the Frankish empire in a time of dynastic crisis.

An Embassy to Harun

After the Persian embassy, the Frankish king in turn sends envoys to Harun. In a scene that again confronts the matter of imperial reputation in far-off lands, the Frankish envoys are successful on a Persian lion hunt. In preparation for the embassy, the Frankish king had put together a gift package that included some hunting dogs that the Persian leader had requested for warding off lions and tigers. Upon the Franks' arrival, Harun immediately invites

---

103. Löwe, "Das Karlsbuch Notkers," 138. The scene also recalls Reischmann's observations on Notker's tendency to use obviously fictionalized dialogues to put words in the mouths of famous figures as a means of conveying his own thoughts and considerations. Reischmann, *Die Trivialisierung*, 43.

them on a lion hunt, an invitation that they eagerly accept. In a moment laden with what could seem like overly obvious symbolism, the German dogs easily capture the Persian lion, and the envoys kill the beast with their swords.[104] The symbolic victory of the Franks is not unqualified, however, since, at least for Notker's reader, the memory of the previous hunting failure looms as a necessary precursor to the parallel hunt in the realm of Harun. The Persian envoys, although they had missed Charles's embarrassing incident, had nonetheless claimed to witness evidence of his political weakness at home. The embassy to the East thus occurs with the understanding that Charlemagne's reputation is vulnerable, especially in the East. Needless to say, the event proves to be far more than a simple case of Frankish superiority manifested in a hunting scene.

By this point in the *Deeds*, it would be naïve to expect a straightforward approach to a familiar triumphal Roman motif such as the lion hunt. Constantine had appeared on a triumphal arch from the fourth century on a lion hunt in Egypt.[105] Charlemagne's own lion hunt happens by proxy, however, leaving the reader to wonder whether the victory in his absence represents a moment of imperial triumph or another instance of Notker's ambivalence expressed within a familiar locus of praise. In the case of Venantius's Saint Martin, the hunting dogs prove ineffectual, as Godman points out, while the Vergil-inspired Paderborn poet grants Charlemagne glorious hunting success.[106] Notker once again concocts a new brand of encomium that falls somewhere between the classical and the Christian. His Charlemagne is victorious, but only because Harun construes the performance of the envoys and the dogs as proof of the Frankish king's superiority:

> Having seen this, Harun (the most powerful of those who had held that name), understood based on this minimal information that Charles was the stronger one, and burst out with these words in his favor: "Now indeed I know those things to be true, which I have heard about my brother Charles, because clearly by hunting so assiduously and by exercising his body and mind with so much tireless zeal, he has the habit of conquering everything under the sun."[107]

---

104. Notker, *GK*, 1.9.
105. David S. Potter, *The Roman Empire at Bay, AD 180–395* (London, 2004), 360–61.
106. Godman, "Poetic Hunt," 584–85.
107. Notker, *GK*, 2.9. "Quo viso nominis sui fortissimus heres Aaron, ex rebus minimis fortiorem Karolum deprehendens, his verbis in eius favorem prorupit: Nunc autem cognosco, quam sint vera, quae audivi de fratre meo Karolo, quia scilicet assiduitate venandi et infatigabili studio corpus et animum exercendi cuncta, quae sub coelo sunt, consuetudinem habet edomandi."

Harun attributes Charlemagne's successful conquests of the whole world to the strength he has gained from so much hunting and other sorts of exercise, but, of course, he has never actually seen the Frankish leader. The reputation of the Frankish king remains robust in the East thanks to the successful embassy, but opinions about him in that part of the world are, as the narrator explains, "*ex rebus minimis*," based only on a small bit of evidence. Moreover, the Persian leader does not know about the earlier debacle in the northern forest. The reader does, though, and that knowledge alters the reception of this second hunting sequence, perhaps enough to have elicited a laugh, especially from a communal listening audience. This is an ambassadorial motif, so it stands to reason that Charlemagne is not present, but Notker uses his absence as an opportunity to show that imperial reputation, the very quality that supposedly inspires foreign leaders to surrender to the emperor, is nothing but a simulacrum.

Notker assumes the existence of two types of witnesses to the deeds of Charlemagne: the internal ones from within the narrative, and the external ones who make up his audience. This division allows for multilayered readings of his rhetorically intricate scenes. The state of the emperor's reputation is a matter of explicit concern during both embassies. In the case of the symbolic besting of Harun, the fact that the envoys do not witness Charles's failure preserves the Frankish king's reputation within the story, while the all-knowing reader can appreciate the interplay between the two embassies. Notker thus achieves a nuanced approach to praising his subject in which the symbolic victory in the East remains intact on one level, but its attainment is undermined in the eyes of those who recognize his reinterpretations of the topoi of imperial praise within which he is writing. For that audience, Harun's glowing praise for Charlemagne's bodily and spiritual strength, the result of much successful hunting, rings hollow and ironically humorous.

After the lion hunt, Harun decides to recognize Charlemagne's newly demonstrated superiority by granting him the Land of Abraham. The transfer of jurisdiction that is implied in Einhard thus emerges in explicit form.[108] Harun's decision follows a period of contemplation to which the reader is privy. At first, he fears that Charles will be too far away to defend the territory, but he is also concerned that if the king were to attend to it excessively, then provinces bordering on the kingdom of the Franks might secede. After wavering a bit, the Persian king decides to hand over the territory, but to rule over it as Charles's faithful steward and to welcome Frankish envoys

108. Kleinclausz argues for Notker's responsibility for propagating the Holy Land protectorate myth, in "La légende du protectorat," 227.

at any time.[109] Charlemagne thus regains Jerusalem after a competition-without-battle that duly establishes the supremacy of the Frankish king over his eastern counterpart.[110] Lurking behind that victory, however, is the fact that Harun came to his decision concerning Charlemagne's merit based on very little evidence.

Notker and the Greeks

To fashion Charlemagne as a new kind of Christian emperor, Notker had to contend with the existence of the titular Roman emperors in Byzantium. In his creation of diplomatic encounters with the Greek East, Notker takes on the delicate issue of the divided empire in the wake of the coronation of 800. The Greek emperor Michael, unlike Harun, is not eager to recognize his new counterpart in the West. While Einhard merely intimates Greek surrender by saying that they sought an alliance out of fear, Notker delves openly into the anxieties surrounding the Frankish assumption of the imperial title. The resulting portrait of the Greeks is not a flattering one. The first inkling of tension occurs in 1.10, when Pope Stephen sends monks from Rome to help the Franks unify their liturgical chant. The embassy includes some devious Greek monks who plot to foil the king's efforts by singing as badly as possible. Notker takes the opportunity to explain the behavior as the product of the unending Greek envy of the glory of the Franks.[111] This early scene inaugurates a tone of hostility that persists throughout the presentation of Franco-Byzantine diplomatic relations, an attitude that has attracted the attention of historians seeking to understand anti–Byzantine sentiment in the Frankish West. Chris Wickham, for example, reads too much into Notker's negative portrayal of Greeks, considering it an unprecedented and trend-setting example of Frankish Hellenophobia, which he sees as the product of southern German provincialism. He charges the monk with placing his account of the Greek embassies "into the equally folkloric account of embassies to and from the 'Persians' (i.e. the caliphate)." For the reader who recognizes Notker's imaginative magnification of the tension

---

109. Notker, *GK*, 2.9. "Si terram promissam Abrahae et exhibitam Iosuae, dedero illi, propter longinquitatem locorum non potest eam defensare a barbaris; vel si juxta magnanimitatem suam defendere coeperit, timeo, ne finitimae regno Francorum provintiae discedant ab eius imperio. Sed tamen hoc modo liberalitati eius gratificari temptabo. Dabo quidem illam in eius potestatem, et ego advocatus eius ero super eam, ipse vero, quandocumque voluerit, vel sibi oportunissimum videtur, dirigat ad me legatos suos et fidelissimum me procuratorem eiusdem provintiae redituum inveniet."
110. Morrissey signals this as the "lutte symbolique" with the East; see *L'empereur*, 60.
111. Notker, *GK*, 1.10.

with the Greeks in chapter 16 of Einhard, this is an obvious pairing of two thematically linked, highly fictionalized accounts. The historian concedes at least some literary strategy to Notker by stating that he places the Franks in an "orientalising mirror" that highlights the laudable traits of the Franks and reveals the negative traits of the Greeks.[112] By leaning on the charge of orientalism, however, he misses the point of Notker's engagement with the discourse of Roman universalism, which involved placing Charlemagne at the helm of the divided empire, to the detriment of the Greeks.[113]

One of Notker's more curious anti–Byzantine moments occurs within his presentation of Charlemagne's journey to Rome for his coronation, which Notker portrays as having been the result of Michael's refusal to answer Pope Leo's calls for assistance against his enemies in Rome. There are very few ninth-century discussions of Charlemagne's imperial coronation, so Notker's heavily fictionalized interpretation of the circumstances leading up to the ceremony is particularly noteworthy.[114] In 1.26, which is otherwise devoted to the administration of ecclesiastical affairs, Notker enlivens his depiction of the Byzantine failure to help Leo through reported dialogue. After the pope secretly makes his predicament known to the Greek emperor through his envoys, Michael tersely tells him to deal with his own problems: "The pope has his own power and it is superior to ours. Let him take revenge on his enemies himself." Leo then turns to the leadership in the West, inviting the "unconquered Charles" to Rome. By divine providence, the narrator offers, the Frankish king was destined to obtain the title of emperor and Augustus by apostolic authority.[115]

In this imagined vignette, Notker reveals the Greeks to be unwilling to stand up for the larger Christian community and thus unworthy of the title of Christian emperors. His presentation of Charlemagne's rescue of Leo is also symptomatic of a larger tendency in the *Deeds* to approach the discourse of universal empire in terms of personal encounters between the leaders of East and West.[116] Hans-Joachim Reischmann identifies Notker's inflation of

---

112. Chris Wickham, "Ninth-Century Byzantium through Western Eyes," in *Byzantium in the Ninth Century: Dead or Alive?* ed. Leslie Brubaker (Aldershot, 1998), 255–56.

113. MacLean also recognizes the characterization of Greeks as lazy and decadent as part of Notker's development of the theme of universalism; see *Kingship and Politics*, 223.

114. Muldoon, *Empire and Order*, 66–67; Folz, *Le souvenir*, 40–41.

115. Notker, *GK*, 1.26. "Quod cum clanculo per familiares suos Michahelo imperatori Constantinopoleos indicari fecissest, et ille omne auxilium ab eo retraheret dicens: Ille papa regnum habet per se et nostro praestantius: ipse se per se ipsum vindicet de adversariis suis."

116. Notker often relies on exploration of psychological issues and on discussion of personality traits in his vignettes, a narrative practice that Reischmann describes as "gap-filling"; see *Die Trivialisierung*, 37.

the binary oppositions between Michael's flaws and Charlemagne's virtues, and rightly argues that the monk's depiction of the Greek emperor's decadent apathy and unwillingness to help is meant to demonstrate Michael's unworthiness as a leader.[117] Notker's depiction of Leo's fruitless call for help to Constantinople appears to be a transposition of events from 752, when Pope Stephen II sent envoys to Constantinople to ask the emperor to liberate the city of Rome. The pontiff had asked the Byzantines for help several times in the first half of that year, but more out of desperation than loyalty, as Thomas F. X. Noble argues. Stephen soon realized that help would not be forthcoming and turned his attention to Pippin and the Franks, thereby initiating the so-called Franco-papal alliance.[118] Pope Stephen displayed his gratitude by consecrating and anointing Pippin, his wife, and his sons at Saint-Denis in July of 754, a ceremony that represented a key moment in the definition of the role of Frankish kingship and its relationship to Rome.[119] The Carolingian kings, from that point on, could be seen as protectors of the papacy whose assumption of the kingdom of the Franks was owed to the Holy See.[120] Pope Leo's coronation of Charles offered further symbolic solidification of this new alliance based on the Frankish mission of protection.[121] By merging elements of these two central moments in the establishment of the Carolingian relationship to the papacy, Notker reaffirms the providential nature of the *translatio ad Francos* and lays the groundwork for his own version of Charlemagne's symbolic defeat of the Greeks.

Notker situates the events leading up to the journey to Rome in 800 within his treatment of the theme of universal empire by describing Charlemagne as the *caput orbis*. Echoing Einhard's claim that the king had not known why Leo had called for him, the monk states, "He [Charles] had always been ready for expeditions and dressed for war; and right away, with his attendants and royal guard, unaware of the reason for the summons, the head of the world set out without delay to the former head of the world."[122] Notker thus

117. Reischmann, *Die Trivialisierung*, 42–43. Cf. Goetz, *Strukturen der Spätkarolingischen*, 77.

118. Thomas F. X. Noble, *The Republic of Saint Peter: The Birth of the Papal State, 680–825* (Philadelphia, 1984), 74.

119. Ibid., 87.

120. Joanna Story, "Cathwulf, Kingship, and the Royal Abbey of Saint-Denis," *Speculum* 74 (1999): 11. Noble argues that the papacy had been emancipated from the Byzantines by the 730s, in *Republic*, 94.

121. Robert Folz, *The Concept of Empire in Western Europe from the Fifth to the Fourteenth Century*, trans. Sheila Ann Oglivie (New York, 1969), 25.

122. Notker, *GK*, 1.26. "Qui, ut semper in expeditione et praecinctu bellico positus erat, statim cum apparitoribus et scola tyronum, causae vocationibus suae penitus ignarus, caput orbis ad caput quondam orbis absque mora perrexit."

refers to Charlemagne the man, who is about to go to Rome, as *caput orbis*, while at the same time referring to his destination, using the same qualifier, "caput orbis ad caput quondam orbis absque mora perrexit."[123] Well aware that *caput orbis* as a metonym for Rome could have a variety of competing referents, Notker leaves his reader to puzzle over which conception of Rome as *caput orbis* he intends to suggest. The passage is intended to be allusive, and he surely meant to evoke the Paderborn poem, which contains the epithet "Rex Karolus, caput orbis" in its celebration of the flowering of a new Rome under Charlemagne.[124] Notker is also celebrating Roman renewal, with his new golden head, but his version demands some redefinition of existing terms. His use of the term *caput orbis* for Charles occurs just after his denunciation of the Greeks and his affirmation of the Franks as the protectors of the papacy. His clever phrasing thus announces the coming ceremony as the moment of transition from a broken and dysfunctional Christian imperium, in which the pope is at the mercy of Greek apathy, to a new and providential conception of empire based on mutual recognition between the Franks and the papacy. Notker's allusions to the Vergilian Paderborn epic, both here and in the hunting scenes, fulfill a specific rhetorical function by tempering the pretensions of the panegyric poem. Charlemagne's status as current *caput orbis* in the *Deeds* becomes tied to his protection of the church.[125]

Notker breathes life into the diplomatic encounters between Charlemagne and the Greeks by revealing the Frankish emperor's concerns after his coronation. He fears, for instance, that as the result of his investiture, the Greeks will be even more full of envy than before, and will therefore try to plot against his kingdom. He also worries that they will be all the more ready to defend against any plans he might have to annex their kingdom. These preoccupations recall Einhard's depiction of the Greek reaction to Charlemagne's new title, as well as the biographer's claim concerning their fear-driven quest for a peace agreement. Notker then builds on Einhard by creating an imagined scenario in which Michael had sought Charles's friendship before the coronation. The encounter seems, at first, to be a sympathetic portrayal of the Greeks, but the scene does not jibe with the larger portrait of Franco-Greek

---

123. Even before Charlemagne was crowned emperor, Alcuin had referred to Rome as *Caput orbis* in poem 25, written around 796. *Poet. Lat.* 1, verses 1–3. "Salve, Roma potens, mundi decus, inclyta mater, / Atque tui tecum valeant in secula nati; / Et caput orbis, honor magnus, Leo papa valeto."
124. *KMLP*, verses 90–96.
125. Cf. Ganz, "Humour as History": "It is God who intervenes in history, making Charles emperor," 178. For Goetz, *caput orbis* signifies that Charlemagne is a new leader of a *Weltreich*; see *Strukturen der Spätkarolingischen*, 74; Siegrist reads Leo's role as secondary, in part because he describes him as "*caput orbis*" even before Charlemagne gets to Rome. Siegrist, *Herrscherbild und Weltsicht*, 115.

relations, and indeed, the mention of past quests for alliance proves to be part of Notker's diminishment of the leadership in Constantinople. Still in a pensive mood concerning the Greeks, Charlemagne looks back to an embassy he received from Constantinople bringing word that the emperor promised loyal friendship. If they were to become closer neighbors, the Greeks explain, their leader intended to treat Charlemagne as a son and relieve him of his poverty. Upon hearing this, Charlemagne had exclaimed: "O would that there were not this little pond between us, for then perhaps we could share the wealth of the East, or else hold it equally in common."[126] Charles seems grateful for the condescending offer, but we are meant to understand that the time of Frankish inferiority and any need for the sharing of Eastern wealth has since passed. Michael's empty offer of an unequal relationship and Charles's eager desire to share the wealth of the East hark back to the time when he was a mere Frankish king and not yet the *caput orbis*.

In another dramatized exchange with the Greek East, which also involves Michael's use of the term *filius* for Charlemagne, the embassy once again provides a fruitful context for the vilification of the Byzantine leadership. Since the visit takes place during Charlemagne's war with the Saxons, it too is understood to have occurred before the imperial investiture. Notker tells of how Charlemagne sent messengers to Constantinople from the scene of the Saxon war, which, in Frankish historiographical tradition, is one of Charlemagne's more glorious military conquests, detailed in Einhard, chapter 15. When the envoys arrive, Michael asks them whether the kingdom of his son Charles is at peace on all fronts. The envoys reply that indeed it is, except for the problem of the Saxons. Michael then wonders aloud why his son bothers with such a petty enemy as the Saxons, when he (Michael) would have gladly just handed them over to the Frankish king.[127] Here Notker depicts the Greeks trying, but failing, to belittle Charlemagne. The Greek offer of the Saxons is empty, and Charles sees it for the taunt that it is. The narrator describes how the extremely warlike Charlemagne (*bellicosissimo*), upon learning of Michael's statement, tells his envoy that the Greek king would have been more helpful if he had offered him a leg wrap for his journey. The back-and-forth between the emperors is petty, even snippy, and all the more humorous given that the retorts in diplomatic time would have taken many

---

126. Notker, *GK*, 1.26. "O utinam non esset ille gurgitulus inter nos, forsitan divitias orientales aut partiremur, aut pariter participando communiter haberemus." Reischmann notes the snub implied by *filius*, in *Die Trivialisierung*, 49. Goetz calls this an outdated term and an empty Byzantine claim of authority, in *Strukturen der Spätkarolingischen*, 77–78.

127. Notker, *GK*, 2.5.

months to reach the ears of their intended victims. Notker's audience, on the other hand, could enjoy the immediacy of these mini-dramas.

Since the Greek emperor's insulting offer occurs during the Saxon war, it shares the same rhetorical context as the catalog of conquests that Einhard had created for the Frankish king, largely in chapter 15. Notker's Charlemagne is "*bellicosissimo*," while Michael, through narrative interjection, is deemed useless, slothful, and worthless in battle, a contrast that Notker deliberately draws with one of Charlemagne's most glorious "deeds in war" as a backdrop. Notker does not lavish praise on Charlemagne for his valor, however. Instead, he embeds an unpleasant diplomatic exchange with Byzantium within an anecdote that should have been about the glorious defeat of the Saxons, once again disrupting an expected locus of praise. The conflict is psychological rather than physical, however, playing out as a war of words between the two leaders that implicitly becomes another one of Charlemagne's victories. Michael's repetition of "my son" is an element of his verbal attack, but Charlemagne is not moved by the Eastern emperor's attempts at debasement. It is the Greeks who are unready to protect, useless in battle, and full of empty promises and worthless offers.

Book 2.6 contains a final embassy from Constantinople that contains Notker's most intricate and allusive meditation on the meaning of Charlemagne's status as Christian emperor. The Frankish leader sends two of his ambassadors, Bishop Heito and Count Hugo, to Greece, where the wicked Greek emperor delays their audience, forcing them to spend their own money while they wait for a meeting.[128] After their return, the Eastern emperor sends some of his own envoys to Charlemagne. As revenge for the inhospitable treatment of his men, the Frankish bishop sets up the usual pomp of a royal audience, but then orders a stable hand to sit on the emperor's throne. When the envoys arrive, they mistake the stable hand for the emperor and prostrate themselves before him. The scene replays itself several times with other members of the court, staff, and servants. Each time, the envoys fall to the ground to worship the person on the throne, and in each instance, they are met with the same refrain: "Non hic est imperator." After the series of false emperors, Charlemagne himself finally appears before the envoys, gleaming in front of a sunlight-filled window, clad in gold

128. The actual embassy of Heito in 811 coincided with the ratification of the peace between Charlemagne and the Byzantines that ultimately yielded recognition of the Frankish imperial title in exchange for jurisdiction over Venice. See Michael McCormick, "Byzantium and the West, 700–900," in *The New Cambridge Medieval History c. 700–c. 900*, vol. 2, ed. Rosamond McKitterick (Cambridge, UK, 1995), 374.

and precious stones and leaning against Heito, the bishop who had returned from Constantinople.[129] When presented with the real Charlemagne in his gleaming finery, the stunned envoys crumble to the ground, almost lifeless, but unlike the arbitrary and malicious Greek emperor, the king takes pity on his visitors, helping them to their feet.

The description of the emperor's appearance in the sunlight in front of the window offers another example of Notker's allusive relationship to the Paderborn epic. Attending Charlemagne are bishops and abbots, but also his daughters, who are "dressed no less in wisdom and beauty than in necklaces," as well as his young sons, who are already partners in the kingdom.[130] The early verses of the Paderborn poem contain an initial reference to Charles as the *pharus Europae* (12): "Beacon of Europe from whom great light shines, / King Charles casts his splendid name to the stars; / the sun shines here with its beams: / indeed as David illuminated his lands with the great light of piety."[131] The passage to which Notker alludes more directly occurs later, however, when the poet describes Charlemagne in the presence of his family: "The beacon of Europe, deserving of veneration, vaunts himself to the sky. / He gleams and shines forth with an extraordinary visage and countenance; / his noble head is circled with precious gold, / towering over all with his tall shoulders."[132] The poet then describes an image of Charlemagne with his daughters in a passage that stretches from verses 212 to 263, a scene that derives from Venantius's panegyric verse description of the Virgin Mary and her court.[133] The poet's vivid descriptions of the king's pious daughters contain frequent references to gold, gems, and the play of light upon them, all of which leads up to another site of inspiration for Notker, Charlemagne's

---

129. "Stabat autem gloriosissimus regum Karolus iuxta fenestram lucidissimam, radians sicut sol in orto suo, gemmis et auro conspicuus, innixus super Heittonem; hoc quippe nomen erat episcopi ad Constantinopolim quondam destinati."

130. Notker, *GK*, 2.6. "In cuius undique circuitu consistebat instar militiae coelestis, tres videlicet iuvenes filii eius, iam regni participes effecti, filiaque cum matre non minus sapientia vel pulchritudine quam monilibus ornatae."

131. *KMLP*, verses 10–15. "Europae quo celsa pharus cum luce coruscat. / Spargit ad astra suum Karolus rex nomen opimum / Sol nitet ecce suis radiis: sic denique David / Inlustrat magno pietatis lumine terras."

132. *KMLP*, verses 169–172. "Europae veneranda pharus se prodit ad auram. / Enitet eximio vultu facieque coruscat; / Nobile namque caput pretioso amplectitur auro / Rex Karolus; cunctos humeris supereminet altis." Godman, "Poetic Hunt," 578.

133. Godman, "Poets and Emperors," 88; Godman, "Poetic Hunt," 581. See also Theodore M. Andersson, *Early Epic Scenery: Homer, Virgil, and the Medieval Legacy* (Ithaca, NY, 1976), 105–20.

departure on the royal hunt. The poem also describes the king as a metaphorical source of light, like King David, shining forth upon his people.[134]

With his gleaming vision of Charlemagne and his family inspired by
the Paderborn poem, Notker continues his reinterpretation of panegyric
themes by humbling the emperor at a moment where a reader of encomium
would expect full-blown praise. The subtle diminishment of Charlemagne
can be identified, for instance, by the fact that Notker emphasizes that
the illuminated emperor is standing in front of a sunlight-filled window.[135]
Morrissey argues that Charlemagne is a celestial king standing before the
window and that he triumphs just by allowing himself to be seen, but Notker's emperor does not enjoy such an unquestioning brand of praise.[136] His
Charlemagne as *pharus Europae* is more equivocal, since, instead of shining forth himself, as a beacon or in the manner of David, he receives his
light from the sun as it shines through the window. Moreover, the king is
physically leaning on Bishop Heito, the same one who has just come back
from Constantinople. Both details reveal Notker's deliberate depiction of
Charlemagne's imperial glory as dependent on other sources, namely God's
light and the prelates of the realm. His imperial authority, we may deduce,
derives from God and is defined by his mandate to protect the church.
For the reader who knew the Paderborn epic, Notker's revisions of scenes
of imperial glory neutralize the memory of the poem's panegyric praise
and redefine imperial encomium in new terms based on his own vision of
Charlemagne's authority as Roman emperor.

Conclusion

In his *Life of Charlemagne*, Einhard presented the emperor's post-coronation
encounters with the East according to a classical topos of praise for a Roman
emperor based the ideal of peaceful surrender of foreign nations. Instead of
offering pure encomium, however, he found a style and tone that allowed him
to recognize the divided state of the empire within the components of the
commonplace that he was employing. With Einhard as his template, Notker
created an intricate elaboration of Einhard's suggestions of Persian and Greek
symbolic surrender, often interweaving references to other instances of praise
for the Carolingian renewal of empire. Despite his playfulness, Notker was

---

134. Godman notes the fusion of Christian and secular traditions in the Paderborn poem, since
the term *pharus Europae* comes from Venantius, and the image of him "towering" is drawn from
Vergil; see "Poetic Hunt," 581.

135. For another example, see Martínez Pizarro, *Rhetoric of the Scene*, 192–94.

136. Morrissey, *L'empereur*, 61.

a theorist of the meaning of the Carolingian inheritance of Rome who confronted the conflicting dictates of Christian and classical imperial praise. In the spirit of dynastic continuity, the monk set out to create a new set of memories of Charlemagne that would affirm the God-ordained status of the Carolingians as the emperors of Christian Rome using his own particular brand of encomium.

Notker's versions of Charlemagne's exchanges with the East demonstrate how the elaboration of Einhard's material could simultaneously preserve, amplify, and meaningfully alter the underlying rhetoric of praise on which the episodes were based. His rewriting of these exchanges through a prism of previous panegyric models reveals a biographical practice that allowed for meditation on the meaning of Christian imperial authority. As a sort of pseudo-imperial *Life* that is itself a commentary on the practice of biographical writing, Notker's work is unique. The monk built his narrative using multiple layers of discourse, participating as an omniscient narrator who sometimes interjects his opinions, while depending mostly on use of direct speech in the scenes between leaders and envoys. His approach succeeds in highlighting the ways in which diplomatic communications are always subject to multiple interpreters and interpretations. The perils of ambassadorial exchanges can then serve as a metaphor for the project of remembering Charlemagne, since everything that was being remembered about the Frankish king was itself the product of multiple voices and subject to various possible interpretations. Notker was himself a sort of ambassador on behalf of Charlemagne, and he wrestles within the pages of his work with how best to deliver his message.

🐌 CHAPTER 2

Relics from the East

By the mid-tenth century, Charlemagne had taken on a more ecclesiastical role in the "imaginative memories" of monastic authors, who depicted him as a pilgrim, founder of monasteries, and donator of relics.[1] Part of this evolution in the recollection of his imperial reign involved the transformation of his alliances with Eastern nations into an actual journey from which he returned with relics. The concept of imperial travel involving the transport of saintly remains was not new at the time, of course, for it had been a motif signifying Christian triumph since late antiquity.[2] The story of Charlemagne's travels in the East, as it evolved in relic *translatio* narratives, preserved this cast of Christian triumph, but the Frankish king also began to embody an even more pronounced eschatological quality than Notker had conveyed in the *Deeds*. By gaining symbolic triumph in Byzantium and then in Jerusalem, the Frankish emperor seemed to be mimicking the predicted final journey of the prophetic Last Emperor of the sibylline tradition, but only in part. Not long after the imperial coronation

---

1. See generally Amy G. Remensnyder, *Remembering Kings Past: Monastic Foundation Legends in Medieval Southern France* (Ithaca, NY, 1995).
2. Sabine MacCormack, *Art and Ceremony in Late Antiquity* (Berkeley, CA, 1981), 64–65; Kenneth G. Holum and Gary Vikan, "The Trier Ivory *Adventus* Ceremonial, and the Relics of St. Stephen," *Dumbarton Oaks Papers* 33 (1979): 119.

of the Saxon emperor Otto II in 967, a chronicle from Italy described how
Charlemagne had peacefully journeyed to meet Harun in Jerusalem and
then the Greek emperors at Constantinople, a voyage from which, as the
chronicler allows, he returned to Francia with relics, having subjugated foreign nations.[3] Charlemagne's first voyage to the East therefore retained the
rhetoric of bloodless victory that had defined his relationship with foreign
nations in the Carolingian sources, but he was now a Holy Land pilgrim who
seemed to be carrying out activities tied to imperial apocalyptic prophecy.
This chapter considers the emergence of "Charlemagne and the East" within
relic *translatio* narratives, and reveals how this evolving episode in the biography of Charlemagne continued in the tenth and eleventh centuries to be
primarily concerned with the definition of Frankish authority in the newly
divided Christian imperium.

An early example of how monastic authors built on the Carolingian versions of Charlemagne's encounters with the East occurs in the *Translatio Sanguinis Domini* from the Benedictine abbey of Reichenau.[4] Dated to about 925,
the document describes the Frankish king's acquisition of relics of the Passion,
including drops of the blood of Christ. In a curious variation on Einhard's
depiction of Charlemagne's relations with the East after his imperial investiture, the document states that a man named Azan, the prefect of Jerusalem, had longed to make an alliance with the emperor.[5] The author works
within the foreign embassy motif, but he makes meaningful changes. For
instance, the story retains the notion that the emperor's reputation is powerful
enough to draw embassies from the East in search of peaceful alliance, but
his name does not inspire awe so much as the desire to behold his imperial
countenance. Azan has heard about the many virtues, miracles, and incomparable battles of Charlemagne, and, moved by great longing to gaze upon
him, decides to come to the West to enact a treaty of friendship.[6] Azan first
approaches Pope Leo to arrange the meeting, promising incomparable treasure from Jerusalem, gifts greater than anything ever before brought to the
West. This is code, we will learn, for relics of the Passion.

Charlemagne is not interested in Azan's proposal, but his initial refusal is
merely a step toward the eventual discussion between Pope Leo and Charlemagne that will lead to the transfer of holy relics from Jerusalem to the

---

3. Benedict, *Chron.*, 116.

4. Folz, *Le souvenir*, 24–25; Nichols, *Romanesque Signs*, 72.

5. In the *ARF, sub anno* 799, the real Azan sends legates to Charles with gifts and keys to the
Spanish city of Huesca. The passage comes just after the patriarch of Jerusalem's gifts from Calvary
sent to Charlemagne on behalf of Harun after the coronation.

6. *Trans. Sang. Dom.*, 447.

Franks. Upset by Charlemagne's negative response, Pope Leo sends word of his dismay. The message appears in direct discourse, which creates a sense of drama and immediacy that recalls Notker's lively representations of Charlemagne's diplomatic exchanges. The messenger speaks to the king, conveying the pontiff's cryptic yet powerful rebuke:

> [Leo responds,] saying, "if you are indeed the one whom the whole world judges you to be, and you are proclaimed as the most famous in the whole universe, you ought to give your life over to danger, if the situation demands it, and walk on foot after him to procure so magnificent a treasure." At length, moved by these words, the heavenly scepter-bearing one, having been moved in his heart, quickly got down from his steed and set out for Rome.[7]

The relationship between Charlemagne and Leo had long inspired the imaginations of Carolingian poets and chroniclers. The above passage offers a vivid example of how authors could impute motives and feelings to accompany the imagined events surrounding the coronation of 800. The initial refusal to meet Azan opens the door for the pope's admonition to Charlemagne to live up to his worldwide reputation. The emphasis on the power of the emperor's renown that characterizes the foreign embassy topos remains a factor here, but the stakes have changed now that the emperor in question is being scolded by the pope who crowned him. Moved by the envoy's message, Charlemagne heeds the papal call and decides to humbly receive the gifts from Jerusalem.

The Paderborn epic had established the relationship between Charlemagne and Leo as an occasion for lofty secular praise. With Pope Leo as the chastising voice, the author of the *Translatio Sanguinis* deflates the sort of Vergilian *fama* celebrated by the Paderborn poet and reframes it in terms of the need for humility. To live up to his reputation, Charlemagne will have to travel, feet on the ground, in spite of the danger, so that he may receive the promised gift. Notker's portrait of Charlemagne represented an early departure from the more secular celebrations of the Carolingian imperial *renovatio*, but Leo's insistence here that the new emperor get down from his horse represents a more explicit call for an imperial model defined by obedience to the

---

7. *Trans. Sang. Dom.*, 447. "Si tu, inquiens, ipse esses, quem te esse totus arbitratur mundus, et universum per orbem celeberrimus diffamaris, vitam tuam, si ita res exigeret, periculo dare et pedum tuorum incessu post ipsum pro adeptione tam magnifici thesauri ambulare debueras. His tandem sermonibus sceptriger caelitus animo commotus, cornipedem celeriter conscendens, Romam profectus est."

Holy See. When Charlemagne initially refuses the offer, he does not know what he is turning down. The transfer of relics of the Passion to the West is thus predicated on the intervention of the pope, whose role in the exchange affirms his place as the necessary mediator in the relationship between the emperor and God.

The author further elaborates the story by having Azan fall ill in Corsica. The envoy sends messages imploring the emperor to meet him on the island, again promising the unnamed treasure of incomparable worth. Charlemagne refuses, citing his fear of sea travel, which greatly disappoints Azan. The emperor sends envoys in his place, with whom he reunites in Sicily, where he finally arrives, having traveled barefoot from Ravenna with a large traveling company. In his new guise as humble pilgrim working in the service of God and the papacy, Charlemagne receives as his reward a collection of relics of the Passion beyond description, most of which go to Aachen, except for the holy blood, destined for the imperial abbey of Reichenau.[8] Stored in an onyx vessel, the relics include, in addition to the drops of blood, a gold, jewel-encrusted reliquary cross with a fragment of wood from the cross, a thorn from the crown of thorns, one of the nails, a bit of the true cross, and a fragment from the Holy Sepulcher.[9] The priceless collection thus appears as the Frankish king's reward for having obeyed the pope by preserving his reputation as emperor and protector of Christendom.[10]

Charlemagne's First Journey to Jerusalem and Constantinople

The oldest extant narrative of Charlemagne making the journey to Jerusalem and Constantinople appeared around 968 in the *Chronicon* of Benedict, an Italian monk from the monastery of Saint Andrew on Mount Soracte, north of Rome. Although often maligned for his Latin skills, there is no question that Benedict marks a crucial juncture in the development of the tradition of Charlemagne's encounters with Harun and the Greeks.[11] We do not know when Charlemagne first began to actually travel to Jerusalem and

---

8. *Trans. Sang. Dom.*, 447.

9. *Trans. Sang. Dom.*, 447; cf. Kleinclausz, "La légende du protectorat," 228.

10. Charlemagne also goes to Jerusalem as a penitent, whence he returns with the Holy Foreskin for the abbey of Charroux. See Matthew Gabriele, *An Empire of Memory: The Legend of Charlemagne, the Franks, and Jerusalem before the First Crusade* (Oxford, 2011), 44–45.

11. Folz recognized that despite Benedict's crude style and confused thinking, his version of the journey to the East was of considerable importance; see *Le souvenir*, 135–36. Gaston Paris, *Histoire poétique de Charlemagne* (Geneva, 1974), 55; cf. Beryl Smalley, *Historians in the Middle Ages* (London, 1974), 84. Paul Aebischer offers a summary of those disgusted by Benedict's "copying" of Einhard,

Constantinople in the minds of chroniclers, but the *Translatio Sanguinis* shows how such an evolution could rather easily occur. Like the tale of Azan, the story that Benedict tells bears witness to a growing practice among monastic authors that involved the manipulation of the story of Charlemagne's post-coronation encounters with the East to a variety of ideological ends. After Charlemagne returns to Italy, the narrator announces that the triumphant king then returned to Francia, "having greatly extended his kingdom and having subjugated foreign nations, and focused assiduously on occupations of this sort."[12] The monk thus makes explicit what others had implied, that the journey to the East was intended to symbolize Charlemagne's symbolic conquest of the Persians and the Greeks.

Like Notker, although with far less literary effort and talent, Benedict also rewrote Charlemagne's alliances with Harun and the Greeks as a meditation on Frankish imperial authority. Notker had done so at a time of uncertainty for the waning Carolingian dynasty, while Benedict remembered the theoretical Frankish conquest of the East in a work that openly lamented the transfer of empire to the Saxons. At the end of his chronicle, Benedict emotionally conveys his unhappiness at the Saxon rise to power, apostrophizing his beloved Rome: "Look, leonine city! A short time ago you were captured by, indeed relinquished to a king of the Saxons."[13] We may presume that he is referring to the recent coronation in 967 of Otto II, who had just been crowned co-emperor with his father Otto I by the pope. His writing of the *Chronicon* would also have coincided with the period not long after Otto I's coronation in 962, the result of a deal struck with the controversial Pope John XII. The pope had agreed to crown Otto emperor at Rome in exchange for protection and return of conquered papal territories in Italy. The Saxon concessions to the papacy were then codified in the *Ottonianum*, a document that would later figure in the polemics between church and state of the late eleventh century.[14]

Charlemagne's journey to the East is based on an established motif of Roman imperial victory without battle that had been adapted to celebrate

---

in *Les versions norroises du "Voyage de Charlemagne en Orient": Leurs sources* (Paris, 1956), 114, 120–21. See also Monteleone, *Il viaggio*, 153–54.

12. Benedict, *Chron.*, 116. "Victor et coronator triumphator rex in *Francia* est reversus. Qui cum tantus in ampliando regno et subiciens esteris nationibus sisteret, et in eiusmodi occupationibus assidue versaretur."

13. Benedict, *Chron.*, 186. "Ve civitas Leoniana! dudum capta fuistis, modo vero a Saxonicum rege relicta."

14. Walter Ullmann, *A Short History of the Papacy* (London, 2002), 119–20; Gerd Althoff, *Die Ottonen: Königsherrschaft ohne Staat* (Stuttgart, 2000), 115; Pierre Riché, *The Carolingians: A Family Who Forged Europe*, trans. Michael Idomir Allen (Philadelphia, 1993), 271–72.

the Frankish monarchy under the Carolingians as the legitimate holders of the Roman imperial title. In Benedict's case, the narrative appears in a chronicle marked by its author's strongly articulated feelings of antipathy toward the new dynasty in power after the transfer of empire away from the Franks. Benedict's dismay over the Saxon usurpation dictates that we read the monk's description of Charlemagne's establishment of his relationship with the papacy and the Christian East in light of his attitude toward the forces of lay authority in the empire at the time. Benedict's Roman Empire is the empire of the church, governed by the papacy in the tradition of the Donation of Constantine. The chronicle opens with a presentation of how the monasteries on Mount Soracte, Saint Sylvester and Saint Andrew, had fared under the various emperors. He condemns Julian, for instance, for his despoiling of Saint Sylvester, an act committed, he insists, out of hatred for what Constantine had built. Benedict also communicates his anti-Saxon stance by linking the two monasteries to Pippin and Charlemagne, exalting the Franks who ruled in Italy as faithful protectors of the papacy. He even rewrites the foundation story of his monastery to make Charlemagne its founder, a process that Remensnyder calls "retrospective dating."[15]

Benedict constructs his narrative of Charlemagne's journey using material from Einhard and the *Royal Frankish Annals*, but there are no envoys. Instead, the emperor travels with a great mass of followers in a manner similar to the voyage described in the *Translatio Sanguinis*. The traveling company will be familiar to readers of Einhard, however, since the ethnic components reflect the list of territories that Charles had conquered in war in chapter 15 of his biography. Having stopped in Rome to receive the blessing of the pope, the king orders boats on the Italian coast to create a bridge across the Adriatic, at which point Benedict hyperbolically announces that the gathering is too large to even be quantified. He then proclaims that the Greeks were not able to offer a comparable show of strength: "All of the nations of the land of the Greeks, having reckoned that their strength amounted to nothing, are praising and blessing God, who directs Charles, servant of Peter, prince of the apostles, on the proper path."[16] The statement recalls Notker's slanderous charges, but it also represents a broader impulse to promote a vision of the Franks working with the Holy See to defend Christendom in response to the Byzantines' inability to do so.

---

15. Benedict, *Chron.*, 168; Remensnyder, *Remembering*, 150.
16. Benedict, *Chron.*, 113. "Molieruntque cuncte nationes terre Grecorum, ut robor eorum pro nichilo computatus, collaudantes et benedicentes Deum, qui via recto dirigit Karulo, servus Petri principis apostolorum."

Benedict's presentation of Harun al Rachid is based closely on Einhard, but he makes significant changes to the story, most strikingly by having the two men meet on Harun's territory.[17] Charlemagne makes a tour of major centers of Christendom, going first to Rome, and then to Jerusalem to meet Harun, who accompanies him to Alexandria before returning by way of Constantinople. In Jerusalem, Harun offers him peace, friendship, and safe passage to visit the Holy Sepulcher, to which he brings many gifts:

> Then he had arrived at the most sacred sepulcher and place of the resurrection of our Lord Jesus Christ, and having decorated the sacred place with gold and gems, he set up a golden standard of astonishing size. Not only did he decorate all of the Holy Places, but also King Harun agreed to assign his power over the Sepulcher of the Lord and the surrounding structure, which they had sought.[18]

Benedict offers a vivid scene of the Frankish king's in-person bestowal of gifts at the sacred site. After completing the decoration, Harun showers Charlemagne with Eastern gifts and finery. When the Franks and the Saracens part ways at Alexandria, it is "as if they were blood brothers."[19] The phrase from Einhard that led to the protectorate myth is present in the passage, but Benedict makes more explicit the idea that the transfer of custody had been one of the objectives of their mission, a detail that could only be inferred from Einhard.

In this new telling, Charlemagne is present, and therefore able to decorate the holy sites himself, placing gifts and an enormous standard at the Holy Sepulcher. The act recalls previous such gestures by Roman emperors who wished to commemorate their imperial stewardship of the Holy City. The practice of bestowing gifts on the Holy Sepulcher was a tradition of Christian emperors beginning with Constantine. The decoration of Golgotha with a standard implied affirmation of the alliance between emperor and cross, and was an instrument of imperial rule that occurred throughout late antiquity and the Middle Ages.[20] The ninth-century Greek chronicler Theophanes described, for instance, how the empress Pulcheria under the

---

17. Benedict, *Chron.*, 113.

18. Benedict, *Chron.*, 114. "Ac deinde ad sacratissimum domini hac salvatoris nostri Jesu Christi sepulchrum locumque resurrectionis advenisset, ornatoque sacrum locum auro gemmisque, etiam vexillum aureum mire magnitudinis imposuit; non solum cuncta loca sancta decoravit, sed etiam presepe Domini et sepulchrum, que petierant Aaron rex potestatis eius ascribere concessit."

19. Benedict, *Chron.*, 114.

20. Muldoon, *Empire and Order*, 69; H. E. J. Cowdrey, "Eleventh-Century Reformers' Views of Constantine," *Byzantinische Forschungen* 24 (1997): 70; Eusebius, *VC*, 4.46; MacCormack, *Art and Ceremony*, 85–88.

influence of Theodosius II had sent donations for the needy in Jerusalem and a golden cross studded with precious stones to be erected during the Persian war of the 420s. The act of decoration was meant to evoke Christ's victory and to announce imminent imperial victory over enemies of the faith.[21] The link between the emperor, the cross, and victory over the Persians was also central to the story of the seventh-century Byzantine emperor Heraclius and his recovery of the true cross, which he returned to Jerusalem in 631.[22] The sending of the banner as a symbol of victory to Charlemagne by the patriarch of Jerusalem described in the *Royal Frankish Annals* probably signified the patriarch's recognition of the new Frankish emperor as protector of the Holy City.[23] By rewriting the episode so that Charlemagne himself brings a banner to the Holy Sepulcher, Benedict joins this tradition of commemorating imperial protection of Christian sites. With Harun presented as the Persian rival of Charlemagne, the scene also symbolizes Charlemagne's peaceful victory over the Persians, which culminates in his "recovery" of the Holy Sepulcher.

Relics from Constantinople

Benedict offers a simplified version of Einhard's discussion of how the Greeks sought an alliance to avoid any *"occasio scandali."*[24] He makes a significant addition, however, when he allows that the Greek emperor gave a relic of Saint Andrew to Charlemagne along with many other gifts.[25] The story is no doubt intended to authenticate a relic for his monastery, just as the author of the *Translatio Sanguinis* does for Reichenau, but both chose to weave their *translationes* into adaptations of scenes from the Carolingian sources having to do with Charlemagne's relations with rivals for his authority as emperor, namely the pope and the Greeks. Relics functioned as instruments of power, guaranteed political authority, and displayed divine approval to those who possessed them.[26] The gift from the Greeks to a Charlemagne who subjugates eastern nations should therefore be viewed as a demonstration of

21. Holum and Vikan, "Trier Ivory," 127–28.

22. John Meyendorff, *Imperial Unity and Christian Divisions: The Church, 450–680 A.D.* (Crestwood, NY, 1989), 334.

23. Robert Folz, *The Coronation of Charlemagne: 25 December 800*, trans. J. E. Anderson (London, 1974), 142. Roger Collins suggests that the gifts may have been inspired by perceived instability in Constantinople and the desire to switch allegiances; see Collins, *Charlemagne*, 149.

24. Benedict, *Chron.*, 114–15.

25. Benedict, *Chron.*, 115. See also Monteleone, *Il viaggio*, 157.

26. Ioli Kalavrezou, "Helping Hands for the Empire: Imperial Ceremonies and the Cult of Relics at the Byzantine Court," in *Byzantine Court Culture from 829 to 1204*, ed. Henry Maguire

Byzantine recognition of a shift in imperial primacy to the West. Moreover, the relic of Saint Andrew held particular significance, for it was Constantius I, father of Constantine, who had brought the bodies of Andrew, Timothy, and Luke to Constantinople to be placed in the church of the Holy Apostles in 357.[27] Paulinus of Nola wrote verses in which he linked the body of Andrew to the establishment of Constantinople as the new imperial city, while the Saxon Poet proclaimed that Charlemagne would be the apostle leading the Saxons on Judgment Day and that Andrew would lead the Greeks.[28] Benedict's presentation of Charlemagne's triumphal return with the remains of Saint Andrew is therefore a component of the chronicler's establishment of Charlemagne's primacy over the East.

Charlemagne returns to the West by way of Rome with many gifts for "Blessed Peter." Heeding orders from the pope, he concedes to the pontiff his power over the city of Rome, all of Pentapolis, Ravenna, and Tuscany.[29] The scene derives from the entry for 756 in the *Royal Frankish Annals*, when Pippin captured Pentapolis and Ravenna from the Lombards and, as promised, returned the recaptured Byzantine territories to Pope Stephen II.[30] Benedict somewhat obsessively repeats this passage nearly word for word for Popes Stephen, Hadrian, and Leo, insisting each time on the Frankish donation to Saint Peter. His interest in the matter may have been related to the contemporary situation between Otto I and John XII, since Otto I had promised to return territory in Italy to the papacy, but had subsequently tried to overthrow the pope to whom he had made the promise. By contrast, Benedict's repeated revisions of the circumstances of the establishment of the Franco-papal alliance convey his appreciation for a Charlemagne whose role as emperor had been defined by his helpful and subservient relationship to the papacy. He even combines the material to give the impression that the journey to the East has yielded a return of territories contested by the Byzantines to the Holy See.

After listing the cities to be handed over to the pope, Benedict describes how Charlemagne thanked God and the prince of the apostles before

---

(Washington, DC, 1997), 55; Holger Klein, "Eastern Objects and Western Desires: Relics and Reliquaries between Byzantium and the West," *Dumbarton Oaks Papers* 58 (2004): 283.

27. Cyril Mango, "Constantine's Mausoleum and the Translation of Relics," *Byzantinische Zeitschrift* 83 (1990): 53.

28. Paulinus of Nola, *Carmina*, 19; Poeta Saxo, bk. 5, verse 683.

29. Benedict, *Chron.*, 116. "Roma veniens, et dona amplissima beato Petro constituit, ordinataque Hurbe et omnia Pentapoli et Ravenne finibus seu Tusscie, omnia in apostolici potestatibe concessit." Benedict repeats a version of this passage four times, in chapters 19, 21, 22, and 23.

30. *ARF, sub anno* 756. Thomas F. X. Noble notes that Pippin did not donate, but rather forced Aistulf to give over the Byzantine territories; see Noble, *Republic of Saint Peter*, 90–94.

accepting the benediction of the pope and the acclamation of the Roman populace as "Augustus." The emperor and the pope then travel together to the monastery of Saint Sylvester.[31] There is no explanation of how the Italian territories came to be Charles's to relinquish, only the implication that his journey had yielded them. This is, in part, because Benedict collapses Charles's journey to the East with the material related to Pippin's return of territories in Italy to the papacy. Benedict deliberately places the scene after, instead of before, the symbolic conquest of the former empires of the East as a way of reinforcing a vision of a more universal imperial Charlemagne who is nonetheless indebted to the papacy for his imperial status.

Charlemagne completes the final stage of the journey from Rome to Mount Soracte accompanied by the pope. The scene recalls the relationship between Constantine and Pope Sylvester, and, in fact, the comparison between the two pairs had already been publicly drawn at Rome. The idealized papal vision of the relationship between Charlemagne and the Holy See appeared early in the ninth century in a mosaic made for the banquet hall of the Lateran Palace in Rome. The lost mosaic, preserved only in sketches, depicts the triad of Christ, Constantine the Great, and Pope Sylvester alongside that of Saint Peter, Pope Leo III, and Charlemagne.[32] Charlemagne appears as heir to Constantine, with Leo in the parallel position to Sylvester, emphasizing the continuity of papal domination over the secular leadership of the empire in a reflection of the tone of the Donation of Constantine.[33] By having Charlemagne travel with the pope to Saint Sylvester after handing over Italian territories, Benedict creates his own image of papal-imperial relations based on the ideal of a subservient temporal leader. The voyage culminates in the deposition of a small bit of the relic of Saint Andrew for the consecration of the eponymous monastery, a donation that Charles must ask the pope's permission to make. The triumphant king then returns to Francia.[34] In the end, Benedict's retelling of Charlemagne's symbolic conquest of the East reveals a monk whose interests were extremely local and, at the same time, preoccupied with the state of lay and ecclesiastical power within the theoretical Christian universe that he inhabited.

---

31. Benedict, *Chron.*, 116. See Gabriele, *Empire of Memory*, 98, for the fact that this is not his imperial investiture.

32. Noble, *Republic of Saint Peter*, 323; Folz, *Coronation*, 115.

33. Cowdrey, "Eleventh-Century," 70; Muldoon, *Empire and Order*, 69.

34. Benedict, *Chron.*, 116.

Charlemagne and the Last Emperor Prophecy

In his quest to explain Benedict's intentions in rewriting Einhard chapter 16 as he did, Robert Folz proposed that in the tenth century no one would have believed that Charlemagne had not already reclaimed the territories that had been lost to the Muslims. This is why, he argued, Benedict transformed the embassies into a single voyage to the East that was neither a conquest nor a crusade, but instead a peaceful mission that ended, as did Einhard's, with the establishment of a Frankish protectorate of the Holy Lands.[35] This explanation not only attributes excessive naïveté to Benedict and his audience, but it also fails to recognize the rhetoric of empire that underlies the episode. The confusion over whether he intended to describe a peaceful mass pilgrimage or perhaps some sort of proto-crusade arises from the fact that the story draws on two competing traditions of Roman universalism. Benedict retains much of Einhard's version, which was based on an ideal of peaceful alliances and willing surrender, but he also drew on the popular sibylline prophecies that promised universal Christian domination through violent conquest of all enemies of the realm.

Benedict's tenth-century chronicle represents a defining moment in the ongoing reframing of "Charlemagne in the East," in large part because the journey that he describes recalls, for the first time that we know of, certain key elements of the apocalyptic Last Emperor prophecy.[36] Sibylline oracles had long spoken of an imperial figure who would reunite the empire before traveling to Jerusalem and laying down his imperial insignia before the Last Judgment. The Charlemagne in the *Chronicon* achieves the symbolic subjugation of the Greeks, thereby uniting East and West under his rule, and he also travels to Jerusalem. In certain ways the echoes are striking, but at the same time, the journey to the East is in no way interested in marking the end of Charlemagne's reign or of the Roman Empire. Benedict's voyage thus offers an early example of adaptation of the prophecy for purposes other than chiliastic speculation.

The sibyls were prophetic texts dating back to antiquity, some of which were concerned with imperial succession and the power structure of the Roman Empire.[37] The Tiburtine Sibyl, one of the most popular works of

35. Folz, *Le souvenir*, 136–37.
36. Ibid., 138; Hannes Möhring, *Der Weltkaiser der Endzeit: Entstehung Wandel und Wirkung einer tausendjahrigen Weissagung* (Stuttgart, 2000), 157; Monteleone, *Il viaggio*, 19; Gabriele, *Empire of Memory*, 114.
37. David S. Potter, *Prophets and Emperors: Human and Divine Authority from Augustus to Theodosius* (Cambridge, MA, 1994), 3.

the Latin Middle Ages, foretold the unification of the East and West under a single messianic ruler and spoke to eschatological concerns related to the leadership of the imperium.[38] The prophetess was said to have wandered for centuries before being called to Rome to interpret a dream about nine suns that had been reported by one hundred Roman senators. She interpreted the suns as generations, and in the final one, she predicted, a *rex Romanorum et Grecorum* named Constans would conquer all enemies of the faith and then go to Jerusalem to relinquish his imperial power before God. The reign of Constans was to be a time of peace and plenitude, but once the enemies of Christianity had been destroyed, he would make his final journey to Jerusalem to lay down the imperial regalia. At that point Antichrist would appear and begin his reign in the Temple at Jerusalem.[39]

The first Latin version of the Tiburtine Sibyl appeared around the year 1000. Largely concerned with political matters in Italy, the Tiburtina may have originated in Lombard circles, but was appropriated and successively rewritten under the Salian and Hohenstaufen kings.[40] Hundreds of versions remain from the Middle Ages, most of which focus on the portion devoted to the coming of the Last Emperor. Despite the many revisions that the sibyl underwent, David Potter points to the oracle's continuity over the centuries, viewing its endurance as "remarkable testimony to the value of the Tiburtine format for social and political commentary throughout these centuries."[41] The various versions of the prophecy were often accompanied by regnal lists, which revisers updated and changed as they kept track of emperors and kings over time. The leaders were identified by initials, with the exception of Constans, a practice that allowed compilers and scribes to make changes when the predicted Last Emperor failed to materialize.[42] The anticipated Constans figure appears in a large number of the redactions, but at a certain point, he ceased to be universally considered Greek, which meant that various peoples in the West could claim for themselves the future great unifier and

38. McGinn, *Visions*, 43–50; Anke Holdenried, *The Sibyl and Her Scribes: Manuscripts and Interpretation of the Latin "Sibylla Tiburtina" c. 1050–1500* (Aldershot, 2006), xviii–xix.

39. Ernst Sackur, *Sibyllinische Texte und Forschungen* (Halle, 1898); Marjorie Reeves, *The Influence of Prophecy in the Later Middle Ages: A Study in Joachimism* (Notre Dame, IN, 1994), 299–300; Daniel Verhelst, "Adso of Montier-en-Der and the Fear of the Year 1000," in Landes, Gow, and Van Meter, *Apocalyptic Year 1000,* 83–84; Paul J. Alexander and Dorothy F. Abrahamse, *The Byzantine Apocalyptic Tradition* (Berkeley, CA, 1985), 151–84.

40. Holdenreid, *Sibyl*, 5; Jeanne Baroin and Josiane Haffen, *La prophétie de la Sibylle Tiburtine: Édition des MSS B.N. Fr. 375 et Rennes B.M. Fr. 593* (Paris, 1987), 19.

41. Potter, *Prophets and Emperors*, 93.

42. Holdenreid, *Sibyl*, xx–xxii; Bernard McGinn, "*Teste David cum Sibylla*: The Significance of the Sibylline Tradition in the Middle Ages," in *Women of the Medieval World: Essays in Honor of John H. Mundy*, ed. Julius Kirshner and Suzanne F. Wemple (Oxford, 1985), 24.

messianic leader. Claims by authors about who would be the Last Emperor thus became a form of political jockeying over the spiritual leadership of Christendom, with some prophecies predicting that he would be from Gaul, while others said he would be a German.[43]

Another important source for the Last Emperor tradition was the *Revelations* of Pseudo-Methodius, a prophetic seventh-century Syriac text that spread in Greek versions before coming to the West in the ninth century.[44] The work was extremely popular and shared the stage over the centuries with the sibylline apocalyptic tradition. After the book of Daniel and the Revelation of John, the Pseudo-Methodius was the most widespread apocalypse story in Europe.[45] Pseudo-Methodius takes the Last Emperor, a figure previously concerned with battling enemies of the faith and barbarians broadly speaking, and introduces him into the context of the fight against the Muslim world. The document also underwent multiple rewritings over time, with the Last Emperor successively fighting Ishmaelites, Arabs, and then Turks.[46] Prior to his battle, the prophecy predicted, the emperor would awaken from a deep sleep in a state of great anger, and then he would conquer the enemies of the faithful before making his final journey as emperor to Jerusalem to depose his imperial regalia on the Mount of Olives.

The Frankish tradition of the Last Emperor witnessed a major development between 949 and 954, not long before Benedict produced his chronicle, when Adso of Montier-en-Der wrote his *De Antichristo* for a concerned Queen Gerberga, the wife of French king Louis IV d'Outremer and sister of Otto I. The letter drew on multiple sources, including Pseudo-Methodius and the exegetical writings of Haimo of Auxerre, but likely not the Tiburtina.[47] Adso wrote that as long as the Franks, the rightful holders of the Roman Empire since Charlemagne's coronation, continued to reign, the end time

43. Marie Tanner, *The Last Descendants of Aeneas: The Hapsburgs and the Mythic Image of the Emperor* (New Haven, CT, 1993), 122.

44. Alexander and Abrahamse, *Byzantine Apocalyptic Tradition*, 152. The manuscripts of these Greek texts were found in the tenth century in the treasury of the court at Constantinople under the title "Visions of Daniel."

45. McGinn, *Visions*, 70.

46. Alexander and Abrahamse, *Byzantine Apocalyptic Tradition*, 156. For Hannes Möhring, the basis for the assimilation of Frankish kings with the *Rex Romanorum* of the Pseudo-Methodius was related to both the issue of the divided empire with the Byzantines and their possession of the title of *patricius romanorum* beginning in 774; see Möhring, "Karl der Grosse und die Endkaiser-Weissagung: Der Sieger über Islam Kommt aus dem Westen," in *Montjoie: Studies in Crusade History in Honour of Hans Eberhard Mayer*, ed. Benjamin Z. Kedar, Jonathan Riley-Smith, and Rudolf Hiestand (Aldershot, 1997), 13–14.

47. Kevin L. Hughes, *Constructing Antichrist: Paul, Biblical Commentary, and the Development of Doctrine in the Early Middle Ages* (Washington, DC, 2005), 167–77.

was not yet upon them.[48] The statement occurs within an explication of the succession of kingdoms theory, during which he describes the progression from the Persians to the Greeks, the second and the third of the four world empires. When he comes to the fourth, the confidant of the West Frankish royal family explains that although the larger part of the Roman Empire has been destroyed, as long the *reges Francorum* reign, Roman dignity will not perish, but will persist in them.[49]

Thus, rather than predicting the arrival of a king from the East who would unite East and West under one leader, Adso supplants the Greek Constans figure, audaciously predicting that one among the kings of the Franks will hold the entire Roman Empire and that a new peaceful time, a *regnum feliciter*, will begin. At the end of that reign, the king of the Franks will come to Jerusalem and place his crown on the Mount of Olives.[50] The timing of Adso's missive during the waning days of the Carolingian dynasty has inspired a variety of theories related to millennial anxiety, declining Carolingian political order, and the influence of monastic reform at the West Frankish court.[51] Whatever the motivation behind the letter may have been, its author made a provocative statement about the preservation of the *translatio ad Francos* that had been effectuated through Charlemagne by reassuring his audience that with the Franks at the helm of the empire, the end time was not near. His more immediate point, however, was that the future of the theoretical Fourth Kingdom was tied to the fortunes of the family of Louis IV. Adso thus confronted the transfer of the Roman Empire from the Carolingian Franks to the Saxons in imperial apocalyptic terms in a document that became widely known and continuously influential.[52]

---

48. Adso, *De ortu*. McGinn, *Visions*, 83–84. Hughes calls the letter an anti-hagiography of Antichrist, in *Constructing Antichrist*, 167. See Daniel Verhelst, "Adson de Montier-en-Der," in *Religion et culture autour de l'an mil: Royaume capétien et Lotharingie*, ed. Dominique Iogna-Prat and Jean-Charles Picard (Paris, 1990). See also E. Ann Matter, "The Apocalypse in Early Medieval Exegesis," in *The Apocalypse in the Middle Ages*, ed. Richard K. Emmerson and Bernard McGinn (Ithaca, NY, 1992), 50; Goez, *Translatio Imperii*, 74; Verhelst, "Adso of Montier-en-Der," 83. Johannes Fried argues, against the grain, that Adso believed he was living in the last days; see "Awaiting the End of Time around the Turn of the Year 1000," in Landes, Gow, and Van Meter, *Apocalyptic Year 1000*, 36.

49. Sackur, *Sibyllinische Texte*, 109.

50. Ibid.,110.

51. McGinn, *Visions*, 82–84; Hughes, *Constructing Antichrist*, 168–72; Arnold, "Eschatological Imagination," 274; Simon MacLean, "Reform, Queenship and the End of the World in Tenth-Century France: Adso's 'Letter on the Origin and Time of the Antichrist' Reconsidered," *Revue belge de philologie et d'histoire* 86 (2008): 645–75

52. MacLean, "Reform, Queenship and the End of the World," 646–47.

Within less than two decades of Adso's letter, the openly anti-Saxon Benedict recalled Charlemagne's symbolic unification of East and West by painting him as a sort of Last Emperor figure. Needless to say, however, Charlemagne's visit to the Holy Sepulcher in the *Chronicon* does not coincide with the culmination of his reign, nor is there any bloody conquest of enemies in an end time scenario. Instead, the journey to the East represents the inauguration of his time as *imperator Christianorum* and serves to define his theoretical realm to include the former empires of the East. The story plainly occurs in the past, and there is no suggestion of a future *Karolus redivivus*. Benedict portrayed Charlemagne fulfilling only certain aspects of the sibylline prophecy, and he did so in a historical rather than a prophetic mode, which raises questions about his ideological motivations. Potter has argued that the importance of the sibyls lay less in the perception of their prophetic powers and more in how they were used to interpret contemporary history.[53] This observation helps to explain Benedict's approach, since we know that he was distressed about the Saxon assumption of the imperial title. Notker had offered a nostalgic vision of Charlemagne as leader of a renewed Fourth Kingdom, and Benedict likewise elides Charlemagne with a figure of Roman universalism as part of his recollection of an idealized time of Frankish leadership. Both were writing during periods of dynastic instability, but Notker was still hoping for Carolingian continuity, while Benedict despaired at the Saxon takeover of Rome.

Benedict's use of apocalyptic discourse needs to be considered in light of the millennial context in which he was writing. There was widespread awareness in monastic circles of Augustine's cautioning against literal readings of signals of the end time and against the sort of apocalyptic speculation that such signs might inspire. The case of Adémar of Chabannes is particularly exemplary. Richard Landes describes how Adémar wrestled with the problem of writing about his own age, arguing that the chronicler confronted the problem of the millennium in part by "domesticating" apocalyptic themes, a major one of which was the problem of imperial continuity. The Ottonians were Saxons who had assumed the Roman imperial dignity, which put Adémar in a complicated situation. As Landes observes, the historian had to make sense of the fact that the current claimants to Roman imperial dignity in the West were neither Franks nor in the line of Charlemagne, or else he had to ignore it. Adémar chose to stress the importance of continuity and to

---

53. Potter, *Prophets and Emperors*, 93.

accept the Ottonian claim.[54] Charlemagne's journey to the East constitutes Benedict's own brand of domestication of apocalyptic matter, but in the opposite direction. The monk used apocalyptic discourse to work against any defense of continuity for the Ottonians by calling them usurpers, while fondly remembering imperial unity under the obedient Carolingians.

Adémar devotes significant attention to Charlemagne in his chronicle and provides his own rewriting of Einhard's vision of Charlemagne's post-coronation foreign relations. His impulse to avoid eschatological themes appears to have also influenced his own depiction of the emperor's dealings with Harun and the Greeks. Relying on the *Royal Frankish Annals* for his details, the chronicler allowed no allusions to the foreign embassy motif or the Last Emperor prophecy. The resulting presentation of the events surrounding the coronation appears comparatively mundane and dryly chronological. There is no mention of the Holy Land protectorate, and the embassies from the East appear in a manner more matter-of-fact than even the *Royal Frankish Annals* entries.[55] The chronicler had intimate knowledge of his Carolingian sources, especially Einhard, which suggests that his elimination of all intimations of imperial universalism was deliberate. In fact, Adémar dismantles the episode so thoroughly that we must conclude that he recognized Einhard's passage as a fictive rhetorical construction. The fact that he reduced the episode to a bare-bones account reminiscent of the annals is also a further indication of the extent to which the construction of "Charlemagne and the East" had become a carefully considered rhetorical act.

Byzantine Dreams and Frankish Imperial Supremacy

After Benedict's chronicle, the trail of Charlemagne's journey to the East goes cold until the late eleventh century. Other chronicles and relic *translatio* narratives make brief mention of his procurement of relics in the East, but they do not involve a newly crowned emperor and his relations with imperial Byzantium and the non-Christian East.[56] The most influential narrative of Charlemagne's journey to Jerusalem and Constantinople appeared

---

54. Landes, *Relics*, 144–49; cf. Michael Frassetto, "The Writings of Ademar of Chabannes, the Peace of 994, and the 'Terrors of the Year 1000,'" *Journal of Medieval History* 27 (2001): 245.

55. Adémar of Chabannes, *Chronicon*, ed. Pascal Bourgain et al., *CC*, Continuatio Mediaevalis, 129 (Turnhout, 1999), 98–100.

56. Matthew Gabriele, "The Provenance of the *Descriptio qualiter Karolus Magnus*: Remembering the Carolingians in the Entourage of King Philip I (1060–1108) before the First Crusade," *Viator* 39 (2008): 1–3; Remensnyder, *Remembering*, 167.

in Capetian France in the early 1080s in a work commonly known as the *Descriptio*, an abbreviation of the lengthy heading "Incipit Descriptio quali-ter Karolus Magnus clavum et coronam Domini a Constantinopoli Aqui-sgrani detulerit qualiterque Karolus Calvus hec ad Sanctum Dionysium retulerit" (Here begins the story of how Charlemagne brought the nail and crown of the Lord from Constantinople to Aachen and how Charles the Bald brought these things to Saint-Denis).[57] The story told in the *Descriptio* is, as its title conveys, a relic *translatio* narrative, but the document also estab-lishes the putative origins of the Lendit (*Indictum*), a festival day devoted to the display of relics that coincided with a highly popular and lucrative fair in France.[58]

Little is known about the authorship of the *Descriptio*, but most scholars agree that the work as we know it dates to the late eleventh century.[59] The document has generally been viewed as the product of Saint-Denis, although Matthew Gabriele has argued for its origins at the court of King Philip I.[60] Whatever its French provenance may have been, it must have existed in an earlier iteration, since there is an obvious narrative and stylistic break in the work after Charlemagne returns to Aachen at the moment when the narrator begins to present the story of how some of the relics from the East had made their way to Francia in the hands of Charles the Bald. The abrupt nature of this transition and the incongruity it creates both reinforce the notion that the pro-Capetian Charles the Bald story had been appended to an existing ver-sion of Charlemagne's acquisition of relics from the East to form the work we read today.[61] There were certainly precedents for fabrications of this sort.

---

57. *Desc.*

58. The Lendit was one of three major fairs at Saint-Denis, which Anne Lombard-Jourdan believes to have appeared spontaneously; see *Montjoie et Saint-Denis: Le centre de la Gaule aux origines de Paris et de Saint-Denis* (Paris, 1989), 273–76, and "Les foires de l'abbaye de Saint-Denis: Revue des données et révision des opinions admises," *Société de l'École des Chartes* 145 (1987): 273–337.

59. Gabriele, "Provenance." Rolf Grosse seems to be alone in arguing for an earlier date in the 1050s, in "Reliques du Christ et foires de Saint-Denis au XIe siècle: À propos de la *Descriptio Clavi et Corone Domini*," *Revue d'Histoire de l'Église de France* 87 (2001): 363. Lombard-Jourdan believes that the document was written to authenticate the relics and to justify the fair as an occasion to adore the relics; see *Montjoie et Saint-Denis*, 225. The fair was so successful that Louis VI organized a second one in 1124, honoring Abbot Suger's request to grant the benefits of this second fair to the monks of Saint-Denis; see Donatella Nebbiai-Dalla Guarda, *La bibliothèque de l'abbaye de Saint-Denis en France du IXe au XVIIIe siècle* (Paris, 1985), 39.

60. Gabriele, "Provenance," 114.

61. Marc Du Pouget argues for a lost original based in part on the abrupt change in style; see "Recherches sur les chroniques latines de Saint-Denis: Édition critique et commentaire de la *Descrip-tio Clavi et Corone Domini* et de deux séries de textes relatifs à la légende carolingienne" (Thèse: École Nationale des Chartes, 1978), 79 and 86; cf. Jacques Nothomb, "Manuscrits et recensions de l'*Iter Hierosolimitanum Caroli Magni*," *Romania* 56 (1930): 201.

The donation of relics of the Passion to ecclesiastical centers in the Frankish West had been recounted in various ways, as we saw with the *Translatio Sanguinis*, going back to the tenth century. On an aesthetic level, the Charlemagne portion of the work is notably richer and more complex than the section containing the transfer of relics to Saint-Corneille and Saint-Denis. Moreover, the Charles the Bald section is also comparatively short, comprising only one and a half of the twenty-two pages of Rauschen's edition in what reads like a hastily created follow-up to an existing work. But given the lack of manuscript evidence for an earlier version of the journey of Charlemagne to the East as told in the *Descriptio*, the circumstances under which such an adaptation occurred remain unknowable. In spite of this mystery, it remains possible to approach the *Descriptio* as the combination of two separate pieces, of which the Charlemagne section provides the most significant rewriting of "Charlemagne and the East" in existence.

The author of the *Descriptio* follows in the footsteps of Benedict by creating a journey that recalls the Last Emperor prophecy. More than a century ago, Franz Kampers noted the sibylline overtones of the story, and Folz later noted that all versions of Charlemagne's journeys to the East were both sibylline and eschatological.[62] The broader ramifications of this observation have not been fully appreciated, however. Scholars have tended to direct their attention toward the *Descriptio*'s role as a proto-crusading document, its relationship to the French royal abbey of Saint-Denis, and finally toward its role in later compilations such as Charlemagne's saintly *Vita* and the *Grandes chroniques de France*.[63] The work has also received attention as a source for the Charlemagne window at Chartres and for the Anglo-Norman poem *The Voyage of Charlemagne to Jerusalem and Constantinople*, to be discussed in chapter 6. In all of this varied scholarship, however, there has never been a close reading of the text itself, in part perhaps because major figures such as Gaston Paris and Joseph Bédier dismissed it as a naïve, clerical fiction designed to authenticate relics.[64] But Bédier, of all scholars, given his theories of the ecclesiastical origins of Old French literature, should not have been so quick to write off this work of Latin prose. A careful reading of the work reveals a set of concerns far less related to relic holdings in France than has previously

---

62. Kampers also saw the Charlemagne of the *Pseudo-Turpin* tradition as a Last Emperor figure; see *Die Deutsche Kaiseridee*, 53; Folz, *Le souvenir*, 138.

63. Gabriele offers a useful summary in *Empire of Memory*, 55–56.

64. Paris, *Histoire poétique*, 55; Joseph Bédier, *Les légendes épiques: Recherches sur la formation des chansons de geste*, vol. 4 (Paris, 1908–13), 134–35.

been believed. Instead the *Descriptio* reflects deep concern about the nature of Charlemagne's status as Christian emperor.

Although the *Descriptio* departs in some ways from previous iterations that drew heavily from Einhard, the document still retains the essential elements of the episode as rhetorical set-piece. These include Charles's worldwide reputation, diplomatic exchanges between East and West, bloodless victory over the Greek East, and the symbolic establishment of imperial supremacy for the West. The document also continues the pattern of using Charlemagne's dealings with the East after the coronation as a forum for addressing the matter of the divided empire. In this version, Charles is the *rex et imperator* of the *regnum Gallicum*, and is summoned to Rome by the Roman people and hailed as emperor. He then receives envoys from Constantinople bearing letters. In one of the missives, the Greek emperor informs Charles that God has revealed to him in a dream that he should call on the Frankish king to help him deal with the plight of Christians in Jerusalem. Having recognized the hand of God in the message, Charlemagne orders the archbishop Turpin to translate the letters for those who are present, and then promptly musters an army of unheard-of magnitude from the realm of the Franks.[65] When Charlemagne and his massive Frankish army arrive in Jerusalem, the pagans flee without a fight, and the Franks return to the West by way of Constantinople.

In the eastern capital, Charlemagne yields to pressure from his hosts and accepts a gift of relics of the Passion from the Greek emperor. With the powerful objects in hand, he performs countless miracles on his way home. Once at Aachen, he announces the establishment of a festival day called the *Indictum* in honor of the new relics, which he wishes for his people to be able to behold.[66] After giving the list of those present for the announcement, including Pope Leo and Archbishop Turpin of Reims, the author describes how Charlemagne ordered a magnificent basilica to be built at Aachen. There follows a short and obviously incongruous section in which Charles the Bald makes a parallel transfer of some of the relics from Aachen to the West Frankish monastery of Saint-Corneille in Compiègne and then delivers the rest to Saint-Denis, where he too establishes the *Indictum*.

---

65. *Desc.*, 108.
66. *Desc.*, 120.

The *Descriptio* and a New *Visio Constantini*

With its careful revisions of Charlemagne's coronation scene and the encounter with the Greek East, the *Descriptio* contains the most intricate revision of the "Charlemagne and the East" episode since Notker's. The most enigmatic of these scenes is the Greek emperor Constantine's description of the dream vision he has experienced that prompts him to call on Charlemagne for help. Charlemagne learns of the dream when an envoy translates the letter for him:

> That night, I was musing about what to do about the invasion of pagans and desiring help from God with all my heart when I was struck, as if in a state of ecstasy; I saw before my bed a young man standing who, addressing me by name in a soft voice, touched me gently and said, "Constantine, you have asked the Lord for the help and counsel of this king; accept here this helper, the emperor Charles the Great, king of France and warrior for God and for the peace of the Church." He then showed me a soldier armed in shin guards, breast plate, and a red shield. Girded to his side was a sword with a purple handle. His spear was very white and emitted flames from its tip, and in his hand he held a golden helmet. He was an old man of full beard, handsome face, and noble stature, whose eyes sparkled like stars and the hairs on his head were turning white. From then on, there was not the slightest doubt that these things were done by the will of God.[67]

The vision is a rich *ekphrasis* that stands out from the rest of the document and, in particular, from the later, more stereotypical scenes related to the transfer of relics.

The communiqué arrives following Charlemagne's imperial investiture, which is an essential detail, since the ceremony forces the division of the empire and creates the need to determine a hierarchy between East and West. The vision thus serves as an expression of divine will articulated to the Greek emperor, after which he acknowledges God's preference for

---

67. *Desc.,* 106–7. "Quippe quadam nocte de invasione paganorum meditans quid agerem et a deo succursum firmo corde postulans et quasi in exstasi effectus, vidi ante lectum meum iuvenem stantem qui me blanda voce vocans nomine meo pauxillum tetigit et ait: 'Constantine, rogasti dominum auxilium et consilium huius rei, ecce accipe adiutorem Karolum magnum imperatorem regem Gallie in domino ac pacis ecclesie propugnatorum.' Et ostendit michi quendam militam ocreatum et loricatum, scutum rubeum habentem, ense precinctum cuius manubrium erat purpureum, hasta vero albissima cuius cuspis sepe flammas emittebat, ac in manu cassidem tenebat auream. Et ipse senex prolixa barba vultu decorus et statura procerus erat, cuiusque oculi fulgebant tanquam sidera, caput vero eius canis albescebat. Unde minime dubitandum non est quin hec Dei voluntate sint facta."

Charlemagne.[68] The plea from the East that follows is constructed through two letters brought by four envoys—two Jews and two Christians—who recognize Charlemagne's new title, addressing him as *nostratem imperatorem Karolum magnum*. One letter is from the patriarch of Jerusalem, who had come to Constantine with news of depredation in the Holy City and dishonorable treatment of the Holy Sepulcher by pagans.[69] The second letter, from the emperor himself, contains the depiction of his vision, including his protestation that he does not seek aid out of any lack of courage or lack of troops.[70] The *Descriptio* narrator conveys that the letters from the East were sent to one "whose fame reverberates, for a long time now, in the ears of people in the East."[71] This is an allusion to the conventional assertion that the emperor's reputation is powerful enough to inspire foreign nations to surrender in peace. After he hears the letters read aloud, Charlemagne acknowledges the hand of God in his renown having reached the East, in the appearance of the divine vision to Constantine, and finally in God's selection of him over the Byzantine leader to protect the empire.[72]

While all of the sources for the *Descriptio* are not identifiable, I have been able to find one likely source for the composition of the Greek emperor's dream. The vision seems to have been created based on the fifth-century document known as the "Letter of Lucianus to the Whole Church." In 415, Palestine was abuzz with the trial of the accused heretic Pelagius. During a spate of relic discoveries, the priest Lucianus claimed to have received visions from the educator of the apostle Paul, the rabbi Gamaliel, who was considered a Christian sympathizer. In the vision, Gameliel told Lucianus where to find the remains of Saint Stephen. Lucianus then told others what he had learned, and the Spanish bishop Avitus of Braga composed a letter about it, telling Orosius the story, which Orosius then passed on to Augustine.[73] The tradition of Lucianus's revelation was well known in the Middle Ages, as Monika Otter has shown in her demonstration of how the letter served as the

---

68. *Desc.*, 107.
69. *Desc.*, 103.
70. *Desc.*, 106.
71. *Desc.*, 104. "ad nostratem imperatorem Karolum magnum, cuius fama orientalium aures iam dudum diverberaverat, legati cum litteris missi sunt."
72. *Desc.*, 108. "intelligens iam se a deo ad hoc negotium preelectum esse et iam usque orientales famam sue probitatis transvolasse, hinc gaudo gavisus est valde, sed oppido, quod dominicum sepulchrum a paganis esset obsessum, condolens lacrimari cepit."
73. E. David Hunt, *Holy Land Pilgrimage in the Later Roman Empire, 312–460* (Oxford, 1982), 213–17.

narrative model for many English relic discovery texts.[74] The work was also available in northern France, appearing in multiple martyrologies, including that of Ado of Vienne.[75]

In the Fleury manuscript, Lucianus describes how at the third watch, a vision appeared to him while he was resting in his bed, on day six of the festival of Parasceve, around the third hour of the night. At a point between wakefulness and sleep, he declares that he was struck, "as if by a departure of my mind." He sees an old man, tall in stature, with a handsome face and a long beard, dressed in white, cloaked in a mantle on top of which are sewn little crosses. He holds a golden staff, and his boots are gold on the outside. Lucianus declares, "He walked up to me and touched me. And when I saw him, he came to me and with the staff in his hand, and touching me lightly, called my name three times."[76] Lucianus, like the Byzantine emperor, is pulled from sleep by the vision. Both emperors are not entirely asleep, but *meditans* and struck as if in ecstasy. The dreamers both experience light touches at their bedsides, and the messenger figure in the vision uses the dreamer's name.

The most striking textual similarity, however, is between the descriptions of the old men. The *Descriptio* reads: "Et ipse senex prolixa barba vultu decorus et statura procerus erat, cuiusque oculi fulgebant tanquam sidera, caput vero eius canis albescebat." (He was an old man with full beard, handsome face, and noble stature, whose eyes sparkled as much as stars, and indeed the hairs on his head were turning white.)[77] The version in the martyrology of Ado of Vienne reads: "vidit virum senem, statura procerum, vultu decorum, prolixa barba," and the Fleury version reads: "vidi virum aetate senem, statura procerum, vultu decorum, promissa barba, in vestitu candido."[78] Although physical descriptions were often based on commonly repeated epithets, the similarities here are undeniable. The example from the Fleury codex is closest to the *Descriptio*, although the beard is *"promissa,"* whereas Avitus's letter and Ado both use *"prolixa,"* as does the *Descriptio*. The description of Charlemagne also contains echoes, but less directly, of the Tiburtina's description of the Constans figure, who is foretold to be tall and handsome with a splendid visage ("erit statura grandis, aspectu decorus, vultu splendidus").[79] The parallel description would have further contributed to

---

74. Monika Otter, *Inventiones: Fiction and Referentiality in Twelfth-Century English Historical Writing* (Chapel Hill, NC, 1996), 26–28.

75. S. Vanderlinden, "Revelatio Sancti Stephani," *Revue des Études Byzantines* 4 (1946): 183.

76. *EL*, Fleury.

77. *Desc.*, 107.

78. *EL*, Ado of Vienne.

79. Sackur, *Sibyllinische Texte,* 185; McGinn, *Visions,* 49.

the sense that the emperor Charlemagne had borne some resemblance to the prophetic emperor figure, perhaps in the spirit of Adso's prediction that the future unifier of East and West would be a Frank.

With the source for the vision available for comparison, it becomes possible to consider the ways in which the *Descriptio* author altered the dream of Lucianus to create Constantine's vision of Charlemagne. Certainly, the major distinction lies in the fact that the old man in Lucianus's vision is the priestly messenger, while the old man in the *Descriptio* is a static image of Charlemagne indicated by a young messenger. The *Descriptio* nonetheless follows the sequence from the ecstatic awakening, to the bedside tapping, and the calling of the dreamer by name. The vision is relatively faithful to its source up until the replacement of the white cloak with the red armor, where the whiteness moves from the cloak of the priestly figure to the hair and beard of Charlemagne. Lucianus describes a figure in a cloak with gold crosses sewn in the top with a golden rod in his hand.[80] The cloak with crosses, rendered in white and gold, is transformed in the *Descriptio* into armor with shades of red and purple, and the rod becomes a flaming lance. The author describes the warrior's eyes as "shining like stars," while there is no mention of the eyes of Gameliel. Finally, the shift from an old man in priestly garb to armor and from white to red signals a deliberate transformation of the vision to suit the story of Charlemagne as the defender of Christendom.

In a divided empire, there was debate over which emperor was the true *vicarius* of God on earth. The *Descriptio* addressed this conundrum by depicting a dream vision that could exist in a typological relationship to the original *visio Constantini* of Constantine the Great. Any dream vision witnessed by a Christian Roman emperor, and in this case, one also named Constantine, necessarily recalls the vision that occurred prior to the battle against the usurping emperor Maxentius in 312 CE. The tradition was known through Eusebius's *Life of Constantine*,[81] which survived in the West largely through the Latin translation by Rufinus, and was also retold in popular versions of his life in the *Acts of Saint Sylvester*.[82] The story also reemerged during bursts of Byzantine iconoclasm in the ninth century. During the reign of Charles

---

80. *EL*, Avitus. "palliatum alba stola, cui inerant gemmulae aureae habentes intrinsecus sanctae crucis signum, et virgam auream in manu habentem." *EL*, Ado of Vienne reads, "in vestitu candido, amictum pallio, in cujus summitatibus erant tanquam aureae cruces contextae; calceatum caligis, in superficie deauratis, et manu tenebat virgam auream." *EL*, Fleury, "amictum pallio, in cujus summitate erant tanquam aureae cruces intextae (et manu tenebat virgam auream), calceatum caligis in superficie deauratis, deambulantem coram me, et tacentem."

81. Eusebius, *VC*, 48–49.

82. Edward T. Brett, "Early Constantine Legends: A Study in Propaganda," *Byzantine Studies* 10 (1983): 69–70.

the Bald, Jonas of Orleans was inspired to write *On the Cult of Images*, which contains a detailed narrative of Constantine's vision.[83]

Jonas describes how Constantine became deeply troubled over a looming war and decided to make a journey during which he looked over and over into the heavens and prayed for divine help. At one point, he sees a cross in the fiery red sky of the East. He later falls into a troubled sleep, in which angels appear. Standing near him, they refer to the image he had seen earlier, and say: "Constantine, in this conquer." After the divine visitation, the emperor feels untroubled about the coming battle. He then places the sign of the cross which he had seen in the sky on his forehead. In other versions of the *Life of Constantine*, the emperor orders copies of the sign made, which leads to the creation of his standard, the Labarum.[84] Jonas comments that since Constantine came to the faith in this way, he can be compared to Paul, who had also received a message from the heavens.[85] The vision of Constantine the Great is marked by several of the same elements that define the vision in the *Descriptio*. Both Constantines are Christian emperors troubled by the plight of the empire and in search of divine aid, and each enjoys the calming voice of a messenger who tells him to have faith in the image before him to bring victory to Christian Rome.

Each dreamer is called out to by name during the vision, a tradition that, as Jonas reveals, goes back to Paul hearing his name from the heavens. The dreams then lead to action: Constantine awakens to order the making of the Labarum, and the *Descriptio*'s Constantine orders the dictation of letters to Charlemagne requesting aid in the East, and the vision of Lucianus facilitates the recovery of the remains of Stephen. The most significant parallel, however, is the fact that both Constantine the Great and the Constantine of the *Descriptio* are pushed to action after expressing despair over the state of the empire. Each is then directed to behold an image that he must understand as a message from God concerning his role as emperor in the protection of the empire. The *Descriptio*'s Constantine is compelled to recognize the image of Charlemagne as the promise of Christian victory in an empire led not by him, but by Charlemagne. The image of Charlemagne is therefore analogous to the cross in the sky as a symbol of the possibility of victory, if the dreaming emperor understands its value and acts on the advice of the

---

83. Eusebius, *VC*, 50; Leslie Brubaker, "To Legitimate an Emperor: Constantine and Visual Authority in the Eighth and Ninth Centuries," in *New Constantines: The Rhythm of Imperial Renewal in Byzantium, 4th–13th Centuries*, ed. Paul Magdalino (Aldershot, 1994), 141. Jonas of Orleans, *De cultu imaginem, PL* 106, cols. 343–48.

84. Eusebius, *VC*, 39.

85. Jonas, *De cultu imaginem*, col. 345.

messenger. In both traditions, then, divinely sent advice to an emperor leads to a turning point in the destiny of the Roman Empire. In the *Descriptio*, this crucial juncture marks the establishment of the primacy of the West over the East under Charlemagne. The power of the vision to convey meaning is therefore dependent upon the recognition of its typological relationship to the tradition of Constantine the Great. The new *visio Constantini* aims to inscribe into Christian history an episode that resolves the problem of a divided empire by designating the Franks as its true protectors.

Medieval dream theorists, relying on works such as Chalcidius's commentary on Plato's *Timaeus* and Macrobius's commentary on the *Dream of Scipio*, provided hierarchies for the various kinds of visions a dreamer could experience, and what those dream visions were meant to convey.[86] J. Stephen Russell cites Macrobius's statement, "We call a dream oracular (*oraculum*) in which a parent, or a pious or revered man, or a priest, or even a god clearly reveals what will or will not transpire, and what action to take or to avoid. We call a dream a prophetic vision (*visio*) if it actually comes true."[87] The visions in the letter of Lucianus and in the *Descriptio* fit Macrobius's definition of an *oraculum*, since the dreamer, in both cases, receives guidance from the figure who speaks to him. The twelfth-century dream interpreter Pascalis Romanus gave Macrobius's categories literary correlations, linking the *visio* to the writing of history and *oraculum* to that of prophecy.[88] As Russell explains, the dream as a narrative event is "fraught with ambiguity and ambivalence," whereas the apocalypse represents "a singular communication from God sent to humanity through the agency of a privileged individual."[89] For Constantine the Great, the vision at the bridge tells him to see the relationship between victory and the cross. For the Constantine in the *Descriptio*, the image of the white-bearded warrior is indicated by the messenger, who clearly advises that he seek help from Charlemagne. The vision is also oracular in that the message is unambiguous and is sent to a "privileged individual" in a singular communication with repercussions for all humanity. There is celestial agency involved in the divine visit to the emperor's bedside, and in the Christian tradition the agent in such dreams was often an angel

---

86. Carolly Erickson, *The Medieval Vision: Essays in History and Perception* (New York, 1976), 11.

87. J. Stephen Russell, *The English Dream Vision: Anatomy of a Form* (Columbus, OH, 1988), 62; Erickson, *Medieval Vision*, 36; Stephen F. Kruger, *Dreaming in the Middle Ages* (Cambridge, UK, 1992), 31–32.

88. Kruger, *Dreaming*, 133.

89. Russell, *English Dream Vision*, 46.

or a priest.[90] In the case of the *Descriptio*, the dream as *oraculum* serves to tie Charlemagne both to the concept of universal empire under Constantine the Great and to the idea of a Last Emperor who is a tall, handsome Frank rather than a Greek.

The Expedition to Jerusalem and Constantinople

The legates from the East bring news of the woeful state of affairs in Jerusalem. The report leads to great sadness in Charlemagne's inner circle, especially after the archbishop Turpin presents the bad news to the laity in their *materna lingua*. The king quickly musters an army of unprecedented size and threatens fines on the heads of those who do not present themselves.[91] On the way to Jerusalem, Charlemagne and his men lose their way and must make camp in a grove filled with nightmarish threats from griffins, bears, lions, tigers, lynxes, and other beasts that "rejoice in the flow of human blood."[92] The Franks are lost both figuratively and physically, for the meaning and motive of their journey have yet to be established. Charlemagne recites from Psalm 119, which, among other things, warns against covetousness, and he implores God to lead him on the proper path, citing the Psalmist's exhortation for God to show him the way.[93] The Frankish leader is concerned that the expedition may be perceived as driven by greed, a sentiment that anticipates the coming encounter between the two emperors in the imperial palace at Constantinople during which the Greek emperor tries to shower Charlemagne with treasure and gifts.

Before the travelers leave the grove, Charlemagne's recitations prove to be the prologue to a strange and miraculous occurrence that foreshadows the encounter with the emperor in Byzantium. As his men sleep, Charles is greeted by human voices coming from birds, a phenomenon so stunning that others awaken and witness the occurrence: "Unexpectedly the voice of a winged thing struck his ears rather vividly, shouting, near his bed, so that certain ones who were present were stunned with great fascination; having been aroused from sleep, they were saying that this was a miraculous sign of something to come, since it seemed to them that the winged ones had made

---

90. See Patrick Geary, "Germanic Tradition and Royal Ideology in the Ninth Century: The 'Visio Karoli Magni,'" *Fruhmittelalterliche Studien* 21 (1987): 282.

91. *Desc.*, 108.

92. *Desc.*, 108.

93. Psalm 119: 35–37.

use of human reason."[94] Like both Constantines, Charlemagne is aroused from sleep by a miraculous communication. The king reacts to the presence of the birds by continuing to recite the Psalm, but once he begins to speak, the birds seem to understand and cry out intelligibly, asking the Frank what he is saying: "France, quid dicis? Quid dicis?"[95] The birds then help the group regain the path to Jerusalem, which the travelers see as divine intervention. The narrator then describes how the locals had claimed that never before had they heard a bird sing with such intelligible reason. The birds had previously been able to perform the salutations of kings in their own language, such as *Chere basileu amachos*, "which in Latin means, 'Greetings, unconquered emperor,'" but it was a miraculous sign from God, he explains, when they spoke with open Latinity (*aperta latinitate*) and responded appropriately to the oration of the king.

The miraculous communication between the birds and the Frankish king does not shed favorable light on the Byzantine leadership. While the talking animals repeat the *laudes* mindlessly in Greek, they display the faculty of human reason only after hearing the emperor of the West reciting from the Psalms. The birds' uncanny ability to communicate in Latin is evidence of God's favor, but it also highlights the emptiness of the parroted *laudes*. The implicit critique of Byzantine practice is akin to Notker's depiction of Greek envoys prostrating themselves at the feet of Charlemagne's various servants and stable hands. Both belittle the Byzantine leadership, while promoting Charlemagne as the divinely chosen Christian emperor. In both works, the Greek emperor is never physically conquered, but instead suffers multiple symbolic defeats.

When the Franks arrive in the Holy City, the pagans flee and the city is restored to Christian control: "Finally, the king with his army reached Constantinople. Afterwards, with the pagans having been put to flight, he came to the city which held fragments of the life-giving cross and the monuments of the passion, death, and resurrection of Christ, he arrived joyful and suppliant and made all things prosperous for the Patriarch and for all the Christian people with the help of God."[96] Having situated his narrative in a time of

---

94. *Desc.*, 109. "ex inproviso ad aures eius evidentius vox cuiusdam alitis prope lectum clamantis ita incussit, ut quidam qui aderant ammiratione magna experrecti a somno stuperant, dicentes hoc esse futurum rei prodigium, quoniam ales uti humana ratione videbatur eis."

95. *Desc.*, 109.

96. *Desc.*, 109. "Tandem rex cum exercitu suo Constantinopolim pervenit. Postea vero fugatis paganis ad urbem, que vexilla vivifice crucis Christique passionis, mortis, ac resurrectionis, retinet monimenta, letus et supplex advenit ac patriarche totique christicole plebi cuncta prospera deo opitulante solidavit."

strife in Jerusalem, the *Descriptio*'s author was caught between the bloodless nature of the Roman foreign embassy motif and the predicted violence of the sibylline tradition. This combination made for a paradoxical situation in which it was difficult to reconcile the peaceful classical ideal of willing alliances with the East and the apocalyptic vision of the Last Emperor's final battle against his infidel enemies. By describing the liberation of Jerusalem in two words, *fugatis paganis*, which gives the impression that the pagans simply flee when Charlemagne arrives, the author retains the ideal of Charlemagne regaining custody of Jerusalem without battle. Harun is not there to greet him, but the ideal of bloodless victory is still implied. Moreover, the idea of Saracens fleeing also recalls Odilo of Cluny's praise-filled imperial address in which he calls for the Greeks to be dumbstruck and for the Saracens to flee, "Sarracenus turbetur et fugiat."[97]

In his influential study of the origins of crusading, Carl Erdmann lists the *Descriptio* as one of a handful of works that provide evidence of an emerging popular crusading spirit in the late eleventh century.[98] Erdmann's view is symptomatic of a broader tendency to view the *Descriptio* in light of the coming crusading movement and to consequently overlook the essential themes of the story.[99] The miraculous flight of the pagans in Jerusalem happens quickly and without elaboration, while the author devotes ample ink to the central concern of the episode, which is the establishment of Charlemagne's authority after his coronation through his reckoning with the Greek East. Charlemagne had been recuperating the Holy Land from the non-Christian East without bloodshed since Einhard, only in this case the sense of menace is more pronounced, and the friendly caliph is gone. The pagan occupation of holy sites has a more urgent feel to it in the *Descriptio*, but the crisis in Jerusalem serves primarily as a pretext for the Greek emperor's divinely inspired call for help from Charlemagne, the newly anointed protector of all Christendom.[100]

The meeting between the emperors of East and West after the liberation of Jerusalem is a rhetorically intricate scene marked by Charlemagne's refusal of lavish Eastern gifts, which then leads to his acquisition of relics of the Passion. After liberating Jerusalem, Charlemagne encounters a grateful Constantine, who is keen to reward him for his deeds. Despite certain

---

97. See Sackur, "Ein Schreiben," 734.
98. Erdmann, *Origin*, 298.
99. See Norman Cohn, *The Pursuit of the Millennium: Revolutionary Millenarians and Mystical Anarchists of the Middle Ages* (Oxford, 1970), 72.
100. Gabriele notes the lack of importance of Jerusalem in the text as well, seeing the primary goal as the acquisition of the relics in Constantinople; see *Empire of Memory*, 55.

ambiguities in the text that have raised questions about whether the two emperors actually meet in Jerusalem, the encounter should be understood as occurring in Constantinople.[101] The Franks, in turn, are eager to return home. The reluctant Greek emperor pleads with them to stay on, and Charlemagne agrees to remain for three more days. During the waiting period, the Greek emperor readies a collection of offerings near the gates of the city, in an open field, so that Charlemagne will see it when he reenters the city. This is a small plot point, but one that reinforces the idea that Charlemagne is visiting Constantinople, where Constantine prepares to greet him on his return with a massive display of his own wealth. The staged spectacle includes expensive animals of many species, beasts and birds, cloaks of many different colors, fineries made of gems and precious stones, and *insignia*.[102] The narrator explains that the emperor considers the gifts to be thanks for the long journey he had made, a statement that would make less sense if they had traveled together to the Holy Land.

When Charlemagne learns of the existence of the display, he fears that the gifts will tempt his men, so he secretly orders his troops to hurry their departure preparations. The king turns to his inner circle for advice on how to respond to the offering. He is pleased when they tell him that since their mission in liberating Jerusalem was solely pious, they should not sully the appearance of their journey by accepting the gifts. They also caution that he would not want people to think that he had undertaken the task out of avarice, or with a desire to expand his kingdom, or to amass gold, silver, and other riches, "which he otherwise lacked."[103] The allusion to the potential desire of the Franks to expand their territory goes back to Einhard. The *Descriptio*, a version of Einhard's original expression of Frankish universalism, depicts a Charlemagne whose protection of Christendom is providential, and whose concerns are neither wealth from the East nor territorial expansion.

---

101. Ronald N. Walpole, *The Old French Translation of the Pseudo-Turpin Chronicle: A Critical Edition*, vol. 1 (Berkeley, CA, 1976), 26. Aebischer, *Les versions norroises*, 148. Monteleone believes that the Constantinople visit is secondary to the liberation of Jerusalem; see *Il viaggio*, 253. For the notion of Constantinople as the New Jerusalem see Evelyne Patlagean, "Byzantium's Dual Holy Land," in *Sacred Space: Shrine, City, Land*, ed. Joshua Prawer, Benjamin Kedar-Kopfstein, and Raphael Jehudah Zwi (New York, 1998), 113.

102. *Desc.,* 110. "Ille Constantinopolitanus imperator pre porta civitatis in aperto campo inque oculorum redeuntis regis intuitu animalia multi generis tam bestiarum quam volucrum cariora variique coloris pallia et meliora gemmarum et preciossissimorum lapidum quoque insignia, hec omnia quasi tanti laboris periculive et longi itineris esse mercedem computans preparari fecit."

103. *Desc.*, 110.

Heeding the commendable decision of his men, Charles refuses the gifts, but the refusal leads to a short and friendly debate with his Byzantine host that the author describes as a *pia altercatio*. Constantine begs, but Charlemagne does not yield. The emperor first warns him of the consequences of coming home empty-handed, but then tries a more thoughtful tactic by saying that Charles's people deserve to know what has occurred, and that he should serve as "someone bearing evidence of the mercy of God."[104] For this new definition of his offerings, Constantine uses the term *pignus* to mean evidence, a word that was also common parlance for relics.[105] The author thus creates a linguistic circumstance in which Constantine does not explicitly offer relics, but alludes to them by encouraging Charlemagne to provide "evidence" of God's mercy, "*misericordie dei pignus.*"[106] Holger Klein has analyzed the literary tradition of Byzantine offerings in diplomatic situations and argues that lavish gifts were usually intended as an assertion of superiority over the visitor that would have presumed reciprocation.[107] The scene in Constantinople suggests a game of hierarchies, but Charlemagne is in no way reduced by an inability to reciprocate. Instead, he will symbolically triumph by refusing sumptuous gifts in the name of piety. Although Constantine is not parading before Charlemagne in surrender, his offerings demonstrate his recognition of what the Frankish king has done to establish himself as the new protector of Christendom. In that sense, the gifts do serve as a form of recognition of the supremacy of the new emperor, but Charlemagne refuses them in favor of a more powerful gift that Constantine can relinquish to him, relics of the Passion.

In his chronicle, Benedict had described Charlemagne's recuperation of holy sites in Jerusalem followed by his triumphal return from Constantinople with relics. The *Descriptio* author also conveys this sense of symbolic triumph marked by the transfer of relics from East to West. The Greek emperor understands Charlemagne's wish to preserve the image of his journey, but will not allow the Franks to leave without ceding in some small way. The diplomatic back-and-forth is really just the prologue, however, to the coming exchange of relics of the Passion from one emperor to the other. Constantine's insistence paves the way for Charlemagne to request the sacred

---

104. *Desc.*, 111.

105. Thomas Head, ed., *Medieval Hagiography: An Anthology* (New York, 2000), 399.

106. Anne Latowsky, "Charlemagne as Pilgrim? Requests for Relics in the *Descriptio Qualiter* and the *Voyage of Charlemagne*," in *The Legend of Charlemagne in the Middle Ages: Power, Faith, and Crusade,* ed. Matthew Gabriele and Jace Stuckey (New York, 2008), 158.

107. Holger Klein, "Eastern Objects and Western Desires: Relics and Reliquaries between Byzantium and the West," *Dumbarton Oaks Papers* 58 (2004): 286–88.

objects instead of accepting jewels and exotic animals. The Greek emperor has carefully rephrased his offer to define it not as a reward, but rather as visual evidence of God's favor on the journey. This redefinition reinforces the idea that Charlemagne's bloodless victory in Jerusalem, like the journey itself, has been orchestrated from above to convey his new designation as God's preferred emperor. As if pondering a riddle, the Frankish leader thinks all night about the offer of something he could accept that would symbolize God's hand in his victory in Jerusalem. In the morning, he reports the results of his ruminations, insisting that he is not moved by avarice and promising to serve as an exemplum of piety for the peoples of the West. Charlemagne then agrees to accept something for those who are unable to come to Jerusalem to expiate their sins, certain visible things that might recall the Passion and inspire piety in them.[108] Although he does not ask for them by name, Charlemagne has requested the most precious relics of all Christendom on behalf of his people.

In typical hagiographical fashion, the whereabouts of the relics are unknown, but their eventual revelation once again ties Charlemagne typologically to Constantine the Great. The Greek emperor understands the roundabout request, but is impeded by the fact that no one knows where Helena, the mother of Constantine, had hidden them. Chroniclers had similarly described how no one knew where Charlemagne was buried at Aachen in the year 1000 until Otto III miraculously gained the knowledge of where to start digging.[109] The allusion to Helena recalls the initial movement of the cross from Jerusalem to Constantinople, a popular story in the eleventh century.[110] After Charlemagne and his men spend three days praying and fasting, the *inventio* occurs when the whereabouts of the relics become miraculously known to Charles. The narrator then allows that, until that point, the precious objects had remained out of view since the time of Constantine. By orchestrating the ceremony in this manner, the author creates a direct link between Charlemagne and Constantine the Great that excludes the Byzantine leadership. Constantinople is therefore, once again, demoted as a center of Christendom in favor of Charlemagne's new empire.

The long list of relics from Constantinople includes numerous Christological relics, including eight thorns from the crown of thorns with the wood in which they were fixed, one of the nails, part of the cross, the *sudarium* or cloth in which Jesus was wrapped after the crucifixion, the tunic Mary

108. *Desc.*, 111–12.
109. Nichols, *Romanesque Signs*, 100.
110. Cowdrey, "Eleventh-Century," 72.

wore at the birth, the swaddling clothes from the manger, and the arm of Saint Simeon, "among other things."[111] With the precious objects in hand, the emperor performs numerous acts of healing on the route home. He also sends messengers ahead to announce to the world his plan to display the relics on the ides of June at Aachen. Upon his arrival, Charlemagne goes to a promontory and announces the establishment of the *Indictum* in honor of the relics. The journey thus ends, as it had in previous relic *translatio* narratives that incorporated the tradition of "Charlemagne and the East," with the donation of the relics.

Although there is ample evidence to show that Charlemagne receives the relics from Constantine in Constantinople, the matter is complicated by two later mentions of their provenance. At the end of the Charlemagne section, when the emperor arrives at Aachen, the relics are described as being from Constantinople and Jerusalem, while in the Charles the Bald section, they are said to have come only from Jerusalem. If these discrepancies show us anything, it is that the *Descriptio* that we read today is the product of multiple authors, who may have had access to varying versions of the story. Later iterations, such as the one produced by the thirteenth-century chronicler Helinand of Froidmont, clarify that the encounter was understood to have occurred in Constantinople. Helinand eliminates the ambiguity by stating that after the events in Jerusalem, the Greek emperor "detained Charlemagne in Constantinople for one day" before offering him lavish treasure.[112] The fact that Constantinople prevailed is significant because the Greek provenance of the relics is crucial to the meaning of the episode. Relics given to Charlemagne by the Greeks are analogous to gifts from surrendering foreign nations in that they symbolize recognition of Charlemagne's superiority. If the relics are said to come from Jerusalem, the story of Charlemagne's journey to the East lacks this essential imperial theme.

Upon his return to Aachen, Charlemagne orders the building of a basilica. After that point, there is a marked shift to a more chronicle-style discussion of Charlemagne's heirs, and an ideological shift toward the interests of Francia. The transfer of relics from the East begun by Charlemagne continues its westward movement as Charles the Bald imitates his grandfather's building projects and moves relics from Aachen to Saint-Corneille and Saint-Denis. The author even adds that Charles the Bald surpassed all Frankish kings, past

---

111. *Desc.*, 120.
112. Helinand of Froidmont, *Chronicon*, 25.4, *PL* 212. "Quem per unum diem retinuit imperator apud Constantinopolim."

and future, in ecclesiastical generosity.[113] The Charlemagne section of the *Descriptio* had been concerned with the new emperor's relationship to Byzantium after his coronation. The author of the Charles the Bald section builds on the theme of *translatio* by according Charlemagne's surviving grandson favored status as the true inheritor of the empire. The passage is punctuated by the announcement that with the death of all the grandsons of Charlemagne but Charles the Bald, the sundered Carolingian Empire returned under one crown and there was peace. The author of the Charles the Bald section perceived the significance of the journey as a transfer of imperial authority through relics. He then extended that journey through the further transfer of the relics to promote Carolingian continuity as it evolved in the West Frankish realm under Charles the Bald.

The *Descriptio*, with its celebration of the donations of Charles the Bald to monasteries in France, has long been associated with the royal abbey of Saint-Denis, but there is reason to suspect that the Charlemagne section had come from elsewhere. As we have seen, Charlemagne's encounters with the East functioned as an adaptable rhetorical set-piece. The *Translatio Sanguinis* and Benedict's version of the journey to the East both reveal that once Charlemagne's new relics arrive in the West, they can go wherever the author of the document chooses to send them. The story told in the *Descriptio* just happens to be best known in the version containing the addition of Charles the Bald's donation of relics to Saint-Corneille and Saint-Denis. The Charlemagne section, which constitutes the vast majority of the work, stands easily on its own. An earlier version of the document, without the Charles the Bald story, could therefore have emerged from a variety of places, including an imperial milieu. Furthermore, the story, even with its focus on Aachen as the center of Charlemagne's realm, could readily have been tied to any number of destinations in the West. To best understand the Charlemagne section of the *Descriptio*, it will be important to extricate it from its French context.

"Charlemagne and the East" as Anti-Reformist Propaganda

During periods of dynastic change and insecurity in the empire, Notker and Benedict had depicted a Charlemagne who unified Christendom without battle while serving as a protector of the papacy and its territorial interests. The *Translatio Sanguinis* had even portrayed Pope Leo as the essential go-between who persuades Charlemagne to receive an indescribable gift from

---

113. *Desc.*, 123.

Jerusalem that will represent, we should deduce, the movement of spiritual leadership to the new emperor in the West. The *Descriptio*, by contrast, gives no place to the pope in the narrative of Charlemagne's assumption of the imperial title and his subsequent bloodless unification of East and West. We do not know exactly when the Charlemagne section of the *Descriptio* was conceived, which makes it difficult to locate its origins in a particular political context. The presentation of Charlemagne's imperial investiture at Rome points, however, to the period of conflict between the Salian emperors and the reform papacy during the turbulent reign of Henry IV in the second half of the eleventh century.[114] The remaining sections of this chapter examine the ideological underpinnings of the Charlemagne section of the *Descriptio*, which prove to have been in harmony with the pro-imperialist polemical literature of the Investiture Contest. We can therefore postulate that the scribe who produced the Capetian-centered version that we read today was working from a document of imperial origins, the provocative prologue to which he chose to preserve.

Charlemagne's encounters with the East provide, in essence, the follow-up episode to the coronation of 800. Like the imperial investiture itself, the reckoning with the East must also be considered as a contested piece of Carolingian memory that fueled the polemics between empire and papacy in the eleventh century. Charlemagne's coronation was the first time that the pope had claimed a role in the process of crowning a Roman emperor; the ceremony had previously been constituted by the acclamation of the Roman people.[115] Leo's addition of a new papal element to the ancient rite led some medieval interpreters of the ceremony to believe that the empire had been, in some way, a gift from the papacy, although modern historians have not reached consensus on the degree to which the pope's participation had represented an assertion of papal primacy over lay leadership. The debate over the meaning of the coronation was particularly vigorous during the Investiture Contest, with authors of pro- and antipapal inclinations offering varying portraits of the ceremony.[116] Within the larger disputes between *regnum* and *sacerdotium* more pointed arguments persisted over how and under what auspices Charlemagne's coronation had taken place, and over what

---

114. Léon Gautier dated it between 1050 and 1080, remarking on its imperialist prologue; see *Les épopées françaises*, vol. 3 (Paris, 1880), 286.

115. Muldoon, *Empire and Order*, 66–67; McKitterick, *Charlemagne*, 115.

116. Folz, *Coronation*; Folz, *Le souvenir*, 142–47; Brian Tierney, *The Crisis of Church and State, 1050–1300* (Englewood Cliffs, NJ, 1964), 17–18; cf. also Goez, *Translatio Imperii*, 141.

shifts in power the ceremony had implied.[117] While the pro-imperial side believed that the imperial dignity had come through divine providence, with a reduced role for the pope, the pontifical view held that it was the popes who chose and made emperors.[118] Both sides claimed the Frankish king's memory, but on different grounds, creating what Folz calls a "*dédoublement*" of the figure of Charlemagne.[119] Spokesmen for the empire, such as Benzo of Alba, put forth a theory of transfer of empire that held that Leo had been a mere instrument of the will of the apostles, while Charlemagne was God's choice. In the pro-papal view, the Carolingians had come to power as protectors of the papacy, having saved it from the Lombards, for which they were rewarded with consecration by Pope Stephen II. The *Descriptio* depicts the investiture scene according to the pro-imperial rhetoric of the late eleventh century by celebrating a Charlemagne who received the empire from the Roman people.

The presentation of the imperial investiture in the *Descriptio*, which directly precedes the journey to the East, provides the earliest clues in the document that point to the imperialist proclivities of its author. With none of the harmonious diplomacy of the friendly Caliph Harun, the *Descriptio* recasts the beginning of Charlemagne's imperial reign as a time of great suffering for the church and for Christians in the East.[120] There follows a carefully worded description of Charlemagne's invitation to Rome and the resulting imperial investiture: "And so, after the reputation for faith and goodness of such a famous man had travelled across nearly the entire world, the Romans, extremely frightened, offered to him the supremely powerful Roman Empire, and indeed even his election of the Pope. Thus by the surpassing providence of God, he was made Roman emperor."[121] Both the invitation to Rome and the nature of the investiture itself demand close reading. In keeping with the classical norm according to which universal dominion is achieved as the result of an unparalleled reputation in foreign lands, the author describes Charles's

---

117. Folz, *Le Souvenir*, 143–44. See I. S. Robinson, *Authority and Resistance in the Investiture Contest: The Polemical Literature of the Late Eleventh Century* (New York, 1978).

118. Mireille Chazan, *L'Empire et l'histoire universelle: De Sigebert de Gembloux à Jean de Saint-Victor (XIIe–XIVe siècle)* (Paris, 1999), 12.

119. Folz, *Le souvenir*, 123.

120. *Desc.*, 103. "Tempore quo rex et imperator Karolus magnus Gallicum regebat regnum, multe quoque contrarietates sancta dei ecclesie inerant."

121. *Desc.*, 103. "Proinde postquam tanti tamque famosi viri per totum fere orbem terrarum fidei probatisve fama transvolavit, Romani magno terrore perterriti potentissimum Romanum imperium, immo etiam pape electionem ipsi prescripserunt. Ita dei providentia precurrente Romanus imperator effectus est." Rauschen links the statement to the Synod of Sutri in 1046, in *Die Legende*, 99; cf. Grosse, "Reliques," 363–64.

worldwide fame. The wording of the invitation establishes his *fama* as resulting from his perceived faith and Christian good works rather than his ability to inspire fear. The passage does contain a certain degree of ambiguity about why the Romans are frightened, but context and later versions show that the Romans do not fear the mighty Charlemagne himself, but rather the looming dangers to Christendom. The passage thus effectuates the same sort of Christianization of the classical theme of imperial reputation that Notker had carried out, and which also occurs in the *Translatio Sanguinis*.

When Charlemagne arrives in Rome, the Roman people reward the king from Gallia with the imperial title. They, and not the pope, have summoned the Frankish king to Rome, and when he arrives, the people of the city relinquish to him not just the imperial title, but control over papal elections. This is a far cry from past visions of a mutilated Pope Leo in distress, with the Frankish king arriving in Rome humbly unaware of why he has been summoned. The investiture with the imperial title is portrayed instead as the result of a combination of divine providence and the acclamation of the Roman people. Pope Leo, typically a major protagonist in the story of Charlemagne's coronation at Rome, is absent from the scene. Rather than rescuing the embattled pope, the Frankish king comes to Rome on behalf of all Christendom. The exclusion of the pontiff constitutes a major modification of the long-engrained story of the Frankish king's willingness to aid the beleaguered pope. Furthermore, the conferral of the right to control selection of the pope represents an echo of contemporary anti-reformist imperialist rhetoric.

The *Descriptio* author was not alone, to be sure, in creating a politically potent new version of the coronation of Charlemagne.[122] As Ian Robinson observes, the polemics of the Gregorian reform saw an unprecedented back-and-forth of pamphlets and letters between the opposing forces.[123] The polemical literature of the Investiture Contest also included false decrees that revised key events in Carolingian memory, including the fabrication of Pope Hadrian's conferral of power over papal elections to Charlemagne. Around 1084, imperialist lawyers at Ravenna were forging documents that promoted the Salian regime, which included invented privileges given by Pope Hadrian I to Charlemagne.[124] The false documents were known at Liège, a major center of pro-imperial propaganda bordering on France, as well as at

---

122. Folz, *Le souvenir*, 142–47.
123. Robinson, *Authority*, 60.
124. Mary Stroll, *Symbols as Power: The Papacy following the Investiture Contest* (Leiden, 1991), 73; Folz, *Le souvenir*, 126–28; Robinson, *Authority*, 160.

Chartres.[125] The false decree of Hadrian is dated to 774, the year of the Peace of Pavia and the Lombard surrender to the Franks. The forger combines material from the period of the Lombard invasions from earlier in the eighth century with details drawn from the sources for the coronation of 800. The result is a new coronation scene that occurs during the papacy of Hadrian I as a reward for Charlemagne's efforts against the Lombard kings.[126] When Hadrian's predecessor, Pope Stephen, dies, the new pope sends legates to Charlemagne asking him to come to Rome to defend the interests of the church. Charlemagne comes to Italy, rescues Pavia, and then arrives in Rome, where Hadrian addresses him as "Charles, perpetual Augustus crowned by God." His imperial power is then univocally acclaimed by all the Roman people.[127] After the ceremony, Hadrian and Charlemagne jointly hold a synod with 150 prelates at the Lateran Palace, where the pope confirms the Frankish king's rights to papal election and investiture.[128] The forgery thus constitutes a major revision of the past in favor of imperialist claims to authority over the papacy. The *Descriptio* author makes similar claims concerning Charlemagne's imperial investiture, which suggests that it too was intended as a pro-imperial tool for redefining the dynamics of power in the empire.

In the *Descriptio*, Charlemagne travels to the East after he learns of the contents of Constantine's dream vision, which deliberately recalls the divine instruction given to Constantine the Great concerning the protection of the empire. The vision at the Milvian Bridge, like Charlemagne's coronation, also served both sides of the debates between empire and papacy during the Investiture Contest. There were thus two competing visions of the relationship between Charlemagne and Constantine. The pro-imperial model reinforced the understanding of the emperor as the vicar of God on earth, who must relinquish his quest for glory in the name of the Christian imperium. On the other hand, beginning in the Carolingian period, evocations of the tradition of Constantine and Sylvester had conveyed the emperor's submission to the papacy, as seen in the mosaic in the *triclinium* of the Lateran Palace in Rome.[129] From a papal standpoint, the image of Charlemagne as heir to

125. Folz, *Le souvenir*, 131–32.
126. *Falschen Investiturprivilegien*, 137.
127. *Falschen Investiturprivilegien*, 142.
128. *Falschen Investiturprivilegien,* 145. "Ad hoc quoque exemplum praefatus Adrianus papa cum omni clero et populo et universa sancta synodo tradidit Karolo augusto omne suum ius et potestatem eligendi pontificem et ordinandi apostolicam sedem, dignitatem quoque patriciatus similiter concessit."
129. See Johannes Fried, *Donation of Constantine and Constitutum Constantini: The Misinterpretation of a Fiction and Its Original Meaning, with a Contribution by Wolfram Brandes: "The Satraps of Constantine"* (Berlin, 2007), 18.

Constantine emphasized the continuity of papal domination over the secular leadership of the empire in the spirit of the Donation of Constantine.[130] The *Descriptio* conforms to the imperial model by depicting a Charlemagne who was not beholden to the papacy for his role as imperial protector of Christendom. Moreover, the dream vision experienced by Constantine illustrates the demotion of the Byzantine leadership, while also depicting God's intervention in the designation of Charlemagne as the protector of the Christian *communitas*, with no role for the papacy.

The Last Emperor and the Investiture Contest

The fact that the Charlemagne who travels to the East mirrors the figure of the Last Emperor is a significant piece of evidence for the antipapal intentions of the *Descriptio*. The Last Emperor prophecy and the story of Charlemagne both celebrate a vision of lay leadership at the helm of a united Christendom. The reform papacy and its theorists also sought to arrogate to the Holy See its own sort of universal imperial authority.[131] Imperial eschatology therefore represented a challenge to the universalizing pretensions of the reformists by positing an end time theory that rivaled papal claims that it was the pope who inherited the role of protector of a universal Christendom. Within their new doctrine, the popes promoted the subordination of temporal authority to spiritual authority in support of their assertions of universal primacy for the church. Pope Gregory VII, in his Dictatus Papae of 1075, adhering to the notion of a papal monarchy that ruled over all churches, asserted that the pope alone could be called "universal" and reserved the use of imperial insignia for the pontiff.[132] This rhetoric also included the fostering of the notion of the pope as *verus imperator* who ruled over assembled nations.[133]

Since emperors had long represented the ideal of Christian universalism, as Brett Whalen argues, the popes needed to co-opt that role to

---

130. Cowdrey, "Eleventh-Century," 71–72; Muldoon, *Empire and Order,* 69; Folz, *Coronation,* 131–33.

131. Whalen, *Dominion of God,* 12; McGinn, *Visions,* 94; Stroll, *Symbols,* xv. Ernst Kantorowicz speaks of the imperialization of the church, in *Laudes Regiae: A Study in Liturgical Acclamations and Medieval Ruler Worship* (Berkeley, CA, 1958), 139.

132. Maureen C. Miller, *Power and the Holy in the Age of the Investiture Contest: A Brief History with Documents* (Boston, 2005), 81–82; Tierney, *Crisis,* 46–50; H. E. J. Cowdrey, *Pope Gregory VII, 1073–1085* (Oxford, 1998), 610–11; Augustin Fliche, *La réforme grégorienne et la reconquête chrétienne (1057–1123)* (Paris, 1946), 394.

133. Chazan, *L'Empire,* 12.

gain credibility as "providential agents."[134] In the spirit of the Donation of Constantine, they put themselves forward as the heirs of the Roman Empire, claiming for it much of the East, including the sees of Jerusalem and Constantinople.[135] They also called into question the schema of the succession of the Four Kingdoms, as well as the tradition of the Last Emperor, which were both, by definition, favorable to a vision of the emperor as supreme leader of all Christendom.[136] The projection of the pope in the position of universal emperor likewise conflicted with the eschatological schema of the Four Kingdoms, which envisioned a Roman emperor shepherding humanity in its final days. The Last Emperor prophecy, which is based on, but distinct from, the idea of Rome as the fourth and last kingdom, also served to counter to the claims of the reform papacy to sole universal authority, since the prophecy also envisioned Christendom under the aegis of a Roman emperor and not the church in the last days.[137] By contrast, the prophecy would have appealed to the imperialist side of the controversy precisely because it featured the emperor at the center of God's plans for the end of time.[138] Voices on the imperial side that refused these universalizing papal claims included Sigebert of Gembloux, whose universal chronicle depicts a world at peace prior to the time of discord under Pope Gregory VII, while celebrating the emperor as the guarantor of universal peace.[139]

Depending on how the story was written, Charlemagne's bloodless reunification of East and West, with its shades of the prophesied journey of the Last Emperor, could also serve as pro-imperial rhetoric. The episode functions as an assertion of universal Christian authority for the emperor, an inherently anti-reformist claim that also ran counter to the spirit of the Donation of Constantine. Benedict had depicted Charlemagne as a precursor to the Last Emperor more than a century earlier, but he also injected a scene with the pope in which a humbled Charlemagne is forced to relinquish to the pontiff the territories that he has gained on his journey. The king even has to ask for permission to share a piece of the relic of Saint Andrew, one of the spoils of his subjugation of the Greeks. With no such assertion of papal dominance, the *Descriptio* reads as a celebration of the providential origins of

134. Whalen, *Dominion of God*, 10–13.

135. John Gilchrist, "The Papacy and War against the 'Saracens,' 795–1216," *International History Review* 10 (1988): 186.

136. McGinn, *Visions*, 94–95; Möhring, *Der Weltkaiser*.

137. McGinn, *Visions*, 94.

138. Christopher Tyerman, *God's War: A New History of the Crusades* (Cambridge, MA, 2006), 69.

139. Chazan, *L'Empire*, 12, 25–27.

Charlemagne's imperial title. During the period of intense conflict between the Salian emperor Henry IV and the reform papacy under Pope Gregory VII, the *Descriptio* would have strongly affirmed a vision of the emperor as the divinely elected protector of Christendom who is in no way beholden to the papacy for his status as emperor.

Conclusion

Within several decades of dissolution of the Carolingian Empire in the late ninth century, adaptations of chapters in the life of Charlemagne began to appear in monastic chronicles, foundation legends, and relic authentication texts. Their authors rewrote the story of his encounters with the East by making it the backdrop for stories of how those relics from the East had found their way to the various monasteries that claimed ownership of the objects. Charlemagne's journey to the East has typically been viewed as not much more than a framework for stories that legitimated the presence of relics in religious houses. The preceding pages have shown that "Charlemagne and the East," when woven into relic *translatio* texts, served as an ever more complex site for meditation on the leadership of the largely theoretical Christian Roman Empire. Authors began to represent a more universally powerful Charlemagne who embodied certain elements of apocalyptic prophecies regarding the coming of a last Roman emperor. The Charlemagne who symbolically conquers the East is a seemingly paradoxical figure, since his journey inaugurates his reign rather than marking its end. What I have shown, however, is that the invocation of imperial apocalyptic discourse did not constitute end time speculation, but served instead to enrich contemporary discourse on the state of the empire. This was especially true during pivotal periods such as the Saxon assumption of the imperial title in the mid-tenth century and the Investiture Contest of the late eleventh century. The following chapter will explore the most striking example we have of the fusion of "Charlemagne and the East" with the Last Emperor prophecy in the work of the prolific imperial propagandist Benzo of Alba.

❧ CHAPTER 3

Benzo of Alba's Parallel Signs

In colorful, poetic, and sometimes foul language, Benzo of Alba promoted the Salian inheritance of the Roman Empire on behalf of Henry IV in his virulently anti-Gregorian *Libri ad Heinricum IV Imperatorem*. Throughout his voluminous work, Benzo composed multiple versions of the foreign embassy motif in a variety of forms and rhetorical contexts, including a version of the Last Emperor prophecy, an eerie visitation by the voice of Charlemagne to explain the prophecy, fabricated diplomatic communiqués, and lofty panegyric verse. More so than anyone before him, Benzo reveals his recognition of the encomiastic function of Charlemagne's symbolic conquest of the East. He began his endeavor during the precarious period of Henry's minority in the early 1060s, and finally completed the project in 1085, after Henry's long-delayed imperial coronation. We have almost no independent evidence of Benzo's career outside of his own writings, at the end of which he portrays himself, as Ian Robinson notes, as "a deserving imperial servant who has yet to receive his just reward."[1] One of the most often evoked passages from Benzo's work involves his adaptation of the Last Emperor prophecy, which seems to promise for Henry a triumphal expedition to Jerusalem and Constantinople. With the timing of the

---

1. I. S. Robinson, *The Papal Reform of the Eleventh Century: Lives of Pope Leo IX and Pope Gregory VII*, trans. and annotated I. S. Robinson (Manchester, 2004), 85.

publication of the *Ad Heinricum* a mere ten years before Urban II's call to arms at Clermont in 1095, Benzo's promise has been, among historians, a favored piece of evidence for the existence of a proto-crusading mentality in the Latin West.[2] A closer examination reveals, however, that the context in which Benzo employed the prophecy had little to do with the Holy Land, and everything to do with his bitter hatred of the reform papacy, its Norman allies, and the combined threat that they posed to Salian imperial authority.

Benzo shared an interest in the discourse of Roman universalism with fellow rhetoricians of the mid-eleventh century who had praised the Salian *renovatio* under Henry III after his imperial coronation at Rome in 1046. He may or may not have been directly associated with the imperial chancery, but his work does resemble that of the short-term imperial chaplain and pro-imperialist scholar Anselm of Besate.[3] Anselm's *Rhetorimachia*, written around 1048, contains an elaborate version of the foreign embassy motif, and we may also note here the coincident composition in 1046 of Odilo of Cluny's praise-filled letter to Henry, which also contains the topos. In his dedicatory letter to the emperor, Anselm likens his task to Vergil's, praising Henry's victories in war and describing his conquests of savage and cruel nations and his crushing of merciless and nefarious souls.[4] After listing Henry's military victories, the panegyrist makes the transition to his deeds in peace by listing the various foreign peoples that had been moved by news of his conquests, such as those in Gaul, Britain, and Hungary. He then proclaims that Greece, Judaea, the Saracen race, and "others across the sea, having learned of his might, await Roman rule, fearful and trembling in servitude."[5]

Anselm's deployment of the surrendering nations motif is not unusual until he makes an unexpected addition to his enumeration of "deeds in peace" that involves the Greeks. The passage is rather vague, but it concerns the Greek emperor, who, as he reminds Henry, had recently sent word ordering that his debts be resolved with the German emperor. The encomiast then praises Henry for having given over the spoils of that unexplained exchange with the Byzantine leadership to Saint Peter in honor of Rome. The addition

---

2. Folz called it an imperial crusade that Benzo sketched out for his master; see *Le souvenir*, 139. See also Sylvia Schein, *Gateway to the Heavenly City: Crusader Jerusalem and the Catholic West (1099–1187)* (Aldershot, 2005), 148–49.

3. Robinson, *Authority*, 72; Tilman Struve, "Kaisertum und Romgedanke in salischer Zeit," *Deutsches Archiv für Erforschung des Mittelalters* 44 (1988): 428; Robinson, *Papal Reform*, 83.

4. Anselm of Besate, *Rhetorimachia*, MGH *Weitere Reihen*, 98.

5. Ibid. "Tuis quide tropheis exultat Italia; cuius virtutibus excitatur Gallia; quem suum regem Francia et imperatorem expectat Brittanniae. Prosperis cuius casibus gens tremat Ungarica, que cito cum aliis tibi iacebit prostrata. Grecia, Iudea, Germania, gens Saracena, transmarina cetera, audita tu potentia Romana expectant imperia et diu laxata iam pavent servitia."

comes just at the end of the enumeration of Henry's bloodless victories, at which point Anselm describes how the conciliatory Greek embassy offered further proof of how nations were gloriously coming together under the new Caesar.[6] This final detail is significant for two reasons. First, it provides another example of implied, symbolic Byzantine surrender to the new emperor in the West presented within the context of the foreign embassy motif. The Greek embassy also foreshadows Benzo's far more elaborate adaptations of the motif, which revolve, in large measure, around invented diplomatic communications from the emperor in Constantinople.

Since late antiquity, the procession of surrendering nations had been a locus of inventive adaptation for commentators on the state of the empire. The writings of panegyrists such as Anselm and Benzo reveal that the motif had remained a prominent piece of imperial discourse with which scholars continued to hone their rhetorical skills, whether playfully or in earnest. For its part, the *Rhetorimachia* was not a serious piece of imperial propaganda, but rather a collection of documents that included mock polemical letters, a common compositional practice among scholars in the eleventh century.[7] The work purports to be a sort of a textbook on rhetoric, but it relies on the presumption of an ongoing competitive exchange of letters between two friends concerning their respective talents in the art of rhetoric.[8] While it would be unfair to compare Benzo's massive literary endeavor too closely to Anselm of Besate's playful handbook on rhetoric, there are nonetheless some aspects of Anselm's work that echo Benzo's massive panegyric to Henry and point to a similar scholarly milieu. Benzo's compilation represents the labor of a scholar who spent decades honing his rhetorical skills in praise of an emperor to whom he most likely did not have access. Anselm, "the Peripatetic" as he called himself, claimed to be Vergil to Henry's Augustus, a pose that Benzo adopts as well. Anselm may also have inspired Benzo to alternate between prose and verse. Anselm is allusive in his writing, and the same can be said of Benzo; but while Anselm offered one version of the foreign embassy motif after the coronation of Henry III, Benzo employed it

---

6. Ibid., 98–99. "Unde spontanea BASYLO nuper direxit mandata, cuius CONSTANTI-NOPOLIS ultra sol vit debita. Que pro signo et meritis ROME Petro tradisti et eius vicariis, ut de gloriis et tropheis his quasi redditis graciis et velut pro memoria remunerationis de tanti revocatione honoris cognoscant etiam gentes et confluentes undique nationes, Romam fore excitatam sub notro cesare Heinrico, quam legimus exaltatem quodam a iulio."

7. Monika Otter, "Scurrilitas: Sex, Magic, and the Performance of Fictionality in Anselm of Besate's *Rhetorimachia*," in *Aspects of the Performative in Medieval Culture*, ed. Manuele Gragnolati and Almut Suerbaum (Berlin, 2010), 108.

8. Ibid., 104.

as a recurring metaphor of imperial power throughout the *Ad Heinricum* in honor of Henry IV.[9]

Benzo of Alba was consumed by the political preoccupations that inspired both his high-blown praise for Henry and his vituperative rants against the reformists at Rome.[10] Throughout his varied compilation, Benzo mounts an ardent defense of the Teutonic inheritance of the empire from the Franks (and before that, the Greeks) with an idealized vision of the continuity of Rome under Salian leadership. The archdeacon Hildebrand, the future Pope Gregory VII, plays the villain throughout the work, functioning as the primary agent of the reformist quest to destroy the German empire. Benzo inserts himself into the battles between empire and papacy, styling himself as a crucial bulwark against the encroachment of rival forces that threaten the survival of the empire of Augustus, Charlemagne, the three Ottos, and the current Henricians. Early in the 1060s, during Henry IV's adolescence, Benzo had been involved, or so he says, in the papal schism between Pope Alexander II and Antipope Honorius II (Cadalus of Parma), which pitted the German court against the Holy See and its new Norman collaborators. In an effort to ensure Cadalus's success in becoming pope, the Salian court, under the direction of Henry's mother, Agnes, had assigned Benzo (so he claims) to promote their interests. Benzo writes at length on the subject of his efforts on their behalf, describing, for instance, how he had led an expedition to Rome to aid the imperial antipope.[11]

The struggle between empire and papacy is a dominant and ongoing theme in Benzo's writings, but his actual role in imperial affairs is difficult to trace, since he is the only one to mention his involvement. It is therefore possible that the relationship with the young king that he describes was largely a product of his own imagination.[12] We know that he became bishop of Alba in the 1050s, but sources do not tie him to the imperial chancery. He was eventually driven from his bishopric by reformist factions in the mid-1070s, but may

---

9. Robinson, *Authority*, 72; Otter, "Scurrilitas," 105.

10. Percy Schramm points to Benzo's deep classical knowledge, in *Kaiser, Rom und Renovatio: Studien zur Geschichte des römischen Erneuerungsgedankens vom Ende des karolingischen Reiches bis zum Investiturstreit* (Leipzig, 1929), 259; cf. Stephen Jaeger, *The Origins of Courtliness: Civilizing Trends and the Formation of Courtly Ideals, 939–1210* (Philadelphia, 1985), 123–25. The author of a nineteenth-century history of Rome, who relies on Benzo as a major source, describes him as a flatterer of the German court and a "vulgar swaggerer" whose prose recalls Rabelais; see Ferdinand Gregorovius, *History of the City of Rome in the Middle Ages*, vol. 4 (London, 1896), 133.

11. On Cadalus, see I. S. Robinson, *Henry IV of Germany, 1056–1106* (Cambridge, UK, 1999), 42–43; Wilhelm von Giesebrecht, *Geschichte der Deutschen Kaiserzeit*, vol. 2 (Leipzig, 1877–95), 574; Cowdrey, *Pope Gregory VII*, 50–51; Fliche, *La réforme grégorienne*, 216–49; G. A. Loud, *The Age of Robert Guiscard: Southern Italy and the Norman Conquest* (London, 2000), 194.

12. Robinson, *Papal Reform*, 83–84.

have regained some degree of access after Gregory VII was deposed in 1084 and the pro-Henrician antipope, Clement III, was finally able to preside over Henry's long-deferred imperial coronation at Rome in 1084.[13] Any analysis of Benzo's self-presentation should therefore consider the panegyrist to have been a potential witness to the events he describes, such as Henry's imperial coronation, but probably not the intimate adviser that he portrays himself to be. Considerable fiction surrounds, for instance, his elaborate presentation of the diplomatic exchanges that he claims to have facilitated between the Byzantine and Salian courts during Henry's adolescence.

There are three main sites in the seven books of the *Ad Heinricum* where Benzo employs versions of the foreign embassy motif to symbolize *dominium mundi* for Henry: in Books 1, 2, and 6.[14] Book 1, which Benzo added during the period of his final revision before 1085, is of primary interest because it includes his version of the sibylline prophecy for Henry. Shortly after detailing the prophecy, Benzo describes an imagined conversation in which the voice of Charlemagne addresses Henry, promising him future victory over all his enemies. In Charlemagne's announcement of the prophecy's promise of universal triumph, the Carolingian emperor draws a series of parallels between his own encounters with Byzantium and the Holy Land and similar incidences in Henry's reign. The intervention thus provides a key to the interpretation of the cryptic message contained in the prophecy. Book 2 contains a letter from the emperor Constantine in Byzantium proposing an alliance with Henry and offering the German king all of his treasure in exchange for cooperation in a future joint imperial expedition to rid Italy of the Normans and Jerusalem of pagans. In Book 6, Benzo presents his verses written in celebration of Henry's campaign in Italy from 1081 to 1084. The poetry represents the most overtly panegyric section of the work, with two versions of the foreign embassy motif, one classical and one post-800 version that describes the concession of authority to the German emperor by the Byzantines. Since the Last Emperor prophecy appears in Book 1, which was written last, Benzo's promise of universal victory, including Henry's coronation in Jerusalem, has frequently been read, by Carl Erdmann most notably, as a harbinger of the coming crusading movement. The actual context for his universalizing rhetoric was really the 1060s, however, in the aftermath of the papal alliance with the Normans in 1056.

13. Robinson, *Authority*, 71–72; *Papal Reform*, 84–85. Robinson states that there is nothing linking Benzo directly to the imperial chancery; see *Authority*, 72, and *Henry IV*, 230.
14. Robinson gives a brief summary of each book, in *Papal Reform*, 85.

Benzo and the Sibyl

Benzo's most enigmatic articulation of Roman universalism on behalf of Henry occurs in Book 1, in which he interprets a sibylline prophecy to mean that Henry will be the future unifier of the empire before the end time.[15] In his version of the Last Emperor prophecy, Benzo promises for Henry his own journey to Constantinople and Jerusalem:

> As the prophecy of the Sibyl tells us, a long road remains in front of him. For when Apulia and Calabria have been put in order and restored to their pristine state, Bizas will see him crowned in his own land. Then, in short order, will be his departure for the city of Jerusalem, where, having visited the Holy Sepulcher and other lordly sanctuaries, he will be crowned to the praise and glory of the one living forever and ever. Stunned, Babylon, desiring to lick the dust from his feet, will come to Zion.[16]

Benzo cites as his source the Cumaean Sibyl, which existed at the time as a reworking of the Tiburtina in favor of Gregory VII.[17] Since antiquity, compilers of sibylline oracles had tended to be either strongly for or against the regime in power, and not necessarily concerned with the actual end of the Roman Empire.[18] There were multiple sibyls in circulation in Germany in the eleventh century, and the different versions served as propaganda both for and against the German kings. Some of the versions of the prophecy were anti-Greek, while others were friendly toward the Greeks.[19] The text on which Benzo based his prophecy is lost, but enough is known of its anti-Salian

---

15. Folz, *Le souvenir*, 139; Robinson, *Authority*, 74; Gabriele, *Empire of Memory*, 112–15. Daniel Verhelst argues that Benzo's prophecy was part of an exhortation to Henry to accept the role of Last Emperor; see "Les textes eschatologiques dans le *Liber Floridus*," in Verbeke, Verhelst, and Welkenhuysen, *Use and Abuse of Eschatology*, 301.

16. *Ad Hein.*, 1.15. "Adhuc enim longa sibi restat via, sicut Sybille testatur prophetia. Nam ordinatis et in statum pristinum collocatis Apulia scilicet atque Calabria, videbit eum Bizas coronatum in sua patria. Deinceps erit egressio eius usque ad urbem Solimorum, et salutato sepulchro ceterisque dominicis sanctuariis coronabitur ad laudem et gloriam viventis in secula seculorum. Stupens igitur Babylon, desiderans lingere pulverem pedum eius, veniet in Syon."

17. Robinson, *Authority*, 74; Reeves, *Influence of Prophecy*, 301–2. Hannes Möhring dates the sibyl to 1042, describing it as Lombard and anti-Ottonian/Salian, in "Benzo von Alba und die Entstehung des Kreuzzugsgedankens," in *Forschungen zur Reichs-, Papst- und Landesgeschichte Peter Herde zum 65. Geburtstag von Freunden, Schülern und Kollegen dargebracht 1998* (Stuttgart, 1998); see also Möhring's *Der Weltkaiser*, 149–56.

18. Potter, *Prophets and Emperors*, 140; Holdenried, *Sibyl*, xxii.

19. Kampers, *Die Deutsche Kaiseridee*, 53; Holdenreid, *Sibyl*. See also Tilman Struve, "Endzeiterwartungen als Symptom politisch-sozialer Krisen im Mittelalter," in *Ende und Vollendung: Eschatologische Perspektiven im Mittelalter*, ed. Jan A. Aertsen (Berlin, 2002), 222.

tone to confirm that Benzo changed it significantly to suit his pro-Henrician agenda. One extant Cumaean Sibyl, for instance, is known to have described a Salian reign of terror that would precede the arrival of a prince from Byzantium who would unite the Greeks and Romans before laying down his regalia at Jerusalem before the end time.[20] Benzo's source predicted that the Last Emperor would destroy Babylon and the Saracens before the time of peace prior to the arrival of Antichrist.[21]

In his revision of the Last Emperor prophecy for Henry, Benzo promises future victory in southern Italy, Byzantium, and Jerusalem, but not through conquest.[22] The prediction stems from his melding of the Einhardian tradition of bloodless submission to Charlemagne with the prediction in the sibylline prophecy that the emperor will unite East and West before journeying one final time to Jerusalem. By predicting that Bizas, the legendary founder of Byzantium, will see Henry crowned "in his [Bizas's] own land," Benzo appropriates for the West the promise from the sibyl concerning the Constans figure who will unite East and West under his rule. Schramm explained this passage by arguing that in a celebration of imperial *renovatio*, there was no room for two emperors.[23] The scene is indeed tied to Benzo's celebration of the Salian claim to Roman *renovatio*, but the image of Byzantium ceding power to the emperor in the West is more complicated than that. The victory over the Greeks is not simply the supplanting of the Constans figure with a German leader. This hybrid motif of symbolic triumph that builds from Einhard, which we first see in Benedict of Mount Soracte, demands that the emperor of the West triumph without battle over both Byzantium and the non-Christian East. Benzo's oracular language concerning the future coronations in Byzantium and Jerusalem fulfills these criteria.

The apparition of Charlemagne in Book 1, despite its appearance in what was the last section to be added to the compilation, most likely reflects an earlier period in Henry's reign and not the triumphal period after his march on Rome and subsequent imperial coronation. The Frankish king begins by comparing the experiences that he and Henry share, such as fighting the Saxons. He speaks to the young king "as one friend to another," addressing him as "*Hymago mea*," as he intones, "Emperor, my image, under whom the substance of the world trembles." Charlemagne also poetically recalls his

---

20. Robinson, *Authority*, 74; Gaston Zeller, "Les rois de France candidats à l'Empire: Essai sur l'idéologie impériale en France," *Revue Historique* 173 (1934): 278; Holdenreid, *Sibyl*, 5.

21. Schein, *Gateway*, 148.

22. For the crucial place of Italy in the Salian conception of German hegemony, see Weinfurter, *Salian Century*, 26–28.

23. Schramm, *Kaiser, Rom und Renovatio*, 261.

own crushing of the Saxons, and promises Henry his own such victory if he continues to wear them down diligently.[24] The voice of the Frankish king addresses Henry, and his father Henry III (d. 1056): "You two, you the greats, the strong ones," he declares: "The world celebrates you both, you the third, him the second."[25] Charlemagne then warns Henry against treachery, telling him to beware, and not to waver in his faith, since the servants of treachery will soon be biting at his heels, lying in wait for the earliest opportunity for "the sacrifice." Charlemagne's tone of paternal admonition, his warnings of looming treachery, and his allusion to thirst for sacrifice all point to the sort of guiding voice that Benzo would have wanted to provide for the boy king as competing factions jockeyed for power during his precarious adolescence in the 1060s. By 1084, on the other hand, the period of major conflict with the Saxons was over, although not resolved in Henry's favor.[26] By then, Henry had waged war in Italy, and had seen enough turmoil in his political life, including being kidnapped as boy, that he would hardly have needed advice whispered from the beyond about the potential for traitors lying in wait.[27] This is not to say that Benzo could not have updated older material for inclusion in his praise-filled introduction to the *Ad Heinricum*. It is important, nonetheless, to recognize that Benzo began creatively revising the sibylline prophecy for Henry in the 1060s, long before Henry's ultimate assumption of the imperial title in 1084.

With the mysterious apparition of Charlemagne, Benzo offers a clear assertion of the connection that he understood to exist between the diplomatic encounters with the East in the Carolingian sources and the rhetorical construction of Roman universal dominion. After his grim admonitions, Charlemagne seeks to reassure Henry about the road that lies ahead for him by laying out further parallels between their two reigns. The similar events he describes are meant to be read as signs pointing to Henry's coming attainment of universal victory: "Divine is the mystery which you grant me, unconquered Caesar, whether in military victories, or in the administration of the Empire. For whatever signs came to me from lands across the seas, almost the same ones are coming to you. The king of the Persians sent an

---

24. *Ad Hein.*, 1.17. "Karolus Heinrico boat hec ut amicus amico. Saxa diu fregi, pedibus fragmenta subegi. Sic sic victor eris, si crebo saxa teris. Cesar, Hymago mea, sub quo tremit orbis hydea."

25. *Ad Hein.*, 1.17. "Vos duo, vos magni, vos fortes, vos velut agni, vos celebrat mundus, tu tercius, ille secundus."

26. The struggles between Henry and Saxony peaked in 1073 but were ongoing, so it is hard to use this statement to date composition of the passage. See Thomas N. Bisson, *The Crisis of the Twelfth Century: Power, Lordship, and the Origins of European Government* (Princeton, NJ, 2009), 215; Robinson, *Henry IV*, 104.

27. For the kidnapping, see Robinson, *Henry IV*, 43.

elephant to me, and to you Africa sent a lion accompanied by marvelous beasts."[28] The scene brings to light the panegyrist's deliberate assimilation of the encounters with Harun and the Greeks with the sibylline tradition of the Last Emperor. Before completing his list of parallel signs, Charlemagne pauses to make a statement referring back to the sibyl in which he clarifies for Henry the fact that the oracle is meant to point to his future assumption of the helm of Christendom: "but this prophecy directs itself to you, who will be the standard bearer of the Christian religion in this undertaking, by the will of God." By establishing the connection between the parallel gifts from the East that have arrived for the two emperors, Charlemagne's enumeration of signs thus elucidates the sparse language of the prophecy and enhances the sibyl's promise of Christian triumph. Charlemagne understands, and he wishes Henry to understand, that the gifts point beyond themselves to a promise of divinely sanctioned victory over the enemies of Christendom. They are not just signs of gratitude, or of the establishment of diplomatic hierarchies, but far more potent indications of Henry's imperial destiny.

In addition to the exotic animals that Charlemagne encourages Henry to read as signs of future universal triumph, the Carolingian emperor also alludes to the two parallel transfers of holy relics from East to West. He presents the diplomatic events in such a way that Henry will see them as providential signs that both have received. He then provides a contemporary analogue to the gifts from the patriarch of Jerusalem that Charlemagne received after his coronation: "The emperor Constantine sent you similar signs, namely parts of the shroud of the Lord, the cross, and the crown of thorns. And so, by these figurative signs, you are able, my friend, to expect certain victory over all enemies. Delight therefore in the Lord and he will grant all the requests in your heart."[29] Benzo's story of the relics being sent from Constantinople to Henry, like the lion, is an invention that forms part of his construction of parallel signs of symbolic conquest of the East. He mentions the relics in Books 1 and 6, two of the later books to be written.

---

28. *Ad Hein.*, 1.17. "Divinum quidem est misterium, quod michi morigeraris, cesar invictissime, sive in bellicis triumphis, seu in dispositione rei publicae. Nam quaecumque signa de transmarinis partibus advenerunt michi, pene eadem occurrunt tibi. Elephantem vero michi direxit rex Persarum, tibi quoque Affrica leonem cum comitatu mirabilium bestiarum."

29. *Ad Hein.*, 1.17. "Basileus autem Constantinus misit tibi signa similia, videlicet de sudario Domini, de cruce, simulque de corona spinea. His itaque figuralibus signis potes, o amice, certam sperare victoriam de omnibus inimicis. Delectare ergo in Domino, et dabit tibi petitiones cordis tui." See Folz, *Le souvenir*, 140–41.

There is no other evidence, however, that Constantine X, who died in 1067, had sent any such gifts.[30]

Since the Charlemagne apparition has usually been interpreted as an example of Benzo's later writings in the 1080s, scholars have sought to show that Henry had recently received relics from Alexius Comnenus, whom Benzo referred to as "Constantine." Some have theorized, for instance, that it was an invention based on a less spectacular offering to the German court in 1082. In that instance, Alexius, under threat from the Normans and in need of help, had sent not relics, but a payment of gold and silks, in the hopes of a united front against the hated Robert Guiscard.[31] To support the claim that Benzo was really referring to Alexius rather than to Constantine, Anatole Frolow attempts to explain away the use of the name Constantine by arguing that we should read the name generically, as "he who sits on the throne of Constantine."[32] This is unlikely, given that gifts of relics from Byzantium to the Salian leadership had occurred even in the 1020s, when Constantine VIII gave a piece of the holy cross to Conrad II, a gift that was widely known in the Salian realm.[33] While Alexius did in fact send an embassy, Benzo's presentation of the parallel signs of universal victory are too closely tied to his imagined diplomatic relations between the Salian and Byzantine courts during the Cadalan schism of the early 1060s to suggest that he was inspired by Alexius's overture of 1082. He seems to have added the relics to the story in the 1080s, but he had been inventing exchanges with Byzantium for two decades prior to his final revision. Sacred objects had come to Charlemagne from Jerusalem in the ninth century, so, to create the sign of future triumph, Benzo invented a parallel gift for Henry from Constantine X, the subject of Benzo's multiple constructions of symbolic Greek surrender to Henry.

Although Charlemagne did indeed receive an elephant from the caliph, Henry probably did not receive a lion from Africa, let alone any of the other marvelous beasts to which Charlemagne alludes. The sending of marvelous beasts to a new emperor had its place in Roman panegyric going back to antiquity as a component of the construction of the procession of surrendering nations. Since Benzo was working within that established tradition

30. See Holger Klein, *Byzanz, der Western und das "wahre" Kreuz: Die Geschichte einer Reliquie und ihrer künstlerischen Fassung in Byzanz und im Abendland* (Wiesbaden, 2004), 86–87, and Klein, "Eastern Objects," 295–96. Cf. Sophia Mergiali-Sahas, "Byzantine Emperors and Holy Relics: Use and Misuse of Sanctity and Authority," *Jahrbuch der Österreichischen Byzantinistik* 51 (2001): 48; Frolow, *La relique de la Vraie Croix: Recherches sur le développement d'un culte* (Paris, 1961), 282.

31. Robinson, *Henry IV*, 214, 222–23.

32. Frolow, *La relique*, 282.

33. Weinfurter, *Salian Century*, 28.

of imperial praise, and there is no evidence of such a gift in the sources, we can be reasonably confident that he invented that detail.[34] Word of such an offering would surely have traveled beyond a brief mention by a panegyrist whose rhetorical needs were so precisely served by its occurrence. The gift of the lion from Africa parallels the gift of the elephant from Harun. Both represent exotic foreign tribute in recognition of the emperor's supremacy and therefore enrich the praise-filled comparison between the two Christian emperors. In fact, all of the parallel signs that point to Henry's attainment of universal victory that Charlemagne enumerates relate to diplomatic exchanges with the East. For both Charlemagne and Henry, those exchanges, which are intended as symbols of the recognition of the emperor's authority by leadership in the East, are both sacred and secular. The Persian elephant and the other exotic animals represent gifts from non-Christian lands, meant to stand in contrast to the sacred objects and relics sent to both emperors from the leadership of the Christian East. The Frankish king recalls how the patriarch of Jerusalem had brought him multiple relics and the keys to the Holy Sepulcher, with a banner, a memory that draws on the *Royal Frankish Annals* rather than Einhard. For Henry, the relics come from Byzantium, acting as politically potent symbols of the recognition of the superior spiritual authority of the new emperor in the West.

The anonymous *Life of Emperor Henry IV*, written after the emperor's death in 1106, offers another example of a pro-Salian version of the foreign embassy motif that sheds light on Charlemagne's discourse on the parallel gifts from the East. The biographer describes how the kings of the East feared the emperor's reputation so much that they chose to be his tributaries rather than his victims: "The king of the Greeks, since he was covering up his fear, sought his friendship, and fearing him as a future enemy, he tried to prevent him from becoming an enemy by means of gifts."[35] He adds that the king of the Greeks sent a beautiful gift to the cathedral of Speyer. The church did in fact boast a splendid Byzantine altar with enamel plaques sent around 1100.[36] The fact that the biographer included the real gift sent from Byzantium to the imperial basilica within a locus of praise designed to convey the idea of the surrender of the Greeks reveals how contemporary events could be integrated into this recognizable motif. When mentioned in this rhetorical context, instead of representing a typical diplomatic offering,

---

34. Seyffert deems the report of the lion plausible, but does so based on the fact that wild animals were a frequent diplomatic gift between rulers in the Muslim East; see *Ad. Hein.*, 555–56, n. 254.

35. *Vita Heinrici Quarti*, MGH *SRG* 58, 12.

36. Krijnie Ciggaar, *Western Travellers to Constantinople: The West and Byzantium, 962–1204: Cultural and Political Relations* (Leiden, 1996), 225.

the altar functions in the passage as implied tribute. For Henry's biographer, the primary aim was to grant to the king the same form of Roman imperial praise that Einhard had composed in honor of Charlemagne, but the mutable nature of the motif allows for the interjection of a detail that ties Speyer, a site dear to the Salian emperors, to the larger imperial ideal.

Charlemagne's explanations of the sibyl reveal that Benzo joined other adapters of "Charlemagne in the East" in integrating two textual traditions of Roman *dominium mundi*, the bloodless alliances of the foreign embassy topos and the violent Last Emperor prophecy. At the end of the enumeration of parallel gifts, Charlemagne announces that the exchanges are meant to be read as signs of Henry's future victory over all his enemies.[37] It is essential to note, however, that all of the victories that Benzo promises for Henry are forecast to occur without conquest. The gifts from the East all represent tribute, and thus submission, with no discussion of conquest of the enemy. Benzo's project was, first and foremost, praise for his emperor, a rhetorical objective that required him to pacify the violent implications of the sibyl by merging the prophecy with the Roman biographical tradition of imperial unity gained without battle.

Future Victories

A closer look at the components of Benzo's revision of the Cumaean Sibyl shows how the encomiast constructed his own particular expression of Roman universalism using the Last Emperor prophecy as a framework. He writes that Apulia and Calabria will return *in statum pristinum*, meaning to the empire and thus no longer be in papal or Norman hands.[38] There are then three future sites of victory in the prophecy as Benzo presents it: Apulia and Calabria, Byzantium, and Jerusalem, but Italy stands apart. The surrender of the Christian East represented by Byzantium and of the non-Christian East represented by Babylon make up the major elements of the prophecy as it was known. Then, for his own purposes, Benzo adds southern Italy as a third locus of triumph, casting the Normans as infidel pagans whose defeat will be

---

37. *Ad Hein.*, 1.17. "His itaque figuralibus signis potes, o amice, certam sperare victoriam de omnibus inimicis."

38. As part of the Norman alliance, Robert Guiscard, duke of Apulia and Calabria, had agreed to hold lands in fief from the papacy in return for support against the empire. See Tilman Struve, "Kaisertum und Romgedanke in salischer Zeit," *Deutsches Archiv für Erforschung des Mittelalters* 44 (1988): 437–38; Brian Tierney, *The Crisis of Church and State, 1050–1300* (Englewood Cliffs, NJ, 1964), 43–44.

a necessary stage in Henry's attainment of universal dominion.[39] The promise of Henry's future victories in the East is merely a function of the melding of contemporary conflicts over southern Italy with the existing components of the sibyl. The prophecy therefore ought not to be read as an actual plan for Salian domination in the East.

The variations on the theme of universal dominion in Benzo's work all reflect what he perceived to be the combined papal and Norman attack on the prerogatives of the empire. Henry IV was nine years old when the Normans, in alliance with the papacy, took possession of Apulia and Calabria in 1059 after the Treaty of Melfi. Under the Norman duke Robert Guiscard, who had become a vassal of Pope Nicholas, the Normans gained papal sanction for their Italian conquests, taking on the obligation to protect the Roman church against the interests of the empire.[40] Benzo depicts himself as having been active in support of Salian interests at the time, working tirelessly to defend the long-standing claims of the empire to overlordship in southern Italy.[41] The loss of the Italian territories was still a fresh wound in the early 1060s, but twenty years later the problem was still far from resolved. The matter remains one of great consternation throughout the *Ad Heinricum*. In Book 7, Benzo makes allusions to contemporary events in the 1080s, but he also continues to fester about the papal politics of the first half of the 1060s. He again decries the loss of Apulia and Calabria and deems the election of Pope Alexander (1061) a travesty, condemning the heretical and illegal assumption of imperial prerogative by the papacy.[42] In support of his claims, Benzo offers his own imperialist interpretation of the Donation of Constantine, describing how Constantine the Great had relinquished custody of Rome not to the papacy, but to the people, "*ad custodiendam rem publicam.*" He then condemns the illegal papacy of Hildebrand before fulminating again about how the emperor must fight to regain Apulia and Calabria.[43]

Benzo is obsessive in blaming Hildebrand/Gregory, although he also harbors continuing resentment toward Godfrey the Bearded for his intervention in favor of Alexander over the imperial antipope Honorius II. He even accuses the duke of "rejoicing in thwarting the cause of the boy king," and

---

39. For the notion that the Normans were worse than the pagans, see Mastnak, *Crusading Peace*, 114–16.

40. Cowdrey, *Gregory VII*, 47.

41. Robinson, *Papal Reform*, 83.

42. *Ad Hein.*, 7.2.

43. *Ad Hein.*, 7.2. See also Giancarlo Andenna, "Il Mezzogiorno normanno-svevo visto dall'Italia settentrionale," in *Il Mezzogiorno normanno-svevo visto dall'Europa e dal mondo mediterraneo: Atti delle tredicesime giornate normanno-sveve, Bari, 21–24 ottobre 1997*, ed. Giosuè Musca (Bari, 1999), 37–39.

of keeping him from donning the imperial crown.[44] In his rant about the machinations of Hildebrand, Benzo describes the then-archdeacon and "his Alexander" grazing in the Lateran "like asses in stable," and refers to the dining hall (*triclinium*) in the Lateran (known for its images of imperial submission to the papacy) as the dung hall (*sterquilinium*).[45] Benzo bitterly relives the outrage of the Norman-papal alliance that threatened Henry's reign and the integrity of the empire. His proposed sibylline journey for Henry must, therefore, be seen in light of this obsession, rather than in relation to any perceived situation in the Christian East and the Holy Land, about which he has nearly nothing to say.

Empire and papacy collided dramatically in the eleventh century over southern Italy, with both entities, along with Byzantium, making pretenses, at various points, to some form of universal Christian authority. The prophecy foretells that after Apulia and Calabria are restored to the empire, Henry will be crowned in Byzantium and again in Jerusalem. The Italian territories thus figure as an essential first stage in the final constitution of his *dominium mundi*. The oracle tells the king that a long road lies ahead of him, a reference, no doubt, to his constitution of a universal empire. The panegyrist is not the first, however, to have woven the issue of jurisdiction over territories in Italy into a journey to Jerusalem and Constantinople with sibylline overtones. Benedict, for instance, had highlighted Charlemagne's return of Italian lands to Rome after his bloodless subjugation of the East. Benzo, as a hater of the papacy, is adamant that the Italian lands be returned to the empire.

A late eleventh-century forgery that accompanied the false decree of Pope Hadrian I, which I discussed in the previous chapter, sheds further light on the role of southern Italy in the polemical literature of the period. As Benzo was completing his compilation, the forgers at Ravenna were fabricating a decree called the Cessio Donationum. The imperialist concoction, which purports to be from Pope Leo VIII in 964, was inspired by the tenth-century Ottonianum, which had laid out the concessions agreed to by Otto I in return for his imperial coronation by Pope John XII.[46] The Cessio Donationum opens with the forger setting the scene in the period when, as he describes it, Charlemagne and Pippin made gifts of territory in Italy to Saint Peter. The decree then lists over one hundred cities, territories, villages, and monasteries to be given to the empire, including Apulia and Calabria, the Exarchate,

44. *Ad Hein.*, 7.2. "Gaudens turbare causam pueri regis."
45. *Ad Hein.*, 7.5.
46. For the document, see Riché, *Carolingians*, 270.

and Pentapolis.[47] At the end, Pope Leo VIII promises the Italian territories to Otto in perpetuity, calling on the emperor to use his military might to protect against the enemies of the church.[48] The tenth-century papal document reflected an emperor bargaining for coronation from a pope using the promise of protection, while the pro-imperial fabrication describes the papacy relinquishing domains in Italy to the emperor, essentially undoing the so-called Donation of Pippin. The forgery thus creates an invented moment in which the first Saxon emperor regained territories in southern Italy that had been contested by the Byzantines, the Lombards, the Carolingians, and the papacy. For an eleventh-century readership, this forged donation served as a declaration that southern Italy had belonged to the empire and not the papacy since the tenth century. By that logic, Apulia and Calabria would not have been the pope's to give away to the Normans in the first place.

In the very early pages of the *Ad Heinricum*, the reader gains crucial perspective on what Benzo perceives to be the major threats to the empire. They are, above all, the "barbarian" invaders (Normans), a treacherous papacy, and, to a lesser degree, the rival Greeks. Most of the crisis for Benzo revolves around the loss of Apulia and Calabria. Should there be any doubt that this loss represents a central theme of Benzo's entire project, the opening lines of the work contain an allusion to the role of Apulia in the Punic Wars that confirms his preoccupation with the region as a symbol of external threats to Roman imperial integrity. Benzo proudly remembers Rome's struggle against Hannibal on the Italian peninsula during the Second Punic War. When Scipio finally defeated the Carthaginian leader, Rome was redeemed and one could speak of her eternal happiness, Benzo announces.[49] Citing Plautus's appellation of Apulia as *"Terra Nostra,"* Serge Lancel speaks of how the region, which had functioned as a major theater of the war in Italy, became symbolic of the larger theme of Rome's struggle to triumph over the dual barbarian worlds of Carthage and the Greeks.[50] Benzo likewise adopts the capture of Apulia for his discourse of universalism, but with Salian Germany as the new Rome, and the Normans as the barbarians in southern Italy who must be driven out if Rome is to endure. The loss of Apulia, for Benzo, encapsulates the major threats to his ideal of Salian imperial unity, namely papal defiance, treachery, and Norman invasion.

---

47. *Falschen Investiturprivilegien*, 157–67.
48. *Falschen Investiturprivilegien*, 167. See also Robinson, *Authority*, 161.
49. *Ad Hein., Dedicatio.*
50. Serge Lancel, *Hannibal*, trans. Antonia Nevill (Oxford, 1998), 213–14.

After the implied comparison between ancient Apulia defended by Scipio and contemporary Apulia under Norman occupation, Benzo sets out to justify his attention to the matter. He declares that he wants to talk about something that not enough people are writing about, the administration of Apulia and Calabria. In an admonition to Henry, he reminds the king that his predecessors never tired in their governance of the two territories, and then gives examples of the various enemies that had needed to be fought off over the centuries. Charlemagne defeated Desiderius, then the Ottonians drove the Saracens off the shores of the Adriatic, and finally Otto beheaded Crescentius and blinded Sergius as punishment, he explains, for their frequent commerce with the Greeks. Benzo's final example of Henry's illustrious imperial forebears and their defense of Apulia involves a series of Henry III's triumphs over various Norman dukes, including Tancred of Hauteville.

The praise for Henry's father includes a meaningful revision of a scene from Paul the Deacon's history of the Lombards, a scene that takes on new significance within Benzo's reconstruction of the past to assert Salian imperial claims to southern Italy. Benzo writes that while in southern Italy, Henry had wanted to see the *"columpna Karoli,"* a monument marking the spot where Charles had thrown his lance in the sea.[51] The column was originally associated with the Lombard king Autari. According to Paul's history, the Lombard leader had reached the far end of Italy in Sicily in his conquests, where he affixed his spear, declaring the spot to be the new outer limit of Lombard territory. The historian then describes a column in the water "still seen today" that is known as the *"columna Authari."*[52] Benzo takes this nugget of Lombard memory and cleverly converts it to a locus of imperialist propaganda by changing the Lombard king to Charlemagne, thereby imagining Charlemagne as a conqueror of the southern reaches of Italy on behalf of the Frankish empire. As with the false donation of Leo VIII to Otto I, here too a propagandist for the empire tries to efface the memory of donations to the papacy made by lay leadership in previous centuries by asserting imperial claims to territories in Italy. Benzo then presumes that Henry must be wondering why he is talking so much about the battles of his predecessors, to which he responds that Henry needs to prepare himself, since God is preparing victory for him. Appealing, as he does on multiple occasions, to the Teutonic inheritance of the Roman Empire as it was passed from the Greeks and Gauls to the Teutons, Benzo declares that the current enemies of Rome

---

51. *Ad Hein.*, 1.13.
52. *Hist. Lang.*, 112.

must be flushed out.[53] This is his prelude to the sibyl that promises universal victory to Henry.

The "Exhortatio ad Proceres Regni"

A poem from the early 1060s offers another example of a sibyl-inflected version of the foreign embassy motif used to condemn the Norman presence in southern Italy. The work is called the "Exhortatio ad proceres regni" (Exhortation to the Princes of the Realm), and while it is anonymous, I agree with those who have proposed that Benzo was the author.[54] The thirty-eight-verse poem is a call to the elites of the realm to support the young Henry during a time of political uncertainty. With its warnings about looming threats of disloyalty and treachery, the poem echoes in its tone the admonitions of Charlemagne in the *Ad Heinricum*. Calling for a united front against the Normans and for loyalty to the young king, the poet promises a parade of surrendering foreign nations if the boy rules over a united empire. The deployment of the foreign embassy motif in the poem therefore functions, as it has in previous examples, as a locus of concern over the continuity of empire during a period of dynastic transition.

The "Exhortatio" demonstrates once again how the foreign embassy motif could be merged with elements of the Last Emperor prophecy as an expression of imperial praise.[55] Schramm, who recognized the enumeration of foreign peoples in the poem as an evocation of *Weltherrschaft*, observed that the domination described in the verses was not gained through violent conquest. He explains that this image of peaceful conquest represented the formation of a new Christian Roman Empire that would be a peaceful *Friedensreich*.[56] It is important to note, however, that the poet was consciously working within an imperial biographical framework in which the willing surrender of foreign nations served as an expression of universal power. The "Exhortatio" focuses first on the promised surrender of the Greek East and the non-Christian East represented by "the Arab":

---

53. *Ad Hein.*, 1.14.

54. Robinson, *Authority*, 83. Erdmann notes the originality of the poem, with its unexpected mixing of Christian themes with the idea of eternal Rome, in *Origin*, 287. See also Natalia Lozosky, "Maps and Panegyrics: Roman Geo-ethnographical Rhetoric in Late Antiquity and the Middle Ages," in *Cartography in Antiquity and the Middle Ages: Fresh Perspectives, New Methods*, ed. Richard J. A. Talbert and Richard W. Unger (Leiden, 2008), 181.

55. Robinson suggests a lost sibylline text from the 1060s, in *Authority*, 74.

56. Schramm, *Kaiser, Rom und Renovatio*, 257.

If the boy is ruler, God is the highest creator, Stand with the one born
of Henry by sacred law. / You have conquered the world, if you have
preserved what is right, / And Libya will be subdued justly / And
Greece having been added, will be present, and there will be no eastern
wars / And the fearful Arab will come running anxiously with gifts.[57]

Among the conquered peoples, the Greeks seem to have a different status,
having been "added" in an ambiguous way that mirrors the fearful alliance
Einhard described when he spoke of the Greeks' fear of Charlemagne's plans
to annex their territory. The phrase "*Grecia iuncta aderit*" creates a parallel sense of peaceful appropriation. After describing the "annexing" of the
Greeks, the poet takes up the theme of conquest without battle by stating
that in an empire united under Henry there will be "no Eastern wars." The
Harun of past iterations appears here as an anonymous quivering Arab bearing gifts. The procession of surrendering nations continues on with Spain, a
common symbol of the western reaches of the Roman Empire: "Brave Spain
will be very reverently submitted to you, and the Cantabrians will accept
Roman laws." The list also includes other symbols of the far West, including
the Britons and the Gauls, but, more significantly, it singles out the Franks,
who will "yield in obsequious servitude." The surrender of the Franks to
Henry thus establishes the distinctly Teutonic inheritance of Roman *dominium mundi* within the poem's enumerative depiction of future Roman rule
under Henry.

After the parade of surrendering nations, the poem contains a striking set
of verses offering an idealized picture of shared authority under Roman law.
The poet imagines a unified world "at peace under the keys of Saint Peter,
safely restored under the laws of the old Roman Empire." Under the reinsti-
tuted system of Roman law, the poet declares, Julius, Augustus, and Charles
will rule equally. In the *Ad Heinricum*, Benzo similarly declares that Henry
will rule in the traditions of both Christian kings and the Roman emperors
of antiquity. He designates these leaders as either *christolicas*, for which his
examples are Charlemagne and Pippin, or *profanes*, such as Theodosius and
Justinian, both of whom were Christian emperors associated with the law
codes of antiquity.[58] In the "Exhortatio," each of the three emperors constitutes a separate element in an amalgam that represents the Salian inheritance
of the Roman Empire. Moreover, the emphasis on the restoration of Roman

---

57. Exhortatio, verses 9–14. "Si puer est rector, deus est altissimus auctor / Heinrici genito sistite
iure sacro / Vicistis mundum, si seruaueritis aequum / Et cum iusticia subdita erit Libia / Grecia
iuncta aderit, nec erunt orientia bella / Et cura muneribus curret Arabs timidus."
    58. *Ad Hein.*, 6.6.

law serves to bolster the legitimacy of the transfer of empire to the Saxons from the Franks as a matter of law in combination with divine election.[59] The poet offers a rich description of the metaphorical scepter that Henry will bear, which embodies the various aspects of imperial authority. Justice and military success will come from the ancient Romans, he explains, while Charles represents sacred authority over Christendom.[60] This hybrid classical/Christian scepter mirrors Benzo's panegyric endeavor in creating an encomiastic model that incorporates both classical and Christian sources.

The celebration in the "Exhortatio" of Henry's Roman imperial antecedents appears alongside the statement that the empire under the Salian king will be at peace "under the keys of Saint Peter." Given the conflicts between empire and papacy of the 1060s, this is a rather unexpected picture of unity between *regnum* and *sacerdotium*.[61] The promise must be viewed, however, in the context of the papal schism of 1061–64. Benzo's vision of harmony relates to his efforts on behalf of Cadalus, the failed antipope Honorius II. The verse in which he describes peace in the empire under the aegis of the Roman church is designed to bolster Benzo's promotion of Honorius's pontificate. The anti-Gregorian subtext to be inferred then is that peace and unity between empire and papacy are possible, but only in a world where the Salian candidate is in possession of the Holy See. By contrast, the reformist world is full of strife and discord that will hasten the disintegration of the empire.

Byzantium: Constantine Seeks an Alliance

Although Benzo's feverish politicking against the papal-Norman alliance pervades the *Ad Heinricum*, Book 2 contains an unusual set of passages purporting to be reproductions of diplomatic exchanges with the East concerning the Norman problem in southern Italy. The letters are fabrications that need to be interpreted in relation to the sibyl and to Benzo's other elaborations on the theme of surrendering foreign nations. The first is from a certain Pantaleus of Amalfi to Benzo, and the other is from the Greek

59. Karl J. Leyser, "The Polemics of the Papal Revolution," in *Medieval Germany and Its Neighbours, 900–1250* (London, 1983), 146–47.

60. Exhortatio, verses 22–32. "Sic fiet mundus sub Petri clauibus aequus / Et uirtus fidei supprimet arma doli / Legibus antiquis totus reparabitur orbis / Iulius et Caesar, Karolus his quoque par / Regnabunt pariles secum ditione potentes / Utetur sceptro magnus honorifico / Par est militia geminis cum uiribus aequa / Par uirtutis opus militie gradibus / Militia una tribus, sotius cum laude triumphus / Tertius est supra religione sacra."

61. For discussion of the conflicts of the 1060s, see Cowdrey, *Pope Gregory VII*, 50–53.

Emperor Constantine X (1059–67) to Honorius, we presume, since it opens
"I, Constantine Doclitus, king of Constantinople, [send] greetings to the
Roman Patriarch, [who was] raised up by the law of kings over the universal
church."[62] This statement reflects the manner in which Cadalus came to be
Honorius II, but it also more generally articulates Benzo's position concern-
ing the role of the emperor in the matter of papal elections.

Benzo makes the only known mention of the letter from Constantine,
but the authenticity of the letter has nonetheless been a matter of debate.[63]
There is ample evidence, however, for Benzo's authorship of the letters, the
most telling of which is the way they conform to his pattern of creating
versions of the foreign embassy topos combined with elements of the Last
Emperor prophecy. Benzo invented other letters as well, including a message
that purports to be from Henry's mother, Agnes, to the Romans, demand-
ing that they return Cadalus to Rome to claim the Holy See and prevent
the Normans from continuing to worship Constantine's horse as an idol.[64]
In the text between the letters, Benzo fulminates against Hildebrand while
describing Cadalus's attempts to attain the Holy See. He then describes his
own march on Rome in 1062 to establish the antipope, an endeavor that was
ultimately thwarted by the then archdeacon. Benzo's various fabrications all
serve his larger anti-Norman, antipapal propaganda project, a major element
of which was the promotion of his own efforts on behalf of Cadalus.

In the first letter, Pantaleus writes to the bishop of Alba to lament the fact
that the Norman invasions in Italy are getting in the way of the once fruitful
and cooperative friendship between the papacy, the Romans, and the Greeks:
"I believe that peace is not unknown among the Latins and Greeks, between
other princes, Roman and Byzantine, with the pope mediating. Now, however, because Normans are coming from the ends of the Earth, disrupting
the fraternal pact of the indivisible empire, to their dishonor and common

62. *Ad Hein.*, 2.12. "Romano patriarche, regia constitutione super universali aecclesia sublimato, Constantinus Doclitius, Constantinopolis basileus, salutem."

63. Hannes Möhring summarizes the earlier debate, in "Benzo von Alba," 185. Some scholars simply declare the letters to be spurious, while others propose that Benzo had doctored an existing document. Folz sees it as a fabrication, *Le souvenir*, 40. Robinson laments the lack of information, noting that Benzo is rather loquacious concerning the proposed alliance, while other sources make no mention of it; see *Authority*, 74. See also Hugo Lehmgrübner, *Benzo Von Alba: Ein Verfechter Der Kaiserlichen Staatsidee Unter Heinrich IV* (Berlin, 1887), 123–24. Tilman Struve refers to the "mys-terious" alliance proposal, in *Salierzeit im Wandel: zur Geschichte Heinrichs IV. und des Investiturstreites* (Vienna, 2006), 222. Krijnie Ciggaar sees Benzo's version as a summary of an existing letter, although it is not clear on what evidence; see *Western Travellers*, 80.

64. *Ad Hein.*, 2.15.

shame, they have dared to invade in our midst with defiant presumption."[65] The letter offers a concise articulation of Benzo's ideal of imperial unity based on a model of cooperation between the papacy and the two sides of the empire. It also offers a further example of how the conflicts over territories in southern Italy that were contested by all three entities functioned within Benzo's discourse of empire as the impediment to Salian domination. The author of the letter extols the ideal of a united empire, an ideal rendered unattainable because the Normans, having transacted with the Holy See, have come between the two sides of the once brotherly and "indivisible empire." The empire could be united and at peace, the letter implies, but only in a world in which the pope cooperates with the emperor and not the Normans, the same message that is implied in the "Exhortatio." The letter from Pantaleus reminds Benzo that the Normans are destroying the eternal friendship between Byzantium and the West that had been successfully mediated by the papacy in the past. Both the "Exhortatio" and the letter thus envision peace between the two sides of the empire and the Holy See. The letter, like the poem, conveys an idealized vision of the triangle of the papacy, Byzantium, and the German empire that would be possible with the pontificate of Honorius II. The missive is also meant to serve as an implied condemnation of the strife and disintegration associated with Alexander II, whom Benzo saw as a puppet of the Normans.

The second letter, the one from Constantine X to the "Roman Patriarch," contains the Greek emperor's proposal for an alliance between the two sides of the Christian empire in response to the Norman occupation in southern Italy, offering financial support (his whole treasury) in return for troops and leadership from the West. Before providing his "reproduction" of the letter, Benzo stages the scene as an East–West diplomatic encounter. He describes the clothing and general appearance of the Byzantine envoys who deliver it, noting that their elaborately decorated purple garb left no doubt that they were from the palace of the *basileus*.[66] Benzo introduces the letter into the text by recounting how the envoys told the pope that they had come in the name of the "common empire" and in the name of the fraternal alliances of its respective princes, echoing the themes of brotherhood in Pantaleus's let-

---

65. *Ad Hein.*, 2.7. "Credo non esse ignotum Latinis et Grecis de concordia inter utrumque principem, Romanum quidem atque Constantinopolitanum, mediante Romano apostolico. Nunc autem quia de finibus orbis terrae venerunt Normanni, conturbantes fraternum foedus indivisibilis imperii, ad dedecus atque communem verecundiam ausi sunt nostra invadere in medio nostrum contumaci praesumptione."

66. *Ad Hein.*, 2.12.

ter. He describes how the ambassadors read out the letter, which allows for
the narrative to be in the first-person voice of the Greek emperor.

During the creatively staged embassy from Constantinople, envoys express
the Greek emperor's desire for an alliance in a manner that recognizes Henry's
authority and superior ability to protect the empire. In proposing a friendly
alliance, Constantine invokes the shared Romanness of the Greeks and the
Germans. "By the hand of our faith, I wish to conclude an eternal pact
of friendship with the boy Henry, Roman king. For I am also Roman, and
therefore let us be as one, both Romans, under you, born of a common father,
conjoined by an indivisible bond of *caritas*."[67] He then invokes their shared
intellectual tradition, now under siege: "Roman wisdom, derived from our
Greek source, which flourished well under the first, second, and third Otto,
is vanishing at the present time, while now it suffers under the Norman
consorts of the empire."[68] The Normans are usurping imperial prerogatives,
he laments, by nominating Bishop Anselm of Lucca, the future Alexander II,
whom he calls "Pseudopope." Although the letter is supposed to be from
Constantine, it addresses in detail what we know to be the preoccupations
that gnawed away at Benzo for decades. The same concerns, although not
insignificant, would not have been nearly so pressing to the emperor in the
East. In any case, they would not have merited a request for military alliance
at the expense of his whole treasury and an imperial son as a hostage offered
in return.

Benzo adopts the voice of the Greek emperor to appeal to a shared higher
ideal of empire, placing the Salians in the long line that went back through
the Ottonians to the Romans and Greeks of antiquity. In this imaginary
encounter between Constantine and Cadalus, Benzo gives his own ideas the
grand forum of a communiqué from the imperial East and conveys a sense
of shared classical heritage between the Greek and German empires. The real
Greek emperor would have had little reason to do either. The reminder to
Honorius of their shared intellectual traditions is also a tacit acknowledgment
that the *translatio studii* had indeed occurred, with *sapienta* having already
passed from the Greeks to the Romans, and is now being perilously guarded
by the Teutons. The Normans in Italy threaten the survival of that tradition,
and so Constantine pleads for the preservation of the glory of the empire
in secular, classical terms. It is difficult to imagine that this argument could

---

67. *Ad. Hein.* 2.12. "Ad hec corrigenda, per manum fidei tuae volo firmare aeternalis amicitiae
pactum cum puero Heinrico, rege Romano. Nam et ego Romanus sum, et ita nos ambo Romani sub
te communi patre simus unum, conligati vinculo indivisae caritatis."

68. *Ad Hein.*, 2.12. "Roma sapientia, a nostro Greco fonte derivata, quae in primo vel secundo ac
tercio Ottone bene floruit, instanti tempore ita defluxit, ut paciatur Normannos consortes imperii."

have emanated from the Byzantine court. In spite of the outlandishness of the letters, Axel Bayer has sought to defend the possible historicity of the alliance proposal using evidence related to contemporary Byzantine relations with Amalfi.[69] His argument for a possible small-scale alliance is plausible, but does not help to authenticate the large-scale proposal from Constantinople, which Benzo created to enhance his vision of Byzantium ceding control to the West.

In his proposed pact with the boy king through Honorius, Constantine offers financial support for the German troops so that they may rid Italy of the Normans and liberate the Holy Sepulcher:

> For this, I will give to him as a hostage my purple-born son, and all of my treasure, so that he may do with it what he wishes for his use and the use of his army, to the extent that there is the ability for us to go to the Holy Sepulcher with you leading, and having purged the filth of the Normans and the pagans, Christian liberty will flower anew, even at the end of time. You, man of God, heir of Saint Peter, keep these words hidden in your heart and do the work of God.[70]

Benzo's revision of the sibyl is, in essence, a figurative version of the same scenario proposed in Constantine's letter. We should therefore embrace Robinson's somewhat tentative suggestion that the letter and the prophecy are related, and both date to the 1060s.[71] If we consider the letter and the prophecy as twin articulations of Greek surrender of imperial authority to Henry, it becomes easier to assert the connection. The sibyl states that Bizas will see Henry crowned in his own land, which is another way to express bloodless conquest of the Greek East by the Christian West. The letter also asks for a unification of the two empires under a single ruler in a manner that implies his conceding of imperial supremacy. Unification of East and West was essential to the Tiburtina's prophecy and to Pseudo-Methodius's as well, but the request also echoes the Greek quest for an alliance that went back to Einhard. The restoration of Apulia and Calabria to its "pristine

---

69. Axel Bayer, *Spaltung der Christenheit: Das sogenannte Morgenländische Schisma von 1054* (Cologne, 2002), 127. Jean-Marie Sansterre recognizes the imperial politicking behind the forged letters, but offers contemporary details as well; see "Byzance et son souverain dans les 'Libri ad Heinricum IV imperatorem' de Benzo d'Alba," *Bollettino della Badia greca di Grottaferrata* 51 (1997): 94–100.

70. *Ad Hein.*, 2.12. "Super hoc filium meum porphyrogenitum dabo sibi obsidem, totumque meum thesaurum, ut ex eo faciat quod voluerit ad suos usus suorumque militum, quatenus te praevio sit nobis facultas ire usque ad sepulchrum Domini, et expurgata spurcicia Normannorum sive paganorum, refloreat christiana libertas vel in fine seculorum. Tu autem vir Dei, heres beati Petri, claude sermones istos in pectore tuo et operare opera Dei."

71. Robinson, *Authority*, 74.

state" in the prophecy is the equivalent of the call to purge the Normans; and, finally, the expulsion of pagans from Jerusalem proposed in the letter is symbolized in the sibyl by Babylon's awe-filled surrender at the feet of the emperor.

In his proposal for an alliance with the West, the Greek emperor suggests that Henry, with support from the Greek East and Honorius II as leader, might rid Italy of the Normans and Jerusalem of pagans. The plan not only represents an example of Greek symbolic surrender similar to what we find in the *Descriptio*, but it also places the Last Emperor–style journey that Benzo describes for Henry within a tangible political context. All three sites of triumph in the sibyl—southern Italy, Byzantium, and Jerusalem—constitute obstacles to the ideal of Roman *dominium mundi* for the West, but southern Italy was the actual site of conflict for the Salian emperor. As in the case of the prophecy, the focus in the letter is on southern Italy, while Byzantium and Jerusalem derive from the existing sibylline tradition. For the letter to convey the potential fulfillment of the prophecy, the suggested alliance needed to include the ceding of control by Byzantium and a journey to Jerusalem, but it is the loss of Apulia and Calabria that matters to Benzo. Constantinople and Jerusalem were engrained components of a well-known sibylline prophecy, but it was the crimes of the reformists regarding southern Italy that motivated so much of Benzo's endeavor.

The vision of Henry's future dual "coronations" in Byzantium and Jerusalem and the proposal of a joint expedition to Jerusalem in Constantine's letter have both been read too literally by historians as references to actual plans for a mission to the East, in some cases as a foreshadowing of the First Crusade. Rather than accounting for his actual political and rhetorical concerns, a significant proportion of Benzo's interpreters have elected to view his sibyl-inflected passages as a reflection of nascent proto-crusading discourse. In an example of how Benzo's writings have served as evidence of mounting crusading fervor, Norman Cohn took the prophecy to mean that Henry would march on Jerusalem to meet and overthrow Antichrist. Cohn even asserts that the idea of the crusade was taking shape in the 1080s, although he at least cautions that Benzo's political predilections are reason not to take his words at face value.[72] The historian moves immediately to Ekkehard of Aura's oft-cited statements concerning the widespread belief among the

---

72. Cohn, *Pursuit*, 71–72. Jonathan Riley-Smith broadly summarizes the scene by saying that Benzo was "advising him" to go to Jerusalem; see *The First Crusade and the Idea of Crusading* (Philadelphia, 1986), 21. Marjorie Reeves also cites Benzo's use of the Last Emperor prophecy as evidence of mounting interest in crusading activity; see *Influence*, 301.

pauperes that Charlemagne had returned to lead them, and ties that detail to a brief outline of the *Descriptio* narrative, which he summons as evidence that "it came to be almost universally believed" that Charlemagne had led a crusade to Jerusalem.[73] Carl Erdmann writes in concrete terms about the plans that Benzo drafted for Henry for a Jerusalem crusade, which he combined in the *Ad Heinricum* with the legend of Charlemagne: "This is a regular plan for crusade, whose special importance consists in translating eschatological speculation into real policy."[74] Erdmann imagines that Benzo first planned for Henry to march against the Normans, and then later, for him to undertake an imperial crusade to Jerusalem, when, as he argues, the idea of crusade was in the air.[75] Finally, Cowdrey proposes that Pope Gregory's own failed plans for a mission to the East in the 1070s were foreshadowed by Benzo's sibylline writings from the 1060s, which in turn foreshadowed the universalizing plans that Benzo describes in Book 1 when he compares Henry to Charlemagne as the standard-bearer of all Christendom.[76]

The connections that scholars have drawn between Benzo's projected journey to Jerusalem and Constantinople and the incipient "crusading" movement have been based on misinterpretations of not only his work, but of the tradition of Charlemagne and the East. More significant, though, is the almost universal failure to properly account for the Norman element of the sibylline language in the *Ad Heinricum*. None of these theories recognizes that outside of the two mentions of Jerusalem, both of which are evinced within the discourse of Roman universalism, the panegyrist shows no interest in the relationship of the empire to the Holy Land. The Holy Land is, in fact, the least politically relevant element of Benzo's sibyl-inflected imperial rhetoric. Benzo's political obsessions were few and focused. His ideal of a renewed Roman Empire under Henry IV was threatened by the

---

73. Ekkehard, *Chronicon Universale*, MGH *SS* 6, 215; Cohn, *Pursuit*, 72.

74. Erdmann, *Origin*, 299. Mastnak writes that Benzo thought of a military march to the Holy Sepulcher, but Urban II made the idea materialize by sending a united Christian army to the Middle East; see Mastnak, *Crusading Peace*, 120.

75. Carl Erdmann, "Endkaiserglaube und Kreuzzugsgedanke im 11. Jahrhundert," *Zeitschrift für Kirchengeschichte* 11 (1932): 403–7; Erdmann, *Origin*, 270. Hannes Möhring suggests the possible influence of Benzo's letter on depictions of the vision of Count Emicho of Flonheim that drove him to lead the massacre of the Jews of the Rhineland in 1096; see Möhring, *Der Weltkaiser*, 165; Matthew Gabriele, "Against the Enemies of Christ: The Role of Count Emicho in the Anti-Jewish Violence of the First Crusade," in *Christian Attitudes toward the Jews in the Middle Ages: A Casebook*, ed. Michael Frassetto (New York, 2006), 62, 68. This scenario, although possible, seems unlikely given the nature of Benzo's work.

76. H. E. J. Cowdrey, "Pope Gregory VII's 'Crusading' Plans of 1074," in *Outremer: Studies in the History of the Crusading Kingdom of Jerusalem Presented to Joshua Prawer*, ed. B. Z. Kedar, Hans Eberhard Mayer, and R.C. Smail (Jerusalem, 1982), 39–40.

alliance between the Normans and the papacy, two entities that receive his vitriol over hundreds of pages. Scholars have, for the most part, mistakenly overlooked the anti-Norman element of his sibylline passages in order to focus on the possible expedition to Jerusalem.[77] Despite the appearance of the work in the mid-1080s, Benzo's use of the Last Emperor prophecy is deeply rooted in the politics of the 1060s. Moreover, his version of the sibyl, Charlemagne's explication of the prophecy, and the letter from Byzantium calling for the purging of pagans are all components of his rhetorical program to claim the role of universal protector of Christendom for Henry. A glance at the seven books of the *Ad Heinricum* reveals that Benzo was more interested in coming up with insulting names for Gregory VII than he was in plotting the Holy Land on Henry's political map.

Although Jerusalem did not figure in Benzo's imagined political landscape, the Holy City plays a significant role in his discourse of imperial unity. The emperor will come in peace to the Holy Sepulcher, and there, he announces, Babylon will bow in awe to Henry. Just as the Charlemagne of the *Descriptio* mimics the Last Emperor's journey, but gains his victories without bloodshed, here, too, the triumph in the Holy City is without battle. Benzo had to reconcile, as did the *Descriptio* author, the competing discourses of Roman universalism by choosing between two models of imperial unity and triumph over the East: the violent conquest of the sibyl or the classical celebration of the emperor's "deeds in peace." For his panegyric offering to Henry, he elected a scenario in which Byzantium and Babylon bow to Henry and cede to his authority, thereby creating a variation on the Last Emperor prophecy that preserves the bloodless surrender of the classical model.

Benzo's intentions concerning the nature of Henry's projected journey to Jerusalem have been a matter of some debate, fueled in part by differing translations of the sparely written oracle. His motives become clearer upon recognition of the fusion of the sibylline prophecy and the classical ideal of willing surrender. For the emperor's future encounter at the Holy Sepulcher, some translate the participle in "*salutato sepulchro*" to give the journey the sense of an armed mission, while others offer the more literal translation of a visit or paying of homage, such as Seyffert's *grüssen*.[78] Benzo makes no

---

77. Cowdrey cautiously supports the notion that Gregory may have wanted to be seen in the Last Emperor role, or at least to preempt the notion of Henry in the role of universal protector of Christendom; see "Pope Gregory," 39. Möhring notes more convincingly that Gregory could just as easily have been influenced by other versions of prophecy, and ties Benzo's sibyl to events in Italy in the early 1040s related to Byzantine rule; see "Benzo von Alba," 186.

78. *Ad Hein.*, 1.15. "Deinceps erit egressio eius usque ad urbem Solimorum, et salutato sepulchro ceterisque dominicis sanctuariis coronabitur ad laudem et gloriam viventis in secula seculorum."

mention of battle or conquest, promising instead that Babylon will come to Jerusalem and surrender in awe, wishing to lick the dust from Henry's feet, a passage drawn from Isaiah 49:23, where Babylon surrenders to the Messiah. The image symbolizes Henry's future triumph over the non-Christian East, which Benzo conveys through transposition of the passage from Isaiah, with Babylon functioning as a metonym for the infidel enemy. In his play of oracular language, Benzo replaces God's feet with Henry's to convey that Henry will receive the willing submission of Babylon. It is the German emperor who inspires the awe of Babylon, while the desire to lick the dust from his feet serves as an allegorical vision of the submission of the East to the new leader.

Despite the apocalyptic nature of the Last Emperor prophecy, Benzo used the oracle to enhance his rhetoric of Roman *renovatio*, not to herald the imminent end time under Henry.[79] Rather than laying down his imperial regalia, as both the Tiburtina and Pseudo-Methodius predict that the Last Emperor will do, Benzo promises that Henry, newly crowned in Constantinople, will be crowned to the glory of God in Jerusalem. There is no suggestion of his relinquishing of the imperial dignity. Instead, the passage conveys the establishment of his universal authority, but not as an end time scenario. In previous instances, such as Notker's *Deeds*, Charlemagne's bloodless triumph over the East had been a central element of the presentation of imperial renewal under the Franks on the heels of the coronation. The same can be said of Benzo and the Salians, whether he was adapting the sibyl during Henry's regency or at the time of the coronation in 1084. Either way, his dream of Salian domination envisioned the preservation of the Roman Empire. Charlemagne is a figure of the past, however, while Henry is still alive and is therefore a potential fulfiller of the prophecy of universal triumph. The voice of Charlemagne in Book 1 points to the signs of universal victory that both received, but the scenario ultimately implies that Henry will surpass his Carolingian predecessor.[80] This does not need to be taken literally, however. Such a comparison between the two providential leaders

---

Seyffert's translation implies a visit and not rescue, as does Robinson's, in *Authority*, 74, "having visited the Holy Sepulcher." McGinn writes, "having rescued," in *Visions*, 90.

79. Folz, in *Le souvenir*, 140, saw the politics behind his use of the prophecy to describe Henry's realization of a universal monarchy; cf. Schramm, *Kaiser, Rom und Renovatio*, 257–61. Struve argues that Benzo meant to depict the emperor as the "Friedenkaiser" of the end time, pointing to the coincidence of the revision of the prophecy with Henry's capture of Rome in 1084 and his subsequent coronation, marking the beginning of a *novum saeculum*; see "Endzeiterwartungen," 224.

80. Folz, *Le souvenir*, 140.

of Christendom functions as its own sort of praise, without implying that Benzo actually saw Henry as the prophesied end time leader.

Modern interpreters run the risk of both over- and underestimating the influence of real apocalyptic speculation on medieval authors. In the case of Benzo, the meaning of the sibyl is best assessed as a product of the rhetorical context in which it occurs. The *Ad Heinricum* is a tireless celebration of secular imperial power, in which Benzo promises Henry an unprecedented future triumph over a universal empire. There is no indication that he intended to herald the imminent arrival of Antichrist by imagining Henry's final journey to Jerusalem to depose the symbols of his power. In fact, he sardonically announces that the Son of Perdition has already come in the form of Gregory.[81] Discussion of apocalyptic signs was often about the present, and the conflict between church and state in the late eleventh century was no exception to this rule.[82] Whatever influence Pseudo-Methodius and the sibyls may have had over the popular crusading movement, Benzo's own particular uses of the sibylline rhetoric of imperial reunification reflected his cultivation of the art of praise.

Constantine, the Normans, and the Preservation of Rome

On multiple occasions in Book 3 of the *Ad Heinricum*, which is often concerned with Cadalus's quest for the Holy See, Benzo tries to lend credence to his story of Constantine's proposed alliance by bringing up the subject to a variety of audiences. He reports the proposal, for instance, in a letter allegedly sent to a fellow prelate, and again in a hortatory passage addressed to Henry, in which Benzo pleads with the young king to fight to preserve the empire. At no point does the subject of going to Jerusalem come up again, for his concerns continue to be the Normans' presence in Italy and their unholy alliance with the papacy that threatens the survival of the empire. The absence of any subsequent mention of the Holy Land, or of any "infidels" other than the Normans, further reinforces the argument that the planned purging of Jerusalem in the letter from Constantine reflects the stock sibylline rhetoric of the letter and was therefore not intended to inspire any actual consideration of an expedition to the Holy Land.

Benzo uses a plea for Rome's survival as an opening to reintroduce the story of Constantine's offer. His first reminder of Constantine's proposal

---

81. *Ad Hein.*, 6, *Narratio* 2. See also Struve, "Endzeiterwartungen," 219.
82. Potter, *Prophets and Emperors*, 219; Struve, "Endzeiterwartungen," 211.

occurs in the opening of Book 3, where he implores the *rectores imperii* to listen to him as he laments the separation of Apulia and Calabria from the empire, like a child torn from its mother. The metaphor precedes one of his more colorful rants against the hated Normans. "They should really be called the 'Nullimanni,'" he insists. They are the "most fetid turds in the world," who seek to subjugate the *castrum* of Saint Paul, and other parts of the empire. He then reminds the Teutons that Appius had declared war on the Carthaginians over Sicily, and implores them to do likewise, and to be the defenders of the Roman people and of Saint Paul. Finally, he asks plaintively why they (the Teutons) do not hurry and bring aid.[83] Benzo then reminds his listeners that the Greek emperor had placed at the feet of his lord (Henry) a massive treasury, amassed by the kings of Byzantium since the dawn of time. With Pantaleus and Cadalus mediating, he recalls, the great emperor had come in a quest for unity and peace. Saint Paul needs to be saved, he declares, from thieves and liars, buffoons, and jesters. Rome, he exhorts, must be purged of this putrid ferment by the hand of Cadalus, so we can bring the *basilieus* into our *communem conventum*.[84]

Slightly later, in 3.3, Benzo again tries to bolster the credibility of his story of Constantine's offer, this time in a letter he claims to have written to Adalbert, archbishop of Bremen.[85] First, he explains why, up until that point, he had not told anyone about the embassy from the Greeks. He explains to Adalbert that since his words seemed delirious and like a laughable piece of mythology, he had decided to keep quiet about the story.[86] This early section of the letter recalls the passage in the letter from Constantine in which the emperor tells Cadalus to keep the matter quiet, "claude sermones istos in pectore tuo." By keeping the embassy from Constantinople a secret, Benzo tells Adalbert, he has forgone the honor that he would have enjoyed had he publicized it. To justify his decision to now bring the embassy to light, he explains that it was Constantine himself who "snatched him from his silence." He therefore no longer wishes to suppress the communication that came to him from across the sea by way of the *patricius* of Amalfi (Pantaleus), addressed to Cadalus, "the elect of Saint Peter."

Benzo's letter to Adalbert, rather than supporting the veracity of the earlier letter from Constantine, offers further evidence of the lengths to which the

---

83. *Ad Hein.*, 3.1. "Fetidissima scilicet stercora mundi."

84. *Ad. Hein.*, 3.1. "expurgate per manus Kadali hoc putribile fermentum, quia sic potestis illum fere nostrum basileum Doclitium adducere ad communem conventum."

85. Sansterre, "Byzance et son souverain," 97.

86. *Ad. Hein.*, 3.3. "Quia mea verba videntur vobis deliramentum et veluti mythologiarum risibile figmentum, decreverum indicem hori imponere, ut immunis persisterem ob omni legationis honere."

panegyrist had gone to concoct his story of a Byzantine alliance proposal in support of Cadalus. Careful to insert himself into the middle of the situation, Benzo lists himself as the other addressee of Constantine's letter, along with Cadalus. This version of the alliance proposal offers far more details than does the letter in Book 2. Benzo describes how the message had been directed to the *portitores* of the boy king, presumably those who dealt with the revenues of the regime and the delegation of troops. The emperor had called on them to act as faithful Teutons and Latins by persuading the boy king to bring one hundred thousand troops to Apulia and Calabria and to supply them with twenty years' worth of food. In return, Constantine promised that one hundred ships from the Sea of Malfi would arrive with more treasure than could be found in all of Italy, unquantifiable amounts of money, horses, an abundance of gold and silver, and cloaks. Once he presents this parody of Byzantine diplomacy, Benzo appeals, once again, to the memory of previous Roman emperors who had rightly attended to the preservation of the empire.[87]

In a passionate admonishment of the young Henry concerning the state of the empire (in 3.13), Benzo yet again recalls the offer from Constantine, although this time his contention that the Greek emperor had offered as a hostage his own purple-born son is decidedly less dramatic. The offer, it now appears, was to treat Henry "as if" he were his own purple-born son, an offer more reminiscent of Notker's Emperor Michael. Benzo wishes that Henry would rise to the occasion and defend the empire, a task that includes acceptance of the Greek proposal. He even tries to claim that he himself had brokered the deal. Speaking directly to the young king, he explains that despite the difficulties in Rome, Henry has reached the age of puberty and must now show his strength by defending the realm that he has inherited from his father.[88] Addressing him as "Cesar Heinrice," Benzo calls on the boy to remember the emperors of the past, scolding him gently for having failed to break a sweat on behalf of the realm, while his predecessors had all done their share of sweating in their many fights. He repeats a familiar list of illustrious imperial predecessors, among them the Ottos and the Henrys who had fought to maintain Italy under their control.

After celebrating the way Henry III had made sure that the church was without the stain of rapaciousness, Benzo once again broaches the topic of Constantine's offer in the name of preserving the realm.[89] His promotion of

---

87. *Ad Hein.*, 3.3.
88. *Ad. Hein.*, 3.13.
89. *Ad. Hein.*, 3.13–14.

the Greek alliance remains a significant element of his campaign on behalf of Cadalus, whose acquisition of the Holy See is the linchpin of his plan for the defense of the empire and German triumph in Italy. "What is certain, O Caesar, is that the holy apostles do not cease to pray for you," he assures Henry, and then launches into another presentation of the Greek emperor's proposal. There are kings whom Henry ought to invite to help him, Benzo explains. Without even being asked, those kings, whom he describes as "unnamed," had already opened their treasuries and offered many gifts to Henry. Constantine Doclitius, king of Byzantium, had even offered to treat Henry as if he were his own purple-born son, Benzo reports to the adolescent king. This is a departure from the letter in Book 2, in which the Greek emperor offers his son as a hostage as part of the anti-Norman pact. Benzo has failed to keep his concocted stories straight. Finally, Benzo reminds him of the *amicitia* sought by the Greek emperor and assures him that the promises made in the letters can be fulfilled right away. He need only decide at what moment he wishes the fulfillment to happen. The offer, he insists, is a sign, not only that God and the apostles Peter and Paul are on his side, but that Apulia and Calabria have their doors open and await liberation.[90]

In an ultimate attempt to promote his personal role in the alleged Byzantine quest for imperial unity (in 3.24), Benzo stages a scene that further exposes the self-aggrandizing fantasy that he had developed around his role in the salvation of the empire. The passage includes his description of the moment at which, in a chamber with three attendants, he personally informed Henry of the offer that had come from the mouth of Constantine. When he had finished his story, Benzo recalls, the king jumped up, dissolved into tears, and beat his chest, thanking him for what he had done in the name of Rome: "O dearest brother bishop Benzo, may he who shines light on the day preserve you."[91] The king then sent legates to all corners of the realm with the announcement. As Seyffert notes, Benzo was an outsider.[92] He would not likely have enjoyed such an audience with the king, even if such an offer had indeed come from the East. Benzo is the only person to ever mention any of these encounters, which were, we may presume, the product of his own imagination.

Benzo's references to the proposed alliance with the Greeks throughout the *Ad Heinricum* are all related to his revision of the sibyl and to Charlemagne's explanation of the meaning of signs of future triumph in Book 1.

---

90. *Ad Hein.*, 3.14.
91. *Ad. Hein.*, 3.24.
92. *Ad Hein.*, 63.

They also echo the rhetoric of imperial unity in the "Exhortatio." Despite the appearance of the sibyl and Charlemagne's intervention in the segment added just before the presentation of the compilation in 1085, the forged letters from Byzantium and the "Exhortatio" demonstrate that Benzo had been writing Henry into a version of the Last Emperor prophecy since the 1060s.[93] As I argued earlier, even the revised prophecy bespeaks the earlier period when Benzo imagined himself to be the councilor of the boy king and protector of the interests of the empire during Henry's precarious adolescence. The interrelationships between the various thematically linked passages concerning Byzantium, including the "Exhortatio," also indicate that Benzo had been thinking about his promotion of Henry in sibylline terms for as long as he had been writing about the ideal of imperial unity under the Salians. Although he added the prophecy and the visit from Charlemagne to the beginning of the work, what we preserve now likely reflects an updated version of material produced much earlier, during the period when Benzo fancied himself at the forefront of the struggle between the imperial court and the reform papacy.

Panegyric Verse and Anti-Gregorian *Vituperatio*

Benzo returns to the rhetoric of Roman universalism in the sixth and penultimate book of the *Ad Heinricum*, displaying an energetic merging of imperial praise and antipapal invective. Book 6 contains a series of seven poems composed in various meters, the last of which credits Henry with surpassing all other emperors. In the years following Henry's excommunication in 1076, Benzo's imperialist fervor had grown, but the triumphal tone reflects more specifically the German king's capture of Rome in 1084. For Benzo, Henry had been appointed by God to rule the world as king and emperor after God, by the assent of the Roman people, and not the papacy.[94] The verses in book 6 represent his most florid celebration of Salian Roman *renovatio*, in which the panegyrist prefaces the verse encomium with some of his more infamous and clever expressions of vituperative hatred of the reform popes. Benzo's idealized emperor, as heir to Caesar, appears starkly juxtaposed to the heretical, conniving, and contemptible Pope Gregory VII. His Henry is also heir to a Charlemagne who was in no way beholden to the papacy for his title. By placing in succession his strongest antipapal rhetoric with his most elaborate articulation of the foreign embassy motif, Benzo employed the

---

93. Erdmann, "Endkaiserglaube," 403–5.
94. Robinson, *Authority*, 71–75.

rhetoric of *dominium mundi* to bring his antipapal discourse into the highest possible relief.

Benzo organizes the sequence of Book 6 in such a way that his expressions of Roman universalism for Henry are surrounded by anti-Gregorian vitriol. His antipapal rhetoric is overt, angry, and sometimes foulmouthed, directed mostly against Hildebrand himself. Benzo sets the anti-Gregorian tone in the prologue to the first poem, in which he claims to have been inspired on the birthday of Saint Andrew to write about the vices of *"Folleprandus Buzi vel Morticio,"* one of his various nicknames for his arch-nemesis. In the first poem, Benzo announces gleefully that Prandellus (also Hildebrand) actually proudly refers to himself as Antichrist. A bit further along, he calls Gregory a false monk and, in a play on the Son of Perdition, dubs the pontiff the *"Homo Perditissimus"* who sits in the temple of Peter.[95] The playfully wicked tone he reserves for discussion of Gregory is then contrasted with his unrestrained praise for Henry in a version of the parade of foreign nations that follows shortly after. Benzo establishes the theme of Roman *renovatio* under Henry in the opening section of the second poem, which he calls the *narratio.* He speaks of the moment of *translatio imperii* under Charlemagne when the Greek emperors lost Rome to the Franks, or, as he poetically describes it, when Lucretia opened the gates of Romulus to the Franks.[96] In a trajectory of imperial transfer that ties Henry to Charlemagne, Benzo credits the Carolingians with the conquests of Aquitaine and Spain, and then moves quickly through the rulers of the Ottonian dynasty and the Henrician kings before reaching the reign of his own subject. He then launches his complex and outlandish construction of the foreign embassy motif, after which begins another diatribe against Hildebrand. The invective as accompaniment to the panegyric verse is essential to his construction of Henry as a universal Roman emperor, for there was no greater threat to Benzo's concept of imperial authority than the papacy, and Hildebrand was, for him, the architect of its destruction.

In leonine hexameter with internal rhyme, Benzo incorporates the theme of Byzantine symbolic surrender and a reference to Constantine's gift of relics also mentioned by the voice of Charlemagne into an elaborate vision of vanquished nations appearing before him in chains. Just as he does with the earlier sibylline material in Book 1, Benzo uses the verses to characterize Henry's future triumph over the world as ordained by God: "It is clear that the ruler of rulers loves him; / Before Rome he gives to him the surrounding

---

95. *Ad Hein.*, 6, *Narratio* 2.
96. *Ad Hein.*, 6, *Narratio* 2.

kingdoms, / Africa and Sicily, and Byzantium which is the equal of Rome."[97]
In the earlier apparition, Charlemagne explains to Henry that Constantine's
gifts are a sign of Henry's future triumph as the standard-bearer of Christendom and conqueror of all enemies.[98] Here too, in recognition of his ceding
of imperial supremacy, the Greek emperor offers tribute in the form of relics
that are without equal on earth, familiar code for relics of the Passion: "The
Basileus sent to him many relics / Which are very useful for temples and
for wars. / No gifts on Earth are considered equal to these."[99] The triumph
over the Greeks, plainly defined here as a gift from God, once again appears
within his fashioning of a divinely elected ruler from the West as presider
over the Christian Roman Empire. Southern Italy, Sicily here, also figures as
one of the "nations" providentially given to Henry. The verses convey that
the surrender of foreign nations is providential, but the territories are specifically Africa, Sicily, and Byzantium, the last of which Benzo specifies as the
equivalent of Rome. This codicil concerning the Greeks makes clear that he
is not referring to the Macedonians, the third of the four empires in Jerome's
schema. Another inference to be drawn, though, is that the current Greeks,
with their competing claim to the Roman imperial dignity, have ceded to
the West, thereby resolving the divide of the post-800 age. In this way, Benzo
recasts the prose material from the early books, continuing in verse his promotion of an ideal of imperial continuity and integrity under Henry, while
decrying the evils of those who seek to thwart his plans.

Constantine's gift of relics becomes a part of Benzo's creative vision of
Byzantine surrender of authority to Henry, this time in the form of a poetic
translatio ad Germanos. The panegyrist conveys the promise of the sibyl in
verse when he writes: "Constantine selected him [Henry] for his command"
(Constantinus optat eum in suo imperio), which is a version of the alliance
proposal in the letter requesting troops and leadership from the West. The
preceding verse describes how foreign kings seek out the emperor "with
great desire."[100] The rhymed pair places Constantine among the eager foreign
kings who seek Henry's favor and offer their submission. Even though the
verse does not starkly indicate surrender, but instead alludes to it, the placement of the Greeks within the context of the foreign embassy topos as one
of the nations eager for an alliance nonetheless confirms their surrender of

97. *Ad Hein.*, 6, *Narratio* 4. "Clarum est, quod eum amat rector dominantium / Ante Romam
confert ei regna circumstantium / Africam Siciliamque, par Romae Bizancium."
98. *Ad Hein.*, 1.17.
99. *Ad Hein.*, 6, *Narratio* 4. "Basileus misit ei multa sanctuaria / Quae in templis seu bellis sat
sunt necessaria / Nulla dona super terram his habentur paria."
100. *Ad Hein.*, 6, *Narratio* 4. "Alieni volunt regem magno desiderio."

authority. Just as Einhard had allowed his reader to deduce the notion of Greek surrender based on the classical model he was imitating, Benzo also avoids a bold assertion, but achieves the same implication through use of an understood rhetorical context. The second of the two verses, the one concerning Constantine's choice of Henry to lead, is the equivalent of the phrase in the prophecy in which the sibyl promises that Henry will be crowned in the land of Bizas. And so, once again, Benzo conveys the ideal of the bloodless surrender of Byzantium, which is also found in the prophecy, in Charlemagne's explanation of the parallel signs, in the "Exhortatio," and in the letter from Constantine.

In the remaining verses of the poem, Benzo remembers Charlemagne's triumphs with references to famous victories, such as his conquest of the Saxons. Then, in the final couplet, he proclaims: "Let our descendants see this whole thing through a mirror / That you have made a New Rome and a new era."[101] The invocation of the mirror serves to reinforce the fact that the concessions of the Greeks, Sicilians, and Africans are meant to be seen as an expression of Roman universal dominion. In Books 1 and 6, Benzo is eager enough for his play of parallel signs of universal victory to be understood that he intervenes with explanatory devices. The voice of Charlemagne appears early on, to set the stage, while the exhortation to Henry's descendants to see the German emperor's deeds in a mirror appears closer to the end. Both remind the reader to view Henry's reign within the panegyric context of *dominium mundi*. After his entreaty to future generations to see the whole thing through a mirror, there is a clear break, after which Benzo begins a much more classical version of the parade of surrendering nations, this time in a more elaborate construction with a longer list of more far-flung peoples. Just before, Benzo had offered a post-800 version of the motif involving the ceding of supremacy to the West by the Byzantines, and so his return to a classical model signals his deliberate attention to both the classical pagan and the Christian imperial models of expression of universal dominion in praise of an emperor. In this regard, the pairing of the two versions of the motif can be interpreted as akin to the scepter described in the "Exhortatio" that embodies the imperial inheritances of both Caesar and Charlemagne, representatives, respectively, of Roman law and Christian sacred duty.

Benzo's classicized version of the foreign embassy motif opens with an address to Henry as Caesar, holder of the imperial scepter, and friend of divine law. The panegyrist then enumerates a long list of conquered peoples

---

101. *Ad Hein.*, 6, *Narratio* 4. "Videant posteri nostri totum hoc per speculum / Quod fecistis novam Romam atque novum seculum."

parading before Henry's new Rome with gifts and tribute.[102] The poet says of Rome and its relations to the rest of the world, "Having bowed to no one, they will come to you, Rome, with tribute / From many kingdoms without a murmur and without fraud."[103] Benzo's list of nations and exotic gifts reaches a level of strangeness that surpasses any of the previous versions we have considered, even the one found in the *Historia Augusta*. The scene is one of "*magna spectacula*," with ambassadors from all corners of the earth bringing gold, silver, cloaks, dyes, and animals, including mules, lions, dromedaries (which he distinguishes from camels with humps), ostriches, and more unusual creatures, such as "baby animals with black hair and little men with naked flesh."[104] Some of the elements of Benzo's elaborate parade plant striking images in the mind. It is hard to imagine precisely what he meant by "*nudae carnis homullos*," on parade as curiosities from the exotic East—perhaps pygmies, as one scholar proposes.[105] In recognition of the new Augustus, peoples arrive from many kingdoms, including the kings of Spain and Galicia, who receive special mention in numerous versions of the motif, and "one after the other rejoice in offering tribute." Spain figures prominently in Orosius's praise-filled construction of Augustus's dominion and his outdoing of Alexander, and, of course, Einhard uses King Alfonso as his surrendering Spaniard.[106] After Spain comes Carthage, preferring to pay the census rather than die, after which come other less well-known peoples such as the Allobroges, the Umbrians, the Cenomani, and the Sicambrians, all of whom willingly return to Rome and "admit that they have sinned." The poet concludes by calling for Rome to seek a great king, and to yield to him forever.[107]

The elaborate procession that Benzo creates may have been influenced by Widukind of Corvey's praise for his Saxon patrons. In his Ottonian-age chronicle, the arrival of ambassadors of the Greeks and Romans bearing tribute for the Saxon king signals the transfer of the Frankish hold of the Roman Empire to the Saxons. Widukind describes how the glorious emperor, after his many victories, received embassies from many fearful kings and peoples who sought his favor. Among them were ambassadors from the Romans,

102. *Ad Hein.*, 6.5.
103. *Ad Hein.*, 6.5. "In nullis nuta; venient tibi, Roma, tributa / De multis regnis sine murmure vel sine tegnis."
104. *Ad Hein.*, 6.5. "Pelle nigra pullos et nudae carnis homullos."
105. *Ad Hein.*, 6.5.
106. Orosius, *Hist.*, 6.21; Einhard, *VK*, 16.
107. *Ad Hein.*, 6.5. "Et pete nobiscum regem, qui cernit abyssum: Augustum talem concedat perpetualem."

Greeks, and Saracens, bearing "many diverse gifts of all sorts," including dyes, perfumes, and animals hitherto unseen in Saxony such as lions, camels, monkeys, and ostriches.[108] The list of exotic animals sent to Otto offers an explanation for Benzo's ostriches, and perhaps for the lion sent to Henry from Africa to which the voice of Charlemagne alludes in Book 1. Benzo took the art of restyling the surrender of foreign nations as a locus of imperial praise to new level of creativity.

Benzo and the *Descriptio*

It is difficult to imagine that Benzo did not know some version of the sibylline-influenced Charlemagne who travels to Jerusalem and Constantinople and achieves imperial unity by allying with a submissive Byzantium. If we compare the *Descriptio* to Benzo's constructions of Byzantine concessions of authority, some striking similarities come to the fore. In both works, relics from Byzantium function as Christianized forms of tribute that symbolize bloodless victory over the Greek East. Each contains a carefully staged scene describing the arrival of envoys bearing rhetorically similar letters from the Greek emperor. The letters in both cases involve a Constantine who calls on the West to provide military leadership to purge the empire of unwanted elements. As the voice of Charlemagne explains to Henry, gifts from the East are the sign that Henry will one day be the leader and standard-bearer of Christendom by the will of God. The message of the *Descriptio* concerning Charlemagne is essentially the same.

Although Benzo began to view Henry's reign through the prism of the sibylline prophecy from early on, the addition of the relics from Constantinople probably coincides with the writing of the verses in Book 6. His specific mention of relics from Constantinople occurs twice, once when Charlemagne explains the parallel exchanges with the East and again in the panegyric verses, both of which were written during the later period of composition and revision in the 1080s. Something had inspired Benzo to incorporate relics of the Passion into the symbolic surrender of imperial supremacy by the Greek East to the West, and the *Descriptio* as we know it could well have been a source of that inspiration. The fact that both works mention the *sudarium* is particularly striking. In the *Descriptio*, Constantine gives Charlemagne the *sudarium*, parts of the crown of thorns, a nail, and a

---

108. Widukind, *Rer. Gest.*, 3.56, *sub anno* 956. See also Karl J. Leyser, "Frederick Barbarossa, Henry II and the Hand of Saint James," in *Medieval Germany and Its Neighbours*, 215.

piece of the cross, among other relics.[109] Benzo's Charlemagne tells Henry, "The emperor Constantine sent you similar signs, namely parts of the *sudarium* of the Lord, the Cross, and the Crown of Thorns." The corresponding verse in the later book describes the same three relics.[110] The cross and the crown of thorns are two of the primary relics of the Passion, so it is not necessary to see much of a coincidence in their mention in both works, but the singling out of the *sudarium* is more noteworthy. It seems unlikely that Benzo would have had direct access to the *Descriptio* produced in France, so one wonders why he emphasizes the *sudarium*, which was so strongly tied to Saint-Corneille, and for which, as Gabriele notes, the *Descriptio* was the only justificatory document.[111]

A possible explanation for Benzo's knowledge of the *Descriptio* lies in his contacts with a French prelate and enemy of Gregory VII named Manasses, whom he encountered at the Salian court. The period of Henry's coronation and ultimate triumph over Gregory in the mid-1080s coincides with the dating of the *Descriptio* to around 1080. A transfer of relics had occurred at Saint-Corneille in 1079, and King Philip, who seems to have known the *Descriptio*, presided over the ceremony.[112] In 1081, Manasses, then the Archbishop of Reims and a leading ecclesiastical figure in France, lost his long battle with Gregory VII over charges of simony, and fled to the imperial court after being chased out of town by the people of Reims. In the preface to Book 6, Benzo speaks of the archbishop's presence at court in the spring of 1081, saying that Manasses, whom he refers to as "the noble and lettered Archbishop of Reims and legate of the venerable King Philip of France," was residing among them.[113] There is reason to think that Manasses and Benzo would have been drawn to one another. The Frenchman was a lover of poetry and also a famous thorn in the side of the pope whom Benzo hated so profoundly. Evidence shows that he had often been in the company of King Philip I, who had himself received angry, condemnatory letters from Gregory about his own conduct in the mid-1070s, and was not an ally of Rome.[114] Manasses could have known about the *Descriptio* story in some form, and been drawn to its imperialist rhetoric. He might then have shared

109. *Desc.*, 120.
110. *Ad Hein.*, 6, *Narratio* 4. See also Gabriele, *Empire of Memory*, 114–15. Folz notes that some of the relics named in the *Descriptio*, including the arm of Saint Simeon, had been named in the collection of relics at Aachen, which Henry had acquired around 1072; see *Le souvenir*, 181.
111. Gabriele, "Provenance," 101.
112. Ibid., 101.
113. *Ad Hein.*, 6, *Praefatio*.
114. John R. Williams, "Archbishop Manasses I of Rheims and Pope Gregory VII," *American Historical Review* 54 (1949): 805, 818–82.

that knowledge with Benzo. Since Benzo was keenly attuned to the symbolic power of gifts sent from the East to emperors in the West, it is easy to imagine why he might have integrated the relics to create a more enhanced version of Charlemagne's exchanges with the East into his nearly completed work.

By the end of the eleventh century, there had been a handful of rhetorically similar fictional letters concocted by Western authors in the name of the emperor of Byzantium. One famous example is the letter purporting to be from Alexius Comnenus to Robert of Flanders, written after the First Crusade. The letter abounds in ecclesiastical exhortations, and for many reasons is unlikely to be the work of an actual Byzantine emperor. The Piacenza letter, as it is often called, contains an imagined version of the Greek emperor's plea for help with an offer of many relics and treasures in return for assistance against the defilers of the Holy Sepulcher. Like Benzo's letter from Byzantium, it too has its defenders, who have argued, for instance, that the extant version is a Latinized version of a real letter in Greek.[115] Scholars have advanced similar theories about the existence of a real version of the letter of Prester John to Manuel Comnenus from 1165, a document that I discuss in detail in chapter 4. In that case, as well, no putative Greek original has ever been found. In fact, the consensus now is that the letter was concocted in the German imperial chancery. None of these missives is likely to have originated in Constantinople. Notker was the first to invent fictionalized diplomatic scenes between Constantinople and the new Frankish empire over the matter of the shared custody and protection of the Christian empire, and that tradition continued for centuries. Rather than looking for clues to the reality behind doubtful communiqués from the imperial East, we need to consider them as an ongoing rhetorical phenomenon within the literature of empire.

Conclusion

In the end, it is possible to tie together all of Benzo's variations on the rhetoric of Roman universalism expressed through the parade of surrendering foreign nations. Whereas the "Exhortatio" constitutes a poetic version of the anti-Norman material from the letter from Constantine, the later sibylline

---

115. M. de Waha, "La lettre d'Alexis I Comnène à Robert le Frison: Une révision," *Byzantion* (1977) 47: 113–12. Cf. Einar Johnson, "The Spurious Letter of Alexius," *American Historical Review* 55 (1949–50): 811–32; Colin Morris, *The Sepulchre of Christ and the Medieval West: From the Beginning to 1600* (Oxford, 2005), 166. Morris says the letter was definitely written by a Latin, perhaps around 1091. Giles Constable argues for composition between 1090 and 1105, based on Urban's sermons and Constantinople's relics catalog, as well as information available in Flanders; see "Forged Letters in the Middle Ages," in *Falschungen im Mittelalter*, vol. 5 (Hanover, 1988), 23.

material in Book 1 (the prophecy and Charlemagne explaining it) mirrors the versified panegyric verses in Book 6. Like those who had preceded him in elaborating Charlemagne's encounters with the East, Benzo combined imperial apocalyptic discourse with the representation of relics as signs of the transferred custody of Christendom from East to West. In this way, relics from the East become the peaceful guarantors of Roman continuity, serving as updated versions of Christianized tribute for the emperor. For Benzo, Charlemagne is Henry's imperial precursor, a Christian emperor who crushed the Saxons, drove the Lombards from Italy, and received symbolic gifts from the East in the name of reestablishing the integrity of the Christian Roman Empire. He is not the Charlemagne who protects the church in return for papal sanctioning of his secular authority. No longer simply the strong arm of the church, indebted to the Holy See for his titles, this Charlemagne is the divinely elected leader of all Christendom. In the age of the Investiture Contest, Benzo's sibyl-inspired exchanges with Byzantium enriched his vision of the Salian emperor as the sole inheritor of a united Christian Rome.

# CHAPTER 4

In Praise of Frederick Barbarossa

In the years following his imperial coronation in 1155, the German emperor Frederick I Barbarossa came into increasing conflict with the papacy. The late 1150s were also a time of heavy promotion of the Hohenstaufen Roman *renovatio,* during which propagandists for the emperor employed a variety of expressions of his universal authority. As the Archpoet proclaimed in the early 1160s after the siege of Milan: "Nobody in his right mind doubts that you, by the assent of God, were set up as the king above all other kings."[1] This first of two chapters exploring the rhetoric of Roman universalism during the reign of Frederick I considers works written prior to or around the time of the canonization of Charlemagne in 1165. With the exception of a passage from the end of the *Deeds of Frederick Barbarossa,* these works do not involve the promotion of the Carolingian emperor as an imperial antecedent to Frederick. Chapter 5 will attend to the role of Charlemagne in Hohenstaufen propaganda. I begin with the influential *Deeds* started by the emperor's uncle, Bishop Otto of Freising, and completed by the chronicler Rahewin. There follows an examination of the anonymous *Play of Antichrist,* and, finally, I look at documents tied to the imperial chancery, including the false Hillin of Trier letters and the letter of Prester John. All of these works address, in different ways, the Hohenstaufen inheritance

---

1. Archpoet, *Kaiserhymnus,* stanza 3.

of the Roman Empire. When taken together, however, they reveal how the discourse of *dominium mundi* continued to be constructed, as it had been for centuries, based on the sometimes awkward melding of the classical ideal of peaceful surrender and the violent end time scenario described in the sibylline tradition.

The promoters of Frederick Barbarossa, including the emperor himself, sought to style the Staufen leader as the next in the long line of Roman emperors, claiming for him a form of universal dominion based on the theory that his reign was a continuation of the Roman Empire.[2] Despite grandiose allusions to the German inheritance of the universal dominion of Augustus, the Roman Empire continued to be, as it had been for centuries, a primarily theoretical concept based on an idealized notion of the protection of all Christendom. In the *History of the Two Cities,* for instance, Otto of Freising speaks of the *patrocinium* or the protection of the whole world belonging to the emperor.[3] Such claims often clashed with papal pretentions to the primary role as guardians of a unified and universal Christendom. After his anointing by Pope Hadrian in 1155, Frederick publicized his belief that his power was God-ordained and had come by way of election by the German princes. His right to the imperial dignity was thus supported by God and Roman law, making him the protector of all Christian people as the vicar of Christ and king of kings on earth.[4] Those charged with praising Frederick provided multiple variations on the theme of his God-given universal authority, but as we shall see, they also addressed rival claims, namely those coming from the papacy and the Greeks.

---

2. Heinrich Appelt, "Friedrich Barbarossa und das Romische Recht," in *Friedrich Barbarossa,* ed. Günther Wolf (Darmstadt, 1975), 58–82; Hans Eberhard Mayer, "Staufische Welterherrschaft," in Wolf, *Friedrich Barbarossa,* 186–87. See generally *Staufisches Kaisertum im 12. Jahrhunder: Konzepte-Netzwerke-Politische Praxis,* ed. Stefan Burkhardt et al. (Regensburg, 2010), especially Burkhardt, "Barbarossa, Frankreich und die Weltherrschaft," 152–58; Roman Deutinger, "Imperiale Konzepte in der hofnahen Historiographie der Barbarossazeit," in Burkhardt et al., *Staufisches Kaisertum,* 25–39. Further bibliography can be found in Horst Furhmann, "*Quis Teutonicos constituit iudices nationum?* The Trouble with Henry," *Speculum* 69 (1994): 354–55.

3. Karl J. Leyser, "Frederick Barbarossa, Henry II and the Hand of Saint James," reprinted in *Medieval Germany and Its Neighbours,* 216.

4. Marcel Pacaut, *Frederick Barbarossa,* trans. A. J. Pomerans (New York, 1970), 57–58. See also Janet Nelson, "Kingship and Empire," in *The Cambridge History of Medieval Political Thought c. 350–c. 1450,* ed. J. H. Burns (Cambridge, UK, 1991), 249; Robert Folz, *Concept of Empire,* 102; Robert L. Benson, "Political *Renovatio:* Two Models from Roman Antiquity," in *Renaissance and Renewal in the Twelfth Century,* ed. Robert L. Benson and Giles Constable (Cambridge, MA, 1982), 359; Sverre Bagge, "German Historiography in the Twelfth Century," in *Representations of Power in Medieval Germany, 800–1500,* ed. Björn Weiler and Simon MacLean (Turnhout, 2006), 180–88; Michael McGrade, "*O Rex Mundi Triumphator:* Hohenstaufen Politics in a Sequence for Saint Charlemagne," *Early Music History* 17 (1998): 183.

Otto of Freising and the French Last Emperor

Benzo of Alba had provided a model for how a revised version of the Last Emperor prophecy could function within the rhetoric of Roman *renovatio.* Otto of Freising also integrated the prophecy into his praise for Frederick Barbarossa, but he did so in an unexpected manner. Instead of applying the prophecy to Frederick himself, Otto, who had studied for years in France, used his highly rhetorical prologue to the *Deeds* to deride a French interpretation of the Last Emperor prophecy that had been popular in the late 1140s, prior to the Second Crusade.[5] The prophecy had appeared in a mysterious letter, the text of which Otto claims to embed within his heavily classicized celebration of Frederick as the next in the long line of Roman emperors going back to antiquity. Written in figurative language, the letter of unknown origin was understood to promise to Louis VII of France the conquest of the entire East, a triumph that would include a journey to Jerusalem and Constantinople.[6] Once again, then, an adaptation of the prophecy of the Last Emperor occurs within an articulation of the rhetoric of Roman universalism in a biographical work produced during a period of imperial renewal.

Despite the condescending tone in which Otto recalls the prophecy and the overtly classical style of his prologue, Marjorie Reeves nonetheless uses the bishop as one of two noteworthy examples of authors in the twelfth century who took the sibyl's promises seriously. Despite its unorthodoxy, she argues, the prophecy of the last world emperor "was cherished not only by the crazy and the fanatical, but by sober historians and politicians."[7] A close reading of the prologue does not bear out her argument. Otto situates his discussion of the letter just after he places himself within the illustrious lineage of those who had recorded the deeds of valiant men in the past.[8] He praises the function of *res gestae,* and then positions himself as a chronicler of deeds in a manner that implies comparisons first between Frederick and Augustus, and then, by extension, between himself and those who had praised the providential

---

5. Otto wrote the first and second of the four books. See *The Deeds of Frederick Barbarossa, by Otto of Freising and His Continuator, Rahewin,* ed. and trans. Charles Christopher Mierow (New York, 1953), 6.

6. Wilhelm von Giesebrecht claimed to know a parchment version of a nearly simultaneous recording of the prophecy in France in 1147. He provides a longer, older one likely used by Otto, and then a shorter one; see *Geschichte der deutschen kaiserzeit,* vol. 4, ed. William von Giesebrecht and Bernhard von Simson (Leipzig, 1877–95), 502–4.

7. Reeves, *Influence of Prophecy,* 302.

8. *GF,* 351. "Omnium qui ante nos res gestas scripserunt haec, ut arbitror, fuit intentio virorum fortium clara facinora ob movendos hominum ad virtutem animos extollere, ignavorum vero obscura facta vel silentio subprimere vel, si ad lucem trahantur, ad terrendas eorumdem mortalium mentes promendo ponere."

peace under Augustus.[9] After establishing this literary link to the classical Roman past, Otto uses the Roman universality topos in a manner similar to what Suetonius, and later Orosius, had done for Augustus by equating his reign with a time of universal peace in the empire. He then further alludes to the classical version of the motif by declaring that peoples living during the reign of his prince tremble in awe under the weight of his *auctoritas.*[10] Proclaiming the whole world to be at peace under Frederick's rule, Otto describes the submission of fearful peoples in the East:

> Therefore I judge those writing at this time to be happy in a certain way, for after a time of troubles, not only does an unheard of serenity of peace shine again, but the authority of the Roman Empire is so strengthened by the virtues of the most victorious prince that the people living under his rule rest humbly in silence, and the barbarian or the Greek living outside his realm trembles, impressed by the weight of his authority.[11]

In an otherwise traditional version of the motif, Otto divides the foreign peoples of the world into two categories, the *barbarus* and *grecus,* thereby interjecting a post-800 detail that serves to assert the transfer of empire from the Greeks to the Germans by placing the Greeks among the trembling foreign nations.

Otto then enhances his celebration of Frederick's Roman renewal with an intricate disparagement of the universalizing pretentions behind the Capetian-friendly version of the Last Emperor prophecy. In a thinly veiled reference to the failed Second Crusade, the bishop associates a recent period of turbulence in the empire with Louis VII, one of the two leaders of the expedition. He describes the endeavor unflatteringly as the time when the Western world,

---

9. Mierow, *Deeds,* 4. Karl F. Morrison characterizes Otto's *History of the Two Cities* from the mid-1140s as morose, eschatological, and focused on the Last Judgment during a time of imperial decline, whereas he sees the *Deeds* as optimistic about better things to come under Frederick; see "Otto of Freising's Quest for the Hermeneutic Circle," *Speculum* 55 (1980): 207. See also Peter Munz, *Frederick Barbarossa: A Study in Medieval Politics* (Ithaca, NY, 1969), 140; Dominique Boutet, "De la *translatio imperii* à la *finis saeculi:* Progrès et décadence dans la pensée de l'Histoire au moyen âge," in *Progrès, réaction, décadence, dans l'Occident médiéval,* ed. Emmanuèle Baumgartner and Laurence Harf-Lancner (Geneva, 2003), 37.

10. *GF, Prologus.*

11. *GF, Prologus.* "Unde hoc tempore scribentes quodammodo iudico beatos, dum post turbulentiam preteritorum non solum pacis inaudita reluxit serenitas, sed et quod ob victoriosissimi principis virtutes tanta Romani imperii pollet auctoritas, ut et sub eius principatu gens vivens humiliter silendo conquiescat et barbarus quique vel Grecus, extra terminus ipsius positus, auctoritatis eius pondere pressus contremiscat."

inspired by "the spirit of the pilgrim God," took up arms against the peoples of the East. This interjection concerning the discord in the world before Frederick's reign constitutes a deliberate disruption of his otherwise conventional encomium, so that he may engage in a bit of its rhetorical opposite, denunciation, of his Gallic neighbors. He then distances himself from his own allusion to the crusade by exhorting his audience not to conclude that he himself believes in any such a thing as "a pilgrim God." Although the term appears in his writing, he assures his reader that he simply borrowed it from the letter that was so "widely read in France in those days."[12]

The letter that he derides is not insignificant for Otto, however, since he features it conspicuously in his prologue to the *Deeds*, where praise for his nephew is the fundamental aim. The reproduction of the oracle concerning Louis's future triumph over the entire East follows just after a brief version of the topos of surrendering nations. The appearance of the prophecy in the otherwise traditional opening thus creates a noticeable stylistic break, which serves to bring the classical nature of his praise for Frederick into higher relief. His addition of the Last Emperor prophecy creates a juxtaposition of two competing models of universal peace in the empire at work in the prologue, both of which are eschatological. One is the providential Augustan peace, the peace praised by Orosius, while the other is the promised reunification to be achieved through violent conquest that is foretold for the last Roman emperor. The encomiast thus creates a comparison between Frederick and the current Augustan-style state of harmony and the French-led calamity in the East, which he ties to the Last Emperor prophecy. The German king, Conrad III, who was the other royal participant in the failed expedition, merits no mention, although both he and Louis had been conspicuous leaders. After celebrating the restoration of peace under Frederick, Otto reveals that he recognizes his decision to write the *Deeds* at that particular moment to have been a providential choice. Indeed, he had even taken up his pen at some point earlier, but then, for inexplicable reasons, had put it down and postponed his writing, as if he had been waiting for the enduring peace that would come under the mightiest of princes of the Roman world.[13] His highlighting of the chaos in the world when Louis tried to take the helm thus serves to enhance his praise for the universal peace under Frederick.

Otto gives a brief paraphrase of the letter containing the prophecy, in which he explicitly ties the French to a predicted triumph over the entire East: "In the course of this letter, in veiled language concerning the storming

---

12. *GF, Prologus.*
13. *GF, Prologus.*

of a royal city and indeed of ancient Babylon, in the manner of Cyrus King of the Persians or of Hercules, a triumph over the entire East was promised to the above-mentioned Louis, King of the Franks."[14] After the summary, he reproduces the letter. In a mystical version of the sibylline prophecy, the missive addresses "L," *pastor corporum,* who is understood to be Louis, and begins with a series of symbolic descriptions using geometric shapes. When L has arrived "at the side of an eternal seated square" and "at the side of eternal standing squares" and finally "to the product of the blessed number plus the first cube," he should raise himself to the place where the angel (or son, as Giesebrecht prefers) of his mother promised to visit, but did not. If we read the two geometrically defined sites as Constantinople and Jerusalem, as Giesebrecht does, the prophecy constitutes a forecast journey to Jerusalem and Constantinople with a conquest of the entire East by a Frankish leader. The passage continues, but with less *involucrum,* as the oracle tells Louis to plant his rose-colored standard as far as the outmost labors of Hercules, at which point the gates of city B (Babylon) will open for him. After directing him to plant his flag in the far reaches of the East, the letter describes Christendom as a ship on the brink of sinking. There is hope, however, in that the bridegroom has made L the mainsail of that ship. Atop that ship will be a triangular sail, so that "he who preceded you may follow you." It finally promises that his L will turn into a C, which is taken to mean that Louis will emulate Cyrus, the king of the Persians, and even become a new C, leader of the Orient, and conqueror of Babylon.[15]

At this point in the prologue, Otto has already alluded to the failure of the expedition, so the reproduction of the letter promising victory is intended to be read against what had already proved to be defeat. Louis traveled to Jerusalem and Constantinople, but did not succeed in uniting the empire by defeating Babylon. The object of Otto's disapproval is not the French king himself, however, but the clerics who appear to have embraced the prophecy. He lambastes those who believed in the oracle's promises, conveying his surprise that so many respected French religious authorities had believed the letter to be of sibylline origin.[16] The bishop then sets forth a challenge

14. *GF, Prologus.* "In cuius scripturae tenore sub quodam verborum involucro de expugnatione regiae urbis necnon et antiquae Babylonis et ad instar Ciri regis Persarum vel Herculis totius orientis triumphus prefato Ludewico Francorum regi promittebatur."

15. *GF, Prologus.* Cf. *HdDC,* 8.20.

16. Some have speculated that the reference is to Bernard of Clairvaux. See McGinn, *"Teste David cum Sibylla,"* 28–29; Hans-Dietrich Kahl, "Crusade Eschatology as Seen by St. Bernard in the Years 1146–1148," in *The Second Crusade and the Cistercians,* ed. Michael Gervers (New York, 1992), 35–36.

to those who had spread the letter's message, calling on those prophets who propagated its contents to make a decision concerning its relationship to the recent failed expedition to the East. He presses them to determine "whether at some point in the future it [the prophecy] is expected to be fulfilled, or, as a thing to be scorned, since it was not fulfilled, the fact that it was able to have any credibility is to be imputed to Gallic credulity."[17] Either way, the underlying message is that true universal leadership lies with Frederick's Roman peace, which was won by Roman virtue.

There follows a cryptic statement in which Otto recognizes the fact that something had in fact motivated the mass expedition: "Knowing such a thing as this, it was not without some measure of reason that the spirit that sent nearly all of the peoples of the West on a pilgrimage was called the 'spirit of the pilgrim God' as much by us as by it [the letter]."[18] Otto had been quick to assert his utter lack of belief in the concept of the "pilgrim God," but he still needed to account for the mass participation of the Christian West in the expedition. To resolve this problem, he divides the term into "spirit" and "pilgrim God," admitting that indeed some sort of "spirit" had been involved. Just as "Eurus brings forth rain," he explains, great men donned pilgrims' garb because of God. By carefully parsing the term, he separates the Christian "spirit" that inspired the Second Crusade from the idea of the "pilgrim God." This allows him to mock the very idea of such an entity, which he ties to the French attempt to attribute potential Last Emperor status to their king, while still acknowledging the godly origins of the expedition. In doing so, he reasserts the fundamental message of his prologue, that universal Christian authority and the achievement of peace in the empire are tied to the German emperor.

Otto ends his digression on the prophecy by declaring that he is living in a time of peace after a period of turbulence, and attributes the improvement to Roman renewal under Frederick, who reigns over an Augustan-style peace.[19] He boastfully concludes that times are now much better, and therefore the moment has come to celebrate the achievements of the most famous of the *Augusti*. This is a task, Otto tells his reader, which he will accomplish by imitating Roman biographical style. His digression about the oracle had created a dramatic stylistic departure, as Otto all but admits here. The promise of a

---

17. *GF, Prologus.* "Sed quisquis fuit ille propheta seu trotannus, qui hoc promulgavit, videat, si in futura adhuc aliqua expeditione implendum expectetur, aut tamquam iam non impletum conculcandum Gallicanae levitati, quod fidem aliquam habere potuit, imputetur."

18. *GF, Prologus.* "hoc tantum sciens, quod non sine rationis proportione spiritus ille omnes pene occidentales in peregrinationem mittens spiritus peregrini Dei tam a nobis quam ab illo vocatus est."

19. *GF, Prologus.*

return to the classical model for the rest of the work reminds the reader of the unusual nature of the digression, thereby highlighting the otherness of the French prophecy and its failed promise of universal victory. The conclusion to the prologue thus reaffirms the association between peace and Frederick as compared to Louis and tumult in the Christian world. Otto is therefore able to twist the knife in the wound for the French by evoking both the failure of the Second Crusade and Louis's failure to fulfill the prophecy, while also realigning Frederick with his glorious predecessors from antiquity.

Otto may have been responding to a growing tendency to recast the Tiburtina's predictions to favor a variety of different origins for the Last Emperor, including French origins. The forecast change of initials from L to C to convey Louis's future assumption of the rule of the entire East reflects the way that scribes updated the regnal lists in the sibyls according to changing political circumstances. Kings were indicated by their initials, which made it easier to manipulate the documents to reflect the times. In the eleventh century, this was a practice most often associated with prophecies related to the role of the German empire in the eschatological progression of Christian history,[20] but the letter that Otto cites is evidence of attempts to apply the prophecy to the French king. Rather than defending a German claim to Last Emperor status, however, Otto returned to the Orosian ideal of universal peace in the empire.

In his complex presentation of the oracle concerning Louis, Otto was either criticizing adherence to the prophecy itself or else deriding the Gallic attempt to appropriate what he saw as German prerogatives. On one hand, there is little to suggest that he was motivated by a jealous desire to remind the French of the German claim to the future Last Emperor. Barbarossa's modern biographer Peter Munz argues, however, that there may have been real hope in Staufen circles that the Last Emperor would be Frederick, but the evidence he musters for this claim is Otto's own "preoccupation" with the prophecy as well as its general popularity. He states: "We cannot avoid the conclusion that Frederick, well acquainted with the ancient prophecy, was confirmed in his belief that he was to be the Last Emperor."[21] Such a conclusion, especially with Otto's prologue as the primary evidence, is not inevitable. Otto does not convey any desire to portray Frederick as a Last Emperor figure. In fact, his emphasis on Roman models, both imperial and biographical, conveys quite the opposite.

---

20. Kampers, *Die Deutsche Kaiseridee*, 49–53; Holdenried, *Sibyl*, 10–17.
21. Munz, *Frederick*, 31.

Frederick himself may have nurtured a long-standing desire to go on crusade again, but that does not mean that he dreamed of shepherding humanity in its final days. The emperor's own plans, which did not materialize until after 1187, are not at issue here, though. At stake is the use of imperial eschatology in constructions of praise for Roman renewal. As I showed in the previous chapter, Benzo's melding of the sibylline prophecy with classical and Carolingian motifs of Roman universalism was both political and literary in that it served as a tool of praise for Henry's preservation of the Salian empire. Otto similarly juxtaposes a version of the Last Emperor prophecy with his own adaptations of classical motifs, and he too reveals an essentially scholarly and propagandistic approach to imperial apocalyptic discourse. If anything, he disparages the universalizing pretensions of the crusading movement and the clerics who promoted it in the 1140s. Benzo's and Otto's works both demonstrate that the expression of conflicting models of universal dominion functioned as an element of the rhetorical project of Romanizing the German regime in power.

Otto had, no doubt, intended his prologue to be a slight against those who applied the Last Emperor prophecy to the French king, but he was not charging the French monarch himself with trying to usurp the status of universal Roman emperor. His aim appears, instead, to have been a ribbing of members of learned circles for buying into the promises of the oracle. Had he wanted to assert Last Emperor status for Frederick, as the major propagandist for the emperor, he could have done so. Instead, Otto could not have been clearer in his affirmation of a classical vision of *dominium mundi,* although this does not mean that he was necessarily against the use of prophecy in general. The Erythraean Sibyl had enjoyed his esteem for her prediction of the coming of Christ in 8.8 of the *History of the Two Cities.* He also believed that the Germans were the inheritors of Rome as the last of the Four Kingdoms, and even provides extensive commentary on Antichrist and the *Discessio* in Book 8 of the *Two Cities.* He was therefore no stranger to imperial apocalyptic themes; he simply did not apply the Last Emperor prophecy to Frederick.

Rahewin

Whereas Charlemagne barely figures in Otto's *Deeds,* the bishop's continuator Rahewin elected to close the work with an adaptation of Einhard's version of the foreign embassy topos. In the final paragraphs, Rahewin paints Frederick as a new Charlemagne by closely imitating Einhard's description of the character, habits, and appearance of his subject.[22] When he describes

---

22. See Mierow, *Deeds,* 331–34.

how Frederick extended his kingdom, the biographer emphasizes that the emperor rebuilt many churches originally constructed by Charlemagne. Although the metaphor is implied rather than explicit, Rahewin is also building, using material about Frederick, on the edifice that was Charlemagne's biography originally built by Einhard. After the enumeration of what would qualify as "deeds in war," and after detailing Frederick's building projects, Rahewin turns to the equivalent of the "deeds in peace" section and rewrites Einhard's chapter 16, adapting it to conform to current events:

> Although the kings of Spain, England, France, Denmark, Bohemia, and Hungary had always been suspicious of his power, Frederick so bound himself to them through friendship and alliance that as often as they sent him letters and envoys, they declared that they yielded to him the authority to rule, and that they did not lack the will to obey. He asked of Manuel, the emperor of Constantinople, who sought friendship and alliance with him from a further distance and called himself Emperor of the Romans in the manner of his predecessors, that he refer to himself as Emperor not of Rome, but of New Rome.[23]

This scene was inspired by the real events of an international courtly gathering before the emperor at Würzburg in 1157. As Karl Leyser argues, the biographer had constructed the scene to give substance to Otto's claims to Frederick's role as protector of the whole world.[24] This is certainly true, and he does so by rewriting the foreign embassy topos as Einhard had employed it. As part of this manipulation, Rahewin recasts the memory of relations in the East as they appear in the ninth-century biography. There is no analogue to Harun and the non-Christian East, however. The intrigue of the passage lies instead in Rahewin's depiction of relations with the Greek emperor, in which Frederick is said to have asked Manuel to stop calling himself *imperator Romanorum* and to essentially share the imperial title by distinguishing between Old Rome and New Rome. The topos of the surrendering leader from the East thus becomes, in 1160, an explicit locus of compromise between the two sides of the empire, rather than an ambiguous suggestion of Byzantine surrender.

---

23. *GF,* 4.76. "Reges Hispaniae, Angliae, Franciae, Daciae, Boemiae atque Ungariae, quamvis suspectam semper eius haberent potentiam, sibi adeo per amicitiam et societatem devinxit, et ad suam voluntatem sic inclinatos habet, ut quoties ad eum litteras vellegatos miserint, sibi cedere auctoritatem imperandi, illis non deesse voluntatem obsequendi denuncient. Imperatorem Constantinopolitanum Manuel, ultro amicitiam et societatem eius expetentem, cum sese, sicut antecessores sui, Romanorum appellaret imperatorem, inflexit, ut se non Romae, sed Neoromae vocet imperatorem."

24. Leyser, "Frederick Barbarossa," 216. He notes that imperializing Anglo-Saxon and Anglo-Norman kings of the eleventh century used it as well.

The discussion of Manuel also recalls Anselm of Besate's unexpected addition of Byzantine capitulation to his version of the Vergilian parade of surrendering nations in the *Rhetorimachia* from a century earlier. Promoters of German emperors seem to have understood from early on that the attribution of universal authority, even the most rhetorically constructed versions, needed a codicil concerning the relative status of the rival Byzantines.

Otto's opening comparison of Frederick to Augustus and Rahewin's elision of Frederick with Charlemagne represent two distinct approaches to conveying the German inheritance of the Roman Empire in a biographical context. The differences between the prologue and the final passages of the *Deeds,* with their two separate authors, reveal significant changes in the construction of the imperial image in the period after Otto's death in 1158 and during the early years of Frederick's conflict with the papacy. Compared to Charlemagne, Augustus was a Roman imperial antecedent less fraught with issues of imperial lineage and shared authority, which is one explanation for the Frankish king's near total absence from Otto's contribution to the *Deeds.*[25] This absence stands in striking contrast to the promotion of the Hohenstaufen emperor during the period of Charlemagne's canonization, an event orchestrated by Frederick's adviser and arch-chancellor, Rainald of Dassel. Rainald exerted crucial influence over intellectual life at the Staufen court until his death in 1167, and it has even been proposed that he was responsible for having Otto write the *Deeds.*[26] Rahewin, also under Rainald's watchful eye, was probably finishing the work in the early 1160s, the period of Rainald's escalation of the detailed imperial program that would lead to the canonization in 1165.[27] The decision to close the biography with an homage to Einhard likely reflects the early stages of the initiative under way at the Staufen court to make Charlemagne the patron saint of Frederick's *sacrum imperium*.

Foreign Embassies and the *Ludus de Antichristo*

Otto of Freising had made sport of the popularity of a pro-French version of the Last Emperor prophecy, while depicting his nephew as a new Augustus. By contrast, an apocalyptic drama known as the *Play of Antichrist*

---

25. *GF,* 2.3. One example is his description of Frederick's royal coronation in 1152 when the then duke sat in the throne placed there by Charlemagne.

26. Joachim Bumke, *Courtly Culture: Literature and Society in the High Middle Ages* (Berkeley, CA, 1991), 462–63.

27. Peter Godman, *The Silent Masters: Latin Literature and Its Censors in the High Middle Ages* (Princeton, NJ, 2000), 200, 218.

(*Ludus de Antichristo*) presents a spectacular, if sometimes equivocal, version of the oracle's message, a version that is largely accepted to be a piece of pro-imperial propaganda.[28] Likely composed at the Bavarian abbey at Tegernsee between 1159 and 1162, the play depicts the Germans at the helm of the Fourth Kingdom as the end time approaches.[29] As a dramatic celebration of the *translatio ad Teutonicos,* the play stakes a loud and unambiguous claim for the primacy of the Germans over the Franks, the Greeks, and everyone else as leaders of the Christian Roman Empire. The *Ludus* dramatizes the conquests of the German emperor and his unification of the empire prior to relinquishing the symbols of his power at Jerusalem. But, as we have seen with previous expressions of universal empire, this work also confronts the competing articulations of Roman universalism that pitted the violent con-quests of the sibylline tradition against the classical ideal of elicited surrender. Likewise, imperial eschatology and the discourse of *dominium mundi* function in the *Play of Antichrist,* as they have elsewhere, primarily as imperial rhetoric rather than as chiliastic speculation.[30]

The earliest of the Antichrist dramas, the play is based on Adso's tenth-century letter, which the author may have known through Lambert of Saint Omer's *Liber Floridus.*[31] As Gerhard Günther notes, the author introduces a vision opposite to that of Adso, since the German emperor is not holding on precariously during a time of threatened *discessio,* but rules instead at a time when the theory of universal monarchy is alive and powerful.[32] The work is unusual in both its format and subject matter with its mixture of the non-liturgical Last Emperor narrative in the first half with the Antichrist story that constitutes the second half. The text combines sung verse and prose passages, with the latter providing a third-person narrative and stage

---

28. Furhmann, "*Quis Teutonicos,*" 362.

29. Schein notes the temptation to tie the play to the *Laetere* Jerusalem events at Mainz when Frederick took the cross in 1188; see *Gateway,* 154. Franco Cardini defends a date of 1159–1160 and refutes theories of a later date of 1188. He also pictures the mise-en-scène occurring in the basilica at Aachen; see "Il 'Ludus de Antichristo' e la teologia imperiale di Federico I," in *Mito e realtà del potere nel teatro: Dall'Antichità classica al Rinascimento: Atti del Convegno di studi del Centro di Studi sul Teatro Medievale e Rinascimentale (Roma, 29 ottobre–1 novembre 1987),* ed. M. Chiabò–F. Dogli (Rome, 1988), 182–83. Munz speculates that it was related to events in 1152, in *Frederick,* 376–77. Cf. Gerhard Günther, *Der Antichrist: Der staufische Ludus de Antichristo* (Hamburg, 1970), 37, 59; Bernard McGinn, *Antichrist: Two Thousand Years of the Human Fascination with Evil* (New York, 2000), 133–34.

30. Kampers, *Die Deutsche Kaiseridee,* 60–61.

31. McGinn notes the author's awareness of the major apocalyptic authors such as Adso and Pseudo-Methodius, in *Antichrist,* 133–34. See also Schein, *Gateway,* 154; Daniel Verhelst, "Les textes eschatologiques dans le *Liber Floridus,*" in Verbeke, Verhelst, and Welkenhuysen, *Use and Abuse of Eschatology,* 301; Penelope Mayo, "The Crusaders under the Palm: Allegorical Plants and Cosmic Kingship in the *Liber Floridus,*" *Dumbarton Oaks Papers* 27 (1973): 29–67.

32. Günther, *Der Antichrist,* 55.

directions.[33] Among the characters, we find a series of kings, their messengers, biblical prophets, and members of the various armies, as well as allegorical characters. The drama begins with the establishment of the supremacy of the German king over all other kings as Roman emperor and ultimately depicts him as a liberator of Jerusalem who has united all other nations in pursuit of that endeavor.[34] The second part is a more traditional eschatological drama about the coming of Antichrist and his eventual destruction by divine intervention in the temple at Jerusalem.

The opening scene depicts the establishment of Teutonic world domination through a series of embassies, and, in fact, much of the intrigue of the early part of the play is composed of ambassadorial exchanges between the emperor and the various kings whose submission he wishes to elicit. The stage directions describe seven royal seats. To the east are those of *Synagoga* and the king of Jerusalem. To the west is the seat of the emperor of the Romans, which is surrounded by the seats of the kings of the Teutons and the Franks, a scene that serves as a visual metaphor of the competition within the West for the imperial throne. To the south are the seats of the kings of the Greeks, the Babylonians, and *Gentilitas.* The Babylonians and *Gentilitas,* the non-Christian representatives of the East, open the drama by singing the praises of the ancient polytheistic system while condemning belief in one god, a chorus that the Jews then join by announcing that salvation in the name of Christ is in vain. The figure of *Ecclesia* then enters, flanked by her rival protectors, on the left by the pope and clergy, and on her right by the emperor of the Romans. When the various kings and allegorical figures take their seats, there is one left vacant, that of the king of the Teutons, who will serve as the emperor of the Romans until his abdication, when he lays down his regalia in Jerusalem.

In a maneuver reminiscent of the life of Aurelian in the *Historia Augusta,* the playwright depicts the reverse of the parade of surrendering nations by having the emperor send his own envoys to demand the submission of foreign kings. In the staging of the scene, the Roman emperor is surrounded by foreign kings, to whom he sends messengers charged with forcing universal recognition of his supreme authority. Unlike imperial propagandists such as Benzo, however, who had chosen to pacify the Last Emperor tradition by envisioning the surrender of the East, the playwright remains faithful to the

33. *Ludus de Antichristo,* ed. Karl Young, in *The Drama of the Medieval Church* (Oxford, 1962); *The Play of Antichrist,* ed. and trans. John Wright (Toronto, 1967).

34. Klaus Aichele, "The Glorification of Antichrist in the Concluding Scene of the Medieval 'Ludus de Antichristo,'" *Modern Language Notes* 91 (1976): 424; Kampers, *Die Deutsche Kaiseridee,* 61; McGinn, *Visions,* 133.

sibylline projection that the emperor will conquer all of his enemies. When the various kings refuse the orders of the messengers to submit, the Roman emperor quickly conquers them. The peaceful nature of the foreign embassy motif, a familiar expression of *dominium mundi* that had appeared in the recently published *Deeds,* is thus turned on its head.

The *Play of Antichrist* emerged during the period of intense cultivation of Frederick's projection of an *imperium sacrum,* but those years were also marked by his conflict with the papacy and by a series of diplomatic contretemps with the French kingdom. Only one full manuscript remains, so it is difficult to discern how well the play was known.[35] Contemporaries of Otto of Freising had used the Antichrist legend for reformist attacks on the empire, so appropriation of the apocalyptic theme in favor of the emperor may have been a response in kind to such denunciations.[36] Some critics have tried to remove the play from any specific historical context, but the drama is best interpreted in light of Hohenstaufen efforts to fashion Frederick as a Christian Roman emperor.[37] With its over-the-top portrayal of the German emperor figure, the play is certainly not pure promotion, however. Praise for emperors, rhetorically speaking, was not meant to be unalloyed, a precept that applies to other forms of promotion of an emperor beyond just *res gestae* or biography.[38] Moreover, it is clear that the discourse of Roman universalism continued to be of interest to clerics and scholars steeped in the rhetorical traditional of imperial praise.

Since the *Play of Antichrist* drew on sources that promised that the Last Emperor would be a Frank, the dramatization of the assertion of German imperial supremacy required some revision. The author needed to refuse somehow Adso's promise that the Last Emperor would be a Frank by creating a new narrative that would depict the Last Emperor as a Teuton. The play fulfills that need by enacting the dramatic crushing of the *rex Francorum* as a central feature of its assertion of Last Emperor status for the *rex Teutonicorum.*[39] The king of the Franks is the first to receive envoys from the Roman emperor / German king, an encounter that eliminates the German

35. Kampers believed that it was popular; see *Die Deutsche Kaiseridee,* 61. See also Wright, *Play,* 24; Fuhrmann, "*Quis Teutonicos*," 346; Zeller, "Les rois de France," 278.

36. McGinn, *Antichrist,* 133.

37. Wright, *Play,* 31, and Aichele, "Glorification," 425, argue against the connections to political reality. Günther argues that it was meant as an allegory of imperial favor at court, in *Der Antichrist,* 60. Cf. Cardini's view, in "Il 'Ludus,'" 187, that the play is an example of political propaganda through theater.

38. See Kempshall, *Rhetoric,* 165–67.

39. In the tenth century the term "*rex Francorum*" designated the Franks in general, but by the twelfth century only the French were using it. The Germans had stopped using the term after Henry IV; see Zeller, "Les rois de France," 277.

emperor's rival in the West and establishes him as the rightful holder of the title of Roman emperor. In the message that he sends with the envoys, the emperor declares, on the authority of historians, that the whole world was once a Roman fief, but that power was squandered.[40] He then demands tribute from each king "according to ancient custom." The *gens Francorum* are an exception, he admits, for they are strong in war and will therefore be allowed to serve the empire in arms, while still being forced to do homage and pledge fealty. The envoys announce, by the order of the supreme empire, that the Frankish king must bow to Roman law, and then summon him into the emperor's service.

To attain his status as the rightful emperor of the world, the German king must gain Frankish recognition of his universal authority. The Frankish king staunchly refuses, invoking historians to support his assertion that the empire has no hold over the Franks. He then vows that the Franks will never bow to the thieving army that seeks to take the empire. The ambassadors report back to their master about the haughty behavior of the Franks who oppose his majesty and weaken his rule, encouraging him to respond by showing them his wrath. The emperor promises to destroy the Franks, stating that if they will not obey him as soldiers, they will soon learn to be his slaves. He swiftly conquers the *rex Francorum,* who is forced to follow him back to the throne and sing for mercy, promising to obey the emperor's command as he begs to keep his crown. The emperor accepts the Frankish oath of homage, allowing the defeated king to keep his kingdom and his royal name as compensation for recognizing his claim to the imperial title. The Frankish king returns to his kingdom, where he sings of his new veneration for the glory of Rome's name and of how he proudly serves its Caesar, whose power is supreme.[41]

The figure of the king of the Franks in the play is at one point charged with the crime of *superbia,* a characterization that has drawn the attention of scholars seeking to tie the play to German relations with the Capetian monarchy. Contemporary tensions could have certainly enhanced enjoyment of the production in imperial circles, but scholars have overstated the direct correlations between the *rex Francorum* and Louis VII. Gaston Zeller, noting that Otto's prologue and the play both contain unfavorable (indirect) allusions to the French king, summons both works as evidence of a reaction on the part of the Germans to the excessive pride of the French under

40. *Ludus,* 373.
41. *Ludus,* 374.

Louis VII.[42] This argument is overly literal with regard to the play, and is simply not borne out by Otto's prologue. The emperor's uncle uses Louis's failure in the East as a foil for Frederick's theoretical achievement of imperial unity and universal peace, while the play enacts the conquest of the world by a German Last Emperor, which includes the crushing of the Franks. These are related rhetorical strategies having to do with the German assertion of universal Roman authority within the context of imperial propaganda. The transfer of empire to the Teutons signified supremacy over the Franks and the Greeks, a scenario related to Adso's promise concerning the stewardship of the Fourth Kingdom that was replayed in various ways over the centuries. Contemporary feelings about the French in the early 1160s need not have been a significant subtext for the play.

Likewise, the defeat of the king of the Franks in this allegorical play ought not to be interpreted as an articulation of Hohenstaufen intentions to conquer their sovereign neighbors. Robert Benson, offering the play as an example of Hohenstaufen inclinations, argues that despite the de facto independence of the surrounding kingdoms, there was still a sense that Frederick might try to extend his empire to match the boundaries of the ancient empire.[43] It is true that Frederick believed that his right to the imperial dignity had been supported by God and Roman law, and that his model of imperial authority presumed the inferiority of other national monarchies, but he did not actually challenge the sovereignty of surrounding kingdoms. Whatever fears of Frederick's intentions may or may not have haunted his rivals in other kingdoms, in his quest to project an image of universal empire, he never disputed the sovereignty of France, Spain, or England. His notion of universality was one of authority and protection in the Christian community, and did not involve any actual capitulation of other leaders.[44]

Although Frederick did not claim sovereignty over the French, there were some infamous diplomatic scuffles that occurred in the early years of his imperial reign. These conflicts occurred, in no small part, because of the personality of Rainald of Dassel, the chief source of Hohenstaufen pretensions to the status of *dominus mundi* for Frederick. In a famous incident, John of

42. Zeller, "Les rois de France," 279. See also Fuhrmann, "*Quis Teutonicos,*" 360, and Bruno Galland, "Les relations entre la France et l'Empire au XIIe siècle," in *Die Staufer im Süden. Sizilien und das Reich,* ed. Theo Kölzer (Stuttgart, 2000), 79–81; Walther Kienast, *Deutschland und Frankreich in der Kaiserzeit (900–1270): Weltkaiser und Einzelkönige* (Stuttgart, 1975), 77; Kampers, *Die Deutsche Kaiseridee,* 60; Günthner, *Der Antichrist,* 58; Cardini, "Il 'Ludus,'" 183.

43. Benson, "Political *Renovatio,*" 378.

44. Galland, "Les relations," 78; Folz, *Concept of Empire,* 108–9; Benson, "Political *Renovatio,*" 378. Kampers observed a real initiative on the part of the Germans to assert imperial authority over the French and other surrounding kingdoms; see *Die Deutsche Kaiseridee,* 60.

Salisbury reported that Rainald had addressed the French king Louis VII as *regulus* or "kinglet" rather than as *rex,* to the French monarch's great annoyance. Scholars have noted that the mocking use of the term *regulus* also bore the connotation of "serpent," a double entendre that echoes the relationship between basilisk and *basileus* in Greek. Rainald was famous for his sharp wit and biting tongue, and even John of Salisbury criticized the chancellor's shameful and scurrilous word play after the "regulus" incident.[45] Not long after that, Rainald referred to the kings of France, England, and Denmark as *provinciarum reges,* implying their status as leaders of provinces of the empire.[46] Both of these diplomatic conflicts point to a tendency in imperial circles to demean neighboring monarchs through clever use of language, especially in matters of theoretical authority. The *Play of Antichrist* does something similar in its depiction of the *rex Francorum,* but the parallels should not be overstated to the point that the play becomes an allegory of the German emperor's real desires to extend the boundaries of the empire into neighboring kingdoms.

As a rule, the incorporation of contemporary details is a defining characteristic of revisions of the foreign embassy topos. The use of such recognizable additions allows the motif to function more effectively as political commentary, but the commonplace remains nonetheless a tool of imperial encomium, rather than a policy statement. The question of whether a new Christian emperor intended to extend his territory through conquest had been a component of the discourse of Christian imperial authority since Einhard. But just as the talk of *dominium mundi* and the conquest of Babylon that sounded like proto-crusading rhetoric in the eleventh century should not be taken at face value, here, too, the theme of world conquest in the *Play of Antichrist* should not be interpreted as a sign of any actual plans for grand-scale territorial expansion. Its function in the twelfth century continued to be what it had been with Benzo, with Einhard, and even with Suetonius, for that matter: the rhetoric of praise.

In his analysis of a much-debated letter sent from Henry II to Frederick I, Karl Leyser offers helpful perspective concerning the need to avoid reading adapted and modernized articulations of the topoi of Roman universalism in Hohenstaufen propaganda as expressions of concrete political aspirations. The communiqué was sent to Frederick for the meeting at Würzburg in 1157, the same gathering of foreign envoys to which Rahewin alludes in his

---

45. Godman, *Silent Masters,* 198. See also Werner Grebe, "Studien zur Geistigen Welt Rainalds von Dassel," in Wolf, *Friedrich Barbarossa,* 283.

46. Folz, *Le souvenir,* 196. Mayer lists the incidence of such insults as a part of the assertion of *dominium mundi* emanating from Staufen circles; see "Staufische Weltherrschaft," 187. Cf. Grebe, "Studien Zur Geistigen Welt," 279.

rewriting of Einhard chapter 16. In the letter, the king of England offers himself as a willing subject of Frederick and bows to his command (*imperium*) in the name of indivisible political unity.[47] Despite previous attempts by others to read the statements literally, Leyser argues convincingly that the letter did not reflect Henry's real intention to recognize Frederick as his imperial overlord. Instead, he was, in essence, acting out the motif of surrendering foreign nations, but in a spirit of courtly participation. Henry's willingness to engage in the universalizing Hohenstaufen rhetoric was intended, Leyser affirms, to foster a sense of solidarity and shared belonging among the princes and counts who attended Frederick's international assembly.[48] Although the *Play of Antichrist* dramatizes a violent and tyrannical vision of the empire's ascendency to world domination, Leyser's call to see Henry's use of universalizing rhetoric as evidence of his language of diplomacy rather than as an actual expression of submission provides a model for interpreting the articulations of imperial dominion in the play.

The Franks are only the first kingdom in the play to receive a menacing embassy from the Roman emperor, but their defeat completes the German conquest of the Christian West. With the Frankish recognition of the German king as *rex Romanorum,* the Greeks are the next people to be forced to submit to his awesome power. The emperor sends his messengers with the same demand of tribute and recognition, coupled with threats of annihilation if they do not submit. Unlike his Frankish counterpart, the king of the Greeks receives no special deal based on a reputation for bravery, and he is quick to submit. Offering his service, the Greek leader promises to venerate the glory of Rome and to recognize the emperor's power as supreme. Like the Frankish king, the Byzantine leader is also allowed to keep his kingdom, for which he is grateful, and so he sings of his wholehearted veneration (the play is quite repetitive in this regard). Next comes the king of Jerusalem, and he is as agreeable and quick to fold as his Greek counterpart. After these serial submissions from the leadership in the East, when the emperor seems to have gathered in much of the world under his supreme rule, the king of Babylonia stands up to decry the vain novelty of the Christian cult that has dethroned the ancient gods. The pagan leader then marshals an army to attack Jerusalem, prompting the king of Jerusalem to send messengers to the Roman emperor to request help for the Holy City under siege. Promising swift aid, the emperor reassures the king of Jerusalem, who then announces to his people that the helping hand of the empire is on the way.

---

47. Leyser, "Frederick Barbarossa," 216.
48. Ibid., 240.

Meanwhile, an angel of God appears to tell the king of Jerusalem and the figure of Judaea not to fear. The emperor's army, which is now a united army of the Christian East and West, defeats the king of Babylonia, at which point the Roman leader proceeds to the temple at Jerusalem, just as the Last Emperor is projected to do after his defeat of the enemies of the faithful. He removes the crown from his head and places it with the scepter and regalia before the altar, relinquishing his rule to the real king of all kings, the *gubernator cunctorum*.[49] At that point, the servants of Antichrist arrive in the forms of Heresy and Hypocrisy, who come to wipe out the memory of Christ. Once the emperor gives up his imperial dignity, the situation in Jerusalem quickly deteriorates. With the arrival of Antichrist, the play begins to sort out the blame for what has befallen Christendom. Two conclusions emerge: things were better before the German emperor abdicated his position, and the pope did nothing to protect the Christian community. After the Hypocrites depose the king of Jerusalem and crown Antichrist instead, the king of Jerusalem comes to the king of the Teutons (the now former emperor of the Romans) crying betrayal and condemning his decision to lay down his regalia.

In a piece of obvious imperialist promotion, the king of Jerusalem insists that under the emperor, the church had been revered, whereas now the law of superstition is gaining ground.[50] The Hypocrites then put Antichrist's throne in the temple, where *Ecclesia* is badly beaten. No longer protected by the emperor, bruised and defeated, she goes back to join the pope, who has offered no assistance. The play's emphasis on the primary role of the emperor in the protection of the Christian imperium is central to the rhetoric of both the German empire and the Last Emperor prophecy, which is why the prophecy functions so effectively within imperialist rhetoric.[51] Earlier in the play, *Ecclesia* had been flanked by the emperor and the papacy, but the pope has essentially no function in the drama of Christendom's final battles. McGinn aptly describes his role as "a walk-on."[52] The pontiff's absence contributes to the celebration of the emperor as the supreme protector of Christendom and helps to refute the sort of universalizing reformist pretensions that had fueled the conflict of the late eleventh century. The play's use of the Last Emperor prophecy to promote the cause of Roman universalism against the claims of the papacy was hardly new, however. In the 1160s, at the

49. *Ludus,* 377.
50. *Ludus,* 379.
51. Friedrich Heer, *The Holy Roman Empire,* trans. Janet Sondheimer (New York, 1968), 73.
52. *Ludus,* 371–72; McGinn, *Antichrist,* 133–34. See also Whalen, *Dominion of God,* 92.

height of Frederick's conflict with the papacy, it had been nearly a century since Benzo's adaptations of the Last Emperor prophecy in the service of his staunchly antipapal praise of Henry IV.

The play ends with the conversion of all peoples to the true faith, but not before the emperor is himself duped by Antichrist. In a sequence that once again travesties the foreign embassy motif and is meant to parallel the opening scene of the play, Antichrist sends out embassies to gather the submission of foreign kings. His first embassy is to the king of the Greeks, who quickly submits, acknowledging the imperial dignity, the *decus imperiale,* of Antichrist.[53] Next, the Franks are easily won over with gifts, a form of wooing about which Adso had warned.[54] The German king requires more aggressive pacification. At first, he is skeptical of the figure claiming to be God, and begins to suspect fraud. Calling the offer a hoax, he accuses Antichrist's messengers of corrupting the Christian faith, and threatens to destroy him. The exchange leads to a pitched battle in which the other kings join the Germans in defeating the army of Antichrist, who then tries a new tactic by performing a series of miraculous healings. With these signs, the king of the Teutons is finally seduced and recognizes Antichrist as God, promising to serve him as a royal knight. The king of Babylonia is then defeated, after which Antichrist orders his messengers to go inform the Jews that the Messiah has come. But when Elijah and Enoch appear, they identify Antichrist as the *"homo perditionis"* and strip off his mask. There is a loud boom above the head of Antichrist, he collapses, and all of his other men flee. *Ecclesia* sings as everyone returns to the faith.[55]

The representation of the defense of Jerusalem by a united Christian army in the *Play of Antichrist* has led scholars to consider the relationship of the play to the theme of crusading.[56] The desire to tie elaborations of the Last Emperor prophecy to the crusading movement once again runs up against a dearth of evidence in Frederick's case, just as it does with Henry IV. Although the play dramatizes the Last Emperor's journey to Jerusalem and the liberation of Christian peoples from the pagan forces represented by Babylon before the end time, actual crusading plans likely did not inspire its composition and reception. With a composition date of around 1160, the work emerged well after the failed Second Crusade and well before Frederick took up the cross at Mainz in 1188 for the Third Crusade. The most ardent Staufen

53. *Ludus,* 379.
54. McGinn, *Visions,* 87.
55. *Ludus,* 387.
56. Schein, *Gateway,* 154.

claims of *dominium mundi* were voiced mainly in the period of the late 1150s after Frederick's coronation and in the 1160s under Rainald of Dassel, the period during which the play was written. These universalizing pretentions coincided with Frederick's carefully orchestrated program of self-promotion, with his campaigns in Italy, and with the early years of his conflict with the papacy. Henry IV had also been in deep conflict with the papacy and had been fighting in Italy. In neither case, though, do we find any real concern about the Christian East in works written in praise of the emperor. Holy Land expeditions did, of course, figure in the mind of Frederick Barbarossa, but the literary configurations of the apocalyptic Last Emperor prophecy were related to a different set of propagandistic concerns.[57]

Both Henry IV and Frederick I defined their reigns according to concepts of theoretical *dominium mundi* and Roman imperial renewal. Just as the Last Emperor prophecy figured within the discourse of imperial praise for Henry, it also appeared in the literature promoting Frederick. The propaganda for these programs was enhanced by adaptations of a prophecy that tied the emperor to a promise of a united Christendom under a Roman emperor, a fantasy that culminated in a scene of either abdication or inauguration at Jerusalem. In both cases, the prophecy served to assert continuity of German imperial authority, not to herald its end or promote any real expedition to the Holy Land. The French and German kings who had gone on crusade in the 1140s, including Frederick himself, surely hoped to succeed in liberating Christians in the East, but there is no evidence that they themselves aspired in concrete terms to the role of Last Emperor. The literary tradition of revised Last Emperor prophecies nourished imperial propaganda, and although such universalizing rhetoric from emperors was not incommensurate with the crusading dreams of the Hohenstaufen leadership, there is little evidence that the two were related during the early decades of Frederick's reign.

Although the *Play of Antichrist* is generally seen as pro-Hohenstaufen propaganda, the depiction of the German king / Roman emperor in the play is not entirely favorable. For instance, since he does not enjoy the awe of foreign kings, the Teutonic king must bully his way into being the sole possessor of the imperial dignity, and he is quick to crush his Christian rivals in his quest for power. This Roman emperor enjoys no procession of gift-bearing envoys, but such a depiction does not mean that the play does not reflect a pro-Hohenstaufen vision of the attainment of *dominium mundi*. Although

---

57. While Munz argued that Frederick had a Holy Land expedition in mind from the very beginning of his reign, Folz argued that the Germans took a long time to incorporate crusading into their idea of empire; see Munz, *Frederick,* 30, and Folz, *Concept of Empire,* 115–16.

the work dramatizes last things, the overarching message that transcends the end time narrative is the insistence on the primacy of the German regime as the best possible unifier of earthly kingdoms and protector of *Ecclesia*. To understand this, one need only recall the cries of regret when the emperor abdicates his imperial status at Jerusalem. There was no doubt some meta-commentary intended by the alteration of the ideal of the parade of foreign nations, a familiar locus of praise. As one scholar notes, the reaction of the German emperor to a performance of the play, if he ever saw one, must be left to the imagination.[58] It is difficult to know exactly what tone the author wished to convey by creating such a bombastic emperor figure, but it seems unlikely that the portrayal could have been intended as a scathing indictment of Frederick Barbarossa. However unflattering the portrait of the German king figure may be, the play is nonetheless a promotion of the Teutonic leader as universal Christian leader and protector, a role in which the papacy had failed.

Fictions and Forgeries in the Imperial Chancery

After the death of Otto of Freising in 1158, Rainald of Dassel was left to his own devices at a time when the emperor was in deep ideological (and sometimes military) conflict with his two main rival claimants to authority over the Christian *imperium*, the Greek emperor Manuel Comnenus and the pope. For more than a decade starting in 1156, Rainald worked to shape and nurture Frederick's imperial image. Under his watch, the first decade of Frederick's imperial reign proved to be a fruitful time in the chancery for the fabrication of documents and decrees related to the legitimation of the German inheritance of the Roman Empire.[59] Two prominent forgeries, the Hillin of Trier letters and the letter of Prester John, both of which contain invented diplomatic exchanges, have recently been identified as products of Rainald's propaganda program during the bitter disputes with the papacy under Popes Hadrian IV and Alexander III. In his contemplation of forgery and apocryphal letters in the Middle Ages, Giles Constable classifies the letter of Prester John in the same group as the Hillin letters, calling them both literary fictions.[60] We should add to that list Benzo's letter from Constantine X to Honorius II. All these letters were propaganda produced for the

---

58. Frank Shaw, "Frederick II as the 'Last Emperor,'" *German History* 19 (2001): 324.

59. Goez, *Translatio Imperii*, 142.

60. Giles Constable, "Forged Letters in the Middle Ages," in *Fälschungen im Mittelalter: Internationaler Kongress der Monumenta Germaniae Historica, München, 16.–19. September 1986*, vol. 5 (Hanover, 1988), 23–24.

German empire, all were concerned with the question of the leadership of Christendom, and all three confront the contested authority of the empire within fictional diplomatic exchanges.

The Hillin of Trier forgeries are a series of three letters that purport to be between Frederick, Pope Hadrian IV, and a group of high-ranking bishops of the German church including the archbishop Hillin of Trier, a legate of Hadrian. The letters appear to be the work of a single author, either Rainald, or else someone related to the chancery, perhaps working for him.[61] The forgeries are in many ways a meditation on the German claim to the Roman Empire. The first letter is from Frederick to Hillin, the second from Hillin to Hadrian, and the third is Hadrian's response to Frederick, which is addressed to the archbishops of Trier, Mainz, and Cologne. As did Benzo, the author of the Hillin letters addresses the conflicts between papacy and empire on a human level, reflecting personal animus, anger, and betrayal through sniping exchanges, all the while invoking the themes and rhetoric of the discourse of Roman universalism. The letter from Hadrian is of particular interest since it contains a deliberately erroneous rewriting of Charlemagne's assumption of the imperial title followed by the pope's claim that he has the power to undo the *translatio* that had moved the imperial dignity from the Greeks to the Franks.

The Hillin letters represent a satirical response to yet another infamous diplomatic incident precipitated by Rainald and his troublemaking manipulations of language. The arch-chancellor's linguistic play had led to Frederick's conflict with Louis VII over the "regulus" statement, but this time Rainald created discord with the papacy through his choice of words in a translation of a genuine letter from Pope Hadrian IV to Frederick. The incident proved to be a turning point in the relationship between the papacy and the empire.[62] A multilingual provocateur, Rainald took the war of words between the imperial court and Hadrian to a new theater by overseeing the production of the Hillin letters. The missives emerged in response to a diplomatic misunderstanding that ensued after Rainald led Frederick to believe that the pope had claimed to have given the emperor his imperial sovereignty as an overlord would to a vassal. At the Diet of Besançon in 1157, Rainald had been outspoken in his assertion of the transcendent powers of the empire and the German church over those of the papacy. In a letter that arrived for

---

61. Goez, *Translatio Imperii,* 142–43. Godman believes they came out of Rainald's chancery after the Diet of Besançon; see *Silent Masters,* 218. See Munz for a summary of earlier scholarship, in *Frederick,* 289.

62. Grebe, "Studien zur Geistigen Welt," 292–93.

Frederick from the pope in the hands of legates from Rome, one of whom
was the future Pope Alexander III, Rainald translated for Frederick, render-
ing the Latin word *beneficia* in a manner that conveyed that the German king
had received the empire in fief from the papacy.[63]

Calling Rainald a "fomenter of schism and despiser of the Church," Peter
Godman invokes this incident as an example of how the chancellor used his
role as mediator between the Roman clergy and the German laity to defend
the interests of the empire against those of the papacy.[64] Rahewin reports the
incident in Book 3 of the *Deeds,* defending Rainald's translation as faithful to
the meaning of the letter, but the chancellor most likely had sought to cause
trouble.[65] And, indeed, the statement provoked the emperor's fury, making him
angry enough to consider taking up arms against the pope. In the end, Frederick settled for sending a manifesto to Hadrian denouncing the pope's crime
in having made such a statement. The pontiff quickly sent legates to explain
the misunderstanding, for he had not intended the meaning that Rainald had
conveyed. A makeshift peace was eventually restored for a time, until Frederick's intervention in the coming papal election after Hadrian's death in 1159.[66]

Despite whatever peace the two sides managed to reach, the Hillin letters
depict an emperor still festering over the assertion of the papal origins of
his status as emperor. Although scholars earlier tried to reduce the missives
to an apolitical writing exercise, it would be a mistake to ignore them on
those grounds.[67] Robert Folz has shown, for instance, that the Hillin letters
were connected to a more prominent confection of the imperial chancery,
the false decree of Charlemagne of January 1166 issued just after the canonization of the Frankish king, a document that I consider in chapter 5.
More recently, scholars have demonstrated that the letters were intended as
a pro-imperial send-up of the vituperative rhetoric that fueled the ongoing
disputes between Frederick and the Holy See.[68] The letters, replete with fiery
polemical accusations and learned classical and scriptural references, combine
antipapal rhetoric with creative presentations of the assumption of empire by
the Germans. And like Benzo's polemical writings, they also convey a deep

63. Godman, *Silent Masters,* 196; Anne J. Duggan, "*Tòtius Christianitatis caput:* The Pope and the
Princes," in *Adrian IV: The English Pope (1154–1159); Studies and Texts,* ed. Brenda Bolton and Anne
J. Duggan (Aldershot, 2003), 128–29.

64. Godman, *Silent Masters,* 198.

65. *GF,* 3.10.

66. Raymonde Foreville, *Latran I, II, III et Latran IV* (Paris, 1965), 110–14; Godman, *Silent
Masters,* 218.

67. *Hillin-Briefe,* 289, Goez, *Translatio Imperii,* 143.

68. Godman, *Silent Masters,* 218; cf. Stephen C. Jaeger, "The Prologue to the *Historia Calamitatum* and the Authenticity Question," *Euphorion: Zeitschrift für Literaturgeschichte* 74 (1980): 11.

sense of personal animus between the figures on both sides of the divide between *regnum* and *sacerdotium*.

The first of the three missives, the one from Frederick to Hillin, is based on a real imperial manifesto issued by Frederick after the events at Besançon.[69] The text of the letter reveals an emperor disgusted by the claim that his power had been conferred by the pope. In this fabricated communication, Frederick calls on Archbishop Hillin to take on added powers for the German church in the name of peace. Asserting his own authority, he exhorts Hillin and the other suffragan bishops of the German bishoprics to rise up and support the teetering column of the *regnum,* and to resist the sons of Belial.[70] Presenting himself as "Fredericus Dei Gratia Romanorum imperator et semper augustus," Frederick proclaims his power to be from God alone.[71] He then describes the state of the church after Saint Peter as a vast sea full of snakes, and characterizes Hadrian as "he who claims to be the vicar of Peter, but is not."[72] Declaring himself unafraid of excommunication, he denounces the house of Peter as a den of thieves and a house of demons.[73] Hadrian had, in fact, been planning to excommunicate Frederick after he refused to recognize papal sovereignty over Rome and the Papal States, but he died in 1159 before carrying out the threat.[74]

The central theme of the letter from Frederick is his refutation of the notion that the empire had been given to him by the papacy. The emperor poses a loaded rhetorical question to Hillin, his go-between, using obvious allusions to recent events: "And what better *beneficium* could there be than the Roman Empire?" The memory of the incident runs through the three letters, but the post-Besançon dust-up is especially present in this passage. Since the use of the term had been interpreted to mean that Hadrian considered the empire to have been given to Frederick in fief, with the emperor in a situation of feudal service, the question "what better gift is there than the Roman Empire?" is a sarcastic lead-in to his argument that there had been no coronation of Frederick by the pope. "We put the crown on ourselves; and in what way did he [the pope] crown us then?" he asks provocatively. Frederick then ties his version of the coronation to the imperialist doctrine that the Roman imperial dignity had come to him directly from God: "Since

69. Robert Folz, "La chancellerie de Frédéric et la canonisation de Charlemagne," *Le Moyen Âge 6* (1964): 20.

70. *Hillin-Briefe,* 321.

71. *Hillin-Briefe,* 318.

72. *Hillin-Briefe,* 318–19.

73. *Hillin-Briefe,* 320.

74. Philippe Levaillain, *The Papacy: An Encyclopedia* (London, 2002), 684.

we put the crown of the realm on us, we took up its rule not from him but from God and not the papacy." He closes with the condemnatory statement, "See then how it is a lie," which could relate either to the *"beneficium"* statement or to the larger lie that he seeks to dispel concerning the papal origins of German imperial power.[75] The second letter is the shortest and least noteworthy, offering little of substance beyond the depiction of the archbishop functioning as a go-between who tells the pope of Frederick's intentions.

The third and most remarkable of the Hillin letters purports to be from Hadrian to the German archbishops, and contains the pope's response to Frederick's letter to Hillin. Letter three contains an angry papal diatribe about the worthlessness of the German kings who owe everything they have to the papacy. The third letter is clearly meant to inflame an imperialist audience with its exaggerated and erroneous papal vision of the origins of the Frankish empire in the eighth century. Letter three also contains thinly disguised allusions to the real Pope Hadrian's betrayal of Frederick in allying with the Greeks and the Sicilians in the mid-1150s. Folz believed that the historical errors in the letter, such as the attribution of the imperial coronation of Charlemagne to Pope Zachary rather than to Leo, had resulted from innocent confusions, but this view sorely underestimates both the astuteness of the author and the complex polemical tenor of the letter.

Hadrian returns to the age of Charlemagne in an attempt to refute Frederick's claims concerning the divine rather than the papal origins of German imperial authority. He asks his interlocutors, the German archbishops, "Was the empire not transferred from the rule of the Greeks to the Germans so that the King of the Teutons, before he was consecrated by the pope, would be acclaimed as emperor and Augustus, as an advocate of Peter?"[76] Calling Frederick a persecutor rather than a protector of Saint Peter, the pope articulates the reformist position that the empire had been given to Charlemagne so that he might serve as the protective arm of the church. The pontiff then offers his version of Charlemagne's assumption of the imperial title:

> Take note of these words: before the consecration, he [Charles] was just a king; after the consecration, he was emperor and Augustus. Whence therefore does he hold the empire, unless it is from us? By the election

75. *Hillin-Briefe*, 320. "An potest esse maius beneficium quam Romanum imperium? Nos ipsi nobis coronam imposuimus et quomodo nos tunc coronavit? Dum coronam regni nobis imposuimus, regnum non ab eo, sed a Deo suscepimus. Videte ergo, qualiter mentitus sit."

76. *Hillin-Briefe*, 326. "Nonne ideo translatum est imperium a regno Grecorum in Alemannos, ut rex Teutonicorum non, ante quam ab apostolico consecraretur, imperator vocaretur et esset augustus et esset advocatus Petri, non persecutor Petri?"

of his princes, meaning the Teutons, he holds the title of king and not
of emperor, by consecration, however, he holds the title of emperor and
Augustus and Caesar.[77]

By analogy to Charlemagne, the letter distinguishes between Frederick's
political power as a king elected by the German princes and his imperial title
based on papal consecration, which Hadrian insists had been a papal decision.

After Hadrian makes his case to the bishops concerning the degraded
origins of the German kings, it becomes clear that the author of the letter
is creating a bond of sympathy between Charlemagne and Frederick at the
expense of the pontiff, whom he depicts as both overwrought and ignorant:
"Remember, before Zachary gave his benediction to Charles, the second one
of that name, the Teutons had the sort of kings who travelled around in an
oxcart like philosophers and like Hilderic and his ancestors." In a sarcastic
tone, he proclaims, "Oh, how glorious was the king of the Germans, sitting
in an oxcart like the head of a synagogue, watching his duke, then called
mayor of the palace, conduct the business of his realm. He was a miserable king, who had nothing else but what his majordomo gave him."[78] This
portrait of the early Germanic kings is rich in political satire, for it seems to
defame the Carolingians, but is really designed to disparage its purported
author, who comes off much worse than the German kings who are being
so unjustly defamed by an incompetent historian.

The reference to the Merovingian kings in the oxcart parodies a passage from the first book of Einhard's *Life of Charlemagne*. The Carolingian
biographer depicts the last Merovingian kings as having been reduced to
doing nothing all day but sitting on their thrones displaying their long hair
and flowing beards while the mayors of the palace conducted the business
of the realm. They also had to ride around in wagons pulled by yoked oxen,
in a rustic manner. Einhard's derisive picture was designed to distinguish the
praiseworthy Carolingians from the last Merovingians, but Hadrian's letter implies continuity or even sameness between the two dynasties by tying

77. Ibid., 326. "Et ecce iste non advocatus, sed persecutor Petri. Notate verba: ante consecrationem solummodo rex, post consecrationem imperator et augustus. Unde igitur habet imperium
nisi a nobis? Ex electione principum suorum, videlicet Teutonicorum, habet nomen regis et non
imperatoris, ex consecratione autem nostra habet nomen imperatoris et augusti et cesaris. Ergo per
nos imperat."

78. *Hillin-Briefe,* 327. "Recolite, antequam Zacharias benedixisset Karolum illius nominis
secundum, quales reges Teutonici habebantur, qui etiam in carpento boum circumferebantur sicut
phylosophi, sicut Hildericus et suis antecessores. Quam gloriosus erat rex Alemannorum, dum in
carpento boum quasi archisynagogus residebat et ducem suum, qui tunc maior domus vocabatur,
tractare regni sui negotia videbat! Rex miser erat, qui nichil aliud habebat, quam quod ei maior
domus sue disponebat."

Charlemagne to the oxcart riders and then lumping them all within the category of "German kings." For Einhard the oxcart was a sign of "ignoble weakness" for the Merovingians.[79] By contrast Hadrian uses the oxcart against the Carolingians by tying Charlemagne to the do-nothing Merovingians. A seemingly diminished Charlemagne and Frederick both appear, then, as representatives of the same miserable race of German kings, but the subtext is pro-Frederick, since the passage reinforces the ties between the German king and Charlemagne.

The revisiting of Charlemagne's coronation was an established tool in the polemics between *regnum* and *sacerdotium,* but Hadrian's letter constitutes a particularly elaborate and multilayered commentary on the Frankish assumption of the Roman Empire. In the letter, Hadrian arranges his information to make Charlemagne's imperial reign appear to follow closely on the age of the penurious wagon riders. It was the arrival of Pope Zachary, he declares, that delivered the German kings from their miserable state when he gave Charles "a grand title and everything else to which he laid claim." The pope then draws a careful distinction between the time before Zachary's arrival and the period after he granted Charles the imperial title:

> These were the laws of the Teuton kingdom since the earliest days when Zachary, sent by God, who calls those things which are not as if they are, raised Charles to Roman emperor and made his name great alongside the names of the great men of his who were in the land, so that, then and now, the king of the Teutons was emperor and protector of the apostolic see, so that all legal matters which touch upon papal matters in the whole of Apulia would be resolved by him; and thus, since a brave armed emperor would guard the doors of the church, all of the things which the church possessed would be at peace.[80]

79. See Alexander C. Murray, "Fredegar, Merovech and 'Sacral Kingship,'" in *After Rome's Fall: Narrators and Sources of Early Medieval History,* ed. Walter A. Goffart and Alexander C. Murray (Toronto, 1998), 130–32. For a useful study of revisions of the Carolingian past in a German imperial context, see Johanna Dale, "Imperial Self-Representation and the Manipulation of History in Twelfth-Century Germany: Cambridge, Corpus Christi College MS 373," *German History* 29 (2011): 557–83.

80. *Hillin-Briefe,* 327. "Hec a primis diebus Teutonici regni iura, quousque Zacharias a Deo missus, qui vocat ea que non sunt tamquam ea que sunt, promovit Karolum in Romanum imperatorem et fecit ei nomen grande iuxta nomen magnorum sui fuerunt in terra, ut et tunc et nunc rex Teutonicorum imperator esset et advocatus apostolice sedis, ut iusticie, que pertinent apostolico in tota Apulia, per eum omnes pacate essent et ita, cum fortis armatus imperator custodiret atria apostolici, in pace, essent omnia, qui apostolicus possideret."

Hadrian reiterates the papal theory that the empire had been a gift of the papacy to the Franks in return for protection, but he has the details wrong. Zachary's pontificate ended in 752, forty-eight years before the imperial coronation of Charlemagne by Pope Leo III. The attribution is obviously inaccurate, and deliberately so, despite Folz's contention that the mistake was a matter of simple confusion between the coronation of 800 and transfer of power from the Merovingians to Carolingians in the 750s.[81]

The real intended victim of the letter is the pope himself, for he appears blustering and ignorant as he makes his justifications for papal primacy over the empire. The letter consists of deliberately weak anti-imperial rhetoric that is designed, by way of its inferior quality, to serve its real function as antipapal rhetoric. While the letter itself, written in the voice of the pope, contains errors in names and dates, the letter's actual author betrays learnedness and wit. For instance, he reveals intimate knowledge of the first book of Einhard's biography of Charlemagne. It is unlikely that the same person who crafted the letters would have actually believed that Pope Zachary had presided over the imperial coronation of Charlemagne. Pope Leo III loomed large in the memory of the Carolingian past. A learned German cleric who had read Einhard would surely have known which pope had been present at the coronation of 800. The mistake was designed to enhance the polemic against the Holy See by making Hadrian's insulting rant against Charlemagne look all the more ridiculous. As a result, Frederick joins Charlemagne as a fellow victim of unschooled and unrestrained papal bluster.

After deriding Charlemagne and his fellow German kings, Hadrian menacingly announces that as pope he holds the power to undo the transfer of empire from the Greeks to the Germans that had occurred with Charlemagne's investiture and give it back to the Greeks. This is another outlandish claim that further reveals the anti-curial subtext of the letters. The threat to reverse the *translatio* is part of the pope's response to an accusation that Frederick makes in the first letter. The emperor bitterly complains that the pope had usurped the *"beneficia,"* meaning the empire, without consultation, and then moved the apostolic see to Viterbo. The real Hadrian had in fact retreated to Viterbo for a few weeks in 1156, but made no such transfer.[82] Frederick's letter also threatens that they, meaning he and the prelates of the German church, intend to take back Apulia. The loss of Apulia is a dominant theme in the letters, serving, as it does for Benzo, as a larger

---

81. Folz, "La chancellerie," 24.

82. Brenda M. Bolton, "*Nova familia beati Petri:* Adrian IV and the Patrimony," in Bolton and Duggan, *Adrian IV,* 165.

symbol of imperial disintegration perpetrated by papal disloyalty. The Treaty of Benevento of 1156, when Hadrian IV chose to join with the Greeks and the Normans of Sicily, represents for the author of the Hillin letters what the Treaty of Melfi of 1059 had represented for Benzo. Both were moments of papal betrayal of the empire regarding territories in southern Italy. In fact, the parallels are strong enough between the rhetoric concerning Apulia in the Hillin letters and in Benzo's writings that it would not be unreasonable to think that Rainald had been inspired by the temperamentally similar Benzo.

The repeated mentions of Apulia in the Hillin letters reflect the period of crisis in Sicily in 1155–56, just prior to Frederick's imperial coronation. The Treaty of Constance in 1153 had sought to create an alliance between the empire and the papacy against the Greeks and the Sicilians over the matter of southern Italy. Three years later, the relationship between Hadrian and Frederick had been deeply damaged when the pope chose to side instead with the Greeks and the Sicilians. Early in his pontificate (1154–59), Hadrian found himself caught between Frederick and King William of Sicily. At one point, the Apulians rebelled against William and turned to Hadrian as their leader. When the Greeks then attempted to regain Apulia and Calabria, they ended up joining with the papacy and with a faction of Apulian rebels.[83] Resolution came in the form of the 1156 treaty that led to papal recognition of the Sicilian monarchy. The accord was perceived by partisans of the empire as Hadrian's great betrayal of Frederick, and his pro-Sicilian alliance permanently damaged the relationship between Barbarossa and the papacy.[84] Anne Duggan even argues that the treatment of relations between empire and papacy in the *Deeds of Frederick Barbarossa* can be read as an extended reflection on Frederick's desire for peace in the face of Hadrian's abandonment and betrayal.[85] The Hillin letters confront this same betrayal, but in a format that allowed for more creative expressions of indignation than had the *Deeds*.

To confront the matter of southern Italy, the Hillin letters invoke the larger theme of *translatio imperii* through allusions to the Carolingian assumption of the empire. Hadrian's threat to give the empire back to the Greeks is the explicit retort to Frederick's statement concerning his plans for an imperial recapture of Apulia, but he includes the Greeks, whom Frederick had not mentioned in the first letter. Hadrian responds to Frederick's accusation concerning his transfer of the Holy See to Viterbo, but his response suggests

83. Duggan, *"Totius Christianitatis caput,"* 114–16.

84. Ibid., 118. Folz notes the plans between the pope and Manuel Comnenus, in "La chancellerie," 24. See also Paul Magdalino, *The Empire of Manuel I Komnenos, 1143–1180* (Cambridge, UK, 2002), 58–60.

85. Duggan, *"Totius Christianitatis caput,"* 107.

that the emperor had also accused him of moving the Holy See to Constan-tinople: "that man [Frederick] says that we transferred the apostolic see to New Rome from the royal chambers of Viterbo, when all of Apulia looked to our power rather than his."[86] The comment refers to the above-mentioned Apulian uprising, which led to Hadrian's temporary role as their leader, and the incorporation of Manuel Comnenus into the alliance. Frederick's accu-sation, as Hadrian cites it, claims that the pontiff had given the papal seat of power to New Rome, or Constantinople. The idea that Hadrian had moved the Holy See to Constantinople is intended as a metaphor for his concession of power in making the alliance with Manuel over the Kingdom of Sicily, about which Frederick felt so angry and betrayed. Hadrian's alliances with Manuel Comnenus were a matter of great indignation for Frederick, some-thing the letter, albeit in the voice of Hadrian, conveys with a level of fervor that more historical and biographical discourses could not achieve. Sicily, for Benzo and for the author of the Hillin letters, represents the primary impedi-ment to unified imperial authority, with the papacy, the Normans, and the Greeks as his rival powers. In its parody of papal bluster, Hadrian's letter con-veys the real Frederick's anger over the real Hadrian's alliance with the Greeks by travestying the discourse of *translatio imperii*. The pope's repeated claim that he holds the power to take back the imperial dignity from the Germans and return it to Constantinople is supposed to bring to mind the treachery of the Holy See in its alliances with the Greeks and the Normans in Sicily.

Hadrian's rant against the German kings continues with a derisive descrip-tion of Aachen. The pontiff describes Frederick's seat of empire as a rural power base lost in the backwoods of Gaul, openly offering it up as the physi-cal analogue to his provincial claims to power. "We have the following divi-sion: us, this side of the Alps, him, the other side of the Alps. Does he not have his seat of power, Aachen, in the Ardennes, which is a forest in Gaul, while ours is in Rome?" The pontiff compares the relative lack of glory of Aachen as compared to Rome, tying the comparison to the men who represent the leadership of the two seats of power. Once again, he reminds the German archbishops that without the pope, the German kings would be nothing: "To the degree that Rome is more worthy than Aachen, so too is the pope better and more worthy than your king. And what makes him equal to us, he who got everything that he has from us?" The diatribe continues with another even more detailed threat to reverse the *translatio imperii*. Hadrian wonders aloud whether, given that it was by papal authority that Zachary consecrated

---

86. *Hillin-Briefe,* 327. "Et iste dicit nos de camera regni Bitervium in novam Romam et apos-tolicam sedem transtulisse, cum tota Apulia nostre auctoritati spectet et non sue."

Charles and transferred the empire from the Greeks to the Germans, under whose watch it has been so greatly reduced, why he would not have the same power to transfer it from the Germans back to the Greeks. He then answers his own question churlishly by stating that it is in his power to hand over whatever he wants, "Ecce in potestate nostra est, ut demus illud cui volumus." In an exaggerated vision of overreaching papal claims to universal dominion, Hadrian announces that the papacy is constituted above all peoples and kingdoms, and that he plans to tear up and destroy what exists so they he may "replant and rebuild."[87] In his threats, Hadrian comes across as insulting and power-hungry, especially in his belief that as pope he can supersede all secular power in his control of the Roman Empire. He does not endure the violent name-calling and insults visited on Gregory VII by Benzo, but the antipapal rhetoric is still successful in painting the portrait of a victimized emperor who only wants what is best for Rome in the face of an overreaching papacy that threatens the very survival of the empire.

Hadrian's letter to the archbishops concludes with an acerbic reminder of the German regime's inability to take hold of southern Italy. Sicily dominates the final passages of the letter as Hadrian wonders aloud to the German archbishops how they can have such faith in the power of German emperors, given that they were unable even to get Roger of Sicily (d. 1154) out of Calabria or Apulia.[88] His calculated musings continue when he questions how Frederick will restrain Greece when he cannot even subjugate Dacia, since the Greeks are stronger than the Dacians. The communiqué closes with Hadrian exhorting the archbishops to call on their king, who, he reminds them, is out of his mind, to come back to him (Hadrian) by way of them, so that he might seek reconciliation, and thereby "mend the schisms between church and state." The three letters all claim to want peace, reconciliation, and an end to the schism, just as Benzo's invented letters from Constantine and Pantaleus convey the overarching desire for harmonious relations between papacy and empire. The conceit of these forgers, however, is that peace in the empire means cooperation on imperial terms.

---

87. *Hillin-Briefe*, 327–28. "Divisum itaque habemus: nos cis Alpes, ille trans Alpes. Nonne ille habet sedem suam Aquis in Arduenna, qui est silva Gallie, sicut est notre Rome? Quanto Roma maior et dignior est quam Aquis Grani, tanto apostolicus maior et dignior est vestro rege. Et unde est, quod se parem facit nobis, qui totum, quod habet, ex nobis habet? Eadem auctoritate, qua Zacharias consecravit Karolum et transtulit imperium de Greco in Teutonicum, nonne et nos poterimus conversam facere, imperium, quod tantum ex Teutonicis regibus adnichilatum est, referre de Teutonico in Grecum? Ecce in potestate nostra est, ut demus illud cui volumus. Propterea constituti sumus super gentes et super regna, et destruamus et evellamus et edificemus et plantemus."

88. See Hubert Houben, *Roger II of Sicily: A Ruler between East and West* (Cambridge, UK, 2002), 97.

The Hillin forgeries make a mockery of Pope Hadrian IV, but they do not paint an entirely favorable picture of Frederick either. The letter from Hadrian to the German archbishops in particular deals some rather severe blows to the emperor, a fact that has led to some questioning of the ideological underpinnings of the whole series. Peter Godman argues, rightly, I think, that the insults to the emperor do not make up for the absurdity of the Hadrian persona, a depiction that undermines papal authority and therefore points to the letter's imperial provenance.[89] Benzo certainly felt free to scold his imperial subject in the *Ad Heinricum,* so there is no reason to think that imperial propagandists, especially within the literary context of faux polemical letters, could not allot themselves the freedom to push certain limits in discussing their subject. Moreover, it is impossible to know what the expectations were for the readership of the letters. The *Play of Antichrist* also presents the emperor figure in a sometimes less-than-favorable light while remaining pro-Hohenstaufen, especially if, as McGinn proposes, the play was meant to be performed before the emperor. In both works, we have evidence of vibrancy in the discourse surrounding Frederick's self-presentation as emperor and of openness to critique rather than of a culture of one-note praise. The producers of these works, much like Anselm of Besate and Benzo, were clerics and scholars steeped in the art of rhetoric, who saw themselves as commentators on the state of the empire.

The Archpoet

A brief foray into the world of the unconventional panegyrist known as the Archpoet offers another example of how the struggle over southern Italy functioned within rhetorical constructions of Roman universalism. As had Benzo and the author of the Hillin forgeries, the poet sets up Apulia as the symbolic missing piece of an idealized universal whole, and thus the obstacle to a unified German imperial landscape. Known for his wine-soaked goliardic persona, the Archpoet bears a pseudonym that reflects the title of his master, Rainald, the arch-chancellor. He did most of his writing between 1162 and 1164, at the end of Frederick's Italian campaign.[90] The laudatory verses of the poem known as the *Kaiserhymnus* celebrate the emperor's victory over Milan in the early 1160s, while taunting the Greeks under Manuel Comnenus who had supported the Milanese against Barbarossa. The panegyric verses, which Rainald commissioned, begin, "Salve mundi domine, Cesar noster, ave." He

---

89. Godman, *Silent Masters,* 218–19.
90. Ibid., 202.

then decries the impious Lombards and compares Frederick to Charlemagne for his success in crushing rebels. Next he menacingly warns Manuel Comnenus and the Greeks, announcing: "In the meantime, Constantine, I am warning you: lower your right hand, cease your threats! Milan is in such ruins that thickets reign in the middle of the city."[91] The victory was so total, he boasts, that the Greeks could have done nothing about it had Achilles himself arrived. The game is over, he gloats, and it is Frederick who has ended it with his rook. After celebrating the fall of Milan, the panegyrist describes universal peace under Frederick, as once again the emperor "makes a census of the whole world." This same motif had served for Orosius as the description of the universal peace that reigned under Augustus at the time of the birth of Christ.[92] Otto of Freising had also proclaimed such a peace under Frederick at the beginning of the *Deeds*. The Archpoet then elaborates further: "The reputation of the emperor travels like a swift horse. The Greek emperor trembles hearing this, and now, blind with fear, does not know what to do; he fears the emperor's name just as the flock fears a lion."[93]

Although the trembling Greeks submit to Frederick, southern Italy eludes him. After taunting the bested Greeks for their attempts to help Milan, the Archpoet addresses the matter of Apulia. In a further allusion to the foreign embassy motif, he describes the Apulians as a people who greatly desire to submit to Frederick, but are denied the opportunity. In emotion-filled verses, he describes the Sicilians' unfulfilled desire to bow to Frederick as their leader rather than to the hated King William of Sicily: "Now the Sicilians are refusing the Sicilian tyrant. The Sicilians thirst for you and wait for you. Now the Apulians freely kneel before you, their eyes tearing up as they wonder what detains you."[94] The Archpoet imagines the rebel Apulians weeping as they hope for the arrival of Frederick to save them from the Sicilian king, but he never comes. Instead, with the Treaty of Benevento, we may infer, the pope recognized William as their king. The moment is thus worthy of great lament, just as Rome's relinquishing of Apulia to Robert Guiscard provoked great sorrow and wrath for Benzo, which he expressed in his own visions of the Salian imperial unity that eluded Henry IV. Within his praise for the

91. Archpoet, *Kaiserhymnus,* stanza 23. "Iterim precipio tibi, Constantine: / iam depone dexteram, tue cessant mine! / Mediolanensium tante sunt ruine, / quod in urbe media modo regnant spine."

92. Orosius, *Hist.,* 6.21.

93. Archpoet, *Kaiserhymnus,* stanza 31. "Volat fama Cesaris velut velox ecus, / hac audita trepidat imperator Grecus; / iam, quid agat nescius, iam timore cecus, / timet nomen Cesaris, ut leonem pecus."

94. Archpoet, *Kaiserhymnus,* stanza 32. "Iam tiranno Siculo Siculi detrectant; / Siculi te siciunt, Cesar, et expectant; / iam libenter Apuli tibi genu flectant, / mirantur, quid detinet, oculos humectant."

emperor, the Archpoet implies that the Apulians would have preferred to bow before Frederick, but they were denied the chance to be among the nations parading before him in willing submission. Instead they were forced to accept a tyrant whom they did not want.

The Archpoet rehearses the familiar topoi of Roman *renovatio* for Frederick in his panegyric for the defeat of Milan, but he ultimately attributes Frederick's successes to Rainald. After the lament for the weeping Apulians longing for Frederick, the poet turns his attention abruptly away from the emperor to offer a paean to Rainald, his own patron and the architect of Frederick's propaganda program. In a striking statement that seems to devalue his previous praise for the emperor, the poet credits his patron with making all things possible for Frederick as well as for himself, a once miserable poet: "The arch-chancellor prepared the way, beat the path, cleared the brush, subjugated the world to the yoke of the emperor and freed me from my pool of wretchedness."[95] In this final verse, the poet manages to amply praise himself by associating Rainald's accomplishments in helping Frederick conquer the world with helping a poor poet by commissioning him to write in praise of the emperor. If Rainald had not helped Frederick conquer the world, then the poet would have had no occasion to sing his praises. Godman proposes that the Archpoet aimed to show his adeptness at using the well-worn commonplaces of imperial praise, but that he also declined to "plod on the pedestrian tracks of encomium." The Archpoet's topoi are deliberately empty, he argues, and the poet only pretends to follow the rules, while insisting tacitly that his reader read between the lines of his clichés.[96] This assessment of the poet's individualized use of a well-known script is convincing, but, as I argue throughout this study, writers of imperial praise had been deviating from the well-worn tracks of the foreign embassy topos for nearly as long the motif had existed. The Archpoet was not the only panegyrist to require careful interlinear readings of praise for Roman universalism; in fact, such expectations were the norm, rather than the exception.

The Letter of Prester John

The Byzantine emperor Manuel Comnenus, Frederick's rival for imperial authority in the Greek East, also fell victim to the learned forgers in the Staufen chancery. The Byzantine emperor figures prominently in a piece of literary

---

95. Archpoet, *Kaiserhymnus,* stanza 33. "Archicancellarius viam preparavit; / dilatavit semitas, vepres extirpavit; / ipse iugo Cesaris terram subjugavit / et me de miserie lacu liberavit."

96. Godman, *Silent Masters,* 209.

fiction known as the letter of Prester John, one of the most famous and oft-reproduced forgeries of the medieval period. The letter is a learned concoction that reflects knowledge of a wide variety of classical and medieval sources. Despite attempts to locate a purported Greek original of the document, no such version has ever emerged, and a convincing argument has been made for its fabrication in imperial circles, involving Rainald of Dassel.[97] The missive began to circulate in 1165, the year of Charlemagne's canonization, but later revisers expanded the narrative to something far more elaborate than what we preserve as its earliest incarnation.[98] The document enjoyed enough publicity in the 1170s to warrant a response from Pope Alexander in 1177, the year when he was finally recognized by the empire after the nearly two-decade-long schism. As recent studies have shown, Alexander's letter to the mythic king probably does not reflect his actual belief in the existence of the ruler from the East.[99] The pope was more likely engaging in a bit of diplomatic repartee, answering one false letter with another.

After the coronation of 800, the rhetoric of Roman universalism ran up against the problem of the divided empire. Authors such as Notker the Stammerer began to use the foreign embassy motif to disparage Byzantine pretensions to the role of protectors of Christendom. The letter of Prester John offers yet another example of this centuries-old rhetorical strategy. While the Hillin forgeries reflect the tone of Staufen anger and betrayal during the period after the Treaty of Benevento in 1156, the letter of Prester John is evidence of ire in the chancery being directed at Frederick's Byzantine rivals. Scholars have set forth a variety of theories about the function of Prester John's extraordinary missive, including anti-Byzantine propaganda, a call for help for Christians in the East, encouragement for crusaders, a school exercise, a contribution to the dossier for the *translatio* of the relics of the Three Kings to Cologne in 1164, and propaganda in support of Frederick against Pope Alexander III.[100] These theories are not mutually exclusive, and parts of some of them have merit, but the letter can be best explained as a piece of pro-imperialist faux diplomacy that is a variation on the universalizing rhetoric of the foreign embassy motif. Composed at the expense of Manuel

97. Bernard Hamilton, "Prester John and the Three Kings of Cologne," in *Prester John, the Mongols and the Ten Lost Tribes,* ed. Charles F. Beckingham and Bernard Hamilton (Aldershot, 1996), 171–85.

98. Suzanne Conklin Akbari, *Idols in the East: European Representations of Islam and the Orient, 1100–1450* (Ithaca, NY, 2009), 58–66.

99. Bernard Hamilton, "The Lands of Prester John. Western Knowledge of Asia and Africa at the Time of the Crusades," *Haskins Society Journal* 15 (2006): 133; *EPJ,* 251. I am working from Wagner's two editions that she based on the earliest twelfth-century manuscripts.

100. Constable, "Forged Letters," 22–23.

Comnenus, the missive is combative, but in an erudite, rhetorically intricate manner that is typical of Rainald of Dassel. Created within the same literary context as that of the Archpoet, himself full of disgust with the Greeks, the letter of Prester John goes even further in travestying previous models of Roman universalism.

The letter from Prester John represents a one-sided epistolary encounter between its author, a self-proclaimed supreme ruler of a peaceful and bountiful kingdom in the Far East, and the emperor of Byzantium. The rich descriptions of Prester John's mythic kingdom have garnered the majority of the scholarly attention on the work, but the relatively neglected dedicatory passage, in which the letter writer addresses the Greek emperor, proves essential to the understanding of the letter.[101] The opening contains Prester John's elaborate debasement of his Byzantine addressee, a process that includes his failure to use Manuel's imperial title, the pretense of his own superiority over the Greek emperor, the questioning of the Greek emperor's orthodoxy, and, finally, his offer to allow Manuel to come and rule under him in his more-than-perfect world beyond the Far East. The carefully worded introduction thus establishes the political stakes of this invented encounter between the East and an imagined Far Far East, a passage without which the entire document would be untethered from its ideological moorings.

Much of the prologue to the grandiose and over-the-top description of Prester John's ideal kingdom consists of a series of affronts, including references, some more veiled than others, to the various needs and lacks of the Greek emperor. From the beginning, Prester John's communication is marked by his arch tone as he diminishes the Byzantine leader and his imperial position. The initial slight involves Prester John's failure to address Manuel as emperor when he presents himself in a lofty manner to his addressee, extending his greetings to his friend Manuel, governor of the Romans.[102] This form of address is an obvious slight, since Manuel is, in fact, the titular emperor. Of course, the rivalry over the title was between the Greeks and the West, so we may read between the lines to identify elements that serve as proxies for the discourse of empire between the Greek East and the Christian West. In the heavily circulated *Deeds,* Rahewin had described a scenario in which East and West would each claim the imperial title, using

101. For further bibliography, see Robert Silverberg, *The Realm of Prester John* (Athens, OH, 1972); Beckingham and Hamilton, *Prester John;* and Michael Uebel, "Imperial Fetishism: Prester John among the Natives," in *The Postcolonial Middle Ages,* ed. Jeffrey Jerome Cohen (New York, 2001), 261–82.

102. *EPJ,* 346.

the designations New Rome and Old Rome, so we know that the issue of the shared title was on the table in Hohenstaufen circles.[103]

After the initial slight, Prester John continues to condescend to Manuel in a very purple passage marked by an exaggerated use of honorifics that is humorously absurd: "It was announced to me, my Majesty, that you were esteeming my Excellence and that there was talk of my Highness in your land. But I learned through this legate that you were wishing to send in my direction certain pleasant things and trifling little gifts, by which my Justice would be charmed."[104] Differently stated, Prester John had heard that his great reputation had reached the Greeks and that the Greeks hoped to win him over with some of their silly little gifts. The letter writer demonstrates familiarity with the established motif of the Byzantines becoming worried after hearing of the mighty reputation of a rival emperor, and then submissively offering gifts as part of an alliance pact. The long-standing reputation for lavish diplomatic gift-giving by the Greeks is lampooned here with the suggestion that anything they might offer would be a mere trifle with which they could only hope to charm his Majesty, Excellency, Highness, and Justice. In the previous chapters, we have seen that gifts sent to the emperor in the West from Constantinople symbolized the bloodless surrender of authority rather than an assertion of superiority. The writer of the letter of Prester John, with its derisive characterization of the gifts with which the Greeks might hope to win the king's favor, engages in this same rhetorical process. The author enriches the tradition on which he builds, however, by adding a new foreign leader to the drama. This new king escapes the dichotomy of East and West by being from farther east than even the East, thereby enlivening the competition for imperial supremacy by humiliating the Greeks from the other side.

The next affront concerns the Greek theory of the divinity of the emperor, another matter of profound disagreement between two sides of Christendom. Prester John implies a comparison between himself, a proud mere human being, and the partly divine Greek *basileus*. He explains that his reason for writing is to find out whether the Greek emperor is a true Christian, the implication being that emperor worship is unorthodox, and by extension that the Greek emperor is not worthy of his title: "For indeed if I am a man, and that is a good thing I believe, and I transmit certain things about my

---

103. *GF,* 4.76.

104. *EPJ,* 347. "Nunciabatur apud maiestatem meam, quod diligebas excellentiam meam et mentio altitudinis meae erat apud te. Sed per apocrisarium istum cognovi, quod mihi volebas iucunda quedam et ludicra munuscula tua dirigere, quibus delectaretur iustitia mea."

affairs to you, because I wish to know whether you have, along with me, the true catholic faith in the Lord and whether you believe through all things in Christ the Lord."[105] Later versions of the letter from the fourteenth and fifteenth centuries recognized the contemptuous tone of the passage and enhanced it by having the king refer to Manuel's subjects as his *Graeculi*.[106]

After mocking the Greek emperor's belief in his own divinity, Prester John implies that Manuel is not wealthy. The Eastern king promises to provide the Greek emperor, by way of his legate the *apocrisarios,* with all that he lacks, proclaiming, "My Magnificence will transmit bounteously, by way of our legates, a supply of things which pertain to joy, that you need."[107] Prester John thus forces the Greeks into the position of receiving demeaning offers of enrichment, a role they usually play with regard to the West, as we saw, for instance, with Notker. After insulting Manuel's diplomatic "trifles," Prester John makes a degrading offer to the Byzantine emperor:

> But if you are willing to come to the realm of my majesty, you will be able to enjoy my abundance, and if you are willing to attend me, I will appoint you as steward of my dominion, but if not, you can go home enriched with these things which I have in abundance. Send to me a note through your ambassador concerning your preference and certify your decision on it for me.[108]

This proposal, while seemingly generous, implies that Manuel would have to rule under him. A similar series of events happens in Notker's *Deeds* when Harun offers Charlemagne the Holy Land as recognition for his superior might, but offers to look after the territory since he is closer. Harun is an important forerunner of Prester John, since he also rules a vast domain in the East, but Harun happily surrenders jurisdiction over the Holy Land to Charlemagne, while Prester John invites the Greek emperor to become, in essence, one of his "*reges provinciarum.*" He ends the proposal by telling Manuel to indicate his decision on a little piece of paper (*scedula*) and send it back with his ambassador. The request further debases the emperor, since it reduces to a

---

105. *EPJ,* 347. "Etenim si homo sum, pro bono habeo, et de meis per apocrisarium meum tibi aliqua transmitto, quia scire volo, si mecum rectam fidem et catholicam habes in domino et si per omnia in Christo deo credis."

106. *EPJ,* 299.

107. *EPJ,* 347. "Magnificentia mea eorum quae ad gaudia pertinent, copiam indigentiae tuae per apocrisarios nostros largiflue transmittet."

108. *EPJ,* 348. "Quotsi velis venire ad dominantionem maiestatis meae, poteris frui habundantia mea et maiorem dominationis meae si mecum stare volueris, te constituam, sin autem in his, quae apud maiestatem sunt habundanter, locupletatus redire. Remitte mihi per apocrisarium tuum scedulam tue dilectionis et in ea certifica me de proposito tuae voluntatis."

little note in the pocket of an envoy the decision of an emperor to relinquish his title and take on an inferior administrative role in a distant kingdom.

After the insult-laden opening, Prester John describes his idyllic kingdom in the East with its exotic animals, precious stones, and fish that bleed purple—in other words, the very sorts of things that we tend to find in visions of the exorbitant tribute brought before the emperor by envoys from the East.[109] Before embarking on the proud description of his realm, Prester John presents himself "Presbiter Johannes, dominus dominantium," or lord of lords, an epithet taken from Apocalypse 19.16. Then, deeming himself a devoted Christian who aids and defends poor Christians everywhere, he claims to have vowed to visit the Holy Sepulcher.[110] At this point, he begins to describe his realm, where he is lord over seven kings and their tributaries, ruling over seventy provinces, few of which are Christian. His realm is his own utopian paradise where everyone gets along, even though they are mostly pagans. One scholar has argued that Prester John's extolling of his own peaceful system in which he controls both *regnum* and *sacerdotium* is evidence that the author composed the letter as an allegory of the problem of shared power between church and state.[111] This theory conforms to the idea that Prester John's letter is a piece of self-promotion from the imperial chancery designed to address the question of divided imperial authority in the empire.

The East in the rhetoric of Roman universalism is the source of all luxurious and exotic gifts and tribute, and therefore we should read the idealized description of Prester John's realm as the source of all that abundance. The underlying implication that must not be forgotten, however, is that all of that wealth and luxury, within the rhetorical context of the foreign embassy motif, is intended to symbolize recognition of the superior status of the receiver. The letter of Prester John represents an elaborate hoax that transforms the motif of the surrendering East by having representatives from the most supreme *dominus* arrive in Byzantium (the West's Christian East) from a further remove that is beyond the farthest reaches of the East. What is more, his kingdom is vaster, richer, more peaceful, and better governed. While the foreign embassy topos celebrates the encompassing of the whole world, including the East, the Prester John letter plays on the major elements of the motif by turning them on their heads. The result is a piece of hyperbolic

---

109. *EPJ*, 349.
110. *EPJ*, 348.
111. Helen Nicholson, *Love, War and the Grail: Templars, Hospitallers and Teutonic Knights in Medieval Epic and Romance, 1150–1500* (Leiden, 2000), 123.

praise for a realm that lies outside the boundaries of Christendom. That new realm provides a mirror that reflects back a negative image of Byzantium. The letter emerged from the same intellectual milieu as the poetry of the Archpoet, the Hillin letters, and the *Play of Antichrist,* a world in which the art of praise could be outrageous, equivocal, and, finally, entertaining.

The letter of Prester John was presumably inspired by a passage from Otto of Freising, who gives the first known report of a leader from the Far East named Prester John. In the *Two Cities,* Otto relates a story that he claims to have heard from the bishop of Antioch. He frames the story with a discussion of how envoys were bringing him grim reports of the mounting problems for the Christian community at Edessa in 1145. Otto then retells an anecdote about a certain John from beyond Persia and Armenia who had defeated the brother kings of the Persians and the Medes, who were leading a combined army of Medes, Persians, and Assyrians.[112] The report of his victory has strong eschatological overtones, since in the schema of the Four Kingdoms, as Otto himself describes it elsewhere in the *Two Cities,* the Assyrians and the Medo-Persians precede the Greek/Macedonian empire, the third in the progression of history toward the Fourth Kingdom, which is the Romans.[113] John's next objective, Otto explains, had been to move his army to aid the church at Jerusalem and to imitate his alleged forebears, the Magi mentioned in the Gospel, by coming from the East to Jerusalem. Bad weather had thwarted his plans, and he was unable to cross the Tigris River, so he turned northward and spent years waiting to try again, but to no avail. Otto then abruptly cuts off his unusual, folkloric digression and moves on to a new topic.[114]

Otto's anecdote and the Prester John letter both originated in the milieu of Staufen propaganda, and the letter was no doubt inspired by Otto's digression. It is even possible to see how the letter takes up where the anecdote left off. Otto had established an eschatological theme by portraying Prester John as a conqueror of the Assyrians and the Medo-Persians who could not get to Jerusalem. The Greeks are the next empire in the familiar sequence, and Prester John comes to them with a proposal that concerns their relative status as emperors in the East and asks them to essentially relinquish their imperial status. We have seen repeatedly that the discourse of empire after Charlemagne's coronation was preoccupied with depicting a bloodless conquest of Byzantium by the West so that the empire might be whole again.

112. *HdDC,* 7.33.

113. *HdDC,* 6.22. "Sicut ergo illud duabus famosis mutionibus, Medorum scilicet et Persarum, succubuisse constat, sic est istud item duabus tantum, Graecorum et Francorum, subiacere debere volunt." See also Goez, *Translatio Imperii,* 114–15.

114. *HdDC,* 7.33. See Hamilton, "Prester John," 174.

Prester John, like the Charlemagne of the *Descriptio* and Benzo's Henry, is meant to symbolically and rhetorically conquer the Byzantine leader. Prester John is not a Roman emperor, but rather a rhetorical construction that serves the cause of empire in the West. As a witty creation of German imperial propagandists seeking to implicitly assert the primacy of Western imperial claims, Prester John is the greatest leader in the world, and should therefore be seen in a mirror as an exaggerated piece of self-representation by the West.

Bernard Hamilton has argued that the political motivations behind the Prester John letter should be seen in light of Rainald of Dassel's establishment of royal cult sites at Aachen and Cologne. The letter appeared just after the canonization of Charlemagne at Aachen in 1165 and not long after the arch-chancellor's orchestration of the establishment of the cult site of the Three Kings at Cologne in 1164.[115] His theory merits further exploration since it situates Rainald's various forgeries within the larger picture of his construction of Frederick's image as Christian Roman emperor. In the *Two Cities,* which appeared in 1157, Otto had emphasized the lineal descent of Prester John from the Three Kings at a time when there was no particular cult of the Magi in the West. In 1158, some relics of three bodies were unearthed in Milan, which were miraculously recognized to be those of the Three Kings. Hamilton sees the orchestration of the transfer to Cologne as part of Rainald's imperial propaganda program.[116] After presiding over the election of the imperial antipope Pascal III, Rainald visited Milan and removed the three bodies, having received them as official gifts from Frederick. He then transferred them to Cologne in July of 1164 after Frederick's Italian campaign.[117] The new shrine of the Magi was meant to be the center of a cult of Christian kingship that would also bolster his imperial program by asserting the prerogatives of lay leadership within the Christian community.[118] The transfer of the relics had been a ceremonial event designed to assert, as one scholar states, a "sanctifying connection" between the biblical kings and the Staufen leadership at a point when the imperial program was faltering

---

115. Hamilton, "Prester John," 177. Robert Trexler warns against overstating the association between the two cult sites, since the arrival of the relics of the Magi was far less significant than the canonization of Charlemagne; see *The Journey of the Magi: Meanings in History of a Christian Story* (Princeton, NJ, 1997), 78.

116. Hamilton argues that the transfer was purely political, noting that Rainald had shown little prior interest in the cathedral at Cologne and that the cult of the Magi in Milan had enjoyed no real popularity; see "Prester John," 177. See also Edina Bozoky, *La politique des reliques* (Paris, 2007), 151–52.

117. Godman, *Silent Masters,* 200; Trexler, *Journey of the Magi,* 78.

118. Hamilton, "Prester John," 177.

and "the sword of Roman imperial ideology had grown rusty."[119] The move was also a precursor to the canonization of Charlemagne, which was proclaimed just a few months after the arrival of the relics in Cologne.

Hamilton proposes that the Prester John letter was commissioned by Rainald as further documentation for the establishment of the cult site for the Three Kings at Cologne. According to this scenario, the arch-chancellor may have hastily ordered the production of the *translatio* narrative for the relics, which included stories of how Helena had brought their bodies from the East to Constantinople. The same scholar working for Rainald may also have written both the Prester John letter and the vitae of the Magi.[120] While the link between the cult of the Magi and the emergence of the Prester John letter is plausible, the theory that the letter was meant as supporting documentation for their saintliness is harder to accept. The document reads much more like a learned hoax inspired by tensions with the Greeks, especially in the wake of their support for the Milanese against Frederick. Moreover, there is little in the letter that would have lent solemnity to the establishment of the cult site at Cologne, nor would it have contributed in any significant way to proving the saintly merits of the biblical kings to whom Prester John claims a remote relationship in Otto's story. Finally, the focus on the imperial East and the anti-Byzantine tone of the letter would also need a better explanation. Hamilton argues that the opening of the missive where Prester John addresses Manuel was merely a literary device to explain how the letter had reached Frederick during a period when Greek envoys had come to court.[121] This is unlikely, given that without the deliberately constructed opening, the description of Prester John's kingdom loses its primary rhetorical function, the debasement of the Byzantines.

Prester John is best understood as a larger-than-life figure who serves as a rhetorical device to belittle the Greek emperor. When seen in that light, the hyperbolic tenor of the letter with its presentation of the idealized kingdom of the East comes into clearer focus. Like the *Play of Antichrist,* the letter has a performative quality that indicates that it was meant to entertain. The Archpoet revealed deep anger at Manuel Comnenus in his panegyric to Frederick after Milan, vaunting Greek defeat within his elaboration of the topos of surrendering foreign nations. The Prester John letter also celebrates symbolic defeat of Byzantium, but in a far more elaborate variation on the

---

119. Joseph P. Huffman, *The Social Politics of Medieval Diplomacy: Anglo-German Relations (1066–1307)* (Ann Arbor, MI, 2000), 73.

120. Hamilton, "Prester John," 180–81.

121. Ibid., 180.

foreign embassy motif. Someone in Rainald's circles, the chancellor himself or another scholar, poet, or learned cleric working around him, likely decided to take the anecdote told by Otto and to create a satirical follow-up. The fact that Pope Alexander then wrote a "response" to Prester John offers further evidence of a culture of witty, highbrow exchanges that took place at the highest levels of clerical intellectual culture.[122]

Conclusion

The early years of the reign of Frederick Barbarossa witnessed a variety of approaches to the theme of Roman universalism. Otto of Freising had made him an Augustus reigning over a providential peace, while the author of the *Play of Antichrist* depicted German universal victory gained through aggressive conquest and intimidation, but both created a vision of Hohenstaufen universalism based on the ideal of Frederick's theoretical *patrocinium*. After Otto, there seems to have been a certain mood in imperialist circles marked by rivalry, anger, and restless intellectual energy that can be sensed in the Hillin series, the Archpoet, and the letter of Prester John. The response to the question of how we should interpret these documents lies in large measure, then, with the imperial chancery and with Rainald himself. The archchancellor and trusted adviser was the provocative and highly ideological mind behind the culture of document production in the period after Frederick's coronation until his death just two years after the canonization of Charlemagne. The circulation of the letter of Prester John coincided with the canonization of Charlemagne in 1165, a political act that was tightly bound up in the imperial politics of the Staufen court and its clash with the papacy. Whereas Charlemagne had not figured in early Hohenstaufen assertions of universal authority and constructions of *dominium mundi,* at a certain point in the early 1160s, the Carolingian emperor gained favor in the chancery as the ideal imperial antecedent of Frederick Barbarossa. The next chapter will consider the incorporation of Charlemagne as universal emperor into the Hohenstaufen discourse of empire.

---

122. For a recent portrait of clerical culture and its relationship to political institutions and court life in the twelfth century, see generally John D. Cotts, *The Clerical Dilemma: Peter of Blois and Literate Culture in the Twelfth Century* (Washington, DC, 2009).

✻ CHAPTER 5

The Emperor's Charlemagne

Otto of Freising made only passing references to Charlemagne in the *Deeds of Frederick Barbarossa,* the most notable one of which occurs in Book 2 when he describes how in 1152 the duke of Swabia, having been raised to the rank of king, sat upon the throne placed by Charlemagne in the church at Aachen. The Archpoet invoked the name of Charlemagne in the *Kaiserhymnus,* but as only one among multiple exempla.[1] Neither Hohenstaufen propagandist presented the Frankish king as an all-encompassing Christian Roman imperial antecedent. A shift occurred in the wake of Frederick's break with the Holy See in 1160, however, and Charlemagne began to emerge as the primary imperial predecessor for the Staufen leader, a movement that culminated in the 1165 canonization of the Carolingian emperor at Aachen.[2] Rahewin's rewriting of Einhard's chapter 16 at the close of the *Deeds* early in the 1160s thus proves to have been a harbinger of the rise to prominence of Charlemagne in the discourse of Roman universalism. In this chapter I consider the emergence of Charlemagne in Hohenstaufen propaganda, first with regard to the canonization of Charlemagne, and then in the saintly biography the *Vita Karoli Magni.* I

---

1. *GF,* 2.3; Archpoet, *Kaiserhymnus,* stanza 16.
2. Folz, *Le souvenir,* 176; Werner Grebe, "Studien zur Geistigen Welt Rainalds von Dassel," in Wolf, *Friedrich Barbarossa,* 273.

conclude with an examination of the writings of Godfrey of Viterbo, whose reinterpretations of the events surrounding the coronation of 800 reveal the extent to which "Charlemagne and the East" continued to serve as a forum for discussion of rival claims to authority in the Christian Roman Empire.

By the mid-twelfth century, the source of Charlemagne's imperial authority had long been a matter of dispute in the polemics between church and state. Propagandists on the imperial side therefore needed to cultivate a particular memory of the Frankish king to fit their political program. Certain memories of the emperor would not have fulfilled their needs, such as the Charlemagne who humbly agreed to protect the interests of the Holy See in return for his title, or the hoary-bearded Charlemagne, king of Saint-Denis in the French vernacular tradition. The version of Charlemagne that they did eventually create was the product of a pastiche of different historiographical and ecclesiastical traditions, including, in particular, the story of how the Frankish emperor received relics from the emperor in Constantinople after his coronation. Benzo of Alba had adapted the memory of Charlemagne's exchanges with the East to promote a concept of lay power over all of Christendom at a time of great struggle between the empire and the Holy See. In the mid-twelfth century, Rainald of Dassel, the architect of Frederick's imperial propaganda program, also recognized the quasi-sibylline Charlemagne who gains symbolic victory over the East as a valuable weapon in his anti-papal arsenal. Both of these learned men were sharp-tongued promoters of Roman renewal, and both were moved by bitter hatred for the popes with whom they clashed.

The worlds of political and ecclesiastical ceremony were intimately intertwined in the Hohenstaufen world.[3] In a grand public gesture, during the Christmas celebration at Aachen in 1165, Frederick had the remains of Charlemagne elevated to the altar in the Church of Saint Mary and placed in a golden casket. Sources say that he moved the body himself. Peter Munz provides a vivid picture of the fraught political drama that led up to the ceremony, including the refusal by the headstrong Rainald to be consecrated as archbishop of Cologne for fear that he would lose his see when the schism was resolved.[4] When he declined a second time in 1164, an angry Frederick publicly called him a traitor and vowed to persecute anyone at court, whether clergy or laity, who supported Pope Alexander III. When the time came for the canonization, Rainald and Frederick had reconciled, and were

---

3. Friedrich Heer, *The Holy Roman Empire,* trans. Janet Sondheimer (New York, 1968), 75.
4. Munz, *Frederick,* 241.

the only ones committed to the antipope Paschal III.[5] The ceremony took place under these tense circumstances, and so rather than serving as a glorious commemoration of the parallels between Frederick and his illustrious predecessor, the canonization of Charlemagne may well have had an air of desperation. The project was nonetheless a bold invocation of the Frankish emperor that was intended to reinforce the idea that Frederick's imperial power came directly from God. The Charlemagne of Staufen memory had been an instrument of providence, not of the papacy, and Frederick likewise answered to God, not to Rome.[6]

A central element of Frederick Barbarossa's self-fashioning as emperor was his refusal of papal authority. His contentious relationship with the papacy had started early in his imperial reign when he refused to carry out the *strator's* duty, which demanded that he lead the pope's horse while on foot with the pope mounted on the horse. The symbolic ritual deliberately recalled the tradition of Constantine's submissive relationship to Sylvester. The defiant refusal was a sign of his intention to reject any role for the clergy in his election, and he remained a staunch proponent of weakened papal influence over the empire.[7] Frederick's troubles with the papacy later escalated over the Treaty of Benevento and the siege of Milan, becoming full-blown after Hadrian died in 1159 and the emperor intervened in the papal election of 1160, setting off a two-decade-long schism.[8] The imperial intervention in the election pitted Alexander III, whom both Louis VII and Henry II favored, against Victor, who was Barbarossa's choice.[9] In March of 1160, after Frederick's unsanctioned election of Victor, for whom the emperor happily performed the service of *strator,* Pope Alexander excommunicated Frederick, along with the other major participants. By 1164, Victor had died, and Frederick's imperial program was not going well. In 1165, at the height of tensions, Rainald organized the canonization of Charlemagne to promote Frederick's *sacrum imperium.* The process was carried out by Victor's unsanctioned replacement, Pope Pascal III, a puppet of the Staufen court.[10]

---

5. Ibid., 241–42.

6. Dietrich Lohrmann, "Politische Instrumentalisierung Karls des Grossen durch die Staufer und ihre Gegner," *Zeitschrift des Aachener Geschichtsvereins* 104/105 (2002/2003): 105. See also Friedrich Hausmann, "Gottfried von Viterbo: Kapellan und Notar, Magister, Geschichtsschreiber und Dichter," in *Friedrich Barbarossa: Handlungsspielräume und Wirkungsweisen Des Staufischen Kaisers,* ed. Alfred Haverkamp (Sigmaringen, 1992), 603–21.

7. Munz, *Frederick,* 81–82.

8. Benson, "Political *Renovatio,*" 378.

9. Goez, *Translatio Imperii,* 142; Kienast, *Deutschland,* 137.

10. Pacaut, *Frederick Barbarossa,* 118–19; Godman, *Silent Masters,* 198; Robert Folz, "Aspects du culte liturgique de Saint Charlemagne en France," in *Karl der Grosse: Lebenswerk und Nachleben IV,*

The canonization of Charlemagne represented a major initiative in Rainald's ongoing and, at times, faltering program to promote Frederick's imperial image. His actions in orchestrating the event were no doubt designed to upset the Holy See by appropriating the papal role in the designation of a saint as illustrious and politically significant as Charlemagne.[11] Timothy Reuter argues that when the imperial chancery invoked Charlemagne and Otto the Great as predecessors of Frederick, those references were intended as implicit responses to Gregorian critiques of German domination.[12] The canonization was as forceful an invocation of the Frankish king as one can imagine, and ought therefore to be seen through the lens of the conflict between empire and papacy. The entire production constituted a bold political act that was essentially a lay canonization presided over by an antipope and an emperor who was in a schismatic relationship with Rome. Despite its importance as an element of the imperial propaganda program, the canonization, it is worth noting, yielded little more than a geographically limited, liturgical tradition for the new pseudo-saint.[13]

A dearth of witnesses has necessitated mostly conjecture about the motivations behind the canonization, but the general consensus holds that, on the most basic level, the move was meant to celebrate Charlemagne as a saintly emperor and to establish him as a Christian imperial antecedent to Frederick.[14] In a decree issued early in 1166, Frederick claims that his decision to canonize Charlemagne was in response to a request by his "most dear friend" Henry (the king of England), but historians tend to credit Rainald with the idea.[15] Another theory holds that the event was largely meant to work against French interests by forging a deliberate Germanification of a Charlemagne

ed. Wolfgang Braunfels and Percy Ernst Schramm (Düsseldorf, 1967), 77. There was a nationalist feeling that went along with the claim to heritage of the holiness of Charlemagne, a sentiment that, according to Grebe, overrode the questionable circumstances under which the canonization had occurred, so much so that Pope Alexander never denied the canonization that his rival antipope Paschal had carried out; see "Studien zur Geistigen," 277–78. See also Munz, *Frederick,* 243; Tischler, "Tatmensch oder Heidenapostel," 7–15.

    11. Godman, *Silent Masters,* 200–201.

    12. Timothy Reuter, "Past, Present and No Future in the *Regnum Teutonicum,*" in *The Perception of the Past in Twelfth-Century Europe,* ed. Paul Magdalino (London, 2003), 23.

    13. Folz, "Aspects du culte."

    14. Godman, *Silent Masters,* 200 and 213; Munz, *Frederick,* 243; Ludwig Vones, "La canonización de Carlomagno en 1165: *La Vita S. Karoli* de Aquisgrán y el Pseudo-Turpín," in *El Pseudo-Turpín, lazo entre el culto jacobeo y el culto de Carlomagno: Actas del VI Congreso Internacional de Estudios Jacobeos,* ed. Klaus Herbers (Santiago de Compostela, 2003), 271; Folz, *Concept,* 101; Monteleone, *Il viaggio,* 214.

    15. Scholars also point to the coincidence of other prominent canonizations of secular leaders such as Henry II of Germany in 1146, Edward the Confessor in 1161, and then, later, Knut of Denmark, in 1169. See Joseph P. Huffman, *The Social Politics of Medieval Diplomacy: Anglo-German Relations (1066–1307)* (Ann Arbor, MI, 2000), 85; Rauschen, *Die Legende,* 155; Mayer, "Staufische

who had become too French. Citing the German orchestrations as reactions to French manifestations of *orgueil,* Zeller went so far as to propose that the canonization of Charlemagne and the birth of Philip Augustus to a mother in the Carolingian bloodline had not been a coincidence.[16] The case for envisioning the German court as weary of France's successful cultivation of the memory of the Frankish king, although appealing as a modern narrative of Franco-German relations, has been overstated. The *Play of Antichrist* offers a helpful lens through which to see the role of the French with regard to the canonization. Both the play and the liturgical ceremony, with its accompanying forged documents, offered staged public articulations of a universalizing concept of German imperial authority. In the play, the king of the Franks is a rival leader in the West with competing historical ties to ancient Rome, who needs to be brought into submission. The scene with the *rex Francorum* is just one element of the play, however, which is more concerned with the larger promotion of the German inheritance of the empire than with the particular challenge to that concept posed by the French kingdom.

Just as it is important to avoiding reading too much into the *Play of Antichrist* as an allegory of relations between Capetian France and Hohenstaufen Germany, we should also see the German relationship with the French in the mid-1160s as but one element, albeit an important one, in the political dramas surrounding the papal schism and the canonization process. The goal of publicly asserting a model of autonomous lay power during a time of papal schism was more important to Frederick and his promoters than establishing Aachen as the center of Charlemagne's world over and against the claims and interests of Saint-Denis. The fact that Rainald and Frederick sought to establish the saintliness of Charlemagne and then carried out the ceremony in the midst of the crisis using their antipope was a deep affront to the Holy See.[17] By contrast, as I argue in chapter 6, there was far less interest in Charlemagne in France during the period of the canonization than has previously been suggested. Frederick needed to keep the French in check, but reclaiming Charlemagne and asserting the primacy of Aachen over Saint-Denis were smaller hurdles to be surmounted as part of the larger program of assertion

---

Welterherrschaft," 190; Jürgen Petersohn, "Saint-Denis–Westminster–Aachen. Die Karls-Translatio von 1164 und ihre Vorbilder," *Deutsches Archiv für Erforschung des Mittelalters* 31 (1975): 420–22.

16. Munz, *Frederick,* 243; Folz, *Le souvenir,* 207; Du Pouget, "Recherches," 14; Zeller, "Les rois de France," 279–80. See also Monteleone, *Il viaggio,* 198–99; Galland, "Les relations," 82. In a more nuanced interpretation, Petersohn notes the similarities between the orchestration of the events of 1165 and a translation of the remains of Saint Denis that occurred at the royal abbey in 1144 under Louis VII, in "Saint-Denis–Westminster," 439.

17. Godman, *Silent Masters,* 200–201.

of Christian imperial authority. Prior to the canonization, a letter linked to Rainald had accused Louis of being an accomplice of Roland (the given name of Pope Alexander) and an enemy of the empire, so there was clearly strife, but Frederick and Rainald had bigger problems than Louis VII and the monks of Saint-Denis.[18]

In a recent study of the liturgical music developed for the feast day of Saint Charlemagne, Michael McGrade demonstrates how the imperial politics of *dominium mundi* were woven into the creation of Charlemagne's liturgical cult. The ceremony, he observes, worked to counter claims by the papacy to the role of protectors of the church, in part by creating a new history that celebrated the cooperation between Charlemagne and Leo in making Aachen the *sedes regni*.[19] Focusing on the chant known as the *Urbs aquensis, urbs regalis,* McGrade shows how the staging of the events in the church, the affirmation of the status of Aachen, the elevation of Charlemagne's remains, and the use of Carolingian symbolism in the basilica all combined to reinforce links to the Carolingian past.[20] The sequence celebrates Charlemagne in the language of Christian victory as the *"rex mundi triumphator"* who subdues barbarian peoples and *"reges superbos."*[21] In the sixth versicle of the chant, Charlemagne is anointed with the crown of glory that places him above all other kings. The liturgical ceremony itself included the lowering of a copper lamp, known as the *corona,* representing the New Jerusalem, which Frederick had donated. The descent of the lamp represented a symbolic coronation that signaled the end of the succession of empires and the coming of the Apocalypse.[22] The ceremony thus looked back to Charlemagne, while celebrating Aachen as the final site of universal Roman dominion and the end of the last of the Four Kingdoms.

The December 1165 ceremony was followed by the issuance of the aforementioned decree of January 1166 issued in Frederick's name, which contained a "found" document written in the name of Charlemagne that granted privileges to the city of Aachen. The document described how, in an assembly at that very church that had been consecrated by Pope Leo III, the pontiff had established Aachen as the *"caput Gallie."*[23] This declaration

---

18. Vones, "La canonización de Carlomagno," 271.

19. McGrade, "*O Rex Mundi,*" 204.

20. Ibid., 202–7.

21. Ibid., 193.

22. Ibid., 205–10.

23. *Karlsprivileg,* 115. See also Monteleone, *Il viaggio,* 202; Rauschen, *Die Legende,* 155–57; Appelt, "Friedrich Barbarossa," 235; Folz, "La chancellerie"; Max Kerner, *Karl der Grosse: Entschleierung Eines Mythos* (Cologne, 2000), 113.

of privileges, a forgery from the imperial chancery, is a first-person narrative offering a rich tale of *inventio* and *renovatio* in which the Frankish leader restores an old Roman site. The site of the church had been built on initially by Granus, a brother of Agrippa and Nero, but that structure had crumbled over time and become overgrown. Charlemagne then tells of how he restored the forgotten Roman foundation, making it into a sanctified Christian site. Through the canonization process and the establishment of the cult site at Aachen, Frederick thus added his own new layer of sanctified Christian imperial *Romanitas*.

In the decree, Charlemagne describes how he had lovingly restored the building, renovating it in marble and adorning it with fine decorations. He had also offered, for its sanctification and protection, multiple relics of the apostles, martyrs, confessors, and the Virgin, objects that he had collected from various lands, most especially from the Greeks. The reference to relics that Charlemagne brought from Constantinople to Aachen certainly derives from the tradition that inspired the *Descriptio* author and Benedict before him. Between the ceremony and the documents, it becomes clear, then, that the Charlemagne whom Rainald and Frederick evoked was the traveling emperor of the "Charlemagne and the East" tradition. Benzo had made it clear that the gifts from Constantinople represented the Greek East's symbolic relinquishing of power to Henry IV as a sign of his triumph over all Christendom. As the decree of 1166 demonstrates, the Salian panegyrist's interpretation continued to be valid when a new generation of antipapal promoters of the German Roman *renovatio* adapted the same rhetorical tradition.

The *Vita Karoli Magni*

Canonizations require documentation to prove the saintly merits of the candidate for sainthood. In 1165, Charlemagne did not have a dossier of such evidence, so one needed to be created. The process took a number of years, although just how many has been a matter of debate. The circumstances of the production of the *Vita Karoli Magni* remain unknown, but the most convincing arguments tie the document to the imperial chancery in the 1170s, and not, as some have argued, to a compilation of documents gathered from various French ecclesiastical centers for Count Baldwin V of Hainaut in the mid-1180s.[24] For instance, the *Descriptio* is reproduced nearly in full in the

---

24. J. B. Gillingham, "Why Did Rahewin Stop Writing the *Gesta Frederici*?" *English Historical Review* 83 (1968): 303; Appelt, "Die Kaiseridee," 236–37. For the Baldwin theory, see H. M. Smyser, *The Pseudo-Turpin: B.N., Fonds Latin, MS 17656* (Cambridge, MA, 1937), 9–10, and Christopher

Vita, and, although we do not know when the *Vita* appeared, there is enough thematic continuity between the *Descriptio* and the decree of January 1166 to indicate that the story told in the eleventh-century document was known in imperial circles in the 1160s. The oldest extant version is found in a codex from sometime after 1179, titled "A new life of Charlemagne written by the order of Emperor Frederick."[25] We do not know to what extent Rainald of Dassel was involved in the production of the *Vita* before he died in 1167, but it seems safe to assume that the arch-chancellor would have remained involved in matters related to his Charlemagne project. It is also impossible to determine how much of the work had been done prior to Frederick's reconciliation with Pope Alexander in 1177.

In spite of the anti-curial atmosphere in which Charlemagne's canonization occurred, little has been said about what might have been the anti-reformist appeal of the documents selected for the *Vita Karoli Magni.* In general, the contents of Charlemagne's saintly *Vita* have not received much scholarly attention, in part because of the mystery of its origins, but also because the compilation has been dismissed as a gathering of preexisting works. A new look at the document that focuses on its thematic organization around a series of divine visions reveals a different story. The *Vita*'s creators were in fact quite deliberate in their presentation of a Charlemagne who had been elected by God, and not the papacy, as the leader and protector of Christendom. The canonization had been an assertion of imperial authority, and Charlemagne's encounters with the East had long been appearing in works devoted to the promotion of Roman imperial renewal. The inclusion of the *Descriptio* in the *Vita,* on those grounds alone, shows that it was perceived as an imperialist vision of Charlemagne's assumption of the empire.

The *Descriptio* appears in the saintly biography in its entirety, except for the Charles the Bald section. In this truncated form, the document celebrates a Charlemagne who achieves symbolic victory over the Greeks and brings the relics from the East back to Aachen, where they stay. This shorter version also ends with a celebration of Charlemagne as the benefactor of Aachen who oversees the building of the basilica and its establishment as the center of Christendom in the Frankish West as the *caput Gallie.* This same scene is central to the January 1166 decree, with its recently "discovered" privileges that Charlemagne had offered to the city of Aachen. The decree also contains the

---

Hohler, "A Note on Jacobus," *Journal of the Warburg and Courtauld Institutes* 35 (1972): 65–66. For those who retain Rauschen's theory of its imperial origins, see Folz, *Le souvenir,* 221; Vones, "La canonización, 98; Kerner, *Karl der Grosse,* 121; Monteleone, *Il viaggio,* 234.

25. "...nova vita Karoli magni jussu Frederici Augusti conscripta," in H. M. Smyser, "An Early Redaction of the *Pseudo-Turpin,*" *Speculum* 11 (1936): 282.

Carolingian king's description of Pope Leo's visit to Aachen to consecrate the Roman edifice that he had lovingly restored to create a splendid basilica. That same narrative figures in Book 1 of the *Vita,* including the mention of his donation of relics from Constantinople.[26] The Charlemagne of the *Vita* is a complex figure constructed with the material of multiple textual traditions, but there is nonetheless clear continuity between the *Descriptio,* the false decree of January 1166, and the *Vita* in the presentation of Charlemagne's establishment of Aachen as the center of his realm. The latter two documents were designed to bolster the political weight of the questionable canonization, and the *Descriptio* had been a key source for their creation.

We have seen in the preceding chapters how epistolary fictions and imagined diplomatic correspondences could serve as a medium for polemical assertions of imperialist doctrine, and Charlemagne's saintly *Vita* participates in this same rhetorical culture. The *Vita* is divided into three books containing a variety of compiled historiographical materials. Each contains a letter describing a divine vision: the vision of Saint Stephen (*Revelatio sancti Stephani*) at the altar of Saint-Denis, Constantine's vision in the *Descriptio,* and Charlemagne's vision in the *Pseudo-Turpin Chronicle* in which Saint James entreats him to liberate his burial site in Galicia. Although the compilers supplemented Charlemagne's saintly biography with other materials, the three visions create an underlying framework as well as a biographical trajectory for the *Vita.* Each conveys a divine message concerning the need for the Carolingian king to render aid to an embattled Christendom. All three letters are presented by the compiler as official documents that have been inserted into the dossier. The *Vita* is therefore based on a series of forged communiqués around which its creators constructed an imperialist revision of the relationship between the papacy and the Carolingian rulers of the eighth and ninth centuries.

Early in Book 1, the author describes Charlemagne's lifetime as an era of great suffering for the papacy. The passage celebrates Rome as "*caput omnium ecclesiarum*" but highlights the difficulties endured during the papacies of Stephen, Hadrian, and Leo, all three of whom are later delivered from their troubles by the Carolingians. The account of papal woes includes what the author describes as the expulsion of Stephen, the oppression of Hadrian, and the blinding of Leo. The passage also serves as a lead-in to the letter describing the vision of Pope Stephen.[27] The story of the vision of Saint Stephen

---

26. *VKM,* 1.16, 41–42. Just as in the 1166 decree, Aachen is described as the *caput Gallie.*

27. *VKM,* 1.1, 21. "per expulsionem Stephani Pape, per oppressionem Adriani, per cacetionem quoque Leonis."

takes place during the pontiff's famous visit to Saint-Denis in 753–54, during which the pope consecrated Pippin and his sons.[28] During his time there, Stephen is said to have fallen gravely ill and received a visitation from Saints Peter, Paul, and Denis. The original version of the vision was commissioned by Louis the Pious and composed in 835 by Abbot Hilduin of Saint-Denis, who, according to one scholar, took great pleasure in counterfeiting papal documents.[29] The dream text is also preserved in the tenth-century chronicle of Regino of Prum and in a formulary at Saint-Denis collated next to a copy of the earlier version of the Donation of Constantine, the Constitutum Constantini. Noting this proximity in the formulary, Johannes Fried argues that some of the language in the description of the dedication of the altar at Saint-Denis that follows the account of Stephen's vision bears remarkable resemblance to language in the neighboring forgery of Constantine's gift of authority in the West to the Holy See.[30] This association between the text of Stephen's vision and the Donation reinforces the importance of the memory of Stephen's consecration of Pippin and his sons as an assertion of papal authority and lay submission to the Holy See.

Since Charlemagne's canonization had been a public assertion of German imperial prerogative during a period of major conflict with the papacy, it is curious that his *Vita* would contain a version of Pope Stephen's famous visit to the French royal abbey. Certainly, the fact that the compilers chose to include a locus of memory that had long served to reinforce the idealized papal vision of a submissive and beholden Frankish king invites a closer reading of the vision story as it appears in the *Vita*. And, indeed, upon closer examination, the cherished piece of ecclesiastical memory had been altered to make the vision less friendly to the papal cause. Although Charlemagne's *Vita* does not adopt nearly as bold an imperialist stance as the apocryphal letters of Pope Hadrian I in the Ravenna forgeries or of Hadrian IV in the Hillin letters, the revised vision of Saint Stephen contains some significant changes that were intended to mold the document to conform to a Staufen vision of lay authority in the empire.

Since the early decades of the Investiture Contest, imperial theorists had been promulgating the belief that God, not the pope, had made Pippin king of the Franks.[31] Moreover, the Ravenna and the Hillin forgeries had articulated

28. Story, "Cathwulf," 11.

29. Johannes Fried, *Donation of Constantine and Constitutum Constantini: The Misinterpretation of a Fiction and Its Original Meaning. With a Contribution by Wolfram Brandes: "The Satraps of Constantine"* (Berlin, 2007), 109.

30. Fried, *Donation,* 109.

31. Goez, *Translatio Imperii,* 97.

adamant refusals of the idea that the papacy had been the source of Charlemagne's imperial power, with the Ravenna forgeries even explicitly dis-
mantling the existing relationship between Charlemagne and Hadrian by
imagining the pope handing over control of papal elections to the king.
Charlemagne's saintly *Vita* is itself a gathering of imperial forgeries that were
deployed in these same ideological battles. The *Vita* version of the vision of
Pope Stephen, in particular, seeks to reshape the memory of the origins of
the Franco-papal alliance. The fact that the papacy had received help from
Pippin and Charlemagne was not a matter of dispute, however. At issue was
the papal role in defining the origins and future of Carolingian kingship, and,
as we shall see, the *Vita* author was careful to excise material that affirmed the
papal origins of that authority.

Charlemagne's *Vita* reproduces much of Hilduin's text, which documented
the events surrounding the consecration of an altar to Peter and Paul in front
of the tomb of Saint Denis. The narrative opens with the characterization of
Stephen's journey to Paris as having occurred during a time of persecution
of the Roman church by the "atrocious and blasphemous" Lombard leader
Aistulf. Having fallen ill on his journey, the pope stands before the altar of
Saint-Denis, where he experiences a vision in which Saints Peter, Paul, and
Denis appear to him.[32] Peter speaks first, saying, "Our brother asks for good
health." Paul, placing his hand on the chest of Denis, tells him that Stephen
will soon be healed by Denis's mercy. Denis then tells Stephen not to fear, for
he will not die, but will return to his seat of power in good health. He then
orders the pope to stand up and be healthy and to dedicate the altar before
him with missals of thanks to the apostles Peter and Paul. Quickly restored to
health, Stephen reports what he experienced to Pippin, his sons, and others.
The people whom he encounters believe that he has lost his mind, until he
carries out his unspecified promises, doing as he was admonished to do in the
vision. The next passage begins rather abruptly in a more annalistic style that
appears to be the work of another author. Here we learn that Pippin and his
sons were consecrated as kings of the Franks in the year 753 at that same altar
where the pontiff had received the vision and was healed. The presentation
of the succession of events makes the consecration appear to be Stephen's
way of proving that he was not crazy by showing gratitude, as instructed by
the saints, for what had occurred.

The *Vita* compilers made a key revision to Hilduin's text by removing
an essential portion of the account of the dedication of the altar. Missing

---

32. *VKM*, 1.1, 22. Cf. Hilduin of Saint-Denis, *Ex Hilduini Abbatis Libro de Sancto Dionysio,*
ed. Wilhelm Wattenbach, MGH *SS* 15.1 (Hanover, 1887), 2–3.

from Charlemagne's saintly *Vita* is Pope Stephen's stipulation concerning the future of Frankish kingship. In consecrating Pippin and the new line of *reges Francorum,* the pope had made a clear assertion of papal control over the election and consecration of Frankish kings in perpetuity.[33] Hilduin had written that after sanctifying the noblemen of the Franks by apostolic benediction, Stephen, on the authority of Saint Peter given to him by Christ, had declared that at no time in the future could anyone from another race (*stirps*) presume to establish himself as king in any other manner. The only exception to that rule was someone who was the progeny of those whom the presiding apostolic see elected by divine providence and whom divine providence deemed worthy of being raised up for royal power and consecration.[34] The creator of Charlemagne's saintly *Vita* removed this essential passage describing how Stephen had established papal election and familial lineage as the only possible modes of succession for Frankish kings.

The alteration to Charlemagne's *Vita* to exclude the establishment of a Frankish kingship as based on both heredity and papal sanction was a logical one, given the ideological aims of those for whom it was being produced. The German emperors based their assumption of Charlemagne's empire on the theory of divinely ordained transfer, and not on their genealogical ties to the Carolingians. Furthermore, the assertion of the primacy of the papacy in the selection and consecration of lay leaders was the very antithesis of the doctrine of imperial authority promulgated by the Hohenstaufen court. If Charlemagne had ruled by divine election, so could Frederick, and matters of bloodlines and papal favor could not get in his way. The *Vita* even contains an added passage that reconfigures Stephen's vision as proof of apostolic approval of Charlemagne's canonization. The narrator explains that the appearance at the altar of Peter, Paul, and Denis had furnished evidence that the three men of apostolic rank who appeared to Stephen had wanted Charlemagne to join them as patron and defender of the church.[35] In its revised form, then, with Stephen's articulation of papal prerogative carefully excised, this politically significant historiographical site of the origins of the Franco-papal alliance conveys instead a divine intervention on behalf of the Germanic line of Roman emperors.

The recasting of the vision of Saint Stephen as a divinely orchestrated event leading to the establishment of Carolingian kingship represents a bold attempt

---

33. Hilduin, *Sancto Dionysio,* 3.

34. Ibid.

35. *VKM,* 23. "Per illum namque apostolice dignitatis et nominis virum tres beate visionis consortes suarum ecclesiarum defensorem et patronum beatum karolum magnum in regum ungi voluerunt."

to undo a long-held memory of the origins of Frankish kingship. It also represents a logical precursor to the presentation of Charlemagne's coronation in Book 2 of the *Vita*. In a combined *explicit* of the first book and prologue to the second, the author claims that he has shown Charlemagne as a *"dei athlete."* He promises that in the next book he will talk about the Frankish king's peregrinations and miracles, including his liberation of the Holy City, which he undertook "after heavenly revelation."[36] This clearly delineated transition to a new section in his biography shows a deliberate progression from one biographical category to the next. These sections can be read as Christianized versions of the Roman biographical categories of "deeds in war" and "deeds in peace" composed for a saintly biography, since Charlemagne goes from being a warrior of God to a pilgrim who performs miracles. The section in Book 1 devoted to depicting Charlemagne as an "athlete of God" focuses heavily on the travails of the papacy and the ways in which Charlemagne saved the pontiffs in distress. These feats do not lead to rewards of temporal authority, however. Instead, Charlemagne is portrayed as working on behalf of God alone, by divine providence, with no papal intermediary. The papacy benefits from his aid, but does not lay claim to having made Charlemagne king or emperor as thanks for his endeavors. Stephen's consecration of Pippin and his sons is portrayed as having been carried out by apostolic order because the three saints wanted Charlemagne to be among them. By canonizing Charlemagne, Frederick fulfills their wish.

The following section, which is essentially the Charlemagne section of the *Descriptio,* is presented as a book that will be devoted to Charlemagne's pilgrimage to the East and the miracles he performed on the way home. The liberation of Jerusalem is portrayed as an unexpected miracle, and therefore does not figure as one of his deeds as a warrior of God. Biographically speaking, the journey is not considered under the rubric of his feats of strength, but rather as one of his deeds in peace. This distinction is significant because it elucidates the question of whether Charlemagne's expedition to Jerusalem was meant to be seen as an armed military expedition. The creator of the *Vita* uses the prologue to the book containing the *Descriptio* to make clear what its source had left somewhat ambiguous, that the journey to Jerusalem was a pilgrimage, and that the flight of the pagan enemy upon his arrival had been an unexpected miracle.[37] The perceived reasons behind Charlemagne's journey to the East were clearly a matter of concern for the author, since,

---

36. *VKM,* 44.
37. *VKM,* 44–45.

in the *incipit,* he insists that the journey was divinely ordered and that the liberation of the city happened during a peregrination.

The third and final book of the *Vita* opens with parts of a version of the *Pseudo-Turpin Chronicle,* which features Charlemagne's vision of Saint James.[38] Although the chronicle is a significant work, I intend to venture only some tentative thoughts regarding its placement in the *Vita.* Charlemagne's saintly career begins in Book 1 with the divine rather than the papal establishment of Carolingian kingship. There follows in the second book his divine election as emperor, his symbolic conquest of the Greek East, and finally his establishment of the seat of spiritual authority in the West, at Aachen. The third vision, in which Saint James implores Charlemagne to rescue his burial site in Spain, reflects the inexorable progression of the Roman Empire from East to West. The expedition also represents the ongoing struggles of the Christian emperor, in this case at the Western reaches of Christendom. In this scenario, the *Pseudo-Turpin* chronicle offers a third divine vision that reasserts the primacy of the emperor as the direct receiver of divine requests for the protection of the empire. That claim to the status of vicar of Christ on earth and king of all terrestrial kings is the unifying theme of all three visions, and of the Staufen conception of Charlemagne as a whole.

In his biography of Frederick II, Ernst Kantorowicz declares that from the moment the Hohenstaufens began to dream of world power, the crusade "became their proudest ambition." To support this claim, the historian cites Conrad's accompaniment of Louis VII on the Second Crusade, after which, he writes, "Twenty years later Barbarossa deliberately treated Emperor and Crusader as synonymous terms."[39] The first step in this process was the canonization of Charlemagne and his commissioning of the saintly *Vita,* "in which much space was given to Charles, the Crusader, and his Pilgrimage to the Holy Land."[40] The German promoters of Frederick borrowed a French legend adapted to imperial concerns, he explains, and then linked it to the Spanish campaign, which became fused with the larger legend of Charlemagne as crusader. In this succinct passage, Kantorowicz reflects the modern conventional wisdom surrounding "Charlemagne and the East," in large part by adducing the canonization as one of his two central pieces

---

38. The first seven chapters of part three of the *Vita* contain chapters 1–4 and 6–8 of the *Pseudo-Turpin Chronicle.* See Smyser, "Early Redaction," 282–83. Smyser argues that the style of these chapters is more elegant than the version in the Codex Calixtinus, but that the content is the same.

39. Ernst H. Kantorowicz, *Frederick the Second, 1194–1250,* trans. E. O. Lorimer (New York, 1957), 167.

40. Kantorowicz, *Frederick the Second,* 167.

of evidence for Frederick's crusading dreams. His reading of the role of Charlemagne in Hohenstaufen propaganda is not the Gallo-centric story of appropriation of the emperor from the French, but it does perpetuate the notion that the Charlemagne who traveled to the East functioned for all who knew the story as a proto-crusader.

Kantorowicz was right to see the appropriation of "Charlemagne and the East" as a tool of Staufen propaganda, but his invocation of the prominence of Charlemagne's Holy Land journey in the German imperial program as evidence of the ongoing dream of crusade demands reconsideration. To say that the crusade was an essential dream of the Staufen leader leaves much room for interpretation. First, it needs to be noted that crusading as a defined concept was in its infancy in the mid-twelfth century, as Christopher Tyerman has shown.[41] What would have constituted a successful "crusade" for a German emperor in 1158 or 1165, for example? How would that victory have been defined within the Staufen imperial program? More important, though, is the fact that the promotion of expeditions to the East, whether the major named crusades or the lesser-known endeavors on behalf of Christians in the East, had been based on a model of papal authority in the Christian world, with temporal leadership providing mainly support.[42]

The use of the words "crusade" and "crusader" has become more nuanced in recent decades, so I do not wish to seem to be simply splitting hairs by arguing that Charlemagne was not seen as a model crusader simply because he did not answer a papal call, take vows, or receive special dispensations for his armed pilgrimage. A distinction does need to be made, however, between viewing crusading as a means toward extending the boundaries of Christendom defined as the German empire, as opposed to viewing it as pope-sanctioned protection of the East as a function of the ecclesiastical dream of Christian universalism. Charlemagne may have served as an exemplum of imperial leadership in the protection of Christendom, but the assertion of a typological relationship between Roman emperors who were protectors of Jerusalem existed long before the crusades and outside of the crusading context. The Charlemagne who conquers the East without bloodshed, as I have argued throughout, is concerned with the reconstitution and preservation of the empire. Beginning with Constantine the Great, protection of the Holy Land was a prominent element of the biographical construction of Christian universalism under an emperor, but this was just one aspect of the expression

---

41. Christopher Tyerman, *The Invention of the Crusades* (Toronto, 1998), 6–12.

42. See Jonathan Phillips, *Defenders of the Holy Land: Relations between the Latin East and the West, 1119–1187* (Oxford, 1996).

of Roman universalism. The rationale behind emphasizing Charlemagne's peaceful liberation of Jerusalem in his dossier of saintly merits lies not in crusade promotion, but in the continuity of imperial biography. The compilers explicitly place the bloodless liberation of Jerusalem among Charlemagne's miracles and pilgrimages, not in the section devoted to his deeds as a warrior of God. The Charlemagne of the *Descriptio* served as a model for lay leadership in the protection of Christendom, not for imperialist expansion of the boundaries of the empire.

While I agree with Kantorowicz's premise that the conquest of the East was fundamental to the concept of world dominion, it is important to distinguish between universalizing rhetoric and the actual crusading movement. The canonization of Charlemagne, which occurred during a fallow period for crusading, was designed to convey the primacy of the emperor as lay leader of Christendom, elected by God and independent of papal control. At the time of the canonization, promoters of Charlemagne as an antecedent of Frederick did not promote the part of the "Charlemagne and the East" story that involved the liberation of Jerusalem. The element of the story that mattered was the arrival of relics from Constantinople that had legitimated the establishment of Aachen as the center of his imperial realm. The theme of crusading also did not figure in the orchestration of the ceremony. In the false donation of Charlemagne to Aachen included in the January 1166 canonization decree, the emperor makes no mention of Jerusalem, although he does discuss the relics he received from Constantinople that he used to beautify the Church of Saint Mary at Aachen. Frederick's decree celebrates Charlemagne as an extender of the boundaries of Christendom, but not as a liberator of Jerusalem.[43] We know from Benzo that the gift of relics from the emperor of Constantinople was code in the discourse of empire for the transfer of authority and for the achievement of imperial unity, with supremacy ceded to the emperor in the West.

The *Descriptio* had made it clear that Charlemagne and his army came to the East for pious reasons, harboring no desire for territorial expansion, and the *Vita* emphasizes that fact even more explicitly in the prologue to the second book. There was a perceptible effort in Hohenstaufen literature to avoid any intimation of military activity by the Franks in the Holy Land. Godfrey of Viterbo, as we shall see shortly, insists on more than one occasion that Charlemagne came to Jerusalem solely to pray, and that his time there was peaceful. The saintly biography reiterates in multiple ways God's preference for the emperor as protector of Christendom by describing how the

---

43. Pacaut, *Frederick Barbarossa*, 119.

Carolingians consistently had to rescue the popes from their various travails. Charlemagne is depicted in the *Vita* as a defender of Christendom, to be sure, but he always had been. The difference lies in who elected him to serve that role, and the German propagandists made sure that it was God, and not the pope.

Both Einhard and the author of the saintly *Vita* respected the difference between "deeds in war" and "deeds in peace" in the life of the emperor, and bloodless conquest of the East, from Einhard on, had been accomplished as a deed in peace. The Hohenstaufen promotion of Charlemagne therefore needs to be considered within the tradition of imperial praise, or we risk attributing concrete intentions to statements born of the rhetoric of empire. The *Descriptio* author had altered Einhard's vision of harmony with the leadership in the Holy Land, but that change was designed to allow for the invention of the dream in which Constantine learns of God's preference for the Latin West as protectors of the earthly empire. The story of Charlemagne's liberation of Jerusalem, which he achieves by simply putting the occupying pagans to flight, was written well before the First Crusade, and was not, nor did it become, commensurate with the ideals of the actual crusading movement.

Godfrey of Viterbo

The story of Charlemagne's bloodless conquest of the East after his coronation received a new narrator in the aspiring panegyrist Godfrey of Viterbo. During the 1180s, near the end of Frederick's long reign, the chaplain and notary produced an unusual history, which he first entitled *Memoria Seculorum* and then changed to *Pantheon*.[44] Like previous authors who had inserted Charlemagne into their rhetoric of Roman universalism, Godfrey deliberately revised familiar motifs of imperial praise. He outdid all his predecessors, however, in redefining the Carolingian origins of Christian imperial authority. Not only did he invent a new genealogy for Charlemagne, but he also radically restaged the events of the coronation and the subsequent encounters with the Greek East to include the bloodless conquest of Sicily.[45]

---

44. Folz, *Le souvenir,* 263; Oliver Killgus, *Studien zum "Liber universalis" Gottfrieds von Viterbo* (Munich, 2010), esp. 80–82; Hans Werner Seiffert, "Otto von Freising und Gotfried von Viterbo," *Philologus: Zeitschrift für klassische Philologie* 115 (1971): 292–301. See also Karl Ferdinand Werner, *Karl der Grosse oder Charlemagne? Von der Aktualität einer überholten Fragestellung* (Munich, 1995), 38. It is not known whether he was German or Italian. See Lucienne Meyer, *Les légendes des matières de Rome, de France et de Bretagne dans le "Panthéon" de Godefroi de Viterbe* (Paris, 1933), 3.

45. Hausmann, "Gottfried," 572–73.

Godfrey is often described as having been an educator of the young Henry VI, but not all believe this to be true.[46] Loren Weber has argued that the historian exaggerated both his proximity to the emperor and his role as tutor of the young king. Godfrey's relationship to his patrons is therefore not entirely clear. He began to work under the Staufen leadership beginning at the end of the reign of Conrad III and continued to do so through much of Frederick's reign, even accompanying the emperor on campaigns in Italy. He dedicated his first work, the *Speculum Regum,* to Henry VI in 1183, but continued to amend it. The project never reached completion, however, and Godfrey turned his attention instead to the *Memoria Seculorum,* later the *Pantheon.*[47] At some point, Godfrey became disenchanted with his dedicatees and decided to revise some of his history and rededicate the work. When he changed the title, he also removed the emperor and his family from the dedication, replacing them with Pope Urban III, a great enemy of Frederick.[48]

The *Memoria* had been intended, at first, to honor the imperial lineage of his patrons, whose feud with the Holy See had only just ended in 1177, so the change was a significant about-face. Weber speculates that Godfrey presented the work in its original form to the court sometime in 1186–87, when Frederick must have refused it. Dejected, he likely then began to change the work to appeal to a wider audience, and, indeed, unlike the *Speculum Regum,* the *Pantheon* proved to be a great success. As imperial chaplain, Godfrey was a member of court society and would have had an audience outside the royal family.[49] The change from an imperial to a papal dedicatee meant that he needed to temper the rhetoric of praise that had characterized the first incarnation of his history. As Weber observes, one of the most identifiable changes was the historian's decision to essentially drown out the existing praise for the emperor rather than remove it. "The panegyrical roots of Godfrey's material are all but smothered under the weight of the new mass of new material," he explains.[50] The interpretation of Godfrey's presentation of Charlemagne must therefore take into account both his invented persona as court intimate as well has his sense of rapprochement with the papacy and growing sense of alienation from the Hohenstaufen family. Since we do not know the exact

---

46. Weber does not support the traditional view that he was an educator of Henry VI held by Bumke, *Courtly Culture,* 460; Loren J. Weber, "The Historical Importance of Godfrey of Viterbo," *Viator* 25 (1994): 153–91.

47. Godfrey of Viterbo, *Speculum Regum,* 131.

48. Weber, "Historical Importance," 186.

49. Ibid., 189–90; Bumke, *Courtly Culture,* 463; Richard Stoneman, "The Medieval Alexander," in *Latin Fiction: The Latin Novel in Context,* ed. Heinz Hofman (London, 1999), 236.

50. Weber, "Historical Importance," 188–89.

timing and nature of the alterations that Godfrey made after changing dedicatees, we can only speculate about how certain scenes reflect his conflicted
relationship with the recipients of his imperial praise.

At the close of the *Deeds,* Rahewin had borrowed Einhard's version of
the foreign embassy topos for Frederick using contemporary allusions to
the nations present at court. Godfrey was working from Otto's *Two Cities,*
which means he surely had access to the *Deeds,* and which also underlines the
importance of reading his revisions of familiar sites of praise against similar
scenes in the sources for the earlier period of Frederick's reign. Early in the
Pantheon, at the end of the prologue, Godfrey demonstrates his adeptness at
manipulating what was, by then, a familiar locus of praise for Charlemagne.
Without mentioning Charlemagne or Einhard, the poet/historian adopts
and transforms the depiction of Greek and Persian legates bringing gifts to
the emperor:

> Often Greeks from Constantinople and Saracens from Babylonia and
> Persians from Persia and Armenians from Armenia came to the impe-
> rial and papal courts bringing large legations, and they instructed me
> and translated for me some of their writings. The work of these books,
> you should know, has taken me ten years, thanks be to God and happily
> has finished, Amen. The name of these books is Remembrance of the
> Ages [*Memoria Seculorum*].[51]

Note here that Godfrey's version of the foreign embassy topos describes legates from the East appearing before both the imperial and papal courts. The
procession of foreign envoys typically served as pure imperial encomium, so
the creation of a scenario in which emperor and pope share the honor surely
reflects the new papal dedicatee.

The more striking adaptation lies, however, in the fact that instead of
using the motif to praise the emperor, Godfrey uses the arrival of envoys
from the East to essentially praise his own authorial endeavor.[52] Godfrey
adapts the motif by adding an element of *translatio studii* to a well-worn scene
of *translatio imperii.* Rather than lamenting that his tongue is not competent
to praise those who have commissioned his work, the confident encomiast
usurps the praise of universality for himself, a rhetorical maneuver that the

51. Godfrey of Viterbo, *Memoria Seculorum,* 105. "Sepe enim Greci a Constantinopoli et Sar-
raceni a Babillonia et Persi a Perside et Armeni ab Armenia ad curiam imperialem et papalem
venientes et magnas legationes ferentes, me instruxerunt et sua scripta aliquando tradiderunt mihi.
Opus autem huius libri scias me spacio annorum agitasse et in decimo, Deo gratias, perfinisse feliciter
amen. Nomen autem huius libri est Memoria seculorum."

52. Hausmann singles out this passage, but seems to take it at face value, in "Gottfried," 605.

Archpoet had also carried out in his hymn to Frederick's defeat of Milan. In Godfrey's version, the envoys come not with tribute and typical gifts of submission, but with written material for him to reproduce in his universal history. In this metaphor of the historiographical process, Eastern gifts that were typically either luxurious finery or precious relics signifying submission are replaced with written materials to enrich his literary endeavor. It is the historian himself who receives this tribute and bounty, not the emperor or the pope. The representatives of the East, both Christian and pagan, hand over materials to the representative of the West, who is the chronicler of the whole world. Instead of ceding political authority, the ambassadors cede control of the historiographical representation of the East. A locus of praise for universal authority thus becomes an expression of praise for Godfrey's writing of a new universal history. Not unlike the Archpoet, Godfrey thus reveals himself as a self-interested poetic manipulator of the established rhetoric of praise for the emperor.

Godfrey's construction of an imperial lineage for his Staufen patrons includes a fanciful new genealogy for Charlemagne. In this new interpretation, the Frankish leader hails from multiple imperial bloodlines, and therefore becomes the embodiment of East/West imperial unity.[53] Godfrey's first work, the *Speculum Regum,* from the early 1180s, places Frederick and his son, the future Henry VI, in the line of Roman emperors. In the *Speculum,* of which a significant amount of material made its way into the *Pantheon,* the author establishes a legitimating set of origins for the German emperors by joining the Romans, Greeks, Franks, and Germans in the person of Charlemagne. He writes that all of the kings and emperors of Italy up to Charlemagne descended from Anchises, Aeneas, and Ascanius. At the same time, the lineage of Priam, king of Troy, from which the German nobility is descended by way of Priam's nephew, also goes all the way to Charlemagne. Bertha, Charles's mother, Godfrey explains, was the granddaughter of the seventh-century Byzantine emperor Heraclius, and was therefore from the line of both Greek and Roman emperors, while Pippin, his father, the king of the Teutons, was descended from Trojan stock. Therefore, he concludes, Charlemagne was born of a Teuton father and a Roman mother.[54] In this

---

53. See also Odilo Engels, "Gottfried von Viterbo und seine Sicht des staufischen Kaiserhauses," in *Aus Archiven und Bibliotheken: Festschrift für Raymund Kottje zum 65. Geburtstag,* ed. Hubert Mordek (Frankfurt, 1992), 337.

54. Godfrey of Viterbo, *Speculum Regum,* 21–22. "Ex Anchise enim Eneas et Ascanius omnesque reges et imperatores Ytalici oriuntur usque ad Karolum regem Magnum; a Priamo autem iuniore, nepote magni Priami ex sorore, universa Theutonicorum nobilitas usque ad eundem Karolum patenter emanat. In ipso Karolo utriusque propaginis genus concurrit Mater enim eius Berta, cum

scenario, Charlemagne manages to be a German king with hereditary claims to the imperial title on both sides of the empire. The *Speculum* also features a list of emperors in which "Eraclius" figures just prior to "Karolus" in an imperial lineage that supports his earlier assertion that Charlemagne was of Byzantine imperial stock.[55] In the *Pantheon,* Godfrey repeats on several occasions his elaborate all-encompassing Greco-Roman-Teutonic genealogy of Charlemagne, of which he appears to have been the inventor.

Godfrey's theory of Charlemagne's origins is given its most detailed and poetic expression in the closing verses of the *Speculum.* In his guise as poet, Godfrey celebrates Charlemagne's embodiment of the combined imperial bloodline, this time with a nod to the legend of big-footed Bertha:

> The wife of the king was Bertha of the large foot. She came from Hungary, but, born of a Greek mother, she was the daughter of the Emperor Heraclius. From this mixture would come the highest crown: Charles the Great, to whom Bertha was going to give birth; the race, once divided, is joined by her craft. Trojan stock, divided in two, is united in the womb of Bertha with the seed of Pippin. With the seed of Pippin, Troy became one. If now you seek Teuton and Trojan seeds, Charles stands as the sole heir from this bud of inheritance, Roman in mother, German in father.[56]

Godfrey creates for his patrons a genealogical relationship to a Charlemagne who embodied the German (not just the Frankish) assumption of the Roman imperial dignity. He also provides Trojan origins for the German nobility and brings further imperial legitimacy to Charlemagne by making him the inheritor of the Byzantine claim to the empire as well.

Promoters of the Salian and Staufen emperors had limited themselves to signaling political analogies to the Carolingian emperor, while also defending the legitimacy of the various transfers that had led to the German claim to the title of Roman emperor. Godfrey did not restrict himself in this way. Instead he invented a new imperial lineage that would make Charlemagne

---

esset filia filie imperatoris Eraclii, de genere imperatorum Romanorum et Grecorum fuit, Pipinus autem pater eius, rex Theutonicorum, a genere Troiano descendit. Fuit itaque Karolus Magnus patre Theutonicus et matre Romanus."

55. Godfrey of Viterbo, *Speculum Regum,* 24; Meyer, *Les légendes,* 159.

56. Godfrey of Viterbo, *Speculum Regum,* 92–93. "Sponsa fuit regi grandis pede nomine Berta: / Venit ab Ungaria, set Greca matre reperta, / Cesaris Eraclii filia namque fuit / Ex hac mistura fit summa corona futura: / Karolus est Magnus, quem Berta fuit paritura, / Stirps divisa prius iungitur arte sua. / In duo divisa Troiana propago parente / Iungitur in Berte Pipini semine ventre; / Semine Pipini Troia fit una sibi. / Si modo Theutonica Troianaque germina queres, / Gemma parentele stat Karolus unicus heres, / Romuleus matre, Theutonicusque patre."

the incarnation of all elements of the Christian Roman Empire as the Germans had inherited it. By making Pippin a Teuton, Godfrey rectifies the problem of the *translatio ad Saxones* and the transfer of the imperial title to the Ottonians as a departure from the Carolingian line.[57] The compilers of Charlemagne's saintly *Vita* had removed the famous passage from Hilduin concerning Pope Stephen's establishment of the *stirps* of Pippin as the only legitimate line of Christian kings. Godfrey addresses the problem of imperial inheritance by redefining Charlemagne's stock in a manner that not only solves the problem of the end of the Carolingian line, but also places the Staufen dynasty as the inheritors of all of the various lines of the Christian *imperium* going back to the Trojans.

In fact, Godfrey's creative family tree would have served imperial interests against both the papacy and the French kingdom. First, the invented genealogy undermines the papal pretense that the Holy See was the source of Charlemagne's imperial title.[58] Second, Godfrey's story goes one step further than contemporary Capetian claims to a return to the *stirps karoli* for the Capetian kings with the marriage of Philip Augustus to a woman of Carolingian stock, Isabelle of Hainaut.[59] Given the timing of the *Speculum* in the early 1180s, especially considering Godfrey's manifest familiarity with French literary traditions, it is possible that the royal French union had inspired Godfrey's genealogical machinations on behalf of the Hohenstaufen family. If this is true, then Godfrey provided something better than a return to Carolingian stock after a long hiatus, which is what some in Capetian propaganda circles were celebrating, by instead offering unbroken and long-standing genealogical ties.

Godfrey sought to create genealogical legitimacy for the Hohenstaufen emperors by recasting the Carolingians as Teutons, Byzantines, and Trojans. Similar motives related to the promotion of the Hohenstaufen dynasty surely lay behind his decision to include in the *Pantheon* a full version of the Tiburtine Sibyl predicting the future 122-year-reign of Constans, the unifier of the Greeks and the Romans. The prophecy appears as an obvious interpolation alongside a brief description of the reign of Alexander the Great, after which his dry enumeration of leaders continues.[60] By including the sibyl, Godfrey broke from his model historian, Otto of Freising, who in the *Two Cities* had placed his German imperial patrons within the schema of

57. Engels, "Gottfried von Viterbo," 337; Folz, *Le souvenir,* 256.
58. Engels, "Gottfried von Viterbo," 340.
59. I address this in chapter 6.
60. Godfrey of Viterbo, *Pantheon,* 145–47.

the Four Kingdoms, but had not included the prophecy of the Last Emperor. The Tiburtina predicts that the Last Emperor will unite East and West and bring all Christendom under his rule. Godfrey's invented genealogy creates a Charlemagne who is, in essence, a *rex Romanorum, Grecorum, Francorum, et Teutonicorum,* and therefore a unifier of East and West. He is also, once again, a sort of forerunner of the future Last Emperor in the same way that he is in the *Descriptio* and in Benzo's *Ad Heinricum.* Godfrey had hailed the birth of Henry VI as the arrival of the foretold Last Emperor, but, here again, as with all previous appearances of the prophecy within the context of imperial encomium, we must consider the celebration of a ruler in eschatological terms to be a matter of praise rather than of actual chiliastic expectation.[61]

Charlemagne's Coronation

Godfrey's creative rewriting of Charlemagne's triumphal journey to Jerusalem, Constantinople, and Sicily cannot be properly understood without consideration of its necessary precursor, his equally inventive version of the coronation of 800. The historian borrows from Otto's *Two Cities* for the initial prose passage, after which he offers his own narrative inventions that are reminiscent of Notker's imagined dialogues and conveyance of the emperor's inner thoughts. Charlemagne speaks in the first person, stating, for instance, that the pope wishes to give him the title of emperor of Rome. He tells of being troubled by Leo's intentions, but also of how he does not wish to appear fearful about the pontiff's plans for him once he arrives in Rome.[62] Godfrey is remembering here, but in his own way, the circumstances evoked by Einhard's famous statement that Charlemagne had not known why he had been called to Rome. The passage thus builds on previous models, creating a more detailed psychological portrait of post-coronation tensions between the Frankish emperor and Constantinople. The historian is not particularly true to Einhard, however. Instead, the still prominent ninth-century biography served more as a framework and source of allusions. Godfrey's Charlemagne insists out loud, for instance, that the pope be the one to crown him, a detail that likely reflects his intention to please his new dedicatee, Urban III. Another more significant departure from Einhard involves Charlemagne's assertion of his supreme displeasure at having to share the imperial title with the Greeks.

61. Kantorowicz, *Frederick the Second,* 4.
62. Godfrey of Viterbo, *Pantheon,* 218. "Imperii nomen qui vult michi promere Rome; / Papaque cesarea voluit me sorte sacrari,/ Ne videar pavidus, suscipiamus, ait."

Imaginative reenactments of the encounter between Charlemagne and Leo joined a long tradition going back to the Paderborn epic in the ninth century. The meaning of the coronation had also been a matter of long-standing dispute between pro- and anti-reformist thinkers, who could creatively depict the event according to their leanings. The author of the mid-century, anti-Hohenstaufen, vernacular *Kaiserchronik* had rewritten the meeting of Charlemagne and Leo, taking significant creative liberties. In this version, Charlemagne and Leo are actually brothers! The work offers a papacy-friendly version of the events of 800, which depicts the notion of an indissoluble fraternal union of emperor and pope. With its creation of a brotherly bond between pope and emperor, the *Kaiserchronik* makes the transfer of empire to the Franks by the pontiff into a kind of family arrangement that is marked by mutual aid and equally proportioned roles in the leadership of Christendom.[63] It is not certain that Godfrey was writing in response to the anti-Hohenstaufen chronicle, but we can nonetheless conclude that competing memories of Charlemagne's coronation were a recognized piece of the contemporary discourse on the origins of German imperial authority.

Einhard had emphasized the Greeks' displeasure over the Frankish assumption of the title, while Godfrey depicts his Charlemagne as openly upset about having to share the imperial dignity with his eastern counterparts: "What Rome does not hold, I will seek with my right hand by the sword. I will choose to extend our strength over the Greeks."[64] In parallel fashion, Godfrey radically alters Charlemagne's famous hesitance to be crowned to make it his forthright insistence on not just accepting the honor, but taking away the imperial dignity from the Greek East: "I do not refuse to take up the name of empire, for we will seize the rights of the crown over the Greeks."[65] Charlemagne eagerly accepts the "*diadem mundi*" and decides that it should be put there by the hands of the pope, but insists that his empire is not complete as long as the Greeks rule in the East.[66]

Godfrey depicts the diplomatic repercussions of the coronation as thoughts in Charlemagne's mind, rather than as historical narrative. Unlike in other imagined depictions of the post-coronation mood in the Frankish West, Godfrey's Charlemagne is adamant about not sharing the imperial title. That honor, when enjoyed solely in Rome, is not enough, the Frankish leader

---

63. Folz, *Le souvenir*, 165–67.

64. Godfrey of Viterbo, *Pantheon*, 219. "Quod non Roma tenet, gladio mea dextra requiret; / Obto super Danaos nostras pretendere vires."

65. Godfrey of Viterbo, *Pantheon*, 219. "Imperii nomen non rennuo tollere Rome / Namque super Danaos capiemus iura corone."

66. Godfrey of Viterbo, *Pantheon*, 218–19.

complains, adding that he has not received the fullness of his imperial dignity. His realm is not complete with only the seat of power in Italy. Godfrey conveys the plan to invade the Greeks as an omniscient narrator revealing Charlemagne's thoughts, but the plan to invade is never realized. When the emperor first decides to take up arms and make the Eastern emperor give up his claim to the title, the Byzantine leader, fearing for his life, concludes a pact with the menacing Frank.[67] This discussion of Charlemagne's potential actions is a recognizable elaboration of the passage in Einhard in which he describes how the Greek emperors were afraid of Charles's plans to annex their territory. While Einhard had merely mentioned their concerns, Godfrey adds depth to the story by discussing his intention to attack, thereby confirming their anxieties. To conform to the story, however, he ultimately has Charlemagne find a peaceful solution.

Certain real-life circumstances may have inspired Godfrey's depiction of Charlemagne's contentious relationship with Constantinople. The treaty of Benevento in 1156 had marked a significant breaking point in imperial-papal relations because Frederick had perceived the alliance between Hadrian IV, Manuel Comnenus, and the Sicilians as a betrayal by Pope Hadrian. Since Godfrey was writing in the 1180s, these events might seem too far in the past to be relevant, but Anne Duggan has argued that Godfrey, who was working from Otto and Rahewin, retained a long-held sense of bitterness over the treaty.[68] Chroniclers from Byzantium and the West discuss the fear among the Greeks that Frederick would invade, and Magdalino even cites the *Play of Antichrist* as evidence of Frederick's aggressive stance.[69] In the 1160s, Pope Alexander had entered into new negotiations with the Greek emperor, who was still seeking a foothold in Italy, while Hadrian may have been in search of an imperial rival to pit against Frederick.[70] Manuel, hoping for an end to the religious divisions in the empire, had proposed a reunion of the Eastern and Western churches, but he overreached when he demanded the imperial crown and recognition as emperor by the West. Imperial unity through alliance with Alexander was tempting for Manuel, but the plan was abandoned by the end of the decade.[71] Godfrey's depiction of a Charlemagne planning

---

67. Godfrey of Viterbo, *Pantheon,* 219–20.

68. Duggan, "*Totius Christianitatis caput,*" 107. See also I. S. Robinson, *The Papacy, 1073–1198: Continuity and Innovation* (Cambridge, UK, 1990), 465.

69. Magdalino, *Empire of Manuel I Komnenos,* 86.

70. Galland, "Les relations," 72–74, 78.

71. Ralph-Johannes Lilie, *Byzantium and the Crusader States, 1096–1204,* trans. J. C. Morris (Oxford, 1994), 310; Pacaut, *Frederick Barbarossa,* 206–8. See also Evelyne Patlagean, "Byantium's Dual Holy Land," in Prawer, Kedar-Kopfstein, and Zwi, *Sacred Space,* 119; Eleni Tounta, "Byzanz

to invade but deciding not to, and the discussion of the sharing of the title that occurs in the works of both Rahewin and Godfrey, may well reflect these contemporary conflicts.

Godfrey's Charlemagne is angry about his incomplete empire, but instead of invading Byzantium, he makes an alliance of "eternal brotherhood and mutual aid" with the Greek emperor, here named Leo. After providing a brief summary of the alliance in prose, Godfrey announces that he will tell the story of the pact in verse. The poetic version contains some revealing details concerning the theme of universal authority.[72] Emphasizing the cooperation between the two emperors, the poet details their decision to be called brothers and to allow for the existence of two universal emperors: "Now there are two highest crowns of the world worn; and whereas once there was one emperor, now there are two. And once there was one *dominus mundi,* now there are two, whereas in the past they used to falsely use the name of brother."[73] Godfrey not only celebrates the willing and equal division of the imperial title, but also throws in a parting comment about how all previous pretenses of East/West alliance had been insincere. His verses recall Einhard, but the pact of brotherhood and shared title raises the possibility that Godfrey was also working from Rahewin's reference to Frederick's offer to share his own imperial title by dividing it between New Rome and Old Rome.[74]

In Godfrey's version, the Greeks still seek an alliance with Charlemagne out of fear, but he tones down the universalizing rhetoric of the episode as Einhard had conceived it by emphasizing the sharing of the empire. This revision bolsters Weber's argument that the encomiast deliberately deflated his panegyric rhetoric when he rewrote the *Pantheon* in honor of the pope. The two emperors hold the empire in a cooperative peace, and he is careful to insist that Charlemagne had gained his status as a co-emperor by right and brotherly pact rather than by seizure, "*quasi praeda.*" Einhard had planted the notion that the envious Greeks feared Charlemagne's plans to invade, a reaction that Notker also elaborated through imagined dialogue. Godfrey further embellishes the story by dramatizing Charlemagne's anger, but in the end celebrates the shared peace on which they are able to finally agree. He well knew that there could be

---

als Vorbild Friedrich Barbarossas," in *Staufisches Kaisertum im 12. Jahrhundert: Konzepte-Netzwerke-Politische Praxis,* ed. Stefan Burkhardt et al. (Regensburg, 2010), 166.

72. See Killgus, *Studien zum "Liber universalis,"* 96.

73. Godfrey of Viterbo, *Pantheon,* 220. "Unde due summe gestantur in orbe corone; / Si fuit una prius, bine sunt ordine Rome, / Unus erat cesar, nunc duo iura colent. / Unus erat dominus mundi, precelsus honore, / Nunc duo sunt, fratrum duplam ratione decores, / Fratris adhuc nomen fingere sepe solent."

74. *GF,* 4.76.

no invasion of the East, but nonetheless pushed the limits of "deeds in peace" by adding extra strife, if only in Charlemagne's mind. Of course, Einhard never explicitly says that the Greeks surrendered to Charlemagne, only that they sought an alliance in fear. He counted on the underlying classical topos to convey their surrender, a strategy used by all who deployed the "Charlemagne and the East" episode. Even Benzo veils Greek surrender in poetic language. As his voice of Charlemagne explains, the West's future attainment of imperial supremacy over the East must be appreciated by way of signs, all of which have to do with imperial exchanges with the East. Godfrey adds a new, less universalizing, dimension to this essential site of Carolingian memory, however, by describing Charlemagne as happy to be crowned by the pope and content to be one of two *domini mundi*.

Charlemagne's Journey to Jerusalem, Constantinople, and Sicily

After the peaceful division of the imperial title between Old and New Rome, Godfrey describes Charlemagne's journey to the East based on the *Descriptio*, which he most likely knew from the saintly *Vita*.[75] He condenses the story down to a brief presentation of the journey, but makes the meaningful addition of a stop in Sicily. The journey first appears in a brief prose passage that tells of how Charlemagne traveled by way of Constantinople as a pilgrim seeking to worship in Jerusalem. In Constantinople he establishes a brotherly peace, and his visit to Jerusalem likewise transpires without conflict. After reaching his destination, "it was said" that on his way back, Charlemagne stayed in Sicily for a while.[76] In the corresponding verse segment, Godfrey offers more detail concerning the pilgrimage. The versified journey to Jerusalem and Constantinople has a *titulus* that emphasizes its pious nature: "Charles hastened as a pilgrim to Jerusalem through Constantinople, but returned through Sicily, Calabria, and Apulia."[77] The emphasis on his status as a pilgrim removes any sense that Charlemagne had been sent by the Greeks to Jerusalem to conquer the enemies of Christendom, and there is no mention of any liberation of the Holy City. The introduction to the journey to the East in the saintly *Vita* emphasizes that the voyage is a

75. Meyer, *Les légendes,* 173.

76. Godfrey of Viterbo, *Pantheon,* 222. "Quibus omnibus in pace compositis, Karolus orationis causa Ierosolimam per Constantinopolim transit factaque ibi oratione, per Siciliam, sicut dicitur, remeavit."

77. Godfrey of Viterbo, *Pantheon,* 222. "Karolus pergit peregrinus Ierosolimam per Constantinopolim, set revertitur per Siciliam, Calabriam et Apuliam."

peregrinatio, and Godfrey likewise insists that Charlemagne had gone to Jerusalem for the sake of prayer and that his time in Jerusalem had been peaceful. The degree of insistence on this matter suggests that Godfrey was trying to make a distinction for those who might mistakenly associate pious journeys to Jerusalem with armed expeditions. The journey for Godfrey is not even a rescue mission, and it certainly does not resemble a crusade. Like the *Vita* authors, he saw the journey as a component of the peaceful establishment of Charlemagne's imperial authority in the East after the coronation, according to biographical norms that had been adapted to tell the story of the life of Charlemagne.

When Godfrey's Charlemagne stops in Sicily on his way back from Jerusalem and Constantinople, he sets up a Christian kingdom. Rather than having taken the land route back through Constantinople, Charlemagne has gone by ship, and the waves carry him to Palermo, which he seizes "without destruction," the narrator emphasizes. The entire land of Sicily offers him gifts. Godfrey thus makes Sicily into one of the foreign nations offering tribute to the new emperor. Charlemagne has the Sicilian king baptized and orders him to adopt the law of the Roman church and the teachings of the God of the Catholic people.[78] The territory in southern Italy therefore joins the nations of the East as part of Charlemagne's empire gathered in through peaceful surrender after his coronation by the will of God and according to Roman law.

For imperial propagandists, Sicily was at once a real political problem and a poetic missing piece in the theory of universal dominion. As a territory contested by the same political entities that jockeyed for position at the helm of Christendom (the papacy, the German empire, and the Byzantines), southern Italy embodied real contested territory and, at the same time, symbolic uncertainty over the inheritance of the Roman Empire. To confront the issue in his universal history, the *Pantheon* author went back to the age of Charlemagne to create a prefiguring event that would mirror an idealized resolution to the political divisions of his own day. The question of southern Italy had been part of the evolution of "Charlemagne and the East" since its earliest known articulation in the chronicle of the anti-Ottonian Benedict of Mount Soracte in the tenth century. Benedict's journey includes a march through Italy, after which the chronicler celebrates Charlemagne's

---

78. Godfrey of Viterbo, *Pantheon,* 223. "Karolus revertitur a Ierosolimis. / Dum rate festina regem vehit unda marina, / Urbe Panormina portum capit absque ruina, / Omne solum Siculi munera solvit ei. / Karolus hic Siculum recreat baptismate regem, / Quem iubet ecclesie Romane sumere legem,/ Catholici populi docma tulere Dei."

relinquishing of once-Byzantine territories to the papacy.[79] Benzo of Alba had been consumed with the matter of Apulia and Calabria, and we see in the Hillin letters and in the verses of the Archpoet how the matter of southern Italy functioned during Frederick Barbarossa's early reign in the debates between the Germans, the Greeks, and the papacy over the theoretical leadership of the Christian imperium.

Like the other imperial propagandists we have seen, Godfrey also highlighted southern Italy as an obstacle to be overcome in the Staufen achievement of imperial unity and *dominium mundi*. Godfrey envisions imperial unity by portraying a submissive Byzantium sharing the empire with Charlemagne. He then creates a fantasized vision of Sicily coming safely and willingly into imperial hands at the end of Charlemagne's journey to Jerusalem and Constantinople. The problem of southern Italy is thus mended in the ninth century by the Carolingian king, who couples the annexing of the territory with his peaceful conquest of the East in the establishment of his new and united empire. One scholar argues that Godfrey's only goal in adding Sicily to the story was to establish a historical basis for Frederick's pretensions in southern Italy, but that reading is too literal.[80] His motives, like those of other encomiasts who creatively envisioned the period after the coronation, were both literary and political. Politically speaking, Godfrey retained a festering resentment regarding the 1156 Treaty of Benevento, when the papacy and the Greeks allied against the empire.[81] A purely political explanation does not account, however, for the encomiastic tradition that Godfrey joined by adding Sicily to his vision of Charlemagne's unified empire.

After describing Charlemagne's establishment of a new Christian kingdom in southern Italy, Godfrey draws on Otto of Freising for Charlemagne's arrival in Rome, where he receives benediction before returning home to Aachen. A large proportion of the historical prose sections, which Godfrey rewrites and versifies, derive from Otto's *Two Cities*, although he does not credit his source.[82] He repeats Otto's report that when Charlemagne returned to Aachen, he built the Church of Saint Mary as part of his establishment of Aachen as his seat of power. He then inserts the following sentence about Charlemagne: "In our own time, he was canonized by Emperor Frederick

79. Roelof Van Waard even argued that Benedict was responsible for creating the legend of Charlemagne's conquests in southern Italy on which the Old French "Chanson d'Aspremont," was based; see *Études sur l'origine et la formation de la Chanson d'Aspremont* (Groningen, 1937), 51–53.

80. Van Waard, *Études,* 51.

81. Duggan, *"Totius Christianitatis caput,"* 107.

82. See Seiffert, "Otto von Freising und Gotfried von Viterbo," 292–301.

and is kept in a golden box under the altar by Pope Alexander at Aachen."[83] Given the acrimonious circumstances of the canonization by antipope Paschal, the fact that Godfrey names Pope Alexander as the keeper of the remains of Charlemagne at Aachen shows that the historian was seeking to bear witness to the recent end to the schism and to Frederick's recognition of Alexander as legitimate pope. It also suggests that he wrote the passage during Alexander's lifetime, and thus prior to the pope's death in 1181. Godfrey's Charlemagne certainly suggests a shift toward a more conciliatory approach to Rome, but by the late 1170s, such an attitude would also have been possible from a pro-Staufen author. Whatever Godfrey's mood may have been when he created his versions of the events surrounding Charlemagne's coronation and subsequent encounter with the East, the very fact that he chose to dramatize those events reveals the extent to which the episode continued to serve as a rhetorical tool for re-remembering the foundational moments of the divided Christian empire.

Conclusion

The preceding two chapters have considered articulations of Roman authority and imperial unity during the reign of Frederick Barbarossa. This current chapter has focused on the construction of Charlemagne as an imperial predecessor to the Staufen leader, primarily with regard to the canonization of 1165. One of the invented memories of Charlemagne's imperial reign that Frederick's propagandists cultivated most vigorously derived from the tale told in the *Descriptio* of how the Greek emperor came to recognize Charlemagne as God's preferred leader and protector of all Christendom. Historical interpretations of the 1165 canonization, notably that of Folz, have long centered on the idea that the Germans wished to wrest the Carolingian emperor from the French.[84] This theory has been buttressed by the fact that the documents that make up the essential backbone of the saintly *Vita* are generally tied to French ecclesiastical centers. A major source for this theory of Franco-German rivalry has been an alleged letter from Archbishop Turpin introducing his chronicle, a document that the creators of Charlemagne's *Vita* reproduced. The introduction to Turpin's narrative in the *Vita* reads: "Now, therefore, we take up the third distinction whose beginning is this letter,

83. *HdDC*, 5.32; Godfrey of Viterbo, *Pantheon*, 220. "Nostro vero tempore per Fredericum imperatorem canonizatus est et in capsa aurea reconditus super altare sub Alexandro papa apud Aquisgrani."

84. Folz, *Le souvenir*, 207.

which we found [*repperimus*] at Saint-Denis in the chronicles of the Franks that Archbishop Turpin of Reims had transmitted to Leobrand, deacon of Aachen."[85] The verb *repperimus* at the end of the passage has been understood to convey that the letter of Turpin was physically found at Saint-Denis by the compilers of the *Vita*. This reading has enhanced the perception that the canonization process fulfilled a desire to undermine Dionysian claims to the memory of Charlemagne, while also fostering the notion that someone had found the document at Saint-Denis and brought it to the imperial court. Christopher Hohler's translation of *repperimus*—"we found out"—provides a preferable alternative, however. Hohler argues convincingly that the passage is meant to convey that the compilers discovered while reading the chronicles of the Franks at Saint-Denis that Archbishop Turpin had sent the letter to Aachen.[86] The passage thus conveys that Turpin's narrative of Charlemagne's journey to Spain had been sent to Aachen in the ninth century rather than recently gathered from the French royal abbey. Moreover, as Elizabeth Brown has shown, the *Pseudo-Turpin* chronicle had not even joined the chronicle tradition of the royal abbey when the *Vita* was compiled.[87]

As we shall see in chapter 6, there was little interest in the *Descriptio* in Capetian circles in the twelfth century. By contrast, we find allusions to Charlemagne's acquisition of relics from Byzantium in Hohenstaufen propaganda as early as the canonization decree of 1166, well before the compilation of the saintly *Vita*. The desire to recuperate Charlemagne from the French simply does not explain the appeal of the "Charlemagne in the East" narrative in German imperial circles. The desire to define German imperial authority, especially with regard to the papacy and the Greeks, offers a much more plausible explanation. The hagiographers of Charlemagne did not reproduce the stories of the apparition of Saint Denis to Pope Stephen, the apparition of Charlemagne to Constantine, and the apparition of Saint James to Charlemagne in order to diminish the royal abbey of Saint-Denis, although that effect would surely have been an added bonus. They chose to compile those particular narratives according to a sequence inspired by imperial biography and based on the eschatological progression of the Roman Empire as the last of the four kingdoms. Each of the three visions, in its own way, projected an image of a Charlemagne who had been elected by God as

---

85. *VKM,* 67. "In presentiarum igitur tercie huius distinctionis inicium ab ea epistola assumemus, quam Tulpinum Remensem archiepiscopum Leobrando Aquisgranensi decano transmisisse in cronicis Francorum apud sanctum Dionysium in Francia repperimus."

86. Hohler, "Note on Jacobus," 66.

87. E. A. R. Brown, "Saint-Denis and the Turpin Legend," in *The Codex Calixtinus and the Shrine of Saint James,* ed. John Williams and Alison Stones (Tübingen, 1992), 51–52, 55.

his representative on earth. The story begins in Rome, the place of origin of his imperial authority. He then travels to the East, peacefully unifying East and West as a precursor to the Last Emperor before establishing Aachen as the center of that new spiritual realm. Finally he answers a divine request to go to Spain, the symbol of the western reaches of Rome in its inexorable movement toward its eventual end.

To make the documents work in their favor, the creators of the *Vita* had to make some changes. Since Saint-Denis had been the birthplace of the Franco-papal alliance, a political event whose memory they sought to redefine, the creators needed to move attention away from that essential site of subservient Carolingian leadership. That way, they could show Aachen as the center of the realm of a Charlemagne who gained imperial unity providentially and to whom the Greeks ceded their authority in recognition of that primacy. The Hohenstaufen cultivation of the imperial cult of Charlemagne was not a matter of taking back Charlemagne from the rival Capetians under Louis VII, but rather the systematic erasure of the memory of the Franco-papal alliance that had established papal authority and genealogical ties as the defining factors of Carolingian royal and imperial power. As we shall see in the following chapter, the Capetians, although eager to affirm genealogical ties to the Carolingian dynasty, were not particularly interested in the imperial Charlemagne.

CHAPTER 6

"Charlemagne and the East" in France

By the twelfth century, Charlemagne had become well known as a pilgrim, a builder and benefactor of churches, and a figure of vernacular epic poetry. Aside from a handful of exceptions, however, the "Charlemagne and the East" tradition proves to have been of little consequence in France until well into the thirteenth century. The relative absence of the "Charlemagne and the East" narrative from the political culture of France, by comparison with its prominence in Hohenstaufen circles, can be largely explained by the fact that the episode would not have enhanced the genealogically based constructions of French kingship that sought to tie the Capetians to the Frankish monarchy under the Carolingians. Charlemagne did, of course, serve as a model leader in the fight against the enemies of Christendom, but he had played that role for centuries, and never in the East. In a study of relative absence rather than presence, this final chapter casts in a new light the fortunes of Charlemagne's journey to the East in twelfth- and early thirteenth-century France.

Charlemagne and the First Crusade

A long tradition of loose translations of a handful of ambiguous phrases from the literature of the First Crusade has led to the overstated claim that participants in the expedition believed themselves to be following the path that

Charlemagne himself had taken to Jerusalem. Edward Gibbon stated, for instance, that the crusaders had sought to emulate their hero Charlemagne, who had liberated Jerusalem in the popular "romance of Turpin."[1] In the 1940s, French historian Paul Rousset, building on Robert Fawtier, exemplified this attitude by urging his readers to appreciate the importance of the memory of Charlemagne in the twelfth century and to recognize that the crusaders had considered the Frankish king to be "the first among them," and the one who had forged the path to the East, "celui qui ouvrit la route."[2] There is an important distinction to be drawn, however, between papal appeals to the largely French-speaking aristocracy to follow the example of their Carolingian ancestors and modern contentions that the participants believed themselves to be walking in Charlemagne's actual footsteps to the East.[3]

The major source for the notion that the crusaders had imagined themselves to be following Charlemagne's road to Jerusalem appears in the anonymous chronicle of the First Crusade known as the *Gesta Francorum*. It reads: "These most valiant knights and many others (whose names I do not know) traveled by the road which Charlemagne, the heroic king of the Franks, had formerly caused to be built to Constantinople."[4] With few exceptions, historians have been eager to interpret this sentence to mean that crusaders saw themselves retracing Charlemagne's path to Constantinople and, by extension, to Jerusalem. But nothing in this wording implies that the travelers were aware of who had built the road or previously traveled upon it. The chronicler is simply adding a piece of historical information about the road. The clerically educated chronicler, especially if he was Italian,[5] was likely

---

1. Edward Gibbon, *The History of the Decline and Fall of the Roman Empire: A New Edition in VIII Volumes* (London, 1821), 7: 217.

2. Paul Rousset, *Les origines et les caractères de la première croisade* (Neuchâtel, 1945), 133; Mastnak, *Crusading Peace*, 67.

3. See Jonathan Riley-Smith, "The First Crusade and Saint Peter," in *Outremer: Studies in the History of the Crusading Kingdom of Jerusalem Presented to Joshua Prawer*, ed. B. Z. Kedar, Hans Eberhard Mayer, and R.C. Smail (Jerusalem, 1982), 47–48; Jonathan Phillips, *The Second Crusade: Extending the Frontiers of Christendom* (New Haven, CT, 2007), 54.

4. "Isti potentissimi milites et alii plures quos ignoro venerunt per viam quam iamdudum Karolus Magnus mirificus rex Franciae aptari fecit usque Constantinopolim," *Gesta Francorum et Aliorum Hierosolimitanorum*, in *The Deeds of the Franks and Other Pilgrims to Jerusalem*, ed. Rosalind Hill (London, 1962), 2–3. Riley-Smith argues that they believed they were marching on the road built by Charlemagne through Hungary; see Riley-Smith, *First Crusade and the Idea of Crusading*, 112. Jonathan Phillips writes, "Numerous writers, such as Robert of Rheims, mentioned him as proto-crusader and noted that the First Crusaders travelled on the road that Charlemagne had constructed for his army"; see *Second Crusade*, 124. Cf. Cohn, *Pursuit*, 72. See also Bédier, *Les légendes épiques*, 131–32.

5. See Jean Flori, *Chroniqueurs et propagandistes: Introduction critique aux sources de la première croisade* (Geneva, 2010), 72–76; Kenneth Baxter Wolf, "Crusade and Narrative: Bohemond and the *Gesta Francorum*," *Journal of Medieval History* 16 (1990): 207–16.

aware of the same legend that had inspired Benedict, but the notion that the crusaders were consciously following the road taken by the Frankish king is an extrapolation that is not supported by the text.

All of the subsequent references to the *"via"* built by Charles, such as those of Peter Tudebode and Robert of Reims, derive from the *Gesta*, but even with their slight elaborations, the later versions offer no new evidence of any awareness among the crusaders of Charlemagne's alleged journey.[6] Robert's chronicle, the most widely read,[7] alters the text slightly to reinforce the notion that Charlemagne had ordered the road to Constantinople to be made for his army, but the monk offers no further clues regarding his sense of the state of mind of the crusaders.[8] Robert, like the anonymous *Gesta* author, is providing antiquarian knowledge about the history of the road rather than asserting that the crusaders were consciously imitating Charlemagne.[9] Since the French chronicler took other liberties with his source, it is fair to say that had he wished to convey that the travelers were aware of the fact that they were following in Charlemagne's footsteps toward the East, he could easily have chosen to say so.

Another piece of evidence from the chronicles of the First Crusade that has fueled the image of Charlemagne as a French proto-crusader comes from Pope Urban II's 1095 exhortation at Clermont to the northern French nobility to remember their Carolingian origins in the fight against the infidel.[10] As recently as 2001, Jean Flori reinvigorated the theory of Charlemagne as first Holy Land crusader by evoking the protectorate story and referring

---

6. Peter Tudebode clearly used the anonymous *Gesta* in his *De Hierosolymitano Itinere, RHC Occ.*, 3: 10–11. Flori, *Chroniqueurs et propagandistes*, 49–63.

7. See Riley-Smith, *First Crusade and the Idea of Crusading*, chap. 6; Marcus Bull, "The Capetian Monarchy and the Early Crusade Movement: Hugh of Vermandois and Louis VII," *Nottingham Medieval Studies* 40 (1996): 41–42; John O. Ward, "Some Principles of Rhetorical Historiography in the Twelfth Century," in *Classical Rhetoric and Medieval Historiography*, ed. Ernst Breisach (Kalamazoo, MI, 1985), 122; Giles Constable, "The Historiography of the Crusades," in *The Crusades from the Perspective of Byzantium and the Muslim World*, ed. Angeliki E. Laiou and Roy Parviz Mottahedeh (Washington, DC, 2001): 5. See also Damien Kempf, "Towards a Textual Archaeology of the First Crusade," in *Narrating the First Crusade: Historiography, Memory and Transmission in the Narratives of the Early Crusade Movement*, ed. Damien Kempf and Marcus Bull (Woodbridge, UK, forthcoming).

8. "Hic, cum fratribus suis Eustachio et Balduino et magna manu militum peditumque, per Hungariam iter arripuit per viam scilicet quam Karolus Magnus, incomparabilis rex Francorum, olim suo exercitui fieri usque Constantinopolim praecipit." *RHC Occ.*, 3:732.

9. John France argues that the historian reported as history the legend that the old Roman road to Constantinople had been built by Charlemagne, in *The Crusades and the Expansion of Catholic Christendom, 1000–1714* (London, 2004), 7. Folz, also skeptical, proposed that someone had misunderstood or assimilated the name Calomanus, the then king of Hungary, and Carlomagnus; see Folz, *Le souvenir*, 142. Jules Coulet believed that the chronicler had made it up; see *Études sur l'ancien poème français du Voyage de Charlemagne en Orient* (Montpellier, 1907), 105.

10. H. E. J. Cowdrey, *Popes, Monks and Crusaders* (London, 1984), 178.

to the Frankish king as the *"prototype du croisé."* Using a familiar pattern of evidence, he lists the allusions to Charlemagne's road in the crusade sources as well as the reference to Charlemagne that Pope Urban II allegedly made at Clermont.[11] In the widely read version of the no-longer-extant speech by Robert of Reims, Urban recalls for his French audience the greatness of their Carolingian stock and reminds them of the glory of others who had conquered the Turks and extended the boundaries of the church.[12] The monk presents Urban's general references to the battles of Charlemagne and his son Louis, but he makes no mention of Jerusalem or Constantinople.[13] The apocryphal story of the Frankish leader's liberation of Jerusalem did not figure in the papal rhetoric designed to inspire the expedition of 1096.

The absence of Charlemagne's encounters in the East from Urban's speech should not be a surprise. The promotion of the memory of Charlemagne's achievement of imperial unity as leader of the Christian imperium would have run counter to the reformist view of papal superiority over lay leadership, a doctrine that Urban had inherited from Gregory VII. The rhetoric of papal reform would also have clashed with a sibyl-inspired vision of an emperor leading a Holy Land expedition without the involvement of the Holy See. Before the relationship between Gregory VII and Henry IV deteriorated beyond repair in 1075, the pope had imagined leaving Henry to protect the Roman church so he himself could set off at the helm of a rescue mission in the Greek East.[14] Twenty years later, after decades of careful articulation of the primacy of *sacerdotium*, and given the long conflict with the German emperor, it would not have been in Urban's interest to invoke the Charlemagne who received his calling to rescue the East directly from God. Half a century later, in the pre–Second Crusade bull issued by Pope Eugenius, Quantum Praedecessores, the pontiff called on the king of the Franks and others to come to the aid of Christians in the East. The pope invoked the Carolingian leaders of the past, speaking of sons following in the footsteps of fathers, but, again, there was no mention of any alleged Carolingian liberation of Jerusalem.[15] Colin Morris has suggested that Urban might have been attracted by prophecies predicting that Jerusalem would be delivered by a godly emperor, and might even have seen himself in that role, especially

11. Jean Flori, *La guerre sainte: La formation de l'idée de croisade dans l'Occident chrétien* (Paris, 2001), 31.

12. *RHC Occ.*, 3:728.

13. Folz, *Le souvenir*, 138; Penny J. Cole, *The Preaching of the Crusades to the Holy Land, 1095–1270* (Cambridge, UK, 1991), 25.

14. H. E. J. Cowdrey, *Pope Gregory VII, 1073–1085* (Oxford, 1998), 610.

15. Letter of 1 December 1145, *PL* vol. 180, cols. 1064–66.

given the lack of a legitimate emperor for the task at the time.[16] If Urban did indeed fancy himself a potential deliverer of the Holy Land, then we have yet another explanation for why the Charlemagne as an avatar of the Last Emperor would not have figured in the papal promotion of a rescue mission to the East. "Charlemagne and the East" is concerned with the establishment of imperial unity under lay leadership. We should not be surprised, then, that this imperialist fantasy did not attract the chroniclers of the pope-sponsored and kingless First Crusade.

Charlemagne's peaceful subjugation of the East began as a tool of imperial propaganda that was often tied to the matter of territory in Italy contested by the empire, the papacy, and the Byzantines. The story continued to be an idealized moment of imperial unity in the German construction of the Carolingian past, figuring, for instance, on the reliquary *châsse* into which Frederick II had the emperor's remains translated in 1215.[17] By contrast, the First Crusade had enhanced the image of the pope, not a king or emperor, at the spiritual helm of a unified Christendom.[18] In his history of the first crusading expedition, *The Deeds of God through the Franks*, Guibert of Nogent underlines on several occasions that the expedition had had no leader and was compelled by God alone, for it had been *"sine domino, sine principe."*[19] Those who wished to vaunt the spectacular successes of a massive lay army heeding papal exhortation to rescue Jerusalem without lay leadership would surely have been drawn to a different locus of Carolingian memory than the one offered by the Charlemagne of the *Descriptio*. Certain aspects of the memory of Charlemagne may well have contributed to the culture of holy war, but his relationship with the East was not one of them.

A final example of how small details from crusade literature have led to overblown assumptions about the memory of Charlemagne as proto-crusader comes from the universal chronicle of Ekkehard of Aura. In an oft-cited comment, Ekkehard describes how preachers around the time of the First Crusade propagated the rumor that Charlemagne had come back from the dead to lead them on their journey to Jerusalem.[20] Norman Cohn

---

16. Colin Morris, *The Papal Monarchy: The Western Church from 1050 to 1250* (Oxford, 1991), 150; see also Whalen, *Dominion of God*, 55.

17. Folz, *Le souvenir*, 280–82.

18. Whalen, *Dominion of God*, 41.

19. *Guibert de Nogent: Dei Gesta per Francos et cinq autres textes*, ed. R.B.C. Huygens (Turnhout, 1996), 86.

20. Ekkehard of Aura, *Chronicon Universale*, ed. Georg Waitz, MGH SS 6 (Hanover, 1844), 215. Monteleone, citing Ekkehard, argues for the memory of Charlemagne as crusader and *Carolus redivivus*; see *Il viaggio*, 33. See also Jean Flori, *La première croisade: L'Occident chrétien contre l'Islam* (Paris, 2001), 236–39.

invokes the chronicler's comments, tying them to the references to Charlemagne's road in the chronicles, and to the story told in the *Descriptio*, which he describes as having enjoyed almost universal popularity.[21] None of this evidence is compelling, however, since the case for the road does not hold up, and there is little to indicate that the *Descriptio* was known to popular audiences in France at the time of the First Crusade.[22] Moreover, the rumor of Charles's return from the dead would not have corresponded to the journey to the East, a story that takes place in a recognizable, if fictionalized, past, not in an anticipated future. The popular belief that Charlemagne might awaken from the dead to lead a massive Christian army is therefore quite distinct from the story of his peaceful journey to the East to unite his new empire. The nature of popular apocalyptic sentiment during the crusading era continues to be much debated among historians.[23] It remains the case, nonetheless, that the motivations behind infusing the memory of Charlemagne's dealings with Byzantium with themes of imperial eschatology continued to be political and contemporary, not popular and apocalyptic.[24]

Saint-Denis and the *Descriptio*

With some fleeting exceptions, the tradition of "Charlemagne and the East" as told in the *Descriptio* did not figure in the propaganda for the French monarchy in the twelfth century. Charlemagne was remembered as a model defender of Christendom and conqueror of pagans, but the specific story of his encounters with Byzantium and the Holy Land did not serve the promotion of the French inheritance of Carolingian kingship. Despite Philip I's troubles with the reformist papacy, by the early decades of the twelfth century, under Louis VI, the French kings for various reasons had allied

---

21. Cohn, *Pursuit*, 72. Coulet asserted early on that people before and after did not think Charlemagne had actually gone on crusade, but he wrongly believed that the *Descriptio* had been influenced by crusade chronicles; see *Études sur l'ancien*, 234.

22. For the limited natures of audiences of medieval historiographical works, see James Powell, "Myth, Legend, Propaganda, History: The First Crusade, 1140–ca. 1300," in *Autour de la première croisade*, ed. Michel Balard (Paris, 1996): 129–30.

23. Whalen, *Dominion of God*, 55. For a skeptical view of the prevalence of apocalyptic thinking among crusaders, see Bernard McGinn, "*Iter sancti sepulchri*: The Piety of the First Crusaders," in *Essays on Medieval Civilization*, ed. Bede Karl Lackner and Kenneth Roy Philp (Austin, TX, 1978), 47. Jay Rubenstein makes a case for the prominence of apocalyptic thinking among the crusaders; see *Armies of Heaven: The First Crusade and the Quest for Apocalypse* (New York, 2011).

24. The idea that the Last Emperor, in the person of Charlemagne, might awaken and come back to lead Christian armies is reflected in the *Song of Roland*, for instance, but only metaphorically; see Matthew Gabriele, "Asleep at the Wheel? Apocalypticism, Messianism and Charlemagne's Passivity in the Oxford *Chanson de Roland*," *Nottingham Medieval Studies* 43 (2003): 46–72.

themselves with the Holy See.[25] The Charlemagne section of the *Descriptio*, with its overt assertions of imperial prerogative, would therefore have clashed with the ideal of French kingship in alliance with the Holy See.

Scholars seeking to shed light on Capetian attempts to forge dynastic links to the Carolingian kings often look to the orchestrations of Abbot Suger, a primary proponent of the cultivation of French spiritual authority in the Christian West. During the battlefield encounter in 1124 between Louis VI, German emperor Henry V, and King Henry I of England, Suger told the French king to raise the banner of Saint Denis, which was said, although scholars are unsure when this appellation arose, to be the banner of Charlemagne. When Louis emerged victorious, the event was celebrated as a glorious episode in the history of French kingship, with its fame heightened by the carefully staged allusions to Charlemagne.[26] Aside from this often-mentioned *lieu de memoire*, there is little evidence that Suger was particularly focused on the emperor Charlemagne. He certainly evoked Carolingian traditions in his construction of Capetian kingship, as Janet Nelson has shown, but the abbot did not direct his attention toward the Carolingian emperor of ecclesiastical legend.[27]

If Suger had wanted to cultivate the memory of Charlemagne as a predecessor of the Capetians and exemplum for French kings, he could have done so in his biography of Louis VI, which he wrote as part of his solidification of the abbey's role as the mouthpiece of the monarchy in the early 1140s.[28] He did not. The abbot makes only a handful of passing references to Charlemagne, listing him as one prince among others who had offered protection to Saint-Denis in the past. Charlemagne appears most prominently in an anecdote about a papal visit. In his description of the encounter between Pope Pascal II, King Philip I, and his son Louis, the future king, in 1107, Suger writes that the pontiff had come to France to discuss the status of the church. He relates that Pascal had entreated the French monarchs to aid and support Saint Peter and his vicar in accordance with the custom

---

25. Galland, "Les relations," 67–68.

26. Folz, *Le souvenir*, 206; Nelson, "Kingship and Empire," 77; Gabrielle Spiegel, "The Cult of Saint Denis and Capetian Kingship," *Journal of Medieval History* 1 (1975): 43–69; Spiegel, *Past as Text*, 153; Robert Barroux, "L'abbé Suger et la vassalité du Vexin en 1124," *Le Moyen Âge* 64 (1958): 1–26; Philippe Contamine, "L'oriflamme de Saint-Denis aux XIVᵉ et XVᵉ siècles: Études de symbolique religieuse et royale," *Annales de l'Est* 25 (1973): 184–85. According to Jean-Pierre Poly and Eric Bournazel, texts do not equate the two banners until end of the twelfth century, and Suger does not name the oriflamme in his discussion of the events of 1124; see *The Feudal Transformation: 900–1200*, trans. Caroline Higgitt (New York, 1991), 191.

27. Nelson, "Kingship and Empire," 77.

28. Suger, *Vie de Louis le Gros*, ed. and trans. Henri Waquet (Paris, 1964).

of their predecessors, the kings of the Franks, Charlemagne, and the others who fought enemies of the church.[29] During his visit, Pascal assured Philip I and Louis VI that it was they who were the true Christian monarchs in the tradition of Charlemagne. He then encouraged them to resist the empire. The pope thus recalled a Charlemagne whose role in relation to Rome was one of protection, based on the idealized memory of the Franco-papal alliance forged during the early days of the Carolingian dynasty. Charlemagne serves Suger primarily as a papal ideal of Frankish kingship in the service of the Holy See, not as a royal predecessor to Louis VI.

The *Descriptio* was clearly known at Saint-Denis in the twelfth century, but its function appears to have been limited to serving as a source for the legitimation of the abbey's holdings of relics. The more political narrative of the circumstances under which Charlemagne had acquired the relics from the leadership in Constantinople was of far less interest. For instance, a charter that contains mention of the relics from the East accompanied King Louis VI's recognition in 1124 of the feast day known as the *Indictum*, the establishment of which is described in the *Descriptio*.[30] Details from the *Descriptio* and the *Pseudo-Turpin* also appear in a handful of forgeries attributed to Charlemagne that contain exaggerated claims of ecclesiastical privileges for the royal abbey. The documents are difficult to date, but likely coincide with the abbacy of Odo of Deuil, Suger's successor, who knew the *Descriptio*.[31] The Dionysian forgeries, which Gabrielle Spiegel sees as evidence of the process of "French monopolization of Charlemagne," also roughly coincide with the period of the canonization and with Frederick's very public decree of January 1166.[32]

Both Aachen and Saint-Denis sought to establish themselves as privileged centers of the realm of Charlemagne, but a major distinction separates the two institutions and their forged ninth-century documents. Whereas Frederick sought to establish Aachen as a center of his *sacrum imperium*, the French documents emphasize the submission of French royalty to the abbey.[33] The

29. Ibid., 54.

30. Gabrielle M. Spiegel, *The Chronicle Tradition of Saint-Denis: A Survey* (Brookline, MA, 1978), 30; Barroux, "L'abbé Suger."

31. Gabriele asserts that Odo knew the *Descriptio* well; see "Provenance," 104. Cf. Brown and Cothren, "Twelfth-Century Crusading Window," 32.

32. Spiegel, *Past as Text*, 124.

33. Co Van de Kieft studies two diplomas falsely attributed to Charlemagne that reflect passages from the *Descriptio*, in "Deux diplômes faux de Charlemagne pour Saint-Denis, du XIIe siècle," *Le Moyen Âge* 64 (1958): 401–37. He ventures that Odo was responsible for K.Kar 286, but can only fix the date between 1156 and 1248. The new privileges were similar to but more generous than those conferred in the *Pseudo-Turpin Chronicle*. Among them were the kingdom of France in fief to

documents related to Saint-Denis served to promote lay submission to ecclesiastical authority, with their discussions of ceremonies such as the king's ritual placement of the four bezants at the altar in recognition of status as vassal of Saint Denis.[34] By contrast, the canonization of Charlemagne had served to shore up the emperor's claims to a form of Christian emperorship for which power and spiritual authority came directly from God. The Hohenstaufen promotion of the cult of Charlemagne in the 1160s occurred at the height of Frederick's conflict with Pope Alexander, and the canonization had represented a loud proclamation of lay independence from ecclesiastical authority.

There is only one conspicuous twelfth-century representation at Saint-Denis of Charlemagne's journey to Jerusalem and Constantinople, and that is the lost crusading window now dated to the late 1150s.[35] The surviving sketches were done in the early eighteenth century, but with no indication of the placement of the images. The sketches depict two scenes of Charlemagne meeting with the emperor in Constantinople, and are believed to have accompanied ten scenes related to major victories during the First Crusade.[36] Both panels contain accompanying inscriptions, but only one is unambiguous. The first reads "Nancii Constantini ad Carolum Parisius" (messengers of Constantine to Charles of Paris), which should be construed as representing the arrival of envoys from Constantinople with the letters urging Charlemagne to bring aid to the East. The second inscription reads:

Saint-Denis, exclusive rights to coronation ceremonies, and the establishment of the ritual placement of the crown and four bezants at the altar of the church. See also Marc Du Pouget, "La légende carolingienne à Saint-Denis: La donation de Charlemagne au retour de Roncevaux," in *La bataille de Roncevaux dans l'histoire, la légende et l'historiographie: Actes du colloque de Saint-Jean Pied de Port 1978* (Bayonne, 1979), 58; Jacques Nothomb, "Manuscripts et recensions de 'l'Iter Hierosolimitatum Caroli Magni,'" *Romania* 56 (1930); Manfred Groten, "Die Urkunde Karls des Grossen für St.-Denis von 813 (D286), eine Fälschung Abt Sugers?" *Historisches Jahrbuch* 108 (1998): 1–36.

34. John W. Baldwin, *The Government of Philip Augustus: Foundations of French Power in the Middle Ages* (Berkeley, CA, 1986), 378. Some versions of the *Pseudo-Turpin Chronicle* contained, for instance, the claim that Saint-Denis had received the French kingdom in freehold and with obedience to the abbot by princes and kings. Brown, "Saint-Denis and the Turpin Legend," 52–53; Smyser, "Early Redaction," 281.

35. Brown and Cothren date the window to as late as 1158, removing it from any pre–Second Crusade context, in "Twelfth-Century Crusading Window," 29–30. Erwin Panofsky did not believe the window had been installed until the late thirteenth century for the crusade of Louis IX; see *Abbot Suger: On the Abbey Church of St.-Denis and Its Art Treasures*, ed. Erwin Panofsky (Princeton, NJ, 1946), 205. See also Colin Morris, "Picturing the Crusades: The Uses of Visual Propaganda, c. 1095–1250," in *The Crusades and Their Sources: Essays Presented to Bernard Hamilton*, ed. John France and William G. Zajac (Aldershot, 1998), 198. Morris disagrees with Brown and Cothren but offers no alternative, as does Jonathan Phillips, *Defenders*, 123–24.

36. Brown and Cothren, "Twelfth-Century Crusading Window," 1–6. For reproductions of the medallions of Montfaucon, see Philippe Verdier, "Saint-Denis et la tradition carolingienne des Tituli: Le *de Rebus in Administratione Sua Gestis* de Suger," in *La Chanson de geste et le mythe carolingien: Mélanges René Louis I*, ed. André Moisan (Saint-Père-Sous-Vézelay, 1982), 349.

"Inperatores. Constantinopolis," which can be interpreted as "Emperors in" or "Emperors of" Constantinople.[37] If we read "emperors in," we must see the panel as a depiction of Charlemagne and the Greek emperor meeting after the liberation of Jerusalem, but the figure who is supposed to be Charles is young with dark features, while in the preceding panel he has a white beard and comes from an entirely different stock figure. If we read "emperors *of* Constantinople," which is preferable, we can interpret the two figures to be the Greek emperor Constantine and his son Leo, which corresponds to the *Descriptio*.[38] In either case, the portraits are clearly based on the imagined encounters with the Greeks.

In their influential work on the window, Elizabeth Brown and Michael Cothren argue that the images of Charlemagne imply his involvement in and approval of the crusading movement.[39] They also suggest the possibility that the window could have been related to the prophecy that Otto of Freising discusses in the prologue to the *Deeds of Frederick Barbarossa*.[40] It is possible to take this a step further though, and to suggest that the window was constructed as a reflection not of the pro-French prophecy itself, but as a rebuttal to Otto's reminder of Louis VII's failure in the East and to his derision of the prelates of France for their belief in the prophecy. Frederick's letter to Otto praising what he had read of the *Deeds* is dated to 1157,[41] so if the window was indeed produced in the late 1150s, as Brown and Cothren conclude, then it could have been constructed in reaction to Otto's prologue. In his hyperbolic praise of his nephew, the bishop had contrasted the world at peace under Frederick with the chaos of Louis's failure on the Second Crusade. The debacle of 1148 was nearly a decade in the past at that point, but Otto had provocatively brought it back to the fore. The critique by the French-educated and well-connected bishop could certainly have created tension in ecclesiastical circles and prompted a desire on the French side to construct an even more public response.

After the death of Suger, Odo of Deuil had become abbot of Saint-Denis and had taken over the promotion of Capetian kingship, a task that would have included the oversight of the window at the royal abbey. By tying the memory of Charlemagne's successes in the East to the success of the First Crusade, he would have created a typological relationship between

---

37. Brown and Cothren, "Twelfth-Century Crusading Window," 14; Verdier, "Saint-Denis," 349.
38. See Mary Jane Schenck, "The Charlemagne Window at Chartres: King as Crusader," *Word & Image* (2012): 143.
39. Brown and Cothren, "Twelfth-Century Crusading Window," 8.
40. Ibid., 23.
41. Mierow, *Deeds*, 17.

the Frankish king and the distinctly Frankish triumph of 1099, a victory achieved with minimal German participation. Moreover, the recent disaster in the East in 1148 was conveniently omitted. Odo, who knew the *Descriptio*, likely saw the propagandistic value of its celebration of Charlemagne as unifier of East and West in the Last Emperor tradition. The difference, of course, was that the French propagandist could point to continuity of Frankishness, whereas German imperial promoters had to forge other kinds of continuity between Charlemagne and the rulers they celebrated. When viewed in this light, the scenes in the window offer yet another example of how allusions to the Last Emperor prophecy functioned within the context of political propaganda. The Charlemagne who conquered the East could indeed belong to the French, but as part of a mandate to protect Christendom under the banner of Frankishness.[42] Given the frequent back-and-forth between the clerical intellectual circles of Aachen and Saint-Denis, the window would have offered, for those who understood it, a visible and assertive retort to Otto of Freising and his universalizing pretentions on behalf of the German emperor.

The *Voyage de Charlemagne*

One of the works that has most defined the modern understanding of Charlemagne's journey to the East is the enigmatic Anglo-Norman poem known as the *Voyage of Charlemagne to Jerusalem and Constantinople*. In this version of the journey, Charlemagne, called king of Saint-Denis, a common appellation for him in the Old French epic tradition, travels to the East to disprove a comment made by his wife, who had publicly repeated a rumor that a certain King Hugo in the East wore his crown better than he did. There is no liberation of Jerusalem in this telling, but while in Constantinople Charles does manage to gain the willing surrender of Hugo, who inhabits a marvelous palace that the Franks then destroy. Upon his oddly triumphal return from the East, Charlemagne displays the relics he has procured on his journey and then prostrates himself before the altar of Saint-Denis, admitting he had been wrong in condemning his wife for her invidious comments. The 870-verse poem, the sole Old French vernacular poetic version of the story, survives in a single facsimile of a lost manuscript from the fourteenth century.[43] Since it features Charlemagne and the Twelve Peers of the Old French epic tradition, but contains no battles, the *Voyage* has long been an intriguing

---

42. Gabriele, *Empire of Memory*, 2011.
43. *The Journey of Charlemagne to Jerusalem and Constantinople*, ed. and trans. Jean-Louis G. Picherit (Birmingham, AL, 1984).

outlier in the canon, and has inspired a rich secondary bibliography.[44] The tone is irreverent and the allusions are richly layered, but we know very little about its production and reception. Some have imagined the poem's origins in the world of oral epic, while others have more convincingly viewed it as a clerical construction.[45] The poem is not a chanson de geste, nor is it a mixture of crusading matter with the Charlemagne legend.[46] The *Voyage* is, however, a version of the story told in the *Descriptio*,[47] and criticism of the poem has failed to recognize the extent to which the work constitutes its own satirical interpretation of the tradition of symbolic surrender by the East that goes back to Einhard.

The place of the *Voyage* within the evolution of Charlemagne as a pseudo–Last Emperor figure falls outside the scope of this study.[48] We can, however, point to the factors that reveal the poem to have participated in the same process of deliberate rewriting that began with Notker's elaboration of Einhard. The poet was well-versed in the Old French epic tradition, possessed intimate knowledge of a version of the *Song of Roland* very close to the Oxford manuscript, and was deeply aware of the rhetorical traditions that underlie the story of Charlemagne's bloodless conquest of the East. Despite the poem's irreverence, it nonetheless embodies the essential elements of the story: the conferral of the imperial title, the encounter with the Eastern emperor, the establishment of the superiority of the West over the imperial East without battle, and the acquisition of some sort of theoretical dominance over the Greek East for the Franks. The final verses of the poem even confirm the poet's adherence to the biographical category of "deeds in peace" when he states that the victory over the Greek emperor was "*sanz bataille campel*"—without pitched battle. The Anglo-Norman context from which the Oxford *Song of Roland* also emerged, although Francophone,

---

44. Anne Elizabeth Cobby presents a useful review of the literature, *Ambivalent Conventions: Formula and Parody in Old French* (Amsterdam, 1995), 82–87. See also Picherit, ix–x. For suggested dates, see John L. Grigsby, *The Gab as Latent Genre in Medieval French Literature: Drinking and Boasting in the Middle Ages* (Cambridge, MA, 2000), 119–20.

45. More recent scholarship has situated the poem much later than the period after 1148, to after the canonization, and perhaps a generation later. Carla Rossi has even suggested a *terminus post quem* of 1204; see *Il viaggio di Carlo Magno a Gerusalemme e a Costantinopoli* (Alessandria, 2006), 124–25.

46. See, for instance, Paul Aebischer, *Le Voyage de Charlemagne à Jérusalem et à Constantinople* (Geneva, 1965), 28; Urban T. Holmes, "The *Pèlerinage de Charlemagne* and William of Malmesbury," *Symposium* 1 (1946/47): 75–81; Alfred Adler, "The *Pèlerinage de Charlemagne* in New Light on Saint-Denis," *Speculum* 22 (1947): 550.

47. Ronald N. Walpole recognized the reliance on the *Descriptio*, in "The *Pèlerinage de Charlemagne*: Poem, Legend, and Problem," *Romance Philology* 8 (1955): 173–86.

48. I am in the process of writing a separate study of the journey to Jerusalem and Constantinople in the Old French tradition.

had long been deeply engaged in the politics of the Hohenstaufen empire. Frederick I even claimed that Henry II had given him the idea to canonize Charlemagne. It was, presumably, in the cosmopolitan world of the Anglo-Angevin court that the imperial-themed *Voyage of Charlemagne to Jerusalem and Constantinople* originated.

The Return to the Carolingian Bloodline

Near the turn of the thirteenth century, Giles of Paris penned the first enco-miastic biography of Charlemagne to be written for a French king. Entitled the *Karolinus*, the work is designed around the four classical virtues, but draws largely on the *Royal Frankish Annals* and Einhard for its content.[49] Giles spent about six months in 1195–96 composing the poem, which he presented to the then-thirteen-year-old Louis VIII in September of 1200.[50] The *Karolinus* is divided into five books, the first four of which are devoted to one of the classical cardinal virtues: *prudentia, iustitia, fortitudo,* and *temperantia.* The virtues serve as an organizing principle, however, rather than as subjects of philosophical meditation, in what is essentially a biographical work based on the Carolingian sources.[51] Giles claims to be offering moral instruction for a young king-to-be, even insisting that it be kept private unless Louis decides otherwise; but given the political nature of the poem, this statement was surely not meant to be taken literally. Writing less than twenty years after the appearance of Charlemagne's saintly *Vita*, but during a time of continued prominence for Einhard's biography, Giles would have confronted conflict-ing biographical models. For his gift to Louis VIII, he elected a classicizing approach, which allowed him to eschew the Charlemagne of the *Descriptio* and *Pseudo-Turpin* traditions that were thriving in rival imperial and Flemish circles. Instead, the poet created a more austere vision of Charlemagne's life, one free of universalizing and prophetic imperial overtones, and therefore

---

49. Giles of Paris, "The 'Karolinus' of Edigius Parisiensis," ed. M. L. Colker, *Traditio* 21 (1973): 199–325. Little is known about Giles of Paris except that he made several trips to Rome and met with Pope Celestine in the late 1180s.

50. Christine Ratkowitsch argues that the extremely virtuous Charlemagne of the *Karolinus* may have been meant as a foil for Louis's not-so-virtuous father. See "Carolus castus. Zum Charakter Karls des Großen in der Darstellung des Egidius von Paris," in *Scripturus vitam: Lateinische Biographie von der Antike bis in die Gegenwart, Festgabe für W. Berschin zum 65. Geburtstag,* ed. Dorothea Walz (Heidelberg, 2002), 369; Colker, "'Karolinus,'" 209, Morrissey, *L'empereur,* 118.

51. Céline Billot-Vilandrau, "Charlemagne and the Young Prince: A Didactic Poem of the Cardinal Virtues by Giles of Paris (c. 1200)," in *Virtue and Ethics in the Twelfth Century,* ed. István P. Bejczy and Richard G. Newhauser (Leiden, 2005), 347.

more in tune with the discourse of Capetian kingship at the turn of the thirteenth century.

Like the English commentator on court life, Walter Map, Giles was full of contempt for the chanson de geste tradition. In the early 1180s, in his lament on the lack of literature of praise for modern kings, Walter had bemoaned the fact that Charlemagne's memory was kept alive by minstrels and buffoons, while the emperors of antiquity had enjoyed the likes of Lucan and Vergil to sing their praises.[52] Giles likewise bemoaned the lack of proper literary praise for Charlemagne, and endeavored to fill the void. He condemns troupes of singers, complaining that they perform songs filled with falsehoods about the battles waged by Charlemagne and the Twelve Peers.[53] Beyond a couple of brief allusions, Giles avoids the story of Charlemagne's expedition to Spain.[54] He does make brief mention of Roland's death, but his Roland dies at the hands of the Basques, a detail drawn from the Carolingian sources that contradicts the popular accounts in the *Song of Roland* and the *Pseudo-Turpin Chronicle*. The chansons de geste about which Walter and Giles complain, as scholars have long shown, demonstrated intense political engagement, and were often critical of royal power.[55] Giles may, therefore, have sought to distance himself from the Charlemagne of popular culture, not simply for esthetic reasons, but also as a demonstration of loyalty to the court that he represented.[56]

One of the two extant manuscripts of the *Karolinus* contains a family tree with allusions to the Carolingian roots of the ruling Capetian family.[57] The doctrine of the return to the Carolingian line, the *reditus regni ad stirpem Karoli*, had become a theme in the political discourse of the realm after Louis VII's marriage to Adela of Champagne in 1160, at which point the assertion of dynastic ties to Charlemagne took on new significance in royal propaganda.[58] The birth of Louis VIII had represented a double return to Carolingian stock, through his grandmother Adela, and then more directly through his Flemish mother, Isabelle of Hainaut. The birth of Louis VIII

52. Walter Map, *De nugis curialium*, ed. M. R. James and R. A. B. Mynors (Oxford, 1983), 404–5.

53. Morrissey, *L'empereur*, 115.

54. *Karolinus*, 273–74.

55. See Dominique Boutet, *La Chanson de geste: Forme et signification d'une écriture épique du moyen âge* (Paris, 1993).

56. See also Morrissey, *L'empereur*, 121.

57. Billot-Vilandrau, "Charlemagne and the Young Prince," 343.

58. Spiegel, *Past as Text*, 112–14; E. A. R. Brown, "Vincent de Beauvais and the *reditus regni francorum ad stirpem Caroli imperatoris*," in *Vincent de Beauvais: Intentions et réceptions d'une oeuvre encyclopédique au moyen âge*, ed. Monique Paulmier-Foucart, Serge Lusignan, and Alain Nadeau (Paris, 1990): 168, 175.

was also seen as the fulfillment of the popular mid-eleventh-century Valerian prophecy, which had promised the eventual return of the French kings to the Carolingian dynastic line.[59] The *reditus* doctrine gained currency with Louis's birth, but historians have downplayed its importance. John Baldwin has argued, for instance, that there were three theories of dynastic succession in Capetian France: the Valerian prophecy, the *reditus* doctrine, and the theory of Trojan origins, but that only the third received serious attention.[60] Moreover, as Elizabeth Brown has shown, Philip Augustus refrained from engaging in dynastic rivalry, doing little to work against the impression that his family lacked a genealogical link to the Carolingians.[61] Instead, she shows that chroniclers encouraged Philip and his son to imitate their predecessors through virtue and laudable acts.[62]

Giles conforms to the model described by Brown in that he does not insist on the ancestral ties between his addressee and Charlemagne. He participates in the movement to tie the young Louis VIII to Charlemagne, but he does so by constructing Charlemagne as an exemplum of virtue, rather than celebrating him as a direct ancestor. In the 1180s, Godfrey of Viterbo had rewritten the circumstances of Charlemagne's birth and his assumption of the empire according to a model of genealogical inheritance rather than God-ordained political transfer. Giles took a far more measured approach, emphasizing emulation over invented family ties. The poet does allude briefly and tentatively, however, to Louis's Carolingian heritage in the prologue to the fifth and last book. The reference is embedded rather than highlighted, appearing after the four books in which the poet systematically ties the deeds of Charlemagne to the four classical virtues. In the opening lines of Book 5, the first one not linked to a specific virtue, Giles addresses Louis as heir to the kingdom by royal blood: "O puer, in regno regalis sanguinis heres." This "virtue," the poet explains, is constituted in the boy through the holy roots of his holy mother. Then, invoking the biblical metaphor, the poet admonishes the boy, stating that since he is from a good tree, he ought to produce good fruit.[63] Giles avoids asserting direct descent from Charlemagne. Instead, he

59. Spiegel, *Past as Text*, 116.

60. Baldwin, *Government of Philip Augustus*, 370.

61. E. A. R. Brown, "La notion de la légitimité et la prophétie à la cour de Philippe Auguste," in *La France de Philippe Auguste: Le temps des mutations*, ed. R.-H. Bautier (Paris: Éditions du CNRS, 1982), 78. See also Brown, "Vincent de Beauvais," 171.

62. Brown, "La notion," 81.

63. *Karolinus, Incipit* to book 5, verses 4–7. "O puer, in regno regalis sanguinis heres, / Hec tibi constituit in te michi credita uirtus, / Qui sancta es soboles sancte genitricis habendus / Et debes prodisse bona bonus arbore fructus." See Andrew W. Lewis, *Royal Succession in Capetian France: Studies on Familial Order and the State* (Cambridge, MA, 1981), 107–10, and Colette Beaune, *The Birth of an*

celebrates Louis's "virtue" that he inherits from his mother. His capacity
for virtue is both something with which he is born and something he must
cultivate by emulating Charlemagne. Giles thus creates thematic continuity
by offering four books of exemplary literature followed by a celebration of
Louis's inheritance of the gift of virtue. The passage does allude, albeit metaphorically, to the Capetian blood-right to Carolingian legitimacy, as Andrew
Lewis has noted, but it does not provide an overt celebration of Carolingian
lineage.[64]

While the *Karolinus* is divided into books based on the virtues, within
those books Giles retains many of the categories and themes of imperial
biography that Einhard had employed. Each book has a prologue, called a
"tenor," consisting of fourteen verses and an epilogue. Early in the poem,
before he defines the cardinal virtues that serve as the framework for his
moral portrait, Giles summarizes each of the five books. Following Einhard's
model, the poet celebrates Charlemagne's territory gained in war followed
by territory gained in peace. Like his predecessors, Giles does not specifically
delineate these sections, but the thematic progression is clear. The "deeds
in war" occur in Book 2, which is devoted to the virtue of justice and cov-
ers Charlemagne's expansion of his dominion through conquest during the
period leading up to his imperial coronation. The encounters with the East
fall within the "deeds in peace" in Book 3, which is devoted to the virtue
of fortitude and narrates Charles's rise to the position of emperor. Here we
find his post-coronation exchanges with foreign princes, including his alliance with Harun al Rachid.[65]

In Book 4, which is devoted to *moderatio* and attends to more personal
matters such as family life, the poet offers a revealing synthesis of his view of
the trajectory of Charlemagne's life.[66] After listing the king's sons and grandsons down to the death of Charles the Bald, Giles returns to Charlemagne.
He reminds his audience that the Frankish king was the first of the Franks to
hold the empire as Augustus and to accept the tribute (*uectigalia*) of the whole
world.[67] Furthermore, he explains, God had arranged Charlemagne's life so
that while he was at his lower status, he waged war, but when he achieved the

Ideology: Myths and Symbols of Nation in Late Medieval France, trans. Susan Ross Huston, ed. Fredric L.
Cheyette (Berkeley, CA, 1991), 190.

64. Lewis, *Royal Succession*, 107–8. Billot-Vilandrau argues that Giles is critical of Philip and
expects Louis to be a better king because he is in the bloodline of Charlemagne, thereby suggesting
a moral significance of royal blood; see "Charlemagne and the Young Prince," 351–53.

65. For Morrissey, Harun's gifts are merely a sign of respect; see *L'empereur*, 119.

66. *Karolinus*, 300.

67. *Karolinus*, 329.

status of emperor, he enjoyed peace. The passage proceeds according to the biographical sequence that places his "deeds in peace" during his imperial reign, which occurred after he fought wars as a mere king, but before he found redemption at the end of this life. In death, Giles adds, he received correction for his life, a reference to the Mass of Saint Giles that appears in Book 4.[68] With the reference to the tribute of the whole world that is offered to Augustus, Giles joins his teleological vision of the progression of Charlemagne's life toward ultimate redemption with a classical rather than an apocalyptic expression of Roman universalism.

The remarks in Book 4 are not the only instance in the *Karolinus* in which the events after the imperial coronation coincide with the expression of the theme of bloodless victory. Prior to the beginning of the first book, there is an introductory section that Giles likely did not write, which provides summaries and commentaries on the books to follow. The explication of Book 3 concerning the virtue of fortitude provides further evidence that biographers thought explicitly about which kinds of deeds should occur in which section of Charlemagne's written life. The commentator announces that the third book is about Charlemagne's rise to emperorship and the favor he enjoyed with all kings and peoples. He then notes that the book includes nothing about wars after the coronation. The author concedes that Charlemagne may have finished off some existing wars after he was crowned emperor, such as the one against Tassilo, adding, "But it is not read in the chronicles that he was engaged in any wars after his assumption of the empire, perhaps because he finished them off quickly, but only that he built churches, supported the poor, and carried out ecclesiastical business."[69] Perhaps not aware of the commonplace that Giles was adapting, the commentator seeks to affirm the validity of Giles's portrait by allowing that there might have been some loose ends that needed tying up after 800. Of course, Charlemagne did fight wars after 800, but Einhard had deliberately created the sense that the assumption of the imperial title had coincided with the peaceful surrender of all nations. This idealized picture of an empire united and at peace after the coronation, a concept born of Roman biographical norms, helps to explain the centuries-old impulse to portray him as an imperial pilgrim rather than as a warrior in the East.

In another introductory segment, which Giles may or may not have written, the author defines the four cardinal virtues. In both extant manuscripts of the *Karolinus*, this section is richly illustrated with images of the female

---

68. *Karolinus*, 207.
69. *Karolinus*, 234.

personifications of the virtues.[70] The discussion of *fortitudo* contains a philosophical version of the foreign embassy topos, in which Charlemagne's
admirable embodiment of that virtue and his peaceful soul are the qualities
that inspire the foreign leaders of the world to seek his friendship. Fortitude,
the author explains, is that which destroys cowardice and storminess of spirit;
regarding the virtue of fortitude, it is said that "it is better to conquer anger
than to capture a city"—which, as the commentator points out, is the lesson
of the third book. Charles had great bodily strength, but it was his mind that
was so great. He was the master of his own soul, which he ruled so force-
fully that by surpassing the souls of all others, he moved them to admire him
and seek his friendship. The author then promises that the previous concepts are more fully described in the third book of the poem.[71] Rather than
gaining the willing surrender of foreign nations through fear of his mighty
reputation, Charlemagne wins alliances because of his mastery of self and
admirable spirit. Godfrey of Viterbo had produced a metaphorical revision
of Einhard's version of surrendering foreign nations by having their tribute
take the form of written material for his universal history. Giles creates his
own poetic revision of the scene by making the willing alliances of foreign
leaders serve as the fruit of his embodiment of *fortitudo*.

In Book 3, Giles gives his account of Charlemagne's foreign relations
after the coronation in a manner that reveals the author's deliberate avoidance of the universalizing discourse of the foreign embassy motif. After a
long adaptation of Einhard's chapter 15, which enumerates the lands that
the king brought under his power, Giles turns to the material of chapter 16
and the peoples Charlemagne conquered in peace. In a familiar rehearsal,
he lists the letters from the Irish, the Scots, King Alfonso, and King Harun
(who is now from Egypt), who are said to have often sent "friendly little
letters."[72] He does not mention the arrival of the patriarch of Jerusalem with
gifts from Calvary. Adhering to his promise to celebrate the cardinal virtues,
Giles celebrates Charlemagne's generosity by talking about his gift exchange
with Harun, but he moves quickly on to his church-building, with no mention of the Greeks' fearful quest for an alliance. He discusses the Greeks
elsewhere, but removes them from the rhetorical context of the enumeration

70. *Karolinus*, 234–35.
71. *Karolinus*, 235. "Fortitudo est que pusillanimatatem et tempestatem spiritus tollit, pro qua
dictum est 'Melior est qui uincit iram quam qui capit civitatem' hec sicut in tertio libro docetur.'
Preter eam quam habuit Karolus in corpore, ita fuit in eius mente quod ipse animus tam fortiter se
gessit quod omnium aliorum animos exuperando in admirationem ipsius Karoli traxit et in gratiam
acquisiuit, et hoc quod dicitur, ibi plenius inuenitur."
72. *Karolinus*, 284.

of surrendering foreign nations. Both the Holy Land protectorate story and the pact with the fearful Greeks are thus excised, which means that Giles's version of Charlemagne's life has no "Charlemagne and the East" and therefore lacks the two audaciously fabricated details that constituted Einhard's deployment of the rhetoric of Roman universalism.

Charlemagne's acquisition of dominion over Jerusalem and the alliance with the submissive Greeks in Einhard had formed the basis for all future iterations of the triumphal journey to Constantinople and Jerusalem. The absences of both cities from Giles's version thus reveal a poet seeking to distance his Charlemagne from the tradition of the invented encounters with the East. Giles likely perceived the apocalyptic overtones that the episode had taken on, especially given that the story had been filtered through Notker and others who had transformed it into an openly eschatological narrative. By eliminating the protectorate story and the Greek emperors, Giles ensures that the centuries-old suggestion of Charlemagne's universal dominion not only loses its universalizing tones, but also any traces of the sibylline reunification of East and West. Instead of choosing a purely classical model, however, Giles emphasizes his subject's generosity, diplomacy, and church-building. In that respect, he conforms to an established pattern of Capetian biography according to which authors such as Suger drew comparisons to Carolingian monarchs without implying dynastic links.

Giles's classicizing aims may have dictated his pared-down depiction of Charlemagne's post-coronation dealings with the East, but there were also political reasons for him to avoid the story of the emperor's symbolic besting of the Byzantines. As I have argued throughout this study, revisions of Charlemagne's apocryphal encounters with the East served as post-800 articulations of imperial continuity and Roman renewal. As a learned propagandist, Giles would likely have been aware of the ways in which the quasi-sibylline Charlemagne had figured in the construction of Frederick Barbarossa's identity as emperor. The decision to remove the Greeks from the context of the foreign embassy topos meant that Giles avoided any participation in the imperialist discourse of Roman *renovatio*. What is more, Capetian propaganda did not identify France with Rome. Alexander the Great was the preferred model for the French monarchy, while Rome was France's imperial enemy. In Guillaume le Breton's anti-imperial rhetoric in the *Philippidos* in celebration of Philip Augustus, the author characterizes the French victory at Bouvines in 1214 in terms of Philip's stopping Rome's lust to dominate the world and asserting Frankish freedom from the yoke of Rome.[73]

---

73. Baldwin, *Government of Philip Augustus*, 383.

The Capetians, for their part, made no claims to Roman imperial authority. Their forged links to the Carolingians were royal, not imperial, and were based on the idea of continuity between the three races of Frankish kings according to the theory of the Trojan origins of Frankish kingship.[74] The assertion of Trojan origins was something quite distinct from the German pretention to being the legitimate embodiment of Rome, the fourth and last of the Four Kingdoms. Finally, it was the papacy under Innocent III at the turn of the century that was making the loudest claims to universal imperial authority. The pontiff asserted, for instance, that the apostolic see had been responsible for the transfer of the Roman Empire from the Greeks to the Germans in the person of Charlemagne, while it was popes who anointed, consecrated, and crowned emperors. Not long after the appearance of the *Karolinus* in 1202, Innocent also proclaimed France's freedom from any subservience to the empire or any other temporal authority in his famous decree, Per Venerabilem.[75] It therefore stands to reason that Giles avoided the discourse of Roman universalism associated with the memory of Charlemagne as it had evolved in the German empire.

Although it appears that the Last Emperor tradition did not exert significant influence during the reign of Philip Augustus, there is evidence for some temporary interest in the prophecy in royal circles near the end of his reign. In 1220, versions of the Valerian prophecy and the Tiburtine Sibyl appeared at the end of the French royal register after a list of French kings, popes, and Roman emperors and all the bishoprics of the realm. Another French document from that period also identifies the French monarchy as the line that will provide the coming Last Emperor.[76] The surreptitious addition to the royal register should not be seen, however, as an official public assertion of any Capetian claim to Last Emperor status for one of their kings. What stands out instead is the fact that the appearance of the sibyl and some passing references to Philip Augustus as a Last Emperor figure happened as quietly as they did and failed to catch on in French circles. Baldwin has puzzled over the choice of the Tiburtina for the register, since both the *Revelations* of Pseudo-Methodius and Adso's letter on Antichrist were in wide circulation at the time. Both

74. Gabrielle M. Spiegel, "Medieval Canon Formation and the Rise of Royal Historiography in Old French Prose," *Modern Language Notes* 108 (1993): 638.

75. Tierney, *Crisis*, 129–33, and Thomas Wetzstein, "La doctrine de la 'translatio imperii' et l'enseignement des canonistes médiévaux," in *Science politique et droit public dans les facultés de droit européennes (XIIIe–XVIIIe siècle)*, ed. Jacques Krynen and Michael Stolleis (Frankfurt am Main, 2008), 192–95.

76. Baldwin, *Government of Philip Augustus*, 384; Brown, "La notion." See also Robert E. Lerner, "Medieval Prophecy and Politics," 418.

prophecies, but especially Adso's, would have provided a more pro-Frankish prophecy than the Tiburtina, which was so strongly associated with Germany and Italy. Baldwin concludes that the reason eludes us, noting only that the insertion of the prophecy happened after the French defeat of imperial forces at Bouvines.[77] Brown confronts the same question and posits that the prophecy was meant as a solution to the perceived genealogical crisis of the Capetians with regard to the Carolingian bloodline.[78] Prophetic speculation was heretical, she notes, but it still may have influenced those seeking to bring legitimacy to the Capetian line enough to put it in the royal register and to thereby propose Philip as the potential Constans figure.[79] The producers of the register may have briefly imagined Philip Augustus as a Last Emperor figure, but it remains the case that neither the Last Emperor prophecy nor the Charlemagne who traveled to the East enjoyed any prominence in Capetian royal propaganda under Philip Augustus and Louis VIII. Imperial eschatology and Trojan genealogy, although both related to the inheritance of Rome, offered two incommensurate visions of dynastic continuity, and the French monarchy espoused the latter.

Giles of Paris's careful avoidance of the Charlemagne who gains symbolic triumph over the East suggests that politically minded authors, whether poets or chroniclers, would have needed to make a choice between the various possible avatars of the emperor Charlemagne. The work of one of Giles's contemporaries, the annalist of Marbach, reveals, instead, that a clear-cut decision was not necessarily required. In the *Annals of Marbach* from the last decades of the twelfth century, the annalist merges Einhard's version of the events surrounding the coronation with the tale told in the *Descriptio*. A historian with close ties to the Staufen court, the annalist pays minute attention to how the empire came to be in German hands. Echoing Otto of Freising, he announces that in the era of the last Carolingians, the rule of the empire had become deficient. As a result of this sorry state of affairs, the empire was transferred from the incompetent Franks to the Teutons. He then echoes the canonization documents concerning the privileges that Charlemagne had accorded to Aachen.[80] For the period after the coronation, the annalist adapts chapters 13–15 of Einhard on Charlemagne's wars and conquests, and then, where material from chapter 16 would be expected, he switches to the

---

77. Baldwin, *Government of Philip Augustus*, 386.

78. Brown, "La notion," 84.

79. Ibid., 85. Jerzy Pysiak cites the appearance in the register of the Tiburtina as evidence that the Capetians saw themselves in the predestined role of source for the Last Emperor; see "Philippe Auguste. Un roi de la fin des temps?" *Annales. Histoire, Sciences Sociales* 57 (2002): 1184.

80. *Annales Marbacenses*, 8.

Descriptio for the "deeds in peace" section. An abbreviated account of the *Pseudo-Turpin* story follows. After the events in Spain, the chronicler then returns to the end of chapter 15 of Einhard and then gives the Carolingian biographer's version of chapter 16.[81]

The interpolation by the Marbach annalist of the abridged *Descriptio* and *Pseudo-Turpin*, which figure side by side in Charlemagne's saintly *Vita*, points to the author's familiarity with the document. Their appearance also bears witness to the fact that in the wake of the publication of the *Vita*, chroniclers were grappling with what to do with the competing sources for the story of Charlemagne's encounters with the East after his imperial investiture. The pro-imperialist historian, according to whom the empire had been transferred to the Germans due to failed governance by the Franks, made a calculated decision to forge his own hybrid interpretation of the post-coronation chapter in Charlemagne's life that included the *Descriptio*'s explicit articulation of the divine conferral of spiritual authority to the emperor. His decision demonstrates that the stories of Charlemagne's journeys to the East and to Spain, especially when paired as they were in the saintly biography, had become ideologically marked as pro-imperialist discourse in the definition of Charlemagne as a political antecedent.

On a political level, it should not come as a surprise, then, that Giles did not choose to incorporate the universalizing discourse of "Charlemagne and the East" into his poem for his Capetian royal patrons. That Charlemagne had been primarily a tool of imperial propaganda. The *Pseudo-Turpin Chronicle*, which was also associated with the saintly *Vita* by the end of the century, was growing in popularity in Flemish aristocratic circles. The members of the family of Hainaut posed a paradoxical threat to Capetian claims to a return to the Carolingian line, for they were at once the source of Louis VIII's maternal claim to Carolingian descent, and at the same time rivals for that honor. Gabrielle Spiegel has demonstrated the social function of the *Pseudo-Turpin* tradition in Flemish court society, revealing how the struggling aristocracy used the famous forgery to both emphasize its genealogical ties to Charlemagne and to appropriate the king as a model of chivalry and virtue over and against the claims of the Capetians.[82] We know that during the reign of Philip Augustus, Flemish courtly audiences were hearing the *Pseudo-Turpin*. Giles, by contrast, chose to hark back to a version of Charlemagne

---

81. *Annales Marbacenses*, 13–14.

82. Gabrielle M. Spiegel, *Romancing the Past: The Rise of Vernacular Prose Historiography in Thirteenth-Century France* (Berkeley, CA, 1993).

that existed long before the *Descriptio* and the *Pseudo Turpin* had become popular in rival courts.

Pierre de Beauvais and the French *Descriptio*

At the turn of the thirteenth century, as Giles was presenting the *Karolinus* to the future king Louis VIII, the tale of Charlemagne's liberation of Jerusalem gained a new voice in Pierre de Beauvais. Pierre, who spent some time at Saint-Denis in the early thirteenth century, produced a handful of works, including a translation of the *Descriptio* from around 1212 for his patrons at Beauvais. The adaptation is based on a version that he claims to have found at the royal abbey, which included the Charles the Bald section.[83] The prologue to the translation offers telling information about the silence in France concerning Charlemagne's travels to the East, as well as crucial insight into the transformation of the *Descriptio* into a piece of vernacular literature destined for a lay Francophone audience.[84]

Pierre begins the prologue by describing how Charlemagne conquered Spain and the Holy Land and then brought back with him "the Crown with which God was crowned."[85] He makes no pretense that the journey to the East was peaceful and augments the relics that Charlemagne obtained to include the entire crown of thorns. He then launches into a complaint concerning the relative neglect of the Holy Land tradition by comparison with the attention being lavished on the story of Charlemagne's exploits in Spain:

> In the books that speak about the kings of France, we find it written that by way of the request of Saint James, our Lord gave the gift to Charlemagne, about which people would speak on and on until the end of time. The truth is that many who willingly listen to stories about Charles know nothing about the trip he made to the East, for the good clerics who have these stories available to them do not care a bit that it is written in three places in France besides Aix-la-Chapelle and Saint-Denis.[86]

---

83. Walpole gives a date of 1212 in "Two Notes on *Charlemagne's Journey to the East*: The French Translation of the Latin Legend by Pierre of Beauvais," *Romance Philology* 7 (1953–54): 132. See also Max L. Berkey, "Pierre de Beauvais' 'Olympiade': A Medieval Outline-History," *Speculum* 41 (1966): 505–15.

84. Pierre de Beauvais, French *Desc.*, 445.

85. Ibid.

86. Ibid. "Es livres qui parolent des roys de France trovons escript que par la priere monseigneur saint Jaque dona nostre Sires cest don a Charlemaine c'on parlerait de lui tant com le siècle dureroit. Voirs est que plusors qui volontiers oient de Charle ne sevent nient de la voie qu'il fist outre mer.

Pierre blames the neglect of the Holy Land narrative on the clerics who attend to the copying and diffusion of written works, claiming that the same ones who make the *Pseudo-Turpin* available for the listening public do not care "one bit" about the liberation of the Holy Land. Although rhetorical, Pierre's complaint is still a useful piece of evidence for the reception of the two works in the French-speaking world.

According to Pierre, the *Pseudo-Turpin* enjoyed wide popularity in its translated versions prepared for Flemish court society, but the *Descriptio* did not have the same appeal.[87] After accusing French clerics of ignoring the story, despite its availability outside of Aachen and Saint-Denis, Pierre insists that it is good for the heart and the soul to hear such stories. This is the reason, he explains, why he looked so hard through the books at Saint-Denis and translated with such great care, from Latin to French, the story of how Charlemagne made the journey to the East before going to Spain. He then invites clerics and lay people alike to lend their ears, "for it [the journey to across the sea] was the way [*voie*] by which France never had more honor, and still does, to this day." He then promises to tell the story from beginning to end according to the Latin he has found.[88] Pierre's assertion that Charlemagne's liberation of Jerusalem was a moment of unparalleled glory for France is symptomatic of the tendency in vernacular culture to view the Carolingian leader as an early French king. His Charlemagne is not just an exemplum, but a piece of France's royal past. The passage also affirms that as late as the early thirteenth century the *Pseudo-Turpin* was being widely heard, while the *Descriptio* had yet to be translated for the ears of lay society. Pierre's goal is to make the neglected work available to a wider public, not to correct the historical record.

The miraculous flight of the pagan occupiers from Jerusalem upon the arrival of Charlemagne is a relatively minor event in the *Descriptio* by comparison with Charlemagne's reckoning with the Greek emperor. Pierre de Beauvais highlights the liberation of the Holy City, presenting it in the prologue to his translation as the central event of the narrative. He thus diverges

---

Car li bon clerc qui les estoires ont en us ne cuident mie qu'il soit ecrit en .iii. lieus en France fors a Ays la Chapelle et a mon seigneur Saint Denis."

87. Spiegel, *Romancing the Past*, 53-98.

88. Pierre de Beauvais, French *Desc.*, 445. "Et por ce qui porfit est au cors et grant biens a l'ame d'oïr les istoires qui enseignent commant on se doit avoir ou siecle et en Dieu, a tant cerchié es livres mon seigneur Saint Denise Pierres, qui l'a mis de latin en romans par grant estuide, comant et par quel achoison Charles ala outre mer devant la voie d'Espaigne. Si doivent clerc et loy, et haut et bas, encliner l'oreilles de lor cuers a oïr cestes estoires, car ce fu la voie dont France ot onques plus d'onor et a encore, si con vos orrés ordeneement selonc le latin de l'estoire qui ci commence. Ou non du Pere du Fil et du saint Esperit."

from all the imperial revisers of the episode, most recently Godfrey of Viterbo, who understood the story to be part of the discourse of *translatio imperii* and, therefore, preserved the classical theme of bloodless surrender. The revisers of Charlemagne's saintly *Vita* were careful to insist that the journey to the East had been a peaceful pilgrimage during which, miraculously and providentially, Jerusalem was liberated. Another more contemporary example of the peaceful interpretation of Charlemagne's journey to Jerusalem, which was inspired by the *Descriptio*, appears on Charlemagne's reliquary *châsse*, revealed in 1215. The reliquary depicts Constantine giving relics to Charlemagne in the Byzantine capital, but no image of anything related to the events in Jerusalem.[89] The essential message of the story in the imperial examples is the ceding of symbolic authority by the Greek East and not the liberation of Jerusalem. By contrast, Pierre lauds Charlemagne's conquest of Spain and the Holy Land, "commant il conquist Espaigne et la sainte terre de promission en la quelle est Jherusalem," as great moments in French history.[90] He was not interested in the imperial politics of the episode, nor was he concerned to preserve the framework of Charlemagne's biography. For the French translator of the Latin *Descriptio*, the salient details of the story of Charlemagne and the East were the liberation of the Holy City and the acquisition of the crown of thorns by a King Charles construed as French.

Truth versus Function

An intriguing bit of evidence about the fortunes of the *Descriptio* in the late twelfth century appears in a proposed outline for a history of the Frankish kings. The resulting work was a new history of the Franks called the *Nova Gesta Francorum*, which can be dated to between 1180 and 1214. The roughly done outline shows that the compilers intended to include works dating from the putative Trojan origins of the Frankish people up to the accession of Louis VI in 1108. A comparison between the outline and the resulting compilation shows that, despite their appearance in the list of intended works, the *Descriptio* and the *Pseudo-Turpin* did not make it into the *Nova Gesta* until the fourteenth century.[91] The dating of the outline corresponds with the appearance of the *Descriptio* and the *Pseudo-Turpin* in Charlemagne's saintly *Vita*, where they figured side by side for the first time. Pro-imperial authors

---

89. Folz, *Le souvenir*, 281.

90. Pierre de Beauvais, French *Desc.*, 445.

91. Spiegel, *Chronicle Tradition*, 42–43; François Béthune, "Les écoles historiques de Saint-Denis et de Saint-Germain-des-Près dans leurs rapports avec la composition des *Grandes Chroniques de France*," *Revue d'histoire ecclésiastique* 4 (1903): 31–33.

such as Godfrey of Viterbo and the Marbach annalist had recognized both the "Charlemagne and the East" episode and the *Pseudo-Turpin* narrative as part of the saintly *Vita's* assertion of Frederick's God-ordained imperial status as the successor of Charlemagne. Capetian biographer Giles of Paris avoided those same traditions in the *Karolinus*, and Pierre de Beauvais's slightly later lament on the neglect of the *Descriptio* provides further confirmation of that rejection. The exclusion of these two episodes from a new Capetian-sponsored history of the Franks was therefore, no doubt, related to their association with Hohenstaufen propaganda.

Other chroniclers who later incorporated the *Descriptio*, such as Helinand de Froidmont, Aubri de Trois-Fontaines, and Vincent de Beauvais, although French, were producers of universal histories and not genealogically based compilations of essentially biographical material. Moreover, all three were strongly influenced by the pro-imperialist universal chronicle of Sigebert of Gembloux, which had been written over a century earlier at the height of the Investiture Contest.[92] Helinand, who was from a Cistercian house near Beauvais, joined Pierre de Beauvais in puzzling over the neglect in France of the story of Charlemagne's liberation of the Holy Land. Vincent de Beauvais later used Helinand's version of the story, although without any of his predecessor's hand-wringing about why no one else seemed to mention it. In his *Chronicon*, written in the early decades of the thirteenth century, Helinand combines the memory of the gifts from the patriarch of Jerusalem described in the *Royal Frankish Annals* with material from the *Descriptio*, which he places in 802. He reproduces segments of the *Descriptio*, beginning with the arrival of messengers from Constantinople, but only up through the rebuilding and consecration of the church at Aachen. There is no mention of the Charles the Bald section, which suggests that Helinand was working from a version resembling the one in the saintly *Vita*.

After describing the establishment of the *Indictum* at Aachen and the arrival of the relics from the East, Helinand makes the following remarks concerning the validity of the story:

> It is astonishing that the whole expedition of Charles to Jerusalem, in which such a great deed was accomplished, that is to say, the acquisition

---

92. Chazan, *L'empire et l'histoire*; Goez, *Translatio Imperii*, 122. The chroniclers most often noted for their use of the *Descriptio* are Vincent de Beauvais, Helinand of Froidmont, Gui de Bazoches, and Petrus Comestor. Of those, only Petrus Comester wrote in the twelfth century (d. 1178), and his allusions to the tradition concerning Charlemagne's gift of the holy foreskin to Charroux are not based on an imperial journey. See Nothomb, "Manuscript et recensions," 193, and Gabriele, "Provenance," for a more complete accounting.

of the land of Jerusalem and so many miracles which were accomplished by the relics, was noted by none among the Latin chroniclers. In this present narrative, however, it seems to result from historical truth that the Patriarch of Jerusalem came to Constantinople to Emperor Constantine and his son Leo at the time when the Roman Empire was given to Charles, but at that time, he [Constantine] had already died.[93]

To legitimate the doubtful story, the chronicler then claims that while Charlemagne may not have officially been emperor during the reigns of Constantine and Leo, he could have been, had he wanted to, since Pope Hadrian had frequently offered him the title.[94] Then, in a show of what Helinand describes as virtuous self-restraint, Charlemagne had managed to content himself with a royal rather than an imperial title during the pontificate of Hadrian.

Helinand's earnest explanation of the anachronism does little to clarify his own stance on the veracity of the story. Either he found the story to be implausible, but still wanted to include it in his chronicle, or else he believed the document to be true and was truly surprised by its neglect. What makes it difficult to determine his mind-set is the fact that the anachronism he chooses to highlight is really the least of the *Descriptio*'s discrepancies with the historical record. Charlemagne never even traveled to the East, let alone liberated Jerusalem. Whether Helinand and Pierre believed the story to be true is hard to ascertain. Both deemed the narrative useful and worth mentioning, and in that regard they mark an important shift in clerical attitudes in France toward the story of Charlemagne in the East. The essential difference between the two, however, is that Pierre emphasized the liberation of Jerusalem as a story destined for a lay audience, while Helinand affirmed its place in a universal history. The chronicle was its logical home, however, since the episode belonged to a conception of history based on the progression of the Roman Empire under the Franks as leaders of the Fourth and Last Kingdom. Universal chronicles that built on an imperial framework, such as that of Helinand's source Sigebert, had a particular need to address the

---

93. Helinand of Froidmont, *Chronicon, PL* 122, col. 843. "Mirum valde est, quod de toto hoc itinere Caroli Jerosolymitano, in quo tam praeclarum opus factum est, ut est acquisitio terrae Jerosolymitanae et tanta miracula quae per has reliquias facta sunt, nihil omnino apud Latinorum chronographos adnotatum reperitur. In hoc autem praesens narratio resultare videtur historicae veritatis, quod dicit patriarcham Jerosolymitanum venisse Constantinopolim ad Constantinum imperatorem et filium ejus Leonem, eo tempore, quo datum est imperium Romanum Carolo, cum uterque istorum, id est Constantinus et Leo filius, eo tempore quo imperium Romanum Carolo datum est jam mortuus fuerit."

94. Ibid.

problem of how the Roman Empire passed from the Greeks to Charlemagne to the Germans. Charlemagne's reckoning with the East functioned within that discourse of *translatio imperii*, since it dealt with the establishment and definition of his imperial authority after the coronation. As a French locus of memory, the story required some redefinition, which Pierre initiated by focusing on the "conquests" of the Holy Land and Spain and the acquisition of the full crown of thorns.

In the decades after the appearance of the canonization *Vita*, the resonance of the saintly life of Charlemagne proved to be different in Capetian France than it had been in the German empire. While chroniclers struggled with whether or not to mention Charlemagne's liberation of the Holy Land, the story gained visibility between 1210 and 1220 as a third of the visual narrative of the Charlemagne window at Notre Dame de Chartres.[95] The window contains three sections based on the hagiographical life of Charlemagne, including the journey to the East, the campaign in Spain, and the Mass of Saint Giles. Recent studies have emphasized the role of the window in legitimating Chartres's most important relic, the holy *chemise* of the Virgin, but questions remain about the sources for the window's pictorial narratives.[96] Scholars have long tied the bottom third of the window to the *Descriptio*, but certain discrepancies point instead to an Old French version of the story. If the images are indeed drawn from a vernacular translation, then we have evidence that Charlemagne's journey to the East had assumed a new function in society and was flourishing in France within vernacular lay culture alongside the popular translations of the *Pseudo-Turpin* tradition, rather than as a political document for chroniclers and royal propagandists.

For decades, criticism about the window has relied on the presumption that the three narrative sequences were based on three Latin texts, the *Descriptio*, the *Pseudo-Turpin Chronicle*, and the *Life of Saint Giles* (*Vita Sancti Aegidii*).[97] In the images of the journey to the East, however, certain details

---

95. Alison Stones, "The *Codex Calixtinus* and the Iconography of Charlemagne," in *Roland and Charlemagne in Europe*, ed. Karen Pratt (London, 1996), 169. The significance of the Charlemagne window has been a topic of intense scholarly interest too vast for satisfactory summary here. See Schenck, "The Charlemagne Window," forthcoming; Nichols, *Romanesque Signs*, 96–105.

96. Elizabeth Pastan, "Charlemagne as Saint? Relics and the Choice of Window Subjects at Chartres Cathedral," in *The Legend of Charlemagne: Power, Faith, and Crusade*, ed. Matthew Gabriele and Jace Stuckey (New York, 2008), 97; Chris Jones, *Eclipse of Empire? Perceptions of the Western Empire and Its Rulers in Late-Medieval France* (Turnhout, 2007), 167.

97. Clark Maines lists the *Descriptio* as the source for the first cycle of six panels, in "The Charlemagne Window at Chartres Cathedral: New Considerations on Text and Image," *Speculum* 52 (1977): 803. See also Emile Mâle, *Religious Art in France of the Thirteenth Century*, trans. Dora Nussey (Mineola, NY, 1913), 408; Ernst S. Grimme, "Das Karlsfenster in der Kathedrale von Chartres," *Aachener Kunstblatter* 19–20 (1960–61): 1–24; Duncan Robertson, "Visual Poetics: The Charlemagne

FIGURE 2.   The Charlemagne window at Notre-Dame de Chartres, c. 1210–20

do not correspond to the Latin text, which in itself would not be striking, were it not for the fact that those same details do correspond to an existing French text. In her study of the Spanish expedition in the window, Mary Jane Schenck has shown that some of the visual narrative was likely based

Window at Chartres," *Olifant* 6 (1978): 107–17; Isabelle Rolland, "Le mythe carolingien et l'art du vitrail: Sur le choix et l'ordre des épisodes dans le vitrail de Charlemagne à la cathédrale de Chartres," in Moisan, *La chanson de geste*, 258.

on the Old French translation of the *Pseudo-Turpin Chronicle* by a certain Johannes from before 1206.[98] A number of the versions of Johannes's translation contain, as an opening, a highly abridged account of the Holy Land journey. It is in this prologue that we find resolution to the discrepancies between the window and the Latin tradition. In the depiction of Constantine's vision in the window at Chartres, a knight in full armor on horseback stands over the bed, brandishing a white lance with a pennant attached and a red shield. His head and face are covered by a helmet with a closed visor, but the *titulus* indicates that he is *Carolus*. Above and to the left is an angel who points to the Charlemagne figure. In the *Descriptio*, the messenger is a youth who is standing and pointing to a white-bearded knight as he tells the Greek emperor that he should call on Charlemagne for help. Johannes describes an angel that appears to the Greek emperor and points to a handsome armed man on a horse.[99] The part of the window devoted to the journey to the East therefore appears to have derived from a bare-bones version of the story that had been appended to a full version of the far more popular Old French version of the *Pseudo-Turpin Chronicle*. The window at Chartres, therefore, does not bear witness to the ongoing influence of the Latin *Descriptio*. Beyond its celebration of Chartres's holdings of relics, the function of the window was more likely to have been in line with the goals of Pierre de Beauvais, who sought to translate for a larger public an edifying and glorious story of France's Carolingian past.

Louis IX

Life began to imitate art in certain ways beginning in the thirteenth century, when the king of France, on more than one occasion, obtained relics of the Passion from Constantinople. In 1205, Philip Augustus acquired relics from Count Baldwin of Flanders, the new Latin emperor of Constantinople, which he donated to Saint-Denis.[100] In 1238, Louis IX purchased the crown of thorns from the cash-strapped Baldwin. Ten years later, the king dedicated the Sainte-Chapelle in honor of the relic before leaving on his own Holy Land expedition. As William Chester Jordan has established, relics did not find their true place in the religion of the French monarchy until Louis

---

98. Mary Jane Schenck, "Taking a Second Look: Roland in the Charlemagne Window at Chartres," *Olifant* 25 (2006): 372.

99. "Donc li aparut uns angles, si li mostra un bel home molt grant armé sor son cheval," in Ronald N. Walpole, *The Old French Johannes Translation of the 'Pseudo-Turpin Chronicle': A Critical Edition*, vol. 1 (Berkeley, CA, 1976), 131.

100. Baldwin, *Government of Philip Augustus*, 377.

took the vow to go on crusade. The association then became strong enough that people came to believe that the pious king had brought the purchased relics back from the East himself. The Sainte-Chapelle later became part of what Jordan calls "the traditional ceremonial apparatus of the French royal crusader."[101]

The story of Charlemagne's acquisition of relics from Constantinople appears, not surprisingly, among the stained-glass images that adorn the Sainte-Chapelle. Alyce Jordan argues that the placement of the story in the window was intended to draw the parallel between instances of acquisition of relics of the Passion by French monarchs, and to provide evidence of what she calls "recurring monarchic activities that were part of a timeless royal agenda."[102] The *Descriptio* had always served Saint-Denis as a relic authentication document. As Jordan shows, the French use of the tradition continued to be focused on the presence of relics of the Passion in the Capetian realm, rather than on the significance of how and why the Greeks had handed over the sacred objects, or on what that relinquishment had signified. Benzo of Alba had clearly explained the typological connections between instances of relics passing from Constantinople to the West as symbolic of the divine sanctioning of the transfer of imperial authority. For the French monarchy, this sort of articulation of the scope and nature of Charlemagne's imperial authority was not the concern.[103] For the Capetians, the story offered a typology of royal acquisition of relics of the Passion and, in some cases, Frankish Holy Land liberation.

Late in the thirteenth century, a version of Charlemagne's biography appeared in Capetian royal propaganda in Primat's *Roman des Rois*. The monk of Saint-Denis, a promoter of the *reditus* doctrine, compiled and then translated the chronicle into French under orders from Louis IX, a task he completed four years after Louis's death in 1274. The monk worked primarily from a Latin compendium from the 1250s housed at Saint-Denis (B.N. lat. 5925) that included Einhard, but not the *Descriptio* and the *Pseudo-Turpin*, which he chose to add.[104] Rather than creating a compilation of histories, Primat was biographically minded, as Anne Hedeman explains, and wanted

101. William Chester Jordan, *Louis IX and the Challenge of the Crusade: A Study in Rulership* (Princeton, NJ, 1980), 107–9.

102. Alyce A. Jordan, *Visualizing Kingship in the Windows of the Sainte-Chapelle* (Turnhout, 2002), 62–63.

103. M. Cecilia Gaposchkin gives no indication that the figure of Charlemagne as Holy Land liberator factored into the construction of the sainthood of Louis IX; see *The Making of Saint Louis: Kingship, Crusades and Sanctity in the Later Middle Ages* (Ithaca, NY, 2008), 233–34, 238–39.

104. Gillette Labory, "Les débuts de la chronique en français (XIIe et XIIIe siècles)," in *The Medieval Chronicle III: Proceedings of the 3rd International Conference on the Medieval Chronicle. Doorn/*

to present a unified whole based on his gathering of lives of Frankish and French kings. He therefore molded the works to his own particular vision of what a history of the kings of France for a lay audience should be.[105] Not surprisingly, his vernacular account of the deeds of the kings of France going back to the Trojans fails to include the first segment of the *Descriptio* that contains the pro-imperial investiture scene at Rome. With the story in its truncated form, the journey to the East ceases to be the implied result of Charlemagne's new imperial status. Primat, or perhaps someone before him, thus neutralized the *Descriptio* to create a less imperialist tone and a less imperial Charlemagne for his version of how the Frankish king first acquired relics from the East. His goal was to create a coherent story for a vernacular audience.[106] In that sense, he likely shared with Pierre de Beauvais a taste for the story of Charlemagne's liberation of Jerusalem in its guise as an exemplary episode in the history of Frankish kingship.

The French monarchy did not seek to establish a strong link between Charlemagne and a concept of empire for itself. As Chris Jones has argued, Primat's inclusion of the *Descriptio* was related to the relics whose transfer it authenticated. The document also reinforced the monarchy's efforts to forge genealogical links to the Carolingians.[107] Jones does, however, point to one of the rare instances of promotion of Charlemagne as emperor in a Capetian context, in this case in relation to Charles of Anjou, the brother of Louis IX who had conquered Sicily in 1266 in a quest to reunite the empire. In the 1270s, there was talk of Charles as the possible coming of a second Charlemagne to restore the empire.[108] The suggestion appeared, for instance, in the universal chronicle of Géraud de Frachet, a copy of which was addressed to Charles of Anjou himself that contained a version of the Last Emperor prophecy. It is unclear when the sibyl was added, but Jones signals that the French copies do not have it, while the Italian copies do.[109] The promotion of Charles of Anjou as a potential unifier of the empire and new Charlemagne in sibylline terms creates a dynamic similar to what Benzo had created in praise of Henry IV. If someone added the prophecy to the version destined

Utrecht 12–17 July 2002, ed. Erik Kooper (Amsterdam, 2004), 18; Brown, "Vincent de Beauvais," 187; Jones, *Eclipse*, 64.

105. Anne D. Hedeman, *The Royal Image: Illustrations of the "Grandes Chroniques de France," 1274–1422* (Berkeley, CA, 1991), 4.

106. Hedeman, *Royal Image*, 5.

107. Jones, *Eclipse*, 167–68. See also Mireille Chazan, "Les lieux de la critique dans l'historiographie médiévale," in *Religion et mentalités au moyen âge: Mélanges en l'honneur d'Hervé Martin*, ed. Sophie Cassagnes-Brouquet et al. (Rennes, 2003), and Alyce Jordan, *Visualizing*, 60–61.

108. Jones, *Eclipse*, 151.

109. Ibid., 152.

for Charles himself, we can deduce that flattery was one motivation for its inclusion. Charlemagne the emperor thus continued to function in an imperial context as part of the discourse of imperial unity and Roman renewal, not as a French royal liberator of the Holy Land.

Despite what would seem to be a likely scenario in which to find the story of Charlemagne's liberation of Jerusalem, the mounting campaign for Holy Land recuperation in France at the end of the thirteenth century did not feature the story told in the *Descriptio*. When recovery of the Holy Land became an increasingly pressing concern, the Second Council of Lyon was convened in 1274 to discuss the matter. At the council, the Dominican cleric Humbert of Romans called for enhanced remembrance of the deeds of Charlemagne and of Godfrey of Bouillon, but he referred to the Frankish king's deeds in Spain based on the *Pseudo-Turpin* tradition and did not invoke the journey to Jerusalem.[110] A rare exception is Pierre Dubois's treatise on the recovery of the Holy Land, from the first decade of the fourteenth century.[111] Dubois wanted to unite East and West to create a universal empire under the French crown, and to promote his dream he invoked the legendary Holy Land crusade of Charlemagne. Dubois not only describes the Carolingian leader as the ancestor of the French kings, but also states that Charles reigned for 125 years—a detail that suggests that the French partisan was not afraid to employ legend in the service of his cause. As part of his ardent support for the French monarchy as members of the bloodline of Charlemagne, Dubois also denounced papal claims to superiority over temporal power.[112] As it had in the past, then, the story of Charlemagne's encounters in the East continued to work against the rival claims of the Holy See to transcendent political power by offering a vision of Christendom under the aegis of temporal leadership in the West.

The next major biographical work devoted to the life of Charlemagne appeared early in the fourteenth century, just as Philip the Fair of France was promoting his brother Charles of Valois as a candidate for the empire.[113] Girart d'Amiens, in his massive *L'Istoire le roy Charlemaine*, a work not terribly beloved by modern scholars, once again dramatized Charlemagne's

---

110. Anthony Leopold, *How to Recover the Holy Land: The Crusade Proposals of the Late Thirteenth and Early Fourteenth Centuries* (Aldershot, 2000), 92. See also Cole, *Preaching*, 214–15.

111. Pierre Dubois, *De recuperatione terre sancte, traité de politique générale*, ed. C.-V. Langlois (Paris, 1891), 130.

112. Jones, *Eclipse*, 170–71. Ernst Kantorowicz, *The King's Two Bodies: A Study in Mediaeval Political Theology* (Princeton, NJ, 1957), 333. For the universalizing pretensions of the French at the time, see Mastnak, *Crusading Peace*, 258.

113. Zeller, "Les rois," 285–88.

encounters in the East in a manner that reflected contemporary questions of imperial continuity and succession.[114] Girart's Charlemagne, the king of Saint-Denis, receives a warm welcome from the pope at Rome on his way to Constantinople, and then Charlemagne and the Greek emperor travel together to liberate Syria. The manuscript is incomplete, so we do not know how Girart chose to end the story, but his revision of the story reinforces the fact that, all along, "Charlemagne and the East" had been intended as a commentary on the custodial responsibilities of the new emperor in the West. Ever since Notker had depicted Pope Leo coming to Charlemagne for help because the Greek emperor had told him to take care of his own problems, the question of which among the three entities should be in charge of the whole empire and therefore of the protection of the Holy Land had been a matter of ongoing discussion. The Frenchman Girart d'Amiens chose to answer that question by depicting harmony between the Holy See, Byzantium, and the West.

Conclusion

Scholars attempting to come to terms with the strange journey of "Charlemagne and the East" have often been stymied by their own excessive focus on the dichotomy between fact and fiction. In his 1865 *Histoire poétique de Charlemagne*, Gaston Paris contemptuously insisted that the *Descriptio* had been accepted as true by the majority of historians from the twelfth century until as late as the Renaissance.[115] Jules Coulet argued the opposite, insisting that the story was able to be interpolated into so many works precisely because the legend was so popular in France, but as a legend, not as fact.[116] Ian Short later pondered the exclusion of the journey to the East from Capetian historical compilations by framing the question in terms of who had or had not been duped by the *Descriptio*. Citing Helinand's concerns over the text's anachronisms, Short argued that such protests were generally forgotten by the early thirteenth century.[117] Bernard Guenée then argued in a similar vein that attitudes toward such invention had been flexible enough in the twelfth

---

114. Daniel Métraux, ed., *A Critical Edition of Girart d'Amiens' "L'Istoire le roy Charlemaine"* (Lewiston, ME, 2004).

115. Paris, *Histoire poétique*, 339.

116. Coulet, *Études sur l'ancien*, 242.

117. Ian Short, "A Study in Carolingian Legend and Its Persistence in Latin Historiography (XII–XVI Centuries)," *Mittellateinisches Jahrbuch* 7 (1972): 132–35. Walpole asserts that critical voices such as that of Helinand of Froidmont had died away by the mid-thirteenth century and the legend continued to gain in popularity; see "Two Notes," 141.

century to allow for the creation at Saint-Denis of Charlemagne's voyage to the Holy Land. Those attitudes later changed, he concluded, and the concept of history ceased to accept such inventions.[118]

Scholars have clearly been at pains to satisfactorily explain the role played by this politically potent episode within French historiographical memory, but this is because they have tended to approach the problem as a matter of fiction rather than function. More recently, Mireille Chazan has argued that the reticence regarding the *Descriptio* endured as it did because of the chronological problems raised by Helinand and others.[119] She concludes that the story nonetheless became a *lieu de critique*, but she too presumes that the fortunes of the document were tied to perceptions of its veracity.[120] The *Descriptio* and the *Pseudo-Turpin Chronicle* continued to grow in popularity, with their reception peaking in the fifteen century, becoming what Short describes as one of the most successful forgeries in literary history.[121] But it would be inaccurate to assert that they either lost or gained credibility over the centuries. The only thing that changed was their perceived rhetorical value within an evolving set of circumstances. In her discussion of the creativity with which humanist historians approached the tradition of Charlemagne in the East, Nancy Bisaha describes how some were eager to tell the story, while others were far more circumspect, given the lack of sufficient evidence. She is able to demonstrate, nonetheless, that those who chose to employ the story of Charlemagne's Holy Land liberation did so for its "rhetorical and inspirational applications."[122]

As this study draws to a close, it will be useful to consider the authors and compilers who found themselves in a position to include or exclude, modify or leave untouched, the story of Charlemagne's liberation of Jerusalem. My aim throughout has been to avoid asking whether these creators of stories did or did not "believe" the narratives that they produced, but to instead understand Charlemagne's post-coronation foreign relations in the East as a mutable, but nonetheless recognizable, rhetorical commonplace. We come full circle, then, to Ruth Morse and her observation of the recurring nature of episodes in medieval biography. Like the Roman parade of surrendering nations, the journey of Charlemagne to the East conveyed an understood set of significations to a community of rhetorically minded authors and

118. Bernard Guenée, *Histoire et culture historique dans l'Occident médiéval* (Paris, 1980), 351–52.
119. Chazan, "Les lieux," 35–37.
120. Ibid., 37.
121. Short, "Study in Carolingian Legend," 151.
122. Nancy Bisaha, *Creating East and West: Renaissance Humanists and the Ottoman Turks* (Philadelphia, 2004), 36–37.

readers. For those who might not have understood this, Benzo of Alba, for one, tried to explain how to read the signs. In doing so, he made explicit what other authors had simply expected us to deduce. Such is the way of rhetorical commonplaces, though; readers are supposed to recognize them. When authors used the rhetoric of Roman universalism, it did not matter, for instance, whether or not elephants, ostriches, or a little naked man had actually paraded before the emperor. Likewise, it did not matter whether Charlemagne had ever gone to the East and received the symbolic submission of the Byzantines. Charlemagne's encounters in the East were the product of biographical thinking, and the deployment of the episode was a rhetorical act unto itself, one that made no pretension of telling the truth.

"Charlemagne and the East" began as a piece of rhetorical invention in a biography, and it flourished for centuries in the context of biography broadly defined to include works that contained episodes in the imagined life of Charlemagne. Much of what we call medieval literature today is essentially biographical, which means that reconstructions of the life of Charlemagne permeated the textual culture of the Latin West. The *Descriptio* should therefore not be seen as a once rejected forgery that authors at some point decided to stop doubting. As a biographical episode, the story had always been adaptable to changing political and social contexts. For imperial propagandists, the Charlemagne of the *Descriptio* was an emperor who represented God-ordained lay leadership and unification of empire that included protection of the Holy Land. On the French side, as the prologue of Pierre de Beauvais reveals, Charlemagne was a French king who had liberated the Holy Land and brought relics of the Passion from Constantinople to France.

Epilogue

The Remains of Charlemagne

On the feast of Saint James, 25 July 1215, the Italian-born grandson of Frederick Barbarossa, Frederick II, was consecrated and crowned king of the Romans. After his initial coronation at Mainz, the twenty-one-year-old decided to stage a second coronation at Aachen, a center of Hohenstaufen support in a German realm still divided after the fall of Otto IV at Bouvines the previous year.[1] Contemporary witnesses tell us that soon after the ceremony, the young king was inspired to take up the cross in the name of aid to the Holy Land.[2] The decision was a controversial one, since he had failed to first gain the approval of the powerful Pope Innocent III, a protocol required by canon law. The pontiff, a vocal proclaimer of his own universal authority and a believer that it was popes who made emperors, was not pleased.[3] Two days after the coronation and pronouncement of

---

1. David Abulafia, *Frederick II: A Medieval Emperor* (Oxford, 1992), 120; Folz, *Le souvenir,* 280; Wolfgang Stürner, *Friedrich II* (Darmstadt, 2000), 168.

2. *Reineri Annales* (ad 1215?) MGH *SS* 16, 673; *Historia diplomatica Friderici Secundi: Sive constitutiones,* 1.2, ed. J. L. A. Huillard-Bréholles (Paris, 1852), 395. See also Abulafia, *Frederick II,* 137–38; Folz, *Le souvenir,* 283.

3. Abulafia, *Frederick II,* 120–21. James Powell calls for some tempering of the theory that Frederick acted alone and in a calculated manner, noting that papal representatives were present; see "Church and Crusade: Frederick II and Louis IX," *Catholic Historical Review* 93 (2007): 253.

the crusading vow, in one of his first acts as king, Frederick presided over the translation of the remains of his ancestor Charlemagne, "*beati Carlo-manni, quod avus suus Fredericus imperator.*" Frederick even removed his royal robes to help the workmen by taking a hammer and driving nails into the silver sarcophagus that had been made for the occasion by local artisans of Aachen.[4] Then on 29 July, Frederick reiterated and even enhanced the privileges that had been accorded to the city and its people in the 1166 diploma of his grandfather, an act that he would repeat on other occasions throughout his reign.[5]

Frederick's decision to take the crusading vow was a surprise to all, including Innocent, who refused to react initially, but later recalled with displeasure the fact that the king had acted without seeking his counsel in advance. Although Frederick would, years later, insist upon the purity of his motives in taking the vow in 1215, Thomas Van Cleve notes that the action of the newly crowned king had been an astute move that had effectively threatened to usurp the leadership of the pontiff's project for a fifth crusade.[6] Five years passed before the Hohenstaufen king was crowned Roman emperor by the pope at Rome in 1220, at which point he restated his earlier promise to go on crusade. At that moment, the Holy See under Pope Honorius III was in a mood favorable to an emperor-led expedition, but that situation quickly changed with the arrival of the new pope, Gregory IX.[7] In 1227, Gregory excommunicated the emperor, ostensibly on the grounds that he had failed to fulfill his crusading vow by delaying his journey one too many times, but the pope's drastic action was probably related to tensions involving the church in Sicily.[8] In a vitriolic encyclical letter, the pontiff listed among the king's many crimes the fact that Frederick had taken up the cross in 1215 without consulting the Holy See.[9]

The coincidence of Frederick's first crusading vow and his translation of the remains of Charlemagne seems, on the surface, to support the notion articulated by Kantorowicz that the German emperors saw Charlemagne as a

---

4. *Reineri Annales,* 673.

5. Folz, *Le souvenir,* 284.

6. Thomas C. Van Cleve, *The Emperor Frederick II of Hohenstaufen: Immutator Mundi* (Oxford, 1972), 96–97.

7. Abulafia, *Frederick II,* 138.

8. Powell, "Church and Crusade," 257.

9. Van Cleve, *Emperor Frederick,* 197.

model crusader.[10] In his biography of Frederick II, David Abulafia also frames the events surrounding the *translatio* in terms of Hohenstaufen crusading dreams, claiming that the emperor had been avowed in his determination to be a new Charlemagne who was "a model emperor and model crusader."[11] As the foregoing chapters have demonstrated, however, the Charlemagne cultivated by the Hohenstaufens in the 1160s had not been intended as a model crusader. Rather he was a divinely chosen, universal leader of all Christendom, who miraculously liberated Jerusalem without bloodshed in an episode designed to articulate the meaning of Frankish authority after the coronation of 800. A similar assessment can be made of the ceremonies of late July 1215. Both the reinterment of Charlemagne's remains and the taking of the crusading vow just after the coronation should be seen as evidence for the king's desire to set a certain tone for his reign by recalling the political program of his grandfather.[12] The *translatio* and the vow were both significant features of the event, but not necessarily intimately related.

At the time of Frederick II's assumption of the title of king of the Romans in 1215, the ambitious Pope Innocent was planning the Fifth Crusade, and the question of responsibility for the protection of Christendom was in the air. A major aspect of the invented narrative of Charlemagne's activities in the East was the promotion of an ideal of lay protection of the empire that was not mediated by Rome. Frederick II therefore likely understood that Charlemagne had served his grandfather as a model of imperial independence during the emperor's great struggle with the Holy See, not as an idealized ninth-century proto-crusader. Although Frederick Barbarossa would later lose his life on the Third Crusade, the concept of a crusading emperor did not really exist during the early decades of his reign.[13] Temporal leaders, including his own father, had certainly led expeditions to the East on behalf of the church, but Barbarossa's promoters had not intended to point to such activities when they invoked the Charlemagne who enjoyed divine favor in his symbolic subjugation of the East.

---

10. Ernst H. Kantorowicz, *Frederick the Second, 1194–1250,* trans. E. O. Lorimer (New York, 1957), 167.

11. Abulafia, *Frederick II,* 120–22. Folz, by contrast, believed that given the lack of discussion of the ceremony in the sources for the period, we may presume that the event had created little resonance and had been essentially liturgical; see *Le souvenir,* 283.

12. See Folz, *Le souvenir,* 283.

13. Tyerman has argued that until the expedition of 1187 there was not even a cohesive idea or institution of crusading; see *Invention of the Crusades,* 6–12; Rubenstein, *Armies of Heaven,* xi.

FIGURE 3. Charlemagne reliquary, Aachen, c. 1215

While it is true that the crusade vow was an important element of Frederick's self-presentation at the crucial moment of his coronation at Aachen in 1215, crusading was merely a subset of the larger definition of his future role at the helm of the theoretical Roman Empire on the model of his grandfather. His summoning of the memory of Charlemagne at the time of his unorthodox crusading vow was no accident, to be sure, but the coincidence of these two public gestures does not reflect the emperor's view of Charlemagne as a crusader. Charlemagne had been an emperor chosen by God to unite the empire without battle, acquire relics of the Passion for ecclesiastical centers in Germany, and make Aachen the center of his realm. Both Fredericks perceived the value of recalling that particular set of feats during the early years of their reigns.

Frederick II's decision to reinter the Carolingian emperor in 1215 may also have been related to the completion of the reliquary that had been prepared for the *translatio* of his remains. The new reliquary, which had been in production perhaps even since the reign of Barbarossa, offers its own set of clues for interpreting the role of Charlemagne in Hohenstaufen memory.[14] For the liturgical ceremony, Frederick had the remains placed in the sumptuous gold and silver reliquary formed in the shape of the nave of a church and covered in ornate relief work.[15] The imagery that adorns the piece reflects the larger ideology of the saintly *Vita,* conveying in pictures the systematic establishment of a vision of divinely ordained lay imperial authority, with Pope Leo and Archbishop Turpin present at his side, though in visibly reduced positions. On the vertical sides, the panels include sixteen portraits of previous German kings crowned at Aachen, eight on each side, all holding the imperial scepter. Charlemagne appears enthroned on the narrow end of the rectangular edifice, surrounded by the pope and archbishop. Both are standing, but are noticeably shorter than the seated Charlemagne, who is being blessed directly by God from above.[16]

The panels that make up the roof include images from the saintly *Vita.* Most of them come from the *Pseudo-Turpin* tradition, but Charlemagne's visit to Constantinople appears as well. The *Descriptio* and the *Pseudo-Turpin* first appeared together in succession in the saintly *Vita,* and would do so more commonly later in the thirteenth century, although the journey to the East usually appeared in greatly abridged form, functioning more as a prologue, as in the aforementioned Old French Johannes translation.[17] The reliquary similarly condenses the journey to the East by comparison with the events in Spain, depicting only two images, both of which relate to Charlemagne's

---

14. Folz, *Le souvenir,* 280.

15. Huillard-Bréholles, *Historia diplomatica Friderici Secundi,* 395.

16. Folz, *Le souvenir,* 281. See also Lisa Victoria Ciresi, "Of Offerings and Kings: The Shrine of the Three Kings at Cologne and the Aachen Karlsschrein and Marienschrein," in *Reliquaire im Mittelalter,* ed. Bruno Reudenbach and Gia Toussaint (Berlin, 2005), 178.

17. For discussion of the combination of the two traditions in thirteenth-century vernacular translations, see Ronald N. Walpole, *The Old French Translation of the Pseudo-Turpin Chronicle: A Critical Edition* (Berkeley, CA, 1976), xvii.

acquisition of relics from the Greek emperor in Constantinople.[18] The panels also include small excerpts of the January 1166 canonization decree, a document that included discussion of how the Frankish leader had brought back relics from Constantinople. The images would therefore have evoked the story of how Charlemagne had donated the precious eastern objects to beautify the Church of Saint Mary at Aachen, the site of the two highly political ceremonies of 1165 and 1215 that tied the German emperors to Charlemagne. There is no reference to the liberation of Jerusalem. It was the meeting of the two emperors and the symbolic transfer of imperial authority that appealed to the promoters of the Staufen emperors.

In 1229, Frederick made his way to Jerusalem as an excommunicate without the pontiff's blessing, finally fulfilling, to his mind, his vow of 1215.[19] He had fallen ill with fever in 1227 along with many of his fellow crusaders, and his wife had died, leaving behind an infant son. Pope Gregory had not been moved by his situation, and punished the emperor with excommunication for his delay in reaching the Holy Land, a move that Frederick saw as a major overstepping of papal authority.[20] Politically, the time was otherwise right for the expedition, however, and so once he was well enough, he set out for the East. The Muslim world was deeply divided at the time, and Frederick took advantage of the situation by coming to the aid of the sultan of Egypt, al-Kamil, who agreed to a deal that would return Jerusalem and the Holy Sepulcher, among other sites, to the West.[21] The church played no role in the negotiations between the two leaders.

The events that transpired when Frederick arrived with his band of crusaders in Jerusalem are known to us largely through a letter that the emperor wrote to King Henry III of England. Dated March 1229, the missive appears in Roger of Wendover's *Flores Historiarum* and later, in revised form, in the *Chronica Majora* of Matthew Paris.[22] In this carefully constructed interpretation of his controversial triumph in the East, Frederick exalts his recupera-

---

18. See *Karl der Grosse und sein Schrein in Aachen,* ed. Hans Müllejans (Mönchengladbach, 1988); *Der Schrein Karls des Grossen: Bestand und Sicherung 1982–1988,* ed. Florentine Mütherich (Aachen, 1998), 8–12; Kerner, *Karl der Grosse,* 120; Monteleone, *Il viaggio,* 203; Elizabeth Pastan, "Charlemagne as Saint? Relics and the Choice of Window Subjects at Chartres Cathedral," in Gabriele and Stuckey, *Legend of Charlemagne,* 108.

19. Abulafia, *Frederick II,* 173, 187. Van Cleve, *Emperor Frederick,* 208–20.

20. Van Cleve, *Emperor Frederick,* 200–201.

21. In reality, the sultan had offered similar truces previously to the leadership in the West; see Powell, "Church and Crusade," 255–56.

22. See Suzanne Lewis, *The Art of Matthew Paris in the "Chronica Majora"* (Berkeley, CA, 1987), 78–79.

tion of Jerusalem and the Holy Sepulcher for Christendom. The missive is self-congratulatory and justificatory in characterizing the emperor's peaceful reacquisition of the Holy City as a miracle. He boasts of having managed to achieve in just a few days through negotiation what so many princes and various rulers had failed to accomplish by means of great force and fear.[23] The agreement had come about after what Frederick describes as much back-and-forth through messengers between him and the "sultan of Babylon."

The letter to the English king also contains Frederick's version of the ceremonial aspects of his time in the Holy City. In a piece of imperial theater that recalls the literary scenes that have populated this study, Frederick's triumphal and bloodless conquest of Jerusalem had been marked by his donning of the imperial crown within the Holy Sepulcher. When he first arrived in Jerusalem, he had adored the Holy Sepulcher in his capacity as emperor. On the next day, he had worn the crown that God had wanted him to have. This action, as he describes it, was both divinely ordained and justified by his sovereign status as emperor, "*iure regni*."[24] In Abulafia's estimation, the ceremony marked the transformation of Frederick from a seeker of peace with the Holy See to an "uncompromising exponent of imperial universalism."[25] The emperor's defiance of the pope to embark on his controversial Holy Land liberation, an endeavor punctuated by his symbolic coronation at the Holy Sepulcher, had thus offered the ultimate expression of Frederick's belief in his universal authority as Roman emperor. He attributed his triumph to the will of God, while making no pretense of ruling as the Last Emperor in the final stage of human history. In a reality that seemed to mimic the pages of Frankish history, the leaders of East and West had struck a friendly deal that would return the Holy Land to the custody of the emperor in the West. While the sultan does not seem to have sent Frederick a cache of exotic gifts or an elephant, for once we can rightly say that Charlemagne had served as a model imperial crusader.

---

23. Letter of March 1229 to Henry III of England, in Roger of Wendover, *Flores Historiarum,* ed. F. Liebermann and R. Pauli, MGH *SS* 28 (Hanover, 1888), 63.

24. For prophecies associated with Frederick II, see Frank Shaw, "Frederick II as the 'Last Emperor,'" *German History* 19 (2001): 321–39.

25. Abulafia, *Frederick II,* 187.

✎ Bibliography

Primary Sources

Adémar of Chabannes. *Chronicon.* Ed. Pascal Bourgain et al. *CC,* Continuatio Mediaevalis, 129. Turnhout, 1999.

Ado of Vienne. *Martyrologium. PL* 123, col. 875.

Adso of Montier-en-Der. *De ortu et tempore antichristi: Necnon et tractatus qui ab eo dependent.* Ed. Daniel Verhelst. Turnhout, 1976.

Annales Marbacenses. Ed. Hermann Bloch. MGH *SRG* 9. Hanover, 1907.

Annales regni francorum. Ed. Friedrich Kurze. MGH *SRG* 6. Hanover, 1895.

Anselm of Besate. *Rhetorimachia.* Ed. Karl Manitius. MGH *Weitere Reihen.* Weimar, 1958.

Archpoet. *Die Gedichte des Archipoeta.* Ed. Heinrich Watenphul and Heinrich Krefeld. Heidelberg, 1958.

Augustus. *Res Gestae Divi Augusti.* Ed. P. A. Brunt and J. M. Moore. London, 1967.

Avitus of Braga. *Epistola ad Palchonium, de Reliquiis Sancti Stephani, et de Luciani epistola a se e graeco in latinum versa. PL* 41, cols. 805–8.

Benedict of Mount Soracte. *Il Chronicon di Benedetto, monaco di Santo Andrea al Soratte e il Libellus de imperatoria potestate in urbe Roma.* Ed. G. Zucchetti. *Fonti per la Storia d'Italia* 55. Rome, 1920.

Benzo of Alba. *Ad Heinricum IV Imperatorem.* Ed. Hans Seyffert. MGH *SRG* 65. Hanover, 1996.

Descriptio qualiter Karolus Magnus clavum et coronam Domini a Constantinopoli Aquisgrani detulerit qualiterque Karolus Calvus hec ad Sanctum Dionysium retulerit. In *Die Legende Karls des Grossen im 11. und 12. Jahrhundert.* Ed. Gerhard Rauschen. Leipzig, 1890.

Dubois, Pierre. *De recuperatione terre sancte, traité de politique générale par Pierre Dubois.* Ed. C.-V. Langlois. Paris, 1891.

Dungal the Recluse. *Hos Karolo Regi versus Hibernicus Exul.* Ed. Ernst Dümmler et al. MGH *Poet. Lat.* 1. Berlin, 1881.

Einhard. *Vita Karoli Magni.* Ed. O. Holder-Egger. MGH *SRG* 25. Hanover and Leipzig, 1911.

Ekkehard of Aura. *Chronicon Universale.* Ed. Georg Pertz. MGH *SS* 6. Hanover, 1844.

Epistola Luciani ad Omnem Ecclesiam, de Revelatione Corporis Stephani Martyris Primi et Aliorum. PL 41, col. 807.

Epistola presbiteri Johannis. Ed. Bettina Wagner. In *Die "Epistola presbiteri Johannis" lateinisch und deutsch: Überlieferung, Textgeschichte, Rezeption und Übertragungen im Mittelalter.* Tübingen, 2000.

Eusebius. *Life of Constantine.* Trans. Averil Cameron and Stuart G. Hall. Oxford, 1999.

Eutropius, *Breviarium ab urbe condita.* Ed. and trans. Joseph Hellegouarc'h. Paris, 1999.

"Exhortatio ad proceres regni." In *Neues Archiv der Gesellschaft für Ältere Deutsche Geschichtskunde,* vol. 1, ed. Georg Waitz. Hanover, 1876.

Die falschen Investiturprivilegien. Ed. Claudia Märtl. MGH *Fontes,* 13. Hanover, 1986.

Florus. *Epitome of Roman History.* Ed. Edward Seymour Forster. Cambridge, MA, 2005 [1929].

Florus of Lyons (Florus Lugdunensis). *Querela de Divisione Imperii.* Ed. Ernst Dümmler. MGH *Poet. Lat.* 2. Berlin, 1884.

Gesta Francorum et Aliorum Hierosolimitanorum: The Deeds of the Franks and the Other Pilgrims to Jerusalem. Ed. Rosalind Hill. London, 1962.

Giles of Paris. *Karolinus.* In "The 'Karolinus' of Edigius Parisiensis," ed. M. L. Colker. *Traditio* 29 (1973): 199–325.

Girart d'Amiens. "L'Istoire le roy Charlemaine." In *A Critical Edition of Girart d'Amiens' "L'Istoire le roy Charlemaine,"* ed. Daniel Métraux. Lewiston, NY, 2004.

Godfrey of Viterbo. *Memoria Seculorum.* Ed. Georg Pertz. MGH *SS* 22. Hanover, 1872.

———. *Pantheon.* Ed. Georg Pertz. MGH *SS* 22. Hanover, 1872.

———. *Speculum Regum.* Ed. Georg Pertz. MGH *SS* 22. Hanover, 1872.

Les Grandes Chroniques de France. 10 vols. Ed. Jules Viard. Paris, 1920–58.

Guibert of Nogent. *Dei Gesta per Francos et cinq autres textes.* Ed. R. B. C. Huygens. Turnhout, 1996.

Helinand of Froidmont. *Chronicon. PL* 122, col. 843.

Hilduin of Saint-Denis. *Ex Hilduini Abbatis Libro de Sancto Dionysio.* Ed. Wilhelm Wattenbach. MGH *SS* 15, Hanover, 1887.

Hillin-Briefe. Ed. Norbert Höing. In "Die 'Trierer Stilübungen.' Ein Denkmal der Früzeit Kaiser Friedrich Barbarossas," *Archiv für Diplomatik, Schriftgeschichte, Siegel-und Wappenkunde 1* (1955): 257–329 and 2 (1956): 125–249.

Historia diplomatica Friderici Secundi: Sive constitutiones, 1.2. Ed. J. L. A Huillard-Bréholles. Paris, 1852.

Jerome. *Hieronymus: Commentariorum in Danielem libri III.* Ed. F. Glorie. *CC* Series Latina 75A. Turnhout, 1964.

Jonas of Orleans. *Jonas Aurelianus: Jonae de Cultu Imaginem. PL* 106, cols. 343–48.

The Journey of Charlemagne to Jerusalem and Constantinople. Ed. and trans. Jean-Louis G. Picherit. Birmingham, AL, 1984.

Karlsprivileg. Aachener Urkunden 1101–1250. Ed. Erich Meuthen. Bonn, 1972.

Karolus Magnus et Leo Papa. Ed. Ernst Dümmler et al. MGH *Poet. Lat.* 1. Berlin, 1881.

Ludus de Antichristo. Ed. Karl Young. In *The Drama of the Medieval Church.* Oxford, 1962.

Moduin. *Ecloga.* Ed. Ernst Dümmler et al. MGH *Poet. Lat.* 1. Berlin, 1881.

Notker of St. Gall. *Gesta Karoli Magni.* Ed. Reinhold Rau. In *Quellen Zur Karolingischen Reichsgeschichte,* vol. 3. Berlin, 1963.

Odo of Deuil. *De profectione Ludovici VII in Orientem.* Ed. and trans. Virginia G. Berry. New York, 1948.

The Old French Johannes Translation of the "Pseudo-Turpin Chronicle": A Critical Edition. Vol. 1. Ed. Ronald N. Walpole. Berkeley, CA, 1976.

Orosius. *Pauli Orosii historiarum adversum paganos libri VII: Accedit eiusdem, Liber Apologeticus.* Ed. Karl Friedrich Wilhelm Zangemeister. *CSEL* 5. Vienna, 1882.

Otto of Freising. *The Deeds of Frederick Barbarossa, by Otto of Freising and his continuator, Rahewin.* Ed. and trans. Charles Christopher Mierow. New York, 1953.

———. *Ottonis episcopi Frisingensis Chronica sive Historia de duabus civitatibus.* Ed. Adolf Hofmeister. MGH *SRG* 45. Hanover, 1912.

Otto of Freising and Rahewin. *Gesta Friderici I imperatoris.* Ed. Roger Wilmans. MGH *SS* 20. Hanover, 1868.

Paul the Deacon. *Historia Langobardorum.* Ed. L. Bethmann and Georg Waitz. MGH *SRL* 1. Berlin, 1878.

Paulinus of Nola. *Sancti Pontii Meropii Paulini Nolani Opera. Pars 2, Carmina.* Ed. Wilhelm von Hartel and Margit Kamptner. *CSEL* 30. Vienna, 1999.

Pierre de Beauvais. French *Descriptio.* Ed. Ronald N. Walpole. In "Charlemagne's Journey to the East: The French Translation of the Legend by Pierre of Beauvais." *Semitic and Oriental Studies* 9 (1951): 445–52.

Poeta Saxo. *Annalium de gestis Caroli Magni imperatoris libri quinque.* Ed. Paul von Winterfeld. MGH *Poet. Lat.* 4. Berlin, 1899.

Reineri Annales. Ed. Georg Pertz. MGH *SS* 16. Hanover, 1859.

Robert the Monk (of Reims). *Historia Iherosolimitana. RHC Occ.* 3. Paris, 1841–95.

Roger of Wendover. *Flores Historiarum.* Ed. E. Liebermann and R. Pauli. MGH *SS* 28. Hanover, 1888.

Scriptores Historiae Augustae. Ed. Ernst Hohl. 2 vols. Leipzig, 1927.

Sedulius Scottus. *Liber de rectoribus christianis.* In *Sedulius Scottus: Quellen und Untersuchungen zur lateinischen Philologie des Mittelalters* 1. Ed. Sigmund Hellmann. Munich, 1906.

Sextus Aurelius Victor. *Liber de Caesaribus.* Ed. Franz Pichlmayr. Leipzig, 1961.

Suetonius. *Vita Augusti.* In *C. Suetoni Tranquilli Opera.* Vol. 1., *De Vita Caesarum Libri VIII.* Ed. M. Ihm. Leipzig, 1907.

Suger. *Vie de Louis le Gros.* Ed. and trans. Henri Waquet. Paris, 1964.

Translatio Sanguinis Domini. Ed. Georg Waitz. MGH *SS* 4, 445–449. Hanover, 1891.

Tudebode, Peter. *De Hierosolymitano Itinere. RHC Occ.* 3. Paris, 1841–95.

Vita Heinrici Quarti. Ed. W. Eberhard. MGH *SRG* 58. Hanover, 1899.

Walter Map. *De nugis curialium.* Ed. M. R. James and R. A. B. Mynors. Oxford, 1983.

Widukind of Corvey. *Rerum Gestarum Saxonicum.* Ed. P. Hirsch. MGH *SRG* 60. Hanover, 1935.

XII Panegyrici Latini. In *In Praise of Later Roman Emperors: The "Panegyrici Latini,"* ed. and trans. C. E. V. Nixon and Barbara Saylor Rodgers. Berkeley, CA, 1995.

Secondary Sources

Abulafia, David. *Frederick II: A Medieval Emperor.* Oxford, 1992.

Aebischer, Paul. *Les versions norroises du "Voyage de Charlemagne en Orient": Leurs sources.* Paris, 1956.

———, ed. *Le Voyage de Charlemagne à Jérusalem et à Constantinople.* Geneva, 1965.

Aichele, Klaus. "The Glorification of Antichrist in the Concluding Scene of the Medieval 'Ludus de Antichristo.'" *Modern Language Notes* 91 (1976): 424–36.

Alexander, Paul J., and Dorothy F. Abrahamse. *The Byzantine Apocalyptic Tradition.* Berkeley, CA, 1985.

Andenna, Giancarlo. "Il Mezzogiorno normanno-svevo visto dall'Italia settentrionale." In *Il Mezzogiorno normanno-svevo visto dall'Europa e dal mondo mediterraneo: Atti delle tredicesime giornate normanno-sveve, Bari, 21–24 ottobre 1997,* ed. Giosuè Musca, 29–52. Bari, 1999.

Andersson, Theodore M. *Early Epic Scenery: Homer, Virgil, and the Medieval Legacy.* Ithaca, NY, 1976.

Appelt, Heinrich. "Die Kaiseridee Friedrich Barbarossas." In *Friedrich Barbarossa,* ed. Günther Wolf, 208–44. Darmstadt, 1975.

———. "Friedrich Barbarossa und das Romische Recht." In *Friedrich Barbarossa,* ed. Günther Wolf, 58–82. Darmstadt, 1975.

Arnold, Benjamin. "Eschatological Imagination and the Program of Roman Imperial and Ecclesiastical Renewal at the End of the Tenth Century." In *The Apocalyptic Year 1000: Religious Expectation and Social Change, 950–1050,* ed. Richard Allen Landes, Andrew Gow, and David C. Van Meter, 271–88. Oxford, 2003.

Bagge, Sverre. "German Historiography in the Twelfth Century." In *Representations of Power in Medieval Germany, 800–1500,* ed. Björn Weiler and Simon MacLean, 180–88. Turnhout, 2006.

Baldwin, John W. *The Government of Philip Augustus: Foundations of French Power in the Middle Ages.* Berkeley, CA, 1986.

Barbero, Alessandro. *Charlemagne: Father of a Continent.* Trans. Allan Cameron. Berkeley, CA, 2004.

Baroin, Jeanne, and Josiane Haffen. *La prophétie de la Sibylle Tiburtine: Édition des MSS B.N. Fr. 375 et Rennes B.M. Fr. 593.* Paris, 1987.

Barroux, Robert. "L'abbé Suger et la vassalité du Vexin en 1124." *Le Moyen Âge* 64 (1958): 1–26.

Bautier, Geneviève. "L'envoi de la relique de la vraie croix à Notre-Dame de Paris en 1120." *Bibliothèque de l'École Nationale des Chartes* 129 (1971): 387–97.

Bayer, Axel. *Spaltung der Christenheit: Das sogenannte Morgenländische Schisma von 1054.* Cologne, 2002.

Beaune, Colette. *The Birth of an Ideology: Myths and Symbols of Nation in Late Medieval France.* Trans. Susan Ross Huston, ed. Fredric L. Cheyette. Berkeley, CA, 1991.

Becher, Matthias. *Karl der Grosse.* Munich, 1999.

Bédier, Joseph. *Les légendes épiques: Recherches sur la formation des chansons de geste.* 4 vols. Paris, 1908–13.

Bender, Karl-Heinz. "La Genèse de l'image littéraire de Charlemagne." *Bolétin de la Real Academia de Buenas Letras de Barcelona* 31 (1995–96): 35–49.

Benson, Robert L. "Political *Renovatio*: Two Models from Roman Antiquity." In *Renaissance and Renewal in the Twelfth Century,* ed. Robert L. Benson and Giles Constable, 339–86. Cambridge, MA, 1982.

Berkey, Max L. "Pierre de Beauvais' 'Olympiade': A Medieval Outline-History." *Speculum* 41 (1966): 505–15.

Berschin, Walter. *Biographie und Epochenstil im lateinischen Mittelalter III: Karolingische Biographie 750–920 n. Chr.* Stuttgart, 1991.

Béthune, François. "Les écoles historiques de Saint-Denis et de Saint-Germain-des-Près dans leurs rapports avec la composition des *Grandes Chroniques de France*." *Revue d'histoire ecclésiastique* 4 (1903): 24–38, 207–30.

Beumann, Helmut. "Topos und Gedankengefüge bei Einhard." *Archiv für Kulturgeschichte* 33 (1951): 337–50.

Billot-Vilandrau, Céline. "Charlemagne and the Young Prince: A Didactic Poem of the Cardinal Virtues by Giles of Paris (c. 1200)." In *Virtue and Ethics in the Twelfth Century*, ed. István P. Bejczy and Richard G. Newhauser, 341–54. Leiden, 2005.

Bisaha, Nancy. *Creating East and West: Renaissance Humanists and the Ottoman Turks.* Philadelphia, 2004.

Bisson, Thomas N. *The Crisis of the Twelfth Century: Power, Lordship, and the Origins of European Government.* Princeton, NJ, 2009.

Bolton, Brenda M. "*Nova familia beati Petri*: Adrian IV and the Patrimony." In *Adrian IV: The English Pope (1154–1159); Studies and Texts*, ed. Brenda Bolton and Anne J. Duggan, 157–79. Aldershot, 2003.

Booker, Courtney M. *Past Convictions: The Penance of Louis the Pious and the Decline of the Carolingians.* Philadelphia, 2009.

Borgolte, Michael. *Der Gesandtenaustausch der Karolinger mit den Abbasiden und mit den Patriarchen von Jerusalem.* Munich, 1976.

Boutet, Dominique. *La chanson de geste: Forme et signification d'une écriture épique du moyen âge.* Paris, 1993.

———. *Charlemagne et Arthur ou le roi imaginaire.* Paris, 1992.

———. "De la *translatio imperii* à la *finis saeculi*: Progrès et décadence dans la pensée de l'histoire au moyen âge." In *Progrès, réaction, décadence, dans l'Occident médiéval*, ed. Emmanuèle Baumgartner and Laurence Harf-Lancner, 37–48. Geneva, 2003.

Bozoky, Edina. *La politique des reliques.* Paris, 2007.

Bredero, Adriaan Hendrik. *Christendom and Christianity in the Middle Ages: The Relations between Religion, Church, and Society.* Grand Rapids, MI, 1994.

Bréhier, Louis. "Les origines des rapports entre la France et la Syrie. Le protectorat de Charlemagne." In *Congrès français de la Syrie, séances et travaux, fasc. II*, 15–39. Marseille, 1919.

Breisach, Ernst. *Historiography: Ancient, Medieval and Modern.* Chicago, 1983.

Brett, Edward T. "Early Constantine Legends: A Study in Propaganda." *Byzantine Studies* 10 (1983): 52–67.

Brown, Elizabeth A. R. "La notion de la légitimité et la prophétie à la cour de Philippe Auguste." In *La France de Philippe Auguste: Le temps des mutations*, ed. R.-H. Bautier, 77–110. Paris, 1982.

———. "Saint-Denis and the Turpin Legend." In *The Codex Calixtinus and the Shrine of Saint James*, ed. John Williams and Alison Stones, 51–88. Tübingen, 1992.

———. "Vincent de Beauvais and the *reditus regni francorum ad stirpem Caroli imperatoris*." In *Vincent de Beauvais: Intentions et réceptions d'une oeuvre encyclopédique au moyen âge*, ed. Monique Paulmier-Foucart, Serge Lusignan, and Alain Nadeau, 167–96. Paris, 1990.

Brown, Elizabeth A. R., and Michael W. Cothren. "The Twelfth-Century Crusading Window of the Abbey of Saint-Denis: *Praeteritorum enim recordatio futurorum est exhibito.*" *Journal of the Warburg and Courtauld Institutes* 49 (1986): 1–40.

Brubaker, Leslie. "To Legitimize an Emperor: Constantine and Visual Authority in the Eighth and Ninth Centuries." In *New Constantines: The Rhythm of Imperial Renewal in Byzantium, 4th–13th Centuries: Papers from the Second Spring Symposium of Byzantine Studies, St. Andrew's, March 1992*, ed. Paul Magdalino, 139–58. Aldershot, 1994.

Buc, Philippe. *The Dangers of Ritual: Between Early Medieval Texts and Social Scientific Theory.* Princeton, NJ, 2001.

Buckler, F. W. *Harun'l-Rachid and Charles the Great.* Cambridge, MA, 1931.

Bull, Marcus. "The Capetian Monarchy and the Early Crusade Movement: Hugh of Vermandois and Louis VII." *Nottingham Medieval Studies* 40 (1996): 25–46.

Bumke, Joachim. *Courtly Culture: Literature and Society in the High Middle Ages.* Berkeley, CA, 1991.

Burkhardt, Stefan. "Barbarossa, Frankreich und die Weltherrschaft." In *Staufisches Kaisertum im 12. Jahrhundert: Konzepte-Netzwerke-Politische Praxis*, ed. Stefan Burkhardt et al., 133–58. Regensburg, 2010.

Campbell, James. "Asser's *Life of Alfred.*" In *The Inheritance of Historiography, 350–900*, ed. Christopher Holdsworth and T. P. Wiseman, 115–35. Exeter, 1986.

Cardini, Franco. "Il 'Ludus de Antichristo' e la teologia imperiale di Federico I." In *Mito e realtà del potere nel teatro: Dall'Antichità classica al Rinascimento: Atti del Convegno di studi del Centro di Studi sul Teatro Medievale e Rinascimentale (Roma, 29 ottobre–1 novembre 1987)*, ed. M. Chiabò–F. Dogli, 175–87. Rome, 1988.

Chastagnol, André. *Histoire Auguste: Les empereurs romains des IIe et IIIe siècles.* Paris, 1994.

Chazan, Mireille. *L'Empire et l'histoire universelle: De Sigebert de Gembloux à Jean de Saint-Victor (XIIe–XIVe siècle).* Paris, 1999.

——. "Les lieux de la critique dans l'historiographie médiévale." In *Religion et mentalités au moyen âge: Mélanges en l'honneur d'Hervé Martin*, ed. Sophie Cassagnes-Brouquet et al., 25–37. Rennes, 2003.

Chesnut, Glen F. "Eusebius, Augustine, Orosius, and the Later Patristic and Medieval Christian Historians." In *Eusebius, Christianity, and Judaism*, ed. Harold W. Altridge and Gohei Hata, 687–713. Leiden, 1992.

Ciggaar, Krijnie N. *Western Travellers to Constantinople: The West and Byzantium, 962–1204; Cultural and Political Relations.* Leiden, 1996.

Ciresi, Lisa Victoria. "Of Offerings and Kings: The Shrine of the Three Kings at Cologne and the Aachen Karlsschrein and Marienschrein." In *Reliquiare im Mittelalter*, ed. Bruno Reudenbach and Gia Toussaint, 165–85. Berlin, 2005.

Classen, Peter. *Karl der Grosse, das Papsttum und Byzanz: Die Begründung des Karolingischen Kaisertums.* Sigmaringen, 1985.

——. "*Res Gestae*, Universal History, Apocalypse: Visions of Past and Future." In *Renaissance and Renewal in the Twelfth Century*, ed. Robert L. Benson and Giles Constable, 387–417. Cambridge, MA, 1982.

Cohn, Norman. *The Pursuit of the Millennium: Revolutionary Millenarians and Mystical Anarchists of the Middle Ages.* Oxford, 1970.

Cole, Penny J. *The Preaching of the Crusades to the Holy Land, 1095–1270.* Cambridge, MA, 1991.

Collins, Roger. *Charlemagne.* Toronto, 1998.

——. *Early Medieval Europe 300–1000.* New York, 1999.

——. "The 'Reviser' Revisited: Another Look at the Alternative Version of the *Annales Regni Francorum.*" In *After Rome's Fall: Narrators and Sources of Early Medieval History; Essays Presented to Walter Goffart,* ed. Alexander C. Murray, 191–213. Toronto, 1998.

Constable, Giles. *Crusaders and Crusading in the Twelfth Century.* Aldershot, 2009.

——. "Forged Letters in the Middle Ages." In *Fälschungen im Mittelalter: Internationaler Kongress der Monumenta Germaniae Historica, München, 16.–19. September 1986,* 11–37. Hanover, 1988–90.

——. "The Historiography of the Crusades." In *The Crusades from the Perspective of Byzantium and the Muslim World,* ed. Angeliki E. Laiou and Roy Parviz Mottahedeh, 1–22. Washington, DC, 2001.

Contamine, Philippe. "L'oriflamme de Saint-Denis aux XIVe et XVe siècles: Études de symbolique religieuse et royale." *Annales de l'Est* 25 (1973): 179–244.

Cotts, John D. *The Clerical Dilemma: Peter of Blois and Literate Culture in the Twelfth Century.* Washington, DC, 2009.

Coulet, Jules. *Études sur l'ancien poème français du Voyage de Charlemagne en Orient.* Montpellier, 1907.

Cowdrey, H. E. J. "Eleventh-Century Reformers' Views of Constantine." *Byzantinische Forschungen* 24 (1997): 63–91.

——. *Pope Gregory VII, 1073–1085.* Oxford, 1998.

——. "Pope Gregory VII's 'Crusading' Plans of 1074." In *Outremer: Studies in the History of the Crusading Kingdom of Jerusalem Presented to Joshua Prawer,* ed. B.Z. Kedar, Hans Eberhard Mayer, and R.C. Smail, 27–40. Jerusalem, 1982.

——. *Popes, Monks and Crusaders.* London, 1984.

Dale, Johanna. "Imperial Self-Representation and the Manipulation of History in Twelfth-Century Germany: Cambridge, Corpus Christi College MS 373." *German History* 29 (2011): 557–83.

De Jong, Mayke. *The Penitential State: Authority and Atonement in the Age of Louis the Pious, 814–840.* Cambridge, UK, 2009.

Deutinger, Roman. "Imperiale Konzepte in der hofnahen Historiographie der Barbarossazeit." In *Staufisches Kaisertum im 12. Jahrhundert: Konzepte-Netzwerke-Politische Praxis,* ed. Stefan Burkhardt et al., 25–39. Regensburg, 2010.

Duggan, Anne J. *"Totius Christianitatis caput:* The Pope and the Princes." In *Adrian IV: The English Pope (1154–1159); Studies and Texts,* ed. Brenda Bolton and Anne J. Duggan, 105–56. Aldershot, 2003.

Du Pouget, Marc. "La légende carolingienne à Saint-Denis. La donation de Charlemagne au retour de Roncevaux." In *La bataille de Roncevaux dans l'histoire, la légende et l'historiographie, Actes du colloque de Saint-Jean Pied de Port, 1978. Bulletin de la Société des Sciences, Lettres et Arts,* 53–60. Bayonne, 1979.

——. "Recherches sur les chroniques latines de Saint-Denis: Édition critique et commentaire de la Descriptio Clavi et Corone Domini et de deux séries de textes relatifs à la légende carolingienne." Thèse: École Nationale des Chartes, 1978.

Dutton, Paul. *Charlemagne's Courtier: The Complete Einhard.* Peterborough, ON, 1998.

———. *Charlemagne's Mustache and Other Cultural Clusters of a Dark Age.* New York, 2004.

———. *The Politics of Dreaming in the Carolingian Empire.* Lincoln, NE, 1994.

Engels, Odilo. "Gottfried von Viterbo und seine Sicht des staufischen Kaiserhauses." In *Aus Archiven und Bibliotheken—Festschrift für Raymund Kottje zum 65, Geburtstag,* ed Hubert Mordek, 327–47. Frankfurt am Main, 1992.

Erdmann, Carl. "Endkaiserglaube und Kreuzzugsgedanke im 11. Jahrhundert." *Zeitschrift für Kirchengeschichte* 11 (1932): 384–414.

———. *The Origin of the Idea of Crusade.* Trans. Marshall W. Baldwin and Walter Goffart. Princeton, NJ, 1977.

Erickson, Carolly. *The Medieval Vision: Essays in History and Perception.* New York, 1976.

Fliche, Augustin. *La réforme grégorienne et la reconquête chrétienne (1057–1123).* Paris, 1946.

Flori, Jean. *Chroniqueurs et propagandistes: Introduction critique aux sources de la Première croisade.* Geneva, 2010.

———. *La guerre sainte: La formation de l'idée de croisade dans l'Occident chrétien.* Paris, 2001.

———. *La première croisade: L'Occident chrétien contre l'Islam.* Paris, 2001.

Foley, John Miles. *A Companion to Ancient Epic.* Oxford, 2005.

Folz, Robert. "Aspects du culte liturgique de Saint Charlemagne en France." In *Karl der Grosse: Lebenswerk und Nachleben IV,* ed. Wolfgang Braunfels and Percy Ernst Schramm, 77–99. Düsseldorf, 1967.

———. "La chancellerie de Frédéric et la canonisation de Charlemagne," *Le Moyen Âge* 6 (1964): 13–31.

———. *The Concept of Empire in Western Europe from the Fifth to the Fourteenth Century.* Trans. Sheila Ann Oglivie. New York, 1969.

———. *The Coronation of Charlemagne: 25 December 800.* Trans. J. E. Anderson. London, 1974.

———. *Le souvenir et la légende de Charlemagne dans l'empire germanique médiéval.* Geneva, 1973.

Foreville, Raymonde. *Latran I, II, III et Latran IV.* Paris, 1965.

France, John. *The Crusades and the Expansion of Catholic Christendom, 1000–1714.* London, 2004.

Frassetto, Michael. "The Writings of Ademar of Chabannes, the Peace of 994, and the 'Terrors' of the Year 1000." *Journal of Medieval History* 27 (2001): 241–55.

Fried, Johannes. "Awaiting the End of Time around the Year 1000." In *The Apocalyptic Year 1000: Religious Expectation and Social Change, 950–1050,* ed. Richard Allen Landes, Andrew Gow, and David C. Van Meter, 17–64. Oxford, 2003.

———. *Donation of Constantine and Constitutum Constantini: The Misinterpretation of a Fiction and Its Original Meaning, with a Contribution by Wolfram Brandes; "The Satraps of Constantine."* Berlin, 2007.

Frolow, Anatole. *La relique de la vraie croix: Recherches sur le développement d'un culte.* Paris, 1961.

Fuhrmann, Horst. "Quis Teutonicos constituit iudices nationum? The Trouble with Henry." *Speculum* 69 (1994): 344–58.

Gabriele, Matthew. "Against the Enemies of Christ: The Role of Count Emicho in the Anti-Jewish Violence of the First Crusade." In *Christian Attitudes toward the Jews in the Middle Ages: A Casebook*, ed. Michael Frassetto. New York, 2006.

———. "Asleep at the Wheel? Apocalypticism, Messianism, and Charlemagne's Passivity in the Oxford *Chanson de Roland*," *Nottingham Medieval Studies* 43 (2003): 46–72.

———. *An Empire of Memory: The Legend of Charlemagne, the Franks, and Jerusalem before the First Crusade*. Oxford, 2011.

———. "The Provenance of the *Descriptio qualiter Karolus Magnus*: Remembering the Carolingians in the Entourage of King Philip I (1060–1108) before the First Crusade." *Viator* 39 (2008): 93–117.

Galland, Bruno. "Les relations entre la France et l'Empire au XIIe siècle." In *Die Staufer im Süden: Sizilien und das Reich*, ed. Theo Kölzer, 57–82. Stuttgart, 2000.

Ganshof, F. L. *The Carolingians and the Frankish Monarchy: Studies in Carolingian History*. Trans. Janet Sondheimer. Ithaca, NY, 1971.

Ganz, David. "Einhard's Charlemagne: The Characterization of Greatness." In *Charlemagne: Empire and Society*, ed. Joanna Story, 38–51. Manchester, 2005.

———. "Humour as History in Notker's *Gesta Karoli Magni*." In *Monks, Nuns and Friars in Medieval Society*, ed. E. B. King, J. T. Schaefer, and W. B. Wadley, 171–83. Sewanee, TN, 1989.

———. "The Preface to Einhard's 'Vita Karoli.'" In *Einhard Studien zu Leben un Werk dem Gedenken an Helmut Beumann gewidmet,* ed. Hermann Schefers, 299–319. Darmstadt, 1997.

Gaposchkin, M. Cecilia. *The Making of Saint Louis: Kingship, Crusades and Sanctity in the Later Middle Ages*. Ithaca, NY, 2008.

Gautier, Léon. *Les épopées françaises*. Vol. 3. Paris, 1880.

Geary, Patrick J. *Furta Sacra: Thefts of Relics in the Central Middle Ages*. Princeton, NJ, 1978.

———. "Germanic Tradition and Royal Ideology in the Ninth Century: The *Visio Karoli Magni*" *Fruhmittelalterliche Studien* 21 (1987): 274–94.

Gibbon, Edward. *The History of the Decline and Fall of the Roman Empire: A New Edition in VIII Volumes*. London, 1821.

Giesebrecht, Wilhelm von, and Bernhard von Simson, eds. *Geschichte der deutschen Kaiserzeit*. 6 vols. Leipzig, 1877–95.

Gilchrist, John. "The Papacy and War against the 'Saracens,' 795–1216." *International History Review* 10 (1988): 173–97.

Gillingham, J. B. "Why Did Rahewin Stop Writing the *Gesta Frederici?*" *English Historical Review* 83 (1968): 294–303.

Glenn, Jason. "Between Two Empires: Einhard and His Charles the Great." In *The Middle Ages in Texts and Texture: Reflections on Medieval Sources*, ed. Jason Glenn, 105–18. Toronto, 2011.

Godman, Peter. "The Poetic Hunt: From Saint Martin to Charlemagne's Heir." In *Charlemagne's Heir: New Perspectives on the Reign of Louis the Pious (814–840)*, ed. Peter Godman and Roger Collins, 565–89. Oxford, 1990.

———. *Poets and Emperors: Frankish Politics and Carolingian Poetry*. Oxford, 1987.

———. *The Silent Masters: Latin Literature and Its Censors in the High Middle Ages.* Princeton, NJ, 2000.

Goetz, Hans-Werner. *Strukturen der Spätkarolingischen Epoche im Spiegel der Vorstellungen Eines Zeitgenössischen Mönchs: Eine Interpretation der "Gesta Karoli" Notkers von Sankt Gallen.* Bonn, 1981.

Goez, Werner. *Translatio Imperii: Ein Beitrag zur Geschichte des Geschichtsdenkens und der politischen Theorien im Mittelalter.* Tübingen, 1958.

Graboïs, Aryeh. "Charlemagne, Rome and Jerusalem." *Revue belge de philologie et d'histoire* 59 (1981): 792–809.

Grebe, Werner. "Studien zur Geistigen Welt Rainalds von Dassel." In *Friedrich Barbarossa,* ed. Günther Wolf, 5–44. Darmstadt, 1975.

Gregorovius, Ferdinand. *History of the City of Rome in the Middle Ages.* Vol. 4. London, 1896.

Grimme, Ernst. "Das Karlsfenster in der Kathedrale von Chartres." *Aachener Kunstblatter* 19–20 (1960): 1–24.

Grodecki, Louis. *Vitraux de Saint-Denis: Étude sur le vitrail au XIIe siècle.* Vol. 1. Paris, 1976.

Grosse, Rolf. "Reliques du Christ et foires de Saint-Denis au XIe siècle: À propos de la *Descriptio Clavi et Corone Domini.*" *Revue d'Histoire de l'Église de France* 87 (2001): 357–75.

Groten, Manfred. "Die Urkunde Karls des Grossen für St.-Denis von 813 (D286), eine Fälschung Abt Sugers?" *Historisches Jahrbuch* 108 (1998): 1–36.

Guenée, Bernard. *Histoire et culture historique dans l'Occident médiéval.* Paris, 1980.

Günther, Gerhard. *Der Antichrist: Der staufische Ludus de Antichristo.* Hamburg, 1970.

Haefele, Hans F. *Notker der Stammler: Taten Kaiser Karls des Grossen.* Berlin, 1962.

Hageneier, Lars. *Jenseits der Topik: Die karolingische Herrscherbiographie.* Husum, 2004.

Hägermann, Dieter. *Karl der Grosse: Herrscher des Abendlandes.* Berlin, 2000.

Hägg, Tomas, and Philip Rousseau. *Greek Biography and Panegyric in Late Antiquity.* Berkeley, CA, 2000.

Halphen, Louis. *Éginhard: Vie de Charlemagne.* Paris, 1947.

———. *Études critiques sur l'histoire de Charlemagne: Les sources de l'histoire de Charlemagne, la conquête de la Saxe, le couronnement impérial, l'agriculture et la propriété rurale, l'industrie et la commerce.* Paris, 1921.

Hamilton, Bernard. "The Lands of Prester John: Western Knowledge of Asia and Africa at the Time of the Crusades." *Haskins Society Journal* 15 (2006): 127–41.

———. "Prester John and the Three Kings of Cologne." In *Prester John, the Mongols and the Ten Lost Tribes,* ed. Charles F. Beckingham and Bernard Hamilton, 171–85. Aldershot, 1996.

Hausmann, Friedrich. "Gottfried von Viterbo: Kapellan und Notar, Magister, Geschichtsschreiber und Dichter." In *Friedrich Barbarossa: Handlungsspielräume und Wirkungsweisen Des Staufischen Kaisers,* ed. Alfred Haverkamp, 603–21. Sigmaringen, 1992.

Head, Thomas, ed. *Medieval Hagiography: An Anthology.* New York, 2000.

Hedeman, Anne D. *The Royal Image: Illustrations of the "Grandes Chroniques de France," 1274–1422.* Berkeley, CA, 1991.

Heer, Friedrich. *The Holy Roman Empire.* Trans. Janet Sondheimer. New York, 1968.

Heffernan, Thomas J. *Sacred Biography: Saints and Their Biographers in the Middle Ages*. Oxford, 1988.

Hellman, Sigmund. "Einhards literarische Stellung." *Historische Vierteljahrschrift* 27 (1932): 81–82.

Herrin, Judith. "Constantinople, Rome and the Franks in the Seventh and Eighth Centuries." In *Byzantine Diplomacy: Papers from the Twenty-fourth Spring Symposium of Byzantine Studies, Cambridge, March 1990*, ed. Jonathan Shepard and Simon Franklin, 91–107. Aldershot, 1992.

———. *Women in Purple: Rulers of Medieval Byzantium*. Princeton, NJ, 2001.

Hoffmann, Heinrich. *Karl der Grosse im Bilde der Geschichtsschreibung des frühen Mittelalters (800–1250)*. Berlin, 1919.

Hohler, Christopher. "A Note on Jacobus." *Journal of the Warburg and Courtauld Institutes* 35 (1972): 31–80.

Holdenried, Anke. *The Sibyl and Her Scribes: Manuscripts and Interpretation of the Latin "Sibylla Tiburtina," c. 1050–1500*. Aldershot, 2006.

Holtzmann, Robert. *Der Weltherrschaftsgedanke des mittelalterlichen Kaisertums und die Souveränität des europäischen Staaten*. Darmstadt, 1953.

Holum, Kenneth G., and Gary Vikan. "The Trier Ivory *Adventus* Ceremonial, and the Relics of St. Stephen." *Dumbarton Oaks Papers* 33 (1979): 115–33.

Houben, Hubert. *Roger II of Sicily: A Ruler between East and West*. Cambridge, UK, 2002.

Huffman, Joseph. *The Social Politics of Medieval Diplomacy: Anglo-German Relations (1066–1307)*. Ann Arbor, MI, 2000.

Hughes, Kevin L. *Constructing Antichrist: Paul, Biblical Commentary, and the Development of Doctrine in the Early Middle Ages*. Washington, DC, 2005.

Hunt, E. David. *Holy Land Pilgrimage in the Later Roman Empire, AD 312–460*. Oxford, 1982.

Innes, Matthew. "The Classical Tradition in the Carolingian Renaissance: Ninth-Century Encounters with Suetonius." *International Journal of the Classical Tradition* 3 (1997): 265–82.

———. "A Place of Discipline: Aristocratic Youth and Carolingian Courts." In *Court Culture in the Early Middle Ages*, ed. Catherine Cubitt, 59–76. Turnhout, 2004.

Jaeger, C. Stephen. *The Origins of Courtliness: Civilizing Trends and the Formation of Courtly Ideals, 939–1210*. Philadelphia, 1985.

———. "The Prologue to the *Historia Calamitatum* and the "Authenticity Question." *Euphorion: Zeitschrift für Literaturgeschichte* 74 (1980): 1–15.

Jones, Chris. *Eclipse of Empire? Perceptions of the Western Empire and Its Rulers in Late-Medieval France*. Turnhout, 2007.

Joranson, Einar. "The Alleged Frankish Protectorate in Palestine." *American Historical Review* 32 (1927): 241–61.

———. "The Spurious Letter of Alexius." *American Historical Review* 55 (1949–1950): 811–32.

Jordan, Alyce A. *Visualizing Kingship in the Windows of the Sainte-Chapelle*. Turnhout, 2002.

Jordan, William Chester. *Louis IX and the Challenge of the Crusade: A Study in Rulership*. Princeton, NJ, 1980.

Kahl, Hans-Dietrich. "Crusade Eschatology as Seen by St. Bernard in the Years 1146–1148." In *The Second Crusade and the Cistericians*, ed. Michael Gervers, 35–48. New York, 1992.

Kalavrezou, Ioli. "Helping Hands for the Empire: Imperial Ceremonies and the Cult of Relics at the Byzantine Court." In *Byzantine Court Culture from 829 to 1204*, ed. Henry Maguire, 53–79. Washington, DC, 1997.

Kampers, Franz. *Die Deutsche Kaiseridee in Prophetie und Sage*. Munich, 1896.

Kantorowicz, Ernst H. *Frederick the Second, 1194–1250*. Trans. E. O. Lorimer. New York, 1957.

——. *The King's Two Bodies: A Study in Mediaeval Political Theology*. Princeton, NJ, 1957.

——. *Laudes Regiae: A Study in Liturgical Acclamations and Mediaeval Ruler Worship*. Berkeley, CA, 1958.

——. "The Problem of Medieval World Unity." *American Historical Association, Annual Report 1942* 3 (1944): 31–37.

Kempf, Damien. "Towards a Textual Archaeology of the First Crusade." In *Narrating the First Crusade: Historiography, Memory and Transmission in the Narratives of the Early Crusade Movement*, ed. Damien Kempf and Marcus Bull. Woodbridge, UK, forthcoming.

Kempshall, Matthew S. *Rhetoric and the Writing of History, 400–1500*. Manchester, 2011.

——. "Some Ciceronian Models for Einhard's *Life of Charlemagne*," *Viator* 26 (1995): 11–37.

Kerner, Max. *Karl der Grosse: Entschleierung Eines Mythos*. Cologne, 2000.

Kershaw, Paul. "Laughter after Babel's Fall: Misunderstanding and Miscommunication in the Ninth-Century West." In *Humour, History and Politics in Late Antiquity and the Early Middle Ages*, ed. Guy Halsall, 179–202. Cambridge, UK, 2002.

Kienast, Walther. *Deutschland und Frankreich in Der Kaiserzeit (900–1270): Weltkaiser und Einzelkönige*. Stuttgart, 1975.

Killgus, Oliver. *Studien zum "Liber universalis" Gottfrieds von Viterbo*. Munich, 2010.

Klein, Holger. *Byzanz, der Western und das "wahre" Kreuz: Die Geschichte einer Reliquie und ihrer künstlerischen Fassung in Byzanz und im Abendland*. Wiesbaden, 2004.

——. "Eastern Objects and Western Desires: Relics and Reliquaries between Byzantium and the West." *Dumbarton Oaks Papers* 58 (2004): 283–314.

Kleinclausz, A. *Charlemagne*. Paris, 1934.

——. "La légende du protectorat de Charlemagne sur la Terre Sainte." *Syria* 7 (1926): 211–33.

Koziol, Geoffrey. *Begging Pardon and Favor: Ritual and Political Order in Early Medieval France*. Ithaca, NY, 1992.

——. "The Dangers of Polemic: Is Ritual Still an Interesting Topic of Historical Study?" *Early Medieval Europe* 11 (2002): 367–88.

Kruger, Stephen F. *Dreaming in the Middle Ages*. Cambridge, UK, 1992.

Kühne, Hartmut. *Ostensio Reliquiarum: Untersuchungen über Entstehung, Ausbreitung, Gestalt und Funktion der Heiltumsweisungen im römisch-deutschen Regnum*. Berlin, 2000.

Labory, Gillette. "Les débuts de la chronique en français (XIIe et XIIIe siècles)." In *The Medieval Chronicle III: Proceedings of the 3rd International Conference on the Medieval Chronicle; Doorn/Utrecht 12–17 July 2002*, ed. Erik Kooper, 1–27. Amsterdam, 2004.

Lair, Jules. "Mémoire sur deux chroniques latines composées au XIIe siècle à l'abbaye de Saint-Denis." *Bibliothèque de l'École des Chartes* 35 (1874): 543–80.

Lancel, Serge. *Hannibal*. Trans. Antonia Nevill. Oxford, 1998.

Landes, Richard. "Lest the Millennium Be Fulfilled: Apocalyptic Expectations and the Pattern of Western Chronography, 100–800 C.E." In *The Use and Abuse of Eschatology in the Middle Ages*, ed. W. D. F. Verbeke et al., 137–211. Louvain, 1988.

——. *Relics, Apocalypse, and the Deceits of History: Ademar of Chabannes, 989–1034*. Cambridge, MA, 1995.

Latowsky, Anne. "Charlemagne as Pilgrim? Requests for Relics in the *Descriptio Qualiter* and the *Voyage of Charlemagne*." In *The Legend of Charlemagne in the Middle Ages: Power, Faith, and Crusade*, ed. Matthew Gabriele and Jace Stuckey, 153–67. New York, 2008.

——. "Foreign Embassies and Roman Universality in Einhard's *Life of Charlemagne*." *Florilegium* 22 (2005): 25–57.

Lehmgrubner, Hugo. *Benzo Von Alba: Ein Verfechter Der Kaiserlichen Staatsidee Unter Heinrich IV*. Berlin, 1887.

Leopold, Anthony. *How to Recover the Holy Land: The Crusade Proposals of the Late Thirteenth and Early Fourteenth Centuries*. Aldershot, 2000.

Lerner, Robert E. "Medieval Prophecy and Politics." *Annali dell'Istituto storico italo-germanico in Trento* 15 (1999): 417–32.

Levaillain, Philippe. *The Papacy: An Encyclopedia*. London, 2002.

Lewis, Andrew W. *Royal Succession in Capetian France: Studies on Familial Order and the State*. Cambridge, MA, 1981.

Lewis, Suzanne. *The Art of Matthew Paris in the "Chronica Majora."* Berkeley, CA, 1987.

Leyser, Karl J. *Communications and Power in Medieval Europe: The Carolingian and Ottonian Centuries*. Ed. Timothy Reuter. London, 1994.

——. "Frederick Barbarossa, Henry II and the Hand of Saint James." In *Medieval Germany and Its Neighbours, 900–1250*, 215–40. London, 1983.

——. "The Polemics of the Papal Revolution." Reprinted in *Medieval Germany and Its Neighbours, 900–1250*, 138–60. London, 1983.

Lifshitz, Felice. "Beyond Positivism and Genre: 'Hagiographical' Texts as Historical Narrative." *Viator* 25 (1994): 95–113.

Lilie, Ralph-Johannes. *Byzantium and the Crusader States, 1096–1204*. Trans. J. C. Morris. Oxford, 1994.

Lohrmann, Dietrich. "Politische Instrumentalisierung Karls des Grossen durch die Staufer und ihre Gegner." *Zeitschrift des Aachener Geschichtsvereins* 104/105 (2002/2003): 95–112.

Lombard-Jourdan, Anne. "Les foires de l'abbaye de Saint-Denis: Revue des données et révision des opinions admises." *Société de l'École des Chartes* 145 (1987): 273–337.

——. *Montjoie et Saint-Denis: Le centre de la Gaule aux origines de Paris et de Saint-Denis*. Paris, 1989.

Loud, G. A. *The Age of Robert Guiscard: Southern Italy and the Norman Conquest.* London, 2000.

Löwe, Heinz. "Das Karlsbuch Notkers von St. Gallen und sein zeitgeschichtlicher Hintergrund." In *Von Cassiodor zu Dante: Ausgewählte Aufsätze zur Geschichtschreibung und politischen Ideenwelt des Mittelalters,* ed. Heinz Löwe, 123–48. Berlin, 1973.

Lozovsky, Natalia. "Maps and Panegyrics: Roman Geo-ethnographical Rhetoric in Late Antiquity and the Middle Ages." In *Cartography in Antiquity and the Middle Ages: Fresh Perspectives, New Methods,* ed. Richard J. A. Talbert and Richard W. Unger, 169–88. Leiden, 2008.

MacCormack, Sabine G. *Art and Ceremony in Late Antiquity.* Berkeley, CA, 1981.

MacLean, Simon. *Kingship and Politics in the Late Ninth Century: Charles the Fat and the End of the Carolingian Empire.* Cambridge, UK, 2003.

——. "Reform, Queenship and the End of the World in Tenth-Century France: Adso's 'Letter on the Origin and Time of the Antichrist' Reconsidered." *Revue belge de philologie et d'histoire* 86 (2008): 645–75

Magdalino, Paul. *The Empire of Manuel I Komnenos, 1143–1180.* Cambridge, UK, 1993.

Maines, Clark. "The Charlemagne Window at Chartres Cathedral: New Considerations on Text and Image." *Speculum* 52 (1977): 801–23.

Mâle, Emile. *Religious Art in France: A Study of the Origins of Medieval Iconography.* Princeton, NJ, 1978.

Mastnak, Tomaz. *Crusading Peace: Christendom, the Muslim World, and Western Political Order.* Berkeley, CA, 2002.

Matter, E. Ann. "The Apocalypse in Early Medieval Exegesis." In *The Apocalypse in the Middle Ages,* ed. Richard Kenneth Emmerson and Bernard McGinn, 38–50. Ithaca, NY, 1992.

Mayer, Hans Eberhard. "Staufische Welterherrschaft." In *Friedrich Barbarossa,* ed. Günther Wolf, 184–207. Darmstadt, 1975.

Mayo, Penelope. "The Crusaders under the Palm: Allegorical Plants and Cosmic Kingship in the *Liber Floridus.*" *Dumbarton Oaks Papers* 27 (1973): 29–67.

Mayr-Harting, Henry. *Ottonian Book Illumination: An Historical Study.* London, 1999.

McCormick, Michael. "Byzantium and the West, 700–900." In *The New Cambridge Medieval History c. 700–c. 900,* vol. 2, ed. Rosamond McKitterick, 349–80. Cambridge, UK, 1995.

——. "Diplomacy and the Carolingian Encounter with Byzantium Down to the Accession of Charles the Bald." In *Eriugena: East and West: Papers of the Eighth International Symposium of the Society for the Promotion of Eriugenean Studies,* ed. Bernard McGinn and Willemien Otten, 15–48. Notre Dame, IN, 1994.

——. *Eternal Victory: Triumphal Rulership in Late Antiquity, Byzantium, and the Early Medieval West.* Cambridge, UK, 1987.

McGinn, Bernard. *Antichrist: Two Thousand Years of the Human Fascination with Evil.* New York, 2000.

——. "*Iter sancti sepulchri:* The Piety of the First Crusaders." In *Essays on Medieval Civilization,* ed. Bede Karl Lackner and Kenneth Roy Philp, 33–71. Austin, TX, 1978.

——. *"Teste David cum Sibylla*: The Significance of the Sibylline Tradition in the Middle Ages." In *Women of the Medieval World: Essays in Honor of John H. Mundy*, ed. Julius Kirshner and Suzanne F. Wemple, 7–35. Oxford, 1985.

——. *Visions of the End: Apocalyptic Traditions in the Middle Ages.* New York, 1998.

McGrade, Michael. "O rex mundi triumphator: Hohenstaufen Politics in a Sequence for Saint Charlemagne." *Early Music History: Studies in Medieval and Early Modern Music* 17 (1998): 183–219.

McKitterick, Rosamond. *Charlemagne: The Formation of a European Identity.* Cambridge, UK, 2008.

——. *History and Memory in the Carolingian World.* Cambridge, UK, 2004.

Mergiali-Sahas, Mergiali. "Byzantine Emperors and Holy Relics: Use, and Misuse, of Sanctity and Authority." *Jahrbuch der Österreichischen Byzantinistik* 51 (2001): 41–60.

Meyendorff, John. *Imperial Unity and Christian Divisions: The Church 450–680 A.D.* Crestwood, NY, 1989.

Meyer, Lucienne. *Les légendes des matières de Rome, de France et de Bretagne dans le "Panthéon" de Godefroi de Viterbe.* Paris, 1933.

Miller, Maureen C. *Power and the Holy in the Age of the Investiture Contest: A Brief History with Documents.* Boston, 2005.

Möhring, Hannes. "Benzo von Alba und die Entstehung des Kreuzzugsgedankens." In *Forschungen zur Reichs-, Papst- und Landesgeschichte Peter Herde zum 65. Geburtstag von Freunden, Schülern und Kollegen dargebracht*, ed. Karl Borchardt and Enno Bünz, 177–86. Stuttgart, 1998.

——. "Karl der Grosse und die Endkaiser-Weissagung." In *Montjoie: Studies in Crusade History in Honour of Hans Eberhard Mayer*, 3–19, ed. Benjamin Z. Kedar, Jonathan Riley-Smith, and Rudolf Hiestand. Aldershot, 1997.

——. *Der Weltkaiser der Endzeit: Entstehung Wandel und Wirkung einer tausendjahrigen Weissagung.* Stuttgart, 2000.

Monteleone, Federica. *Il viaggio di Carlo Magno in Terra Santa.* Fasano di Brindisi, 2003.

Morris, Colin. *The Papal Monarchy: The Western Church from 1050 to 1250.* Oxford, 1991.

——. "Picturing the Crusades: The Uses of Visual Propaganda, c. 1095–1250." In *The Crusades and Their Sources: Essays Presented to Bernard Hamilton*, ed. John France and William G. Zajae, 195–209. Aldershot, 1998.

Morrison, Karl F. "Otto of Freising's Quest for the Hermeneutic Circle." *Speculum* 55 (1980): 207–36.

Morrissey, Robert. *L'empereur à la barbe fleurie: Charlemagne dans la mythologie et l'histoire de France.* Paris, 1997.

Morse, Ruth. *Truth and Convention in the Middle Ages: Rhetoric, Representation and Reality.* Cambridge, UK, 1991.

Muldoon, James. *Empire and Order: The Concept of Empire, 800–1800.* New York, 1999.

Müllejans, Hans., ed. *Karl der Grosse und sein Schrein in Aachen.* Mönchengladbach, 1988.

Munz, Peter. *Frederick Barbarossa: A Study in Medieval Politics.* Ithaca, NY, 1969.

Murray, Alexander C. "Fredegar, Merovech and 'Sacral Kingship.'" In *After Rome's Fall: Narrators and Sources of Early Medieval History*, ed. Walter A. Goffart and Alexander C. Murray, 121–52. Toronto, 1998.

Musca, Giosuè. *Carlo Magno e Harun al Rashid*. Bari, 1963.

Mütherich, Florentine, ed. *Der Schrein Karls des Grossen: Bestand und Sicherung 1982–1988*. Aachen, 1998.

Nebbiai-Dalla Guarda, Donatella. *La bibliothèque de l'abbaye de Saint-Denis en France du IXe au XVIIIe siècle*. Paris, 1985.

Nees, Lawrence. "Charlemagne's Elephant." *Quintana: Revista do Departamento de Historia da Arte, Universidade de Santiago de Compostela* 5 (2006): 13–49.

——. *A Tainted Mantle: Hercules and the Classical Tradition at the Carolingian Court*. Philadelphia, 1991.

Nelson, Janet L. "Kingship and Empire." In *The Cambridge History of Medieval Political Thought c. 350–c. 1450*, ed. J. H. Burns, 211–51. Cambridge, UK, 1991.

——. "Kingship and Empire in the Carolingian World." In *Carolingian Culture: Emulation and Innovation*, ed. Rosamond McKitterick, 52–87. Cambridge, UK, 1994.

Nichols, Stephen G. *Romanesque Signs: Early Medieval Narrative and Iconography*. New Haven, CT, 1983.

Nicholson, Helen. *Love, War and the Grail: Templars, Hospitallers and Teutonic Knights in Medieval Epic and Romance, 1150–1500*. Leiden, 2000.

Nicol, Donald M. *Byzantium and Venice: A Study in Diplomatic and Cultural Relations*. Cambridge, UK, 1988.

Noble, Thomas F. X. *Charlemagne and Louis the Pious: Lives by Einhard, Notker, Ermoldus, Thegan, and the Astronomer*. University Park, PA, 2009.

——. *Images, Iconoclasm and the Carolingians*. Philadelphia, 2009.

——. *The Republic of Saint Peter: The Birth of the Papal State, 680–825*. Philadelphia, 1984.

Nothomb, J. "Manuscripts et recensions de 'l'Iter Hierosolimitatum Caroli Magni,'" *Romania* 56 (1930): 191–211.

O'Leary, Stephen D. *Arguing the Apocalypse: A Theory of Millennial Rhetoric*. New York, 1994.

Otter, Monika. *Inventiones: Fiction and Referentiality in Twelfth-Century English Historical Writing*. Chapel Hill, NC, 1996.

——. "Scurrilitas: Sex, Magic, and the Performance of Fictionality in Anselm of Besate's *Rhetorimachia*." In *Aspects of the Performative in Medieval Culture*, ed. Manuele Gragnolati and Almut Suerbaum, 101–24. Berlin, 2010.

Pacaut, Marcel. *Frederick Barbarossa*. Trans. A. J. Pomerans. New York, 1970.

Paris, Gaston. *Histoire poétique de Charlemagne*. Geneva, 1974.

——. "La traduction de la légende latine du voyage de Charlemagne à Constantinople par Pierre de Beauvais." *Romania* 21 (1895): 734–36.

Paschoud, François. *Roma Aeterna. Étude sur le patriotisme romain dans l'Occident latin à l'époque des grandes invasions*. Rome, 1967.

Pastan, Elizabeth. "Charlemagne as Saint? Relics and the Choice of Window Subjects at Chartres Cathedral." In *The Legend of Charlemagne in the Middle Ages: Power, Faith, and Crusade*, ed. Matthew Gabriele and Jace Stuckey, 97–136. New York, 2008.

Patlagean, Evelyne. "Byzantium's Dual Holy Land." *In Sacred Space: Shrine, City, Land*, ed. Joshua Prawer, Benjamin Kedar-Kopfstein, and Raphael Jehudah Zwi. New York, 1998.

Petersohn, Jürgen. "Saint-Denis—Westminster—Aachen. Die Karls-Translatio von 1164 und ihre Vorbilder." *Deutsches Archiv für Erforschung des Mittelalters* 31 (1975): 420–54.

Phillips, Jonathan. *Defenders of the Holy Land: Relations between the Latin East and the West, 1119–1187.* Oxford, 1996.

———. *The Second Crusade: Extending the Frontiers of Christendom.* New Haven, CT, 2007.

Pizarro, Joaquín Martínez. "Images of Church and State: Sulpicius Severus to Notker Balbulus." *Journal of Medieval Latin* 4 (1994): 25–38.

———. "The King Says No: On the Logic of Type-Scenes in Late-Antique and Early-Medieval Narrative." In *The Long Morning of Medieval Europe: New Directions in Early Medieval Studies,* ed. Jennifer R. Davis and Michael McCormick, 181–92. Aldershot, 2008.

———. *A Rhetoric of the Scene: Dramatic Narrative in the Early Middle Ages.* Toronto, 1989.

Poly, Jean Pierre, and Eric Bournazel. *The Feudal Transformation, 900–1200.* Trans. Caroline Higgitt. New York, 1991.

Potter, David S. *Prophets and Emperors: Human and Divine Authority from Augustus to Theodosius.* Cambridge, MA, 1994.

———. *The Roman Empire at Bay, AD 180–395.* London, 2004.

Powell, James. "Church and Crusade: Frederick II and Louis IX." *Catholic Historical Review* 93 (2007): 251–64.

———. "Myth, Legend, Propaganda, History: The First Crusade, 1140–ca. 1300." In *Autour de la première croisade,* ed. Michel Balard, 127–41. Paris, 1996.

Purkis, William J. *Crusading Spirituality in the Holy Land and Iberia, c. 1095–c. 1187.* Woodbridge, UK, 2008.

Pysiak, Jerzy. "Philippe Auguste. Un roi de la fin des temps?" *Annales: Histoire, Sciences Sociales* 57 (2002): 1165–90.

Rankin, Susan. "Ego itaque Notker scripsi." *Revue Bénédictine* 101 (1991): 268–98.

Ratkowitsch, Christine. "Carolus castus. Zum Charakter Karls des Großen in der Darstellung des Egidius von Paris." In *Scripturus vitam. Lateinische Biographie von der Antike bis in die Gegenwart, Festgabe für W. Berschin zum 65. Geburtstag,* ed. D. Walz, 369–77. Heidelberg, 2002.

Reeves, Marjorie. *The Influence of Prophecy in the Later Middle Ages: A Study in Joachimism.* Oxford, 1969.

Reischmann, Hans-Joachim. *Die Trivialisierung des Karlsbildes der Einhard-Vita in Notkers "Gesta Karoli Magni": Rezeptionstheoretische Studien zum Abbau der Kritischen Distanz in der spätkarolingischen Epoche.* Konstanz, 1984.

Remensnyder, Amy G. *Remembering Kings Past: Monastic Foundation Legends in Medieval Southern France.* Ithaca, NY, 1995.

———. "Topographies of Memory: Center and Periphery in High Medieval France." In *Medieval Concepts of the Past: Ritual, Memory, Historiography,* ed. Gerd Althoff, Johannes Fried, and Patrick J. Geary, 193–214. Cambridge, UK, 2002.

Reuter, Timothy. "Past, Present and No Future in the *Regnum Teutonicum.*" In *The Perception of the Past in Twelfth-Century Europe,* ed. Paul Magdalino, 15–36. London, 2003.

Reynolds, Leighton D., ed. *Texts and Transmission: A Survey of the Latin Classics*. Oxford, 1983.

Riché, Pierre. *The Carolingians: A Family Who Forged Europe*. Trans. Michael Idomir Allen. Philadelphia, 1993.

Riley-Smith, Jonathan. "The First Crusade and Saint Peter." In *Outremer: Studies in the History of the Crusading Kingdom of Jerusalem Presented to Joshua Prawer*, ed. B. Z. Kedar, Hans Eberhard Mayer, and R. C. Smail, 41–55. Jerusalem, 1982.

———. *The First Crusade and the Idea of Crusading*. Philadelphia, 1986.

Robertson, Duncan. "Visual Poetics: The Charlemagne Window at Chartres." *Olifant* 6 (1978): 107–17.

Robinson, I. S. *Authority and Resistance in the Investiture Contest: The Polemical Literature of the Late Eleventh Century*. New York, 1978.

———. *Henry IV of Germany, 1056–1106*. Cambridge, UK, 2003.

———. *The Papacy, 1073–1198: Continuity and Innovation*. Cambridge, UK, 1990.

———, ed. and trans. *The Papal Reform of the Eleventh Century: Lives of Pope Leo IX and Pope Gregory VII*. Manchester, 2004.

Rohrbacher, David. *The Historians of Late Antiquity*. London, 2002.

Rolland, Isabelle. "Le mythe carolingien et l'art du vitrail: Sur le choix et l'ordre des épisodes dans le vitrail de Charlemagne à la cathédrale de Chartres." In *La chanson de geste et le mythe carolingien: Mélanges René Louis I*, ed. André Moisan, 255–77. Saint-Père-Sous-Vézelay, 1982.

Rossi, Carla. *Il viaggio di Carlo Magno a Gerusalemme e a Costantinopoli*. Alessandria, 2006.

Rousset, Paul. *Les origines et les caractères de la première croisade*. Neuchâtel, 1945.

Rubenstein, Jay. *Armies of Heaven: The First Crusade and the Quest for Apocalypse*. New York, 2011.

Runciman, Steven. "Charlemagne and Palestine." *English Historical Review* 50 (1935): 606–19.

Russell, J. Stephen. *The English Dream Vision: Anatomy of a Form*. Columbus, OH, 1988.

Sackur, Ernst, ed. "Ein Schreiben Odilos von Cluni an Heinrich III. Vom October 1046." *Neues Archiv* 24 (1899): 732–35.

———. *Sibyllinische Texte und Forschungen*. Halle, 1898.

Sansterre, Jean-Marie. "Byzance et son souverain dans les 'Libri ad Heinricum IV imperatorem' de Benzo d'Alba." *Bollettino della Badia greca di Grottaferrata* 51 (1997): 93–111.

Schein, Sylvia. *Gateway to the Heavenly City: Crusader Jerusalem and the Catholic West (1099–1187)*. Aldershot, 2005.

Schenck, Mary Jane. "The Charlemagne Window at Chartres: King as Crusader." *Word & Image* (2012): 135–60.

———. "Taking a Second Look: Roland in the Charlemagne Window at Chartres." *Olifant* 25 (2006): 371–86.

Schmid, Karl. "Aachen und Jerusalem: Ein Beitrag zur historischen Personenforschung der Karolingerzeit." In *Das Einhardkreuz: Vorträge und Studien der Münsteraner Diskussion zum arcus Einhardi*, ed. Karl Hauck, 122–42. Göttingen, 1974.

Schmitt, Jean Claude. *The Conversion of Herman the Jew: Autobiography, History, and Fiction in the Twelfth Century.* Philadelphia, 2010.

Schramm, Percy. *Kaiser, Rom und Renovatio: Studien zur Geschichte des römischen Erneuerungsgedankens vom Ende des karolingischen Reiches bis zum Investiturstreit.* Berlin, 1929.

Seiffert, Hans Werner. "Otto von Freising und Gotfried von Viterbo." *Philologus: Zeitschrift für klassische Philologie* 115 (1971): 292–301.

Shaw, Frank. "Frederick II as the 'Last Emperor.'" *German History* 19 (2001): 321–39.

Shepard, Jonathan. "Byzantine Diplomacy, A.D. 800–1204: Means and Ends." In *Byzantine Diplomacy: Papers from the Twenty-fourth Spring Symposium of Byzantine Studies, Cambridge, March 1990,* ed. Jonathan Shepard and Simon Franklin, 41–71. Aldershot, 1992.

Sholod, Barton. "Charlemagne—Symbolic Link between the Eighth and Eleventh Century Crusades." In *Studies in Honor of M. J. Benardete (Essays in Hispanic and Sephardic Culture),* ed. Izaak A. Langnas and Barton Sholod, 33–46. New York, 1965.

Short, Ian. "A Study in Carolingian Legend and Its Persistence in Latin Historiography (XII–XVI Centuries)." *Mittellateinisches Jahrbuch* 7 (1972): 127–52.

Siegrist, Theodor. *Herrscherbild und Weltsicht Bei Notker Balbulus: Untersuchungen zu den Gesta Karoli.* Zürich, 1963.

Silverberg, Robert. *The Realm of Prester John.* Athens, OH, 1972.

Smalley, Beryl. *Historians in the Middle Ages.* London, 1974.

Smith, Julia M. H. "Rulers and Relics c. 750–c. 950: Treasure on Earth, Treasure in Heaven." *Past & Present* 206 (2010): 73–96.

Smyser, H. M. *The Pseudo-Turpin: B.N., Fonds Latin, MS 17656.* Cambridge, MA, 1937.

Spiegel, Gabrielle M. *The Chronicle Tradition of Saint-Denis: A Survey.* Brookline, MA, 1978.

——. "The Cult of Saint Denis and Capetian Kingship." *Journal of Medieval History* 1 (1975): 43–69.

——. "Medieval Canon Formation and the Rise of Royal Historiography in Old French Prose." *Modern Language Notes* 108 (1993): 638–58.

——. *The Past as Text: The Theory and Practice of Medieval Historiography.* Baltimore, 1997.

——. "The Reditus Regni ad Stirpem Karoli Magni: A New Look." *French Historical Studies* 7 (1971): 145–74.

——. *Romancing the Past: The Rise of Vernacular Prose Historiography in Thirteenth-Century France.* Berkeley, CA, 1993.

Steltzmann, Arnold. "Rainald von Dassel und seine Reichspolitik." *Jahrbuch des Kölnischen Geschichtsvereins* 25 (1950): 60–82.

Stiennon, Jacques. "L'iconographie de Charlemagne." In *Charlemagne et l'épopée romane. Actes du VIIe Congrès International de la Société Rencesvals, Liège, 28 août– 4 septembre 1976,* ed. Madelaine Tyssens et al., 159–76. Paris, 1978.

Stoneman, Richard. "The Medieval Alexander." In *Latin Fiction: The Latin Novel in Context,* ed. Heinz Hofman, 238–52. London, 1999.

Story, Joanna. "Cathwulf, Kingship, and the Royal Abbey of Saint-Denis." *Speculum* 741 (1999): 1–21.

Stroll, Mary. *Symbols as Power: The Papacy following the Investiture Contest.* Leiden, 1991.

Struve, Tilman. "Endzeiterwartungen als Symptom politisch-sozialer Krisen im Mittelalter." In *Ende und Vollendung: Eschatologische Perspektiven im Mittelalter,* ed. Jan A. Aertsen, 207–26. Berlin, 2002.

——. "Kaisertum und Romgedanke in salischer Zeit." *Deutsches Archiv für Erforschung des Mittelalters* 44 (1988): 424–54.

Stuckey, Jace. "Charlemagne as Crusader? Memory, Propaganda, and the Many Uses of Charlemagne's Legendary Expedition to Spain." In *The Legend of Charlemagne in the Middle Ages: Power, Faith, and Crusade,* ed. Matthew Gabriele and Jace Stuckey, 137–52. New York, 2008.

Sturm, Sara. "The Stature of Charlemagne in the *Pèlerinage.*" *Studies in Philology* 72 (1974): 1–18.

Stürner, Wolfgang. *Friedrich II.* Darmstadt, 1992–2000.

Tanner, Marie. *The Last Descendants of Aeneas: The Hapsburgs and the Mythic Image of the Emperor.* New Haven, CT, 1993.

Tierney, Brian. *The Crisis of Church and State: 1050–1300.* Englewood Cliffs, NJ, 1964.

Tischler, Matthias. *Einharts Vita Karoli: Studien zur Entstehung, Überlieferung und Rezeption.* Hanover, 2001.

——. "Tatmensch oder Heidenapostel: Die Bilder Karls des Grossen bei Einhart und im Pseudo-Turpin." In *Jakobus und Karl der Grosse: Von Einards Karlsvita zum Pseudo-Turpin,* ed. Klaus Herbers, 7–15. Tübingen, 2003.

Trexler, Robert. *The Journey of the Magi: Meanings in History of a Christian Story.* Princeton, NJ, 1997.

Tyerman, Christopher J. *God's War: A New History of the Crusades.* Cambridge, MA, 2006.

——. *The Invention of the Crusades.* Toronto, 1998.

Uebel, Michael. "Imperial Fetishism: Prester John among the Natives." In *The Postcolonial Middle Ages,* ed. Jeffrey Jerome Cohen, 261–82. New York, 2001.

Ullmann, Walter. *A Short History of the Papacy in the Middle Ages.* London, 2003.

Vance, Eugene. "Semiotics and Power: Relics, Icons, and the *Voyage de Charlemagne à Jérusalem et à Constantinople.*" *Romanic Review* 79 (1988): 164–83.

Van Cleve, Thomas C. *The Emperor Frederick II of Hohenstaufen, Immutator Mundi.* Oxford, 1972.

Van de Kieft, Co. "Deux diplômes faux de Charlemagne pour Saint Denis du XIIᵉ siècle." *Le Moyen Âge* 13 (1958): 401–36.

Vanderlinden S. "Revelatio Sancti Stephani." *Revue des Études Byzantines* 4 (1946): 178–217.

Van Oort, Johannes. *Jerusalem and Babylon: A Study into Augustine's "City of God" and the Sources of His Doctrine of the Two Cities* (Supplements to Vigiliae Christianae). Leiden, 1991.

Vantuch, A. "La légende de Charlemagne aux IXe–Xe siècles." In *Mélanges offerts à Rita Lejeune,* vol. 2, 919–28. Gembloux, 1969.

Van Waard, Roelof. *Études sur l'origine et la formation de la "Chanson d'Aspremont."* Groningen, 1937.

Velaza, Javier. "Le *Collectaneum* de Sedulius Scotus et l'*Histoire Auguste.*" In *Histoire Augustae Colloquium Argentoratense,* ed. Giorgio Bonamente et al., 339–47. Bari, 1998.

Verdier, Philippe. "Saint-Denis et la tradition carolingienne des Tituli: Le *de Rebus in Administratione Sua Gestis* de Suger." In *La chanson de geste et le mythe carolingien: Mélanges René Louis I*, ed. André Moisan, 341–59. Saint-Père-Sous-Vézelay, 1982.

Verhelst, Daniel. "Adso of Montier-en-Der and the Fear of the Year 1000." In *The Apocalyptic Year 1000: Religious Expectation and Social Change, 950–1050*, ed. Richard Allen Landes, Andrew Gow, and David C. Van Meter, 81–92. Oxford, 2003.

——. "Adson de Montier-en-Der." In *Religion et culture autour de l'an mil: Royaume capétien et Lotharingie*, ed. Dominique Iogna-Prat and Jean-Charles Picard, 25–30. Paris, 1990.

——. "Les textes eschatologiques dans le *Liber Floridus*." In *The Use and Abuse of Eschatology in the Middle Ages*, ed. Werner Verbeke, Daniel Verhelst, and Andries Welkenhuysen, 299–305. Leuven, 1988.

Vignéras, L. A. "L'abbaye de Charroux et la légende du pèlerinage de Charlemagne." *Romanic Review* 32 (1941): 121–28.

Vones, Ludwig. "La canonización de Carlomagno en 1165, *La Vita S. Karoli* de Aquisgrán y el Pseudo-Turpín." In *El Pseudo-Turpin, lazo entre el culto jacobeo y el culto de Carlomagno: Actas del VI Congreso Internacional de Estudios Jacobeos,* ed. Klaus Herbers, 271–83. Santiago de Compostela, 2003.

Waha, M. de. "La lettre d'Alexis I Comnène à Robert le Frison: Une révision." *Byzantion* 47 (1977): 113–25.

Walpole, Ronald N. "Charlemagne's Journey to the East: The French Translation of the Legend by Pierre of Beauvais." *Semitic and Oriental Studies* 9 (1951): 445–52.

——. *The Old French Translation of the Pseudo-Turpin Chronicle: A Critical Edition.* Berkeley, CA, 1976.

——. "The *Pèlerinage de Charlemagne*: Poem, Legend, and Problem." *Romance Philology* 8 (1955): 173–86.

——. "Two Notes on *Charlemagne's Journey to the East*: The French Translation of the Latin Legend by Pierre of Beauvais." *Romance Philology* 7 (1953–54): 130–42.

Ward, John O. "Some Principles of Rhetorical Historiography in the Twelfth Century." In *Classical Rhetoric and Medieval Historiography*, ed. Ernst Breisach, 103–65. Kalamazoo, MI, 1985.

Weber, Loren J. "The Historical Importance of Godfrey of Viterbo." *Viator* 25 (1994): 153–91.

Weinfurter, Stefan. *The Salian Century: Main Currents in an Age of Transition.* Philadelphia, 1999.

Werner, Karl Ferdinand. *Karl der Grosse oder Charlemagne? Von der Aktualität einer überholten Fragestellung.* Munich, 1995.

Wetzstein, Thomas. "La doctrine de la 'translatio imperii' et l'enseignement des canonistes médiévaux." In *Science politique et droit public dans les facultés de droit européennes (XIIIe–XVIIIe siècle)*, ed. Jacques Krynen and Michael Stolleis, 185–221. Frankfurt am Main, 2008.

Whalen, Brett Edward. *Dominion of God: Christendom and Apocalypse in the Middle Ages.* Cambridge, MA, 2009.

Wickham, Chris. "Ninth-Century Byzantium through Western Eyes." In *Byzantium in the Ninth Century: Dead or Alive?* ed. Leslie Brubaker, 245–56. Aldershot, 1998.

Williams, John R. "Archbishop Manasses I of Rheims and Pope Gregory VII." *American Historical Review* 54 (1949): 804–24.

Wolter, Heinz. "Intention und Herrscherbild in Einhards 'Vita Karoli Magni.'" *Archiv für Kulturgeschichte* 68 (1986): 295–317.

Wright, John, ed. and trans. *The Play of Antichrist*. Toronto, 1967.

Zeller, Gaston. "Les rois de France candidats à l'Empire: Essai sur l'idéologie impériale en France." *Revue Historique* 173 (1934): 273–311.

Ziolkowski, Jan M., and Michael C. J. Putnam, eds. *The Virgilian Tradition: The First Fifteen Hundred Years*. New Haven, CT, 2008.

❦ Index

Note: Page numbers followed by letter *f* indicate figures.

Lightning Source UK Ltd.
Milton Keynes UK
UKHW041245290320
361016UK00013B/214